Nebuchadnezzar's Dream

Nebuchadnezzar's Dream

THE CRUSADES, APOCALYPTIC PROPHECY, AND THE END OF HISTORY

Jay Rubenstein

OXFORD
UNIVERSITY PRESS

OXFORD
UNIVERSITY PRESS

Oxford University Press is a department of the University of Oxford.
It furthers the University's objective of excellence in research, scholarship,
and education by publishing worldwide. Oxford is a registered trade mark of
Oxford University Press in the UK and certain other countries.

Published in the United States of America by Oxford University Press
198 Madison Avenue, New York, NY 10016, United States of America.

Library of Congress Cataloging-in-Publication Data

Names: Rubenstein, Jay, 1967– author.
Title: Nebuchadnezzar's dream : the Crusades, apocalyptic prophecy, and the
end of history / Jay Rubenstein.
Description: New York, NY : Oxford University Press, [2019] | Includes
bibliographical references and index.
Identifiers: LCCN 2018008319 | ISBN 9780190274207 (hardback : alk. paper)
Subjects: LCSH: Crusades—First, 1096–1099. | Crusades—Second, 1147–1149. |
Jerusalem—History—Latin Kingdom, 1099–1244. | End of the world—History
of doctrines—Middle Ages, 600–1500.
Classification: LCC D161.2 .R746 2019 | DDC 956/.014–dc23 LC record available at
https://lccn.loc.gov/2018008319

3 5 7 9 8 6 4 2

Printed by Sheridan Books, Inc.
United States of America

FOR EDWARD

CONTENTS

CONCLUSION: The Ongoing Madness of Antichrist   208

LIST OF FIGURES

LIST OF TABLES

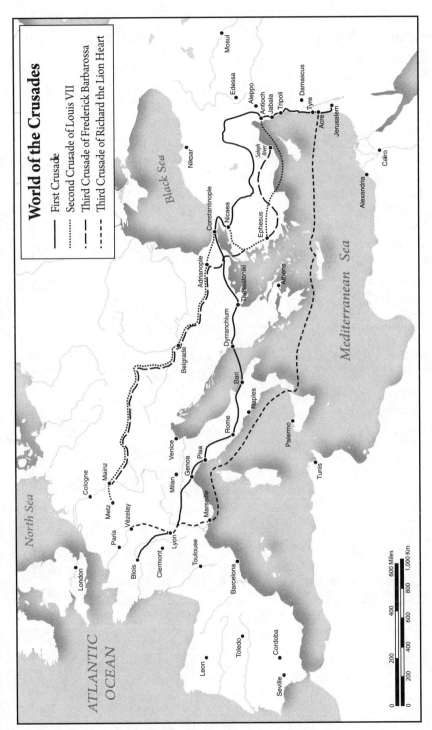

World of the Crusades

—— First Crusade
········· Second Crusade of Louis VII
— · — Third Crusade of Frederick Barbarossa
– – – Third Crusade of Richard the Lion Heart

North Sea

ATLANTIC OCEAN

Black Sea

Mediterranean Sea

London
Cologne
Mainz
Metz
Paris
Vézelay
Blois
Clermont
Lyon
Toulouse
Milan
Venice
Genoa
Pisa
Marseille
Rome
Naples
Bari
Dyrranchium
Belgrade
Adrianople
Thessaloniki
Athens
Palermo
Tunis
Barcelona
Leon
Toledo
Cordoba
Seville

Constantinople
Nicaea
Ephesus
Niksar
Edessa
Mosul
Aleppo
Antioch
Jabala
Tripoli
Damascus
Tyre
Acre
Jerusalem
Cairo
Alexandria

Saleph river

0   200   400   600 Miles
0   200   400   600   800   1,000 Km

MAP 1

Europe in the Crusade Era

North Sea

German Empire

Bruges

Flanders

Cologne

English Channel

Saint-Omer

Mainz

Nogent-sous-Coucy

Caen

Reims

Paris

Dol

Saint-Evroul

Freising

Reichersberg

Chartres

Troyes

Clairvaux Abbey

Schäftlarn

Tours

Bourgueil

FRANCE

Cîteaux Abbey

Tegernsee Abbey

Saint-Léonard de Noblat

Cluny Abbey

Montferrat

Ferrara

ITALY

Mediterranean Sea

Rome

0   100   200 Miles
0   200   400 Km

MAP 2

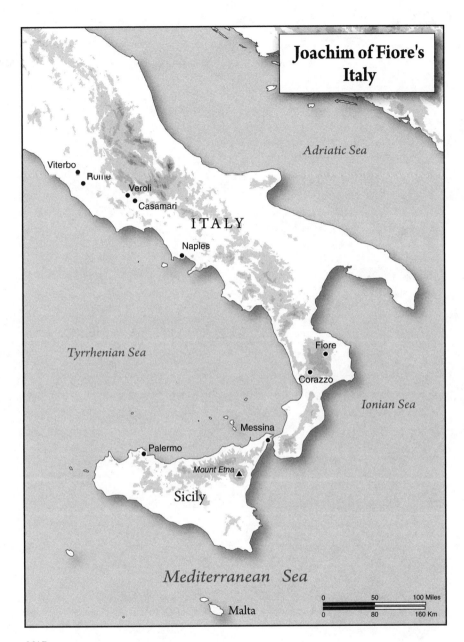

Joachim of Fiore's
Italy

Adriatic Sea

Viterbo
Rome
Veroli
Casamari
ITALY
Naples

Tyrrhenian Sea

Fiore
Corazzo

Ionian Sea

Messina
Palermo
Mount Etna ▲
Sicily

Mediterranean Sea

Malta

0   50   100 Miles
0   80   160 Km

MAP 3

PREFACE

This book began with an observation and the question that followed upon it. The observation involves one of the most creative historians of the Middle Ages, Guibert of Nogent (ca. 1060–1125), and how he looked at the key event of his lifetime, the First Crusade. In addition to being one of the most perceptive writers of his day, Guibert was also one of the most melancholic and dyspeptic, not often given to enthusiasm about the state of human affairs. Upon first hearing the news of the campaign for Jerusalem's capture, he became uncharacteristically excited about the crusade. By the end of his life, however, his attitude toward it had grown more jaundiced. He had become disillusioned with the whole enterprise.[1] The question then followed from this observation: Was Guibert's disillusionment widely shared? How did his contemporaries look upon the event that has come to define their age?

To answer this question in full, which this book will try to do, requires first addressing another question. If disillusionment such as Guibert's followed the First Crusade, what was the illusion that had originally inspired it? The First Crusade, and in particular the capture of Jerusalem, had changed the course of history. Indeed, it represented in the eyes of contemporaries probably the most important event ever. But more fundamentally, it changed not just perceptions of the past but of the future. Human potential seemed limitless, but time itself was winding down. Divine closure, in the form of the Apocalypse, was at hand.

That is where my work ended, but when I began, I was confident that the Apocalypse and the crusades had nothing to do with one another. Recent historians have almost all agreed on this point: When talking about the crusade movement, it is best to avoid prophecy. Such an attitude, more importantly, conformed to Guibert's prejudices, too. It was a point of principle for him. Rather than a prophetic framework, the most meaningful level of interpretation of any event or idea was, for him, moral, or tropological, something akin to what modern readers think of when they hear the word *psychological*: How is the human mind structured, and what makes people behave as they do? Guibert's goal as a teacher and writer was to change hearts. Promises of heavenly reward and threats of hellfire, he thought, were ineffective tools for reaching listeners and teaching them how to behave. Whatever the reason for Guibert's disillusionment, it could not be because it didn't meet his apocalyptic expectations. Guibert had none to begin with.

Yet during the course of my work, I kept noticing exceptions in the foundational sources for crusade history to what I believed the anti-apocalyptic rule. Eventually, I had made note of so many instances of apocalyptic language that I had to throw the rule out altogether. That earlier, skeptical consensus was understandable. Historians try to empathize with their sources, to treat them (with rare exception) respectfully, or to at least assume that historical figures with whom they are engaged were rational actors, that they had sound reasons for what they thought and wrote, and weren't prone to lunacy. In our age, those who believe in the Apocalypse are dismissed as mad, the kind of people who reject reality and retreat into allegorical or literal bunkers.

For most historians, it has been far easier to see the crusades as driven by a desire for wealth, territorial expanse, or colonial dreams. Or if religion drove them, it would likely be a need for penance on the part of the soldiers, a desire for salvation, a dream of redemption for themselves or their families. In the halcyon days of the early 1990s, when history supposedly had ended and liberal democracies stretched into the future as far as the prophetic eye could see, this sort of modernizing, empathetic retelling of crusade history seemed the only rational approach. Now that we have reentered an age where religious violence is not so foreign, where its enactors openly dream of bringing about the End Times in some form or other, an apocalyptic reading of crusade sources seems compelling, or at least pardonable.

The story told here, however, is not about the rage for apocalyptic thinking that erupted in 1099. It is rather an examination of the question that animated Guibert and other contemporary writers, and one with revived relevance. What had the capture of Jerusalem changed and would these changes endure? Behind it is the question of how to live with an ongoing apocalyptic war, one that seemingly can end only with the destruction of institutions of human judgment and secular government and their transformation into something eternally enduring. That was the illusion that Guibert embraced and then gradually let go.

Part 1 lays the foundation for this project by laying bare the illusion. In its initial conception, the First Crusade was understood and interpreted in biblical, prophetic language. This vision originated not with theologians. It came, rather, from Bohemond of Antioch, from soldiers who had helped lead the crusade and who proclaimed that by taking Jerusalem, the crusaders had fulfilled prophecies from the book of Daniel, prophecies involving the ancient Babylonian King Nebuchadnezzar and a dream about statues and a magical rock. The dream's interpretation had long been shrouded in obscurity, but now those meanings were coming clear, according to Bohemond. A man of remarkable charisma—he was tall and uncommonly handsome, it was said—Bohemond was a brilliant field tactician without whose leadership the crusade would have likely failed during the long siege of Antioch (October 1097–June 1098).

But for all his charm and genius, as well as his facility at self-promotion, Bohemond was a soldier—and a mercenary's son—not a scholar. And he was an opportunist, too, having abandoned the crusade shortly after the fall of Antioch, preferring to remain as the city's ruler rather than to continue on the road to Jerusalem. Even in 1106, as he preached about the prophetic significance of the crusade, his eyes were fixed on not a Muslim but a Christian enemy, the Byzantine ruler Alexius Comnenus, whose empire he hoped to claim. Bohemond's presentation was therefore, for multiple reasons, a bit rough around the edges. Better-educated historians needed to put a nicer gloss on it. None did more in this cause than Lambert of Saint-Omer, a Flemish canon who is one of the principle figures in this narrative. Lambert placed the conquest of Jerusalem at the culmination of world history. That was the illusion; that was the grand hope. European soldiers had fulfilled prophecies of both the Old and New Testaments.

But this view of history had consequences, which form the subject of Part 2. These consequences also help to explain the sources of Guibert's disillusionment. Because of their achievements, born of personal purgation and purity, veteran crusaders were being held to impossible standards of conduct and virtue. The turbulent and at times pathologically brutal behavior of some of these men—justified by appeals to their status as crusaders—would have given any thoughtful observer cause to question how they or their achievements could possibly fit into God's plan. Additionally, the triumph of the crusade carried in its wake hundreds of stories of tragedy, now mostly lost to view but certainly known to contemporaries. It is not a question of whether the First Crusade remained popular or else a target of scathing criticism. It is, rather, a recognition that the idealized version of the story crafted in the years following 1099 was from the start vulnerable to doubt, and that such doubt would have been present well before the first great failure in the crusade movement, the Second Crusade (1146–49).

The Second Crusade was indeed a monumental disaster, and its impact on the memory of the First Crusade is the primary focus of the third part of this book. It was the moment when the disillusionment experienced earlier by Guibert became widespread. The mismanagement of the campaign and its shockingly fast and dire denouement alone would have undercut the idealistic memory of the First Crusade.

Perhaps more startling than the historical and political changes inspired by the Second Crusade were the concomitant changes in prophetic thought itself. Effectively, Christian theologians and intellectuals began writing Jerusalem and the Holy Land out of their apocalyptic narratives. Revelation, the advent of Antichrist, the Second Coming of Christ—all looked more likely to be events that would occur inside Europe, products of ongoing battles between popes and emperors, rather than the result of wars fought in the distant East.

Christian Europe might have continued down this self-critical road and eventually lost interest altogether in the settlements in the Holy Land and in continuing the crusade project. In 1187, however, the Muslim general Saladin conquered Jerusalem, an event shocking enough to demand yet another revision of history and another reinvention of prophecy. That is the subject of the fourth and final part of this book. The fiction that the First Crusade had been a transformational moment in salvation history could no longer be maintained. It was just another battle. Armageddon might yet occur in Jerusalem, but if so, the First Crusade would be only a footnote to it. It surely is no coincidence that at this precise moment, when external events dictated a complete rethinking of the Apocalypse, the most influential prophetic thinker in the Middle Ages, Joachim of Fiore, began writing in earnest. Among his many other achievements, which have been widely recognized and even celebrated, Joachim forced a complete reevaluation of the importance of both the First Crusade and of the ongoing crusade movement. Despite his reputation as a medieval thinker unusually tolerant toward outside groups, including Muslims, Joachim's vision embraced an inevitable and probably endless conflict between Christendom and Islam, between West and East.

A final word on terminology. The word *apocalypse* literally means "revelation." In the Latin tradition, it is the title of the last book of the Bible, written by John of Patmos (an obscure figure who, in the Middle Ages, became conflated with John the Apostle). It also refers to a genre of literature about the End Times and Last Judgment, a genre to which Jewish, Christian, and Muslim writers have all contributed. Among students of the Middle Ages, "apocalypse" refers to a belief that the Last Days are imminent (as opposed to *eschatology*, which refers to a general interest in the Last Days, without a sense that they are at hand). A related concept is *millennialism* or *millenarianism*, a belief based on Revelation 20 that Christ will return to earth to rule for one thousand years before the Last Judgment actually occurs. Because of the association between this last belief and socialist utopias, millennialism has been the focus of most histories of apocalyptic thought—the lead character, as it were.[2] In this book, by contrast, millennialism plays only a minor part.

The ongoing fascination with millennialism does help to explain why historians of apocalyptic thought have taken so little interest in the crusades. And although I will make frequent use of the word *apocalypse*, the book of the Apocalypse proper did not exert significant influence on twelfth-century thinkers who tried to isolate the intersections between prophecy and current events. The most important text was instead the book of Daniel, specifically the story of that dream of King Nebuchadnezzar of Babylon, a dream with whose historical context this story shall begin.

PART I

Prophecy and the First Crusade

CHAPTER 1

Nebuchadnezzar's Dream, 600 BCE

ACCORDING TO DANIEL, in the second year of his reign King Nebuchadnezzar II of Babylon had a troubling dream. He wished to know its meaning, even though the king himself seems to have forgotten its details. Thus when Nebuchadnezzar called together his soothsayers, he set them a double task: describe the dream and then interpret it. Understandably, the soothsayers complained, "There is no one on earth, O king, who can accomplish your command! Nor does any king, though great and mighty, ask such a thing of any diviner, or wise man, or Chaldean."[1] Nebuchadnezzar, unmoved, ordered them all put to death.

It is a singular moment in a legendary, near-mythical career. During Nebuchadnezzar's reign, Babylon assumed an imperial grandeur, which it had never previously possessed. At his command, architects and engineers created the Hanging Gardens, one of the Seven Wonders of the World. The wealth and splendor of his court attracted merchants, diplomats, and settlers from many lands, a diversity of peoples and tongues that itself was a wonder too. Their presence beneath a three-hundred-foot ziggurat, dedicated to the god Marduk, and their incessant multilingual chatter inspired the city's enslaved Jews to invent a tall tale, that of the Tower of Babel—a fantasy of divine vengeance and destruction that remains a potent explanation for the world's ongoing discord.[2]

Those Jews' presence in Babylon, during the period called "the Babylonian Captivity," has become likewise proverbial. Historically, it was the culmination of a series of wars beginning in 605 BCE.

Nebuchadnezzar, returning from a successful campaign against Egypt, forced the kingdom of Judah to accept status as a tributary state. Eight years later, he suppressed a Jewish rebellion and brought the Judean King, Jeconiah, to his capital as a prisoner. He did so with God's blessing, according to the Old Testament, since Jeconiah's father, Jehoiakim, "filled Jerusalem with innocent blood, which the Lord would not pardon."[3] In 587 BCE, after another rebellion, Nebuchadnezzar ordered the city of Jerusalem destroyed and its people forcibly relocated. More distressing, he had the Temple of Jerusalem, built at the command of Solomon, razed and its treasures and vessels broken into pieces.[4]

To return to the dream: Alone among Babylon's wise men, a Jewish exile named Daniel met both of Nebuchadnezzar's challenges. "For there is a God in heaven," Daniel proclaimed, "who opens mysteries and who has revealed to you, King Nebuchadnezzar, what will transpire in the Last Days. Here are your dream and the visions of your head seen while you lay in bed."[5] The king had gazed upon a colossal statue made of various metals. The head was gold, the chest and arms silver, the belly and thighs bronze, and its legs iron. Its feet were made partly of iron and partly of clay. Then a stone, cut from the side of a mountain without the intervention of human hand, struck the statue's feet. The entire thing crashed to the ground, making it as chaff on the summer's threshing floor. In its place, the stone grew into a mountain and filled the earth.

That statue, Daniel explained, symbolized all the kingdoms and empires that ever would exist, the times and ages that God alone can change. The golden head was Nebuchadnezzar, a king among kings to whom God had given strength, power, and glory. After Nebuchadnezzar's death, a new kingdom would arise, inferior to his rule, symbolized by the silver chest and arms, to be succeeded by still another, again less impressive, bronze kingdom, one that would nonetheless rule the entire earth. The fourth kingdom, of iron, would be the least splendid of all, but prove more powerful than any of its predecessors, and it would dominate and destroy whoever might challenge it. Yet that kingdom, too, would grow vulnerable. Its people would mix their seed with that of other nations, and, like iron and clay, they would not cohere. At last, God himself would strike it down and set up his own kingdom, one that would consume all earthly rulers and that would endure forever. "God has shown to the king what is going to happen," Daniel concluded. "The dream is true and its interpretation faithful." Nebuchadnezzar abased himself before Daniel and ordered animals and incense sacrificed to him.[6]

Some questions about the dream remained unanswered—chiefly, who were the successor states, the silver, bronze, and iron kingdoms? Clarity emerged only during two later visions in the same book, ones that Daniel himself experienced. In the first he saw four beasts—a lioness, a bear, a leopard, and an unnamed creature, "wonderful and terrible," with slashing claws and iron teeth. The second one involved a bloody clash between a ram and goat. Based on correspondences among these animals and between them and the four metals, and thanks as well to explanations given by an angel, it is possible for careful readers to fully interpret Nebuchadnezzar's dream.[7] The silver chest symbolized Persia, whose ruler, Darius, allowed the Jews to rebuild Jerusalem. The bronze midsection was the kingdom of Alexander the Great. And the iron legs were the Hellenistic successor states, particularly the Seleucids, who dominated the former Babylonian Empire, and the Ptolemies, who ruled Egypt. And what of the stone uncut by human hand or the mountain that would fill the earth? These figures were to remain veiled. In the words of the angel, they would be "closed and sealed until the appointed time."[8]

The original readers of Daniel—completed more than four hundred years after the book's events were supposed to have occurred—believed that the appointed time had begun. They were residing in and around the city of Jerusalem, where the Seleucid monarch Antiochus IV Epiphanes had outlawed the practice of Judaism. His decree sparked a new uprising, the Maccabean Revolt. The book of Daniel was compiled at this time as an act of intellectual resistance.[9] As such, Antiochus was the fourth, nameless beast in Daniel's vision, a creature more fearsome than any that had come before. More precisely, he was that beast's eleventh horn, uttering blasphemies before God. He was also the last ruler of the iron empire, whom God would strike down. In his place would emerge a new kingdom, one to dominate historical events and preserve Jerusalem till the end of time.

The Maccabean Revolt succeeded, but it did not initiate the Last Days. Antiochus IV died in 164 BCE, about three years after the composition of the book of Daniel. The Maccabees established a dynasty that governed Judea for nearly a century, but it did not fill the earth as a mountain. Instead, in 63 BCE, Judea became a client state of Rome, just as it had once been a tributary of Babylon. The symbolism of the vision, the meaning of the last three metals and the stone, were opened anew for debate.

About 450 years later, the biblical translator and exegete St. Jerome developed what would become the standard interpretation of Nebuchadnezzar's dream. The golden head and silver chest were still Babylon and Persia. The bronze belly and thighs, however, now incorporated both Alexander the Great and the various Hellenistic successor states. In hindsight, the iron legs stood for Rome. Once ferocious and indomitable, her empire had, in Jerome's eyes, weakened. Barbarians had overrun it. Yet Rome depended on those same barbarians to fight its wars. Iron and clay, Romans and barbarians, mixed together. The stone that would bring Rome down was Christ. Uncut by human hand, that is to say born of a virgin and unstained by sex, Christ and his church would grow into a mountain and fill the earth. His heavenly kingdom would stretch into eternity, long after all earthly rule had ceased.[10]

So elegant was Jerome's reading that it stood unchallenged for centuries, one of the fundamental building blocks of Christian historical and apocalyptic thought. But in 1103, in a castle in northern Anatolia, modern-day Turkey, in the city of Niksar, a prisoner named Bohemond had an epiphany about Nebuchadnezzar's dream. It happened while he was speaking with his friend Richard of the Principate, like Bohemond a Norman and a veteran of the First Crusade. In the midst of their conversation, Bohemond realized something remarkable about that stone uncut by human hand. It was not a symbol for Christ. It was instead a symbol of Bohemond himself. He and his friends—they were the stone. The prophet Daniel had been talking about them.

CHAPTER 2

Nebuchadnezzar's Dream, 1106 CE

Bohemond

The prisoner, Bohemond, had been locked away in Niksar for three years. His actual name was "Mark," but when his father realized just how fast his boy was growing, he started calling by the nickname "Bohemond," taken from a tale about a giant.[1] As the Byzantine princess Anna Comnena, in a biography of her father, Emperor Alexius Comnenus, remembered Bohemond's appearance, it was, "unlike that of any other man whether Greek or barbarian seen in those days on Roman soil. The sight of him inspired admiration, the mention of his name terror. I will describe in detail the barbarian's characteristics. His stature was such that he towered almost a full cubit over the tallest men. He was slender of waist and flanks, with broad shoulders and chest, strong in arms; overall he was neither too slender, nor too heavily built and fleshy, but perfectly proportioned.... There was a certain charm about him, but it was somewhat dimmed by the alarm his person as a whole inspired. There was a hard, savage quality in his whole aspect, due, I suppose, to his great stature and his eyes; even his laugh sounded like a threat to others."[2]

Shortly after his revelation about Nebuchadnezzar's dream, Bohemond was released from captivity. A few months later still, in 1105, he would return to Europe, first to Italy and then to France, where he would go on a preaching tour. His words stirred up such excitement that people began to write books about how the Franks conquered Jerusalem, with Bohemond as the hero, though Bohemond

7

had actually quit the expedition early, before it reached Jerusalem. Three monastic writers—Baldric of Bourgueil, Guibert of Nogent, and Robert of Reims (or Robert the Monk)—were especially important in this process.[3]

And suddenly it seemed people everywhere wanted a piece of Bohemond. As a monk from the storied monastery of Monte Cassino, birthplace of Benedictine monasticism, remembered the scene, "everyone rushed to him in crowds, longing to gaze on him, as if they were about to see Christ Himself."[4] According another monk named Orderic Vitalis—whose church was close enough to Bohemond's itinerary to feel the blowback from his speeches—French nobles invited him to stand at baptisms as godfather for their children. His strange name became trendy, "popularized in Gaul, although previously it had been almost unknown to westerners."[5]

Bohemond's purpose in 1105/6 was to organize a new expedition to the East, a second crusade.[6] In theory, he wanted to shore up the settlements founded during the original campaign, including his own principality of Antioch. In practice, he had more personal goals. Most of his life had been spent at war against the Greek emperor Alexius Comnenus. In the 1080s, Bohemond and his father, the legendary Norman mercenary Robert Guiscard, had fought against Alexius in the Balkans. Robert had already captured an impressive collection of territories and aimed at that time to expand his authority eastward, at the expense of the Greek Empire. The campaign, under Bohemond's leadership, eventually foundered. When Bohemond joined the First Crusade in the late 1090s, he decided to change his approach. This time he struck an alliance with the emperor but predictably broke their agreement barely a year later in order to claim Antioch for himself. The crusaders had earlier promised that if they captured cities like Antioch—Byzantine possessions that had only recently been lost to the Turks—they would hand them back over to the empire. Claiming that Constantinople had reneged on its promises of military support, Bohemond decided that he could now found a new principality at Antioch in his own name.

In 1106, he was hoping to take his career trajectory to its logical conclusion. As his father had attempted twenty-five years earlier, he intended to overthrow Alexius and make himself emperor—lofty ambitions for the disinherited bastard son of a Norman freebooter.

Bohemond was doing so, moreover, with the blessing of Pope Paschal II, who had dispatched one of his most important advisers, Bishop Bruno of Segni, to accompany him on his tour. Known mainly as a biblical commentator, Bruno was also a veteran of many of the papacy's wars. Alongside Gregory VII in 1084, he had survived a siege of Rome led by the German emperor Henry IV. Bruno and Gregory owed their rescue and their lives, in fact, to, Robert Guiscard, Bohemond's father. About a decade later, Bruno was helping Urban II plan the original crusade, and he traveled with him into France to promote it.[7] Now, once again ten years later, Bruno was in France, still preaching war, advising not a pope but a freakishly large, fantastically charismatic mercenary. Their goal was to remake history. The lever to move hearts and worlds toward a second crusade was Nebuchadnezzar's dream.

Their first performance came in February 1106, in central France in the town Saint-Léonard-de-Noblat. The church there was a popular destination for pilgrims, especially those who had escaped imprisonment, wrongful or otherwise. Grateful visitors left behind chains from their captivity, some so massive that it seemed miraculous anyone had been able to move them at all.[8] In 1106, the interior of the church was so full of shackles that the more recent pilgrims had had to hang their offerings outside from a tree in the churchyard. The branches "shimmered with symbols all made out of iron."[9] Amid all this iron, one set of chains was made instead of silver. Bohemond himself had had his friend Richard of the Principate, with whom he had discussed Nebuchadnezzar's dream in Niksar, lay them at St. Léonard's shrine and claim that they were the very shackles with which the Turkish warlord had held him captive. By the time Bohemond arrived at the church, everyone would have been buzzing about his gift to the saint and wondering what it was he would have to say.[10]

When he finally did speak at Noblat, the sermon was impressive enough that the monks commissioned a visiting dignitary, Bishop Galeran of Naumburg, to write it down.[11] Part propaganda piece, part apology, part grand adventure, Galeran's account offers an unusually clear window onto what an actual crusade sermon looked like—rarer still, what a crusade sermon preached by a layman looked like. Galeran also reveals the moment Nebuchadnezzar's dream first intersected with the crusades.

Tall Tales

As Galeran tells the story, it started with a chance to convert Muslims, or Saracens, as European Christians preferred to call them. In the summer of 1100, a certain "duplicitous Gentile," by which Galeran meant a Muslim, had told Bohemond that he had begun to hate

Saracen law and that he wished to be baptized. He framed the request in terms of prophecy, recognizing the inevitability of Christ's rule on earth. "'I am a king,' he said, 'and up to now it has seemed ridiculous to me to worship a crucified man. But all the kings of the earth will one day worship him, so why not me? All peoples will serve him, so why must my people wait?'"[12]

But there was a problem. Another Muslim ruler, known as "the Danishmend," an honorific meaning "the wise man," had given protection to the Gentile king in the past.[13] If the Danishmend learned of his conversion to Christianity, it would lead to a bitter war. The king needed protection. And Bohemond naturally, heroically, agreed to help, not seeing that it was a ruse—"Persian trickery."[14] For the unnamed Gentile king was in fact conspiring with the Danishmend, to whom he would betray Bohemond and thus strike a fatal blow against the Christian world.

This story is a highly fictionalized account of something that actually did happen.[15] The Gentile leader who sought Bohemond's aid was not an unnamed Saracen but rather an Armenian Christian called Gabriel, governor of the city of Melitene, or Malatya, in the patchwork frontier region of Eastern Anatolia, divvied up among a variety of ethnic and religious groups at the time, Turks and Franks among them. Armenian leaders like Gabriel had survived by playing one side off against another, not always successfully. For example, a former Armenian governor of Edessa named T'oros had requested military aid from the crusade leader Baldwin of Boulogne, only to have Baldwin depose him in a coup a month later.[16] One of Gabriel's daughters had been married to the same T'oros, so Gabriel knew the risk he was taking by getting involved with the Franks.[17]

Bohemond's journey in 1100 from Antioch to Melitene was a long one, about two hundred miles, much of it through difficult mountainous terrain. And while cutting through one pass, "whose narrow entry was something akin to jaws,"[18] as if entering the mouth of hell, Bohemond fell into an ambush. The story as reported crackles with authentic detail, suggesting that Galeran's rendition is close to what Bohemond had actually said at Noblat: "The Persians did not draw their battle lines together into a tight formation but instead scattered about hither and thither like hunters, striking with sudden force whenever opportunity permitted, pressing against everyone who fled, turning their backs to anyone standing his ground. So skilled were they that they could fire arrows while retreating, thus inflicting great damage on anyone who recklessly pursued them. Their troops carefully avoided our charges. If any of them was thrown from his horse, he could do nothing but be cut down like a helpless lamb."[19]

Bohemond tried to rally his men with a speech, one he likely reenacted outside the church of Saint-Léonard in 1106, maybe beneath a tree of glittering fetters. "'If we live,'" he said,

> "we live for the Lord. If we die, we die for the Lord—but rather than *to die for the Lord*, I should say *to live*, since truly anyone who dies for Christ lives and gains eternal blessedness. Oh happy state of battle, where faith overcomes idolatry; justice, injustice; temperance, impudence; and the whole army of virtues, the monstrous collection of vices—where [the archangel] Michael comes to our aid with a host of angels. For a long time now the Prince of Persians has opposed us and hindered our battles and obstructed our prayers and blocked Michael's aid. But the Prince of Persians will not prevail, because Michael will rise up with a vast force and fight for us against the ancient serpent. Yet, if the Prince of Persians is allowed to postpone our victory through this battle, let the Lord make happen what is good in his eyes, because we still will return joyfully from the fight, because through death we will conquer. Death will be transformed into victory, and we will be granted true life. There can be no happier outcome for the dead, whom Michael will lead exultantly into Paradise."[20]

The language might have been lifted from any of the dozen surviving chronicles of the First Crusade—with one slight difference. Bohemond places an unusual emphasis on St. Michael, a popular saint among the Normans, though not actually much mentioned in First Crusade narratives—another indication of the authenticity of Galeran's account. It is also suggests an apocalyptic outlook. Michael was best known as a dragon slayer in the book of Revelation (see fig. 1).[21]

Bohemond rallied his men repeatedly with words such as these, struck at the Muslims where they appeared strongest, cut down enemies left and right, creating what Galeran describes as "an amusing spectacle" for his followers. Dead Persians fell in piles. Streams of blood trickled down the mountain pass, but to no purpose. However many of the enemy died, more arose "like the poisonous heads of a hydra," creating many new martyrs for Michael to escort to heaven. "Almost everyone, pierced with arrows, had fallen to the ground—horses, riders, infantry—until Bohemond, as the situation now demanded, surrendered to the Danishmend's custody."[22] Thus it was that Bohemond came to be imprisoned in Anatolia.

Despite religious differences, it was customary, in both East and West, for armies to hold valuable prisoners for ransom. Bohemond certainly fit this category, but his case was difficult. He commanded a high price, and no one wanted to pay it. The king of Jerusalem, Baldwin of Boulogne, former lord of Edessa, did not have the money, and anyway Bohemond was a rival for the throne. Alexius Comnenus, the Greek emperor, did have the money, but his support carried an unacceptable proviso. Bohemond would have had to restore Antioch to his control.[23] As for the citizens of Antioch, they were probably happy for Bohemond to stay in prison and to keep as their leader Bohemond's nephew Tancred: "a man fierce and resolute, wise in council, ever ready for battle, like a lion cub, he feared no engagement with the enemy."[24] Tancred and his men reportedly sent prayers to St. Léonard in heaven to free Bohemond but did nothing in the earthly realm to move the process along.[25]

Fortunately for Bohemond, captivity proved comfortable. Even though he was kept in a tower and closely guarded, he could receive visitors and maintained a small retinue of servants—sometimes ten, sometimes twenty. All of these arrangements were made, according to Galeran, because of a truce between the Franks and the Turks, the existence of which would have surprised listeners at Saint-Léonard-de-Noblat, who likely would have been primed to think of Saracens only as blood-drinking monsters.[26] In return for mild treatment, Frankish prisoners promised not to try to escape—but it was a mixed blessing. Due to this treaty, St. Léonard could not intervene. If there had been no such agreement, Léonard could have shattered Bohemond's chains, broken the locks, and smashed the doors, as Christians all over the Latin world were reportedly praying for him to do. But ethics were ethics. Léonard had to control his miraculous impulses, and Bohemond had to stay in his tower, unable to receive "assistance from God, saint, or friend."[27] At Noblat, where monks kept abreast of news from the Holy Land, they prayed every Friday for Bohemond's release,[28] but neither escape nor ransom was an option, and his imprisonment dragged on for more than three years.

One of Bohemond's visitors toward the end of this time was the aforementioned Richard of the Principate. Like Bohemond, Richard had also been captured in battle, and Bohemond had thought him dead, killed not by the Turks but by Alexius Comnenus. Even in the Danishmend's prison, Bohemond considered Alexius his most hated adversary, a man far worse than the Saracens.[29] It was a topic on which he was happy to declaim, as Galeran reports. "O cruelest emperor! His wicked treachery has oppressed many thousands of Christians, some consigned to shipwreck, many to poison, more still to exile, and countless others he has handed over to pagans. This emperor is not a Christian at all but a mad heretic, Julian the

Apostate, another Judas, like a Jew, pretending peace but inciting war, cutthroat to his brothers, a bloody Herod against Christ. He persecutes Christ through his limbs, he slaughters the innocent, he pours out the blood of saints like water, and he makes their remains food for birds of the air."[30] Such a man was unworthy of high office— a usurper who had to go. And in that case, listeners might conclude, who better to install in his place than Bohemond?

In a scene reminiscent of a symposium in ancient Athens, Bohemond reclined on a bed surrounded by "chosen heroes" who had gathered together to enjoy his sweet discourse.[31] Soldiers marveled to one another that God had worked miracles through their own actions in battle. To explain how, they latched onto a specific biblical story—the dream of Nebuchadnezzar. The Bible gave Daniel's interpretation, but Bohemond and his men discovered a new meaning. "Now, just as in the vision of King Nebuchadnezzar, the stone cut from the mountain without human hands has shattered and laid low the pagans. That multifarious statue has been struck by a blow from that stone and been reduced to dust—iron, clay, bronze, silver, and gold. The iron Persians of Nicea and Antioch were laid low. The clay Egyptians of Jerusalem and Ascalon, the Bronze and silver Chaldeans, the golden Arabs, partly put down by the sword, partly reduced to ashes in fires, countless others cast down headlong as if by a storm's wind into the sea."[32]

This reading breaks badly with scripture. According to Daniel, as noted already, the four different metals symbolized four different kingdoms that succeed one another. In Bohemond's reading, according to Galeran, they existed all at once, and the Franks had destroyed them all at once, too. The first great sieges of the crusade (Nicea, which surrendered in 1097 and was returned to Alexius, and Antioch to which Bohemond laid claim in 1098) were fought against a single ethnic group, the Turks, who in this passage become "iron Persians." The last battles of the crusade (Jerusalem, which the Franks conquered in July 1099, and Ascalon, where a month later they defeated another Muslim army) were fought against "clay Egyptians." Where the Chaldeans and Arabs fit into this picture is unclear, but all are Eastern kingdoms, and all had been brought low in the space of three years.

Bohemond then asks, "And why did this happen? Since [the Saracens] stumbled upon the stumbling block [1 Peter 2:8], cut without the hands of cutters, just as he was born from a virgin without the touch of another's hand. This stone verily fell upon those infinite legions of warriors and laid them low by the hands of the lowly and the poor."[33] The first half of this reading is conventional. The stone, uncut by human hand, represented Christ, born of a Virgin and hence created without human agency. But that stone also symbolized the crusade: it was Bohemond, Richard of the Principate, and all the heroes who had liberated Jerusalem from God's enemies.

What Bohemond leaves unclear, as Galeran presents him, is where these prophecies were leading. In Daniel, the statue's collapse represented the end of all earthly rule. It is an apocalyptic moment in the most technical sense—the transformation of the world in the Last Days when the eternal kingdom of God will be realized. Did Bohemond mean to say that the world was ending? It is hard to see how he might credibly have done so. Wars against unbelievers and schismatics were ongoing, and the Saracens—Bohemond assured audiences in 1106—still worshipped idols, effigies intended to recall the monster from Nebuchadnezzar's dream. "The Gentiles have rejected you by building their multifarious statues and have insulted you: 'Go away from us! We don't want to know your ways....You beggar dogs, stupid foreigners trusting in a crucified man who cannot free you! What help has he been to you?'"[34] History had not ended. There were battles yet to be fought.

On another level, though, Bohemond's commentary does argue for the apocalyptic character of the crusade. By so thoroughly defeating Islam, the Franks had fulfilled Nebuchadnezzar's dream, an event that would happen only, according to the Bible, in *novis temporibus*—the Last Days (Daniel 2:28). Perhaps Bohemond made reference to Daniel only because he wished to give his war stories an added sense of grandeur (though since he was traveling through France with the biblical scholar Bruno of Segni, it is unlikely that he would have been entirely ignorant of his words' implications). Regardless, he had offered the clergy in his audience some profoundly exciting ideas to sift through. The crusaders were Christ, the stone whose trajectory in the East had brought down the great edifices of Persian, Chaldean, Arab, and Egyptian empires.

Peace with Honor

Back in Niksar in 1100, the philosophic dialogue drew to a close, and Bohemond fell asleep. Like Nebuchadnezzar, he had a vision. St. Léonard stood before him. "Bohemond!" he said. "Do not despair! Do not continue wasting away in daily sadness because of your imprisonment. God chastises every child whom he shall receive."[35] The moment of liberation was at hand, provided that Bohemond was willing to visit Léonard's shrine as soon as he was able.

The sleeping Bohemond wept so loudly that he roused everyone in the room. Some of his companions suggested shaking the warrior awake to discover the reason behind his tears, but Richard of the Principate stopped them. For Bohemond "might be learning something in a vision, and if we interrupt, it could go very badly for everyone." Richard knew what he was talking about, for he, too, had had visions of St. Léonard before his own liberation from a Greek prison, as Galeran tells elsewhere in his collection of the miracles of St. Léonard.[36]

Eventually, Bohemond awoke, but he refused to answer questions. Instead, he took the Psalter kept at the head of his bed (a shocking detail to audiences, no doubt—here was a warrior who could read his own prayers!), sang songs, and offered thanks to God and St. Léonard. Calm restored to his followers, Bohemond explained that he had been crying not out of sadness but of joy, for "St. Léonard is going to free us through the same Danishmend who captured us."[37]

At the same time, unknown to Bohemond, the Danishmend was preparing to make war against a neighboring emir called "Solomon." "There existed," Galeran writes, "between the Danishmend and Solomon an inveterate, incurable hatred. It originated before the coming of the Christians and continued afterward, too, with regular clashes in battle, as well as acts of plunder, arson, and slaughter."[38] Solomon was the usual Latin name for Qilij-Arslan, the Sultan of Rûm, another Turkish dynasty in Anatolia founded by Qilij-Arslan's father (who really was called Solomon, or "Suleiman," in Arabic). The Danishmend and Qilij-Arslan were bitter enemies, though they had put aside their differences long enough to, among other things, capture Bohemond in 1100 and to destroy a second wave of crusading armies in 1101. By 1103 their truce had broken down, and when Qilij-Arslan challenged the Danishmend to battle, according to Galeran, the Danishmend's advisers urged him to avoid the fight, believing they could never win.[39]

The only person who did not panic was the Danishmend's wife, a closet Christian, Galeran explains, or imagines. St Léonard visited her, too, and delivered this message: "Your faith will save your husband, free your homeland, drive off the enemy, return liberty, restore lost goods, and expand your power into the lands of your enemies. As a faithful counselor to your husband, give him useful advice. Let him take as much money as he wishes from his prisoner and strike a treaty and a fast friendship. If he releases Bohemond, he will have victory in battle."[40] Some sources put the actual ransom as high as one hundred thousand bezants.[41] In Galeran's retelling, the Danishmend's wife negotiated her husband down to five thousand bezants. And Bohemond did not even pay that amount. Rather, the Danishmend's wife covered some of the ransom from her own resources. The rest she raised from Turks anxious to have the crusade's most famous hero fighting on their side.[42] The Danishmend still had concerns, but a nocturnal visit from St. Léonard—who else?—closed the deal.[43] If any audience member at one of Bohemond's performances still questioned whether it was a good bargain, Bohemond added a further detail, that the Danishmend had promised to release four thousand prisoners.[44]

For three continuous months in 1103, according to Galeran, Bohemond and his men made war against Qilij-Arslan, driving his armies back deep into his territories and expanding the Danishmend's realm the equivalent of a four-day ride on horseback.[45] And then, liberated and ever victorious, Bohemond returned to the West, ready to initiate a new phase in the crusade.

Historically speaking, whether Bohemond ever really did help the Danishmend is unclear. After his return to Antioch, he seems to have directed his energies against yet another Turkish ruler, Ridwan of Aleppo, probably in the hopes of winning enough plunder to pay off his ransom (which of course had not been settled by his own captors). The campaign went badly. In May 1104, a joint Christian army from Antioch and Edessa under Bohemond's command was defeated near Harran, located close to the modern border between Turkey and Syria. The Turks used the venerable strategy of false retreat, drawing the Franks into an ambush—the type of maneuver that a reputed genius like Bohemond should have foreseen. Instead, two Frankish leaders, Count Baldwin II of Edessa and Joscelin of Courtnay, were captured, while Bohemond and Tancred escaped back to Antioch, a city now surrounded by enemies—Aleppo, Mosul, the Sultanate of Rûm, and his old archenemy, Alexius Comnenus.[46]

Even in failure, though, Bohemond inspired gripping stories. The emperor's daughter Anna Comnena, says that he left Antioch so terrified of capture that he faked his own death, hiding inside a coffin.[47] He kept a dead rooster locked up with him, to create an appropriate stench. At every port the men aboard his ship tore their hair and cried in despair, so that everyone would know of the giant warrior's death. Finally at Corfu, still in Byzantine territory but near Apulia, Bohemond felt safe enough to rise from his grave and to send a message back to Alexius:

I want you to know that, although I was dead, I have come back to life again; I have escaped your clutches. In the guise of a dead man I have avoided every eye, every hand, every plan. And now I live, I move, I breathe the air, and from the island of Corfu I send to Your Majesty offensive, hateful news. It will not make very pleasant reading for you. I have handed over the city of Antioch to my nephew Tancred, leaving him a worthy adversary for you and your generals. I myself will go to my own country. As far as you and your friends are concerned, I am a corpse; but to myself and my friends it is manifest that I am a living man, plotting a diabolical end for you.[48]

This charade was the set up for the grand, theatrical tour of France, whose opening act occurred in the churchyard of Saint-Léonard de Noblat in 1106.

The Epic Hero

For a time, in 1106 and 1107, everything again seemed possible for Bohemond, now not just a crusading hero but a scholar and prophet. And he had become a member of a royal family, too, for during his tour he married a French princess, Constance, daughter of Philip I of France and sister to the future Louis VI.[49] He was now fully qualified to claim a crown. According to one rumor, the mother of his archenemy Alexius Comnenus, also a sorceress, had foreseen "that a man of Frankish origin would take away his rule and his life." Guibert, who recorded this story, explained its meaning: "Bohemond now wishes to fulfill this oracle. He frequently attacks the emperor and in battle has often forced him to turn tail and run, and he has annexed the greater part of his lands to his command. His people come from Normandy, which is part of Francia. For this reason as well he will qualify as a Frank: because he is marrying the daughter of the king of the Franks."[50]

Such would be the sequel to the First Crusade—the creation of a Frankish empire that stretched from Paris to Jerusalem, a Christian kingdom standing against the future attacks of Antichrist.[51]

But why stop there? A contemporary poet called Marbod of Rennes wrote a short tribute to Bohemond, presumably in the wake of the same 1106 itinerary. The entire world was about to fall under Bohemond's sway. The king of Constantinople already paid him tribute, and of course Nicaea and Antioch had surrendered to his armies. But his reach might extend farther still, embracing lands and peoples whose histories reached back to the days of Nebuchadnezzar. "Syria serves him, and the Sabines send him new gifts. The Parthian, the Arab, the Median, all wish to enter into an alliance with him. The resplendent king of Babylon appeases him with gifts. The Persian sultan fears him and flees his sword. Africa trembles and devotedly gives him tribute."[52] At the beginning of the poem, Marbod observes, "In the whole world, no man is equal to Bohemond." He concludes it, "Through the whole world, redounding rumor bellows 'Bohemond!' And again the world bellows at Bohemond's great deeds."[53]

This campaign to remake the world in Bohemond's image began in 1107. As his father had done in 1082, Bohemond launched his grand enterprise with a siege to Alexius's city of Dyrracchium. on the eastern Adriatic coast.

He went no farther.

A year later, as the Franks had made no progress and disease was breaking out in their camps, Bohemond and Alexius negotiated the Treaty of Devol, essentially a record of Bohemond's abject surrender.[54] Among its terms, Bohemond promised to restore Antioch to Alexius, but after Dyrracchium he never returned to the East. Instead, he went home to southern Italy, where he passed his final years. In doing so, he allowed his nephew Tancred to keep Antioch and to leave open the possibility that one of his own children with Constance might someday inherit it, as eventually did happen.[55]

Observers in France tried to ignore the giant failure of Bohemond's last "crusade." One account notes only that Bohemond left France in triumph, and that his son by Constance, Bohemond II, would later die while campaigning around Antioch. A Latin account of the failed siege of 1107, written at the monastery at Fleury—a community with close connections to the French monarchy—says that contrary to report, the emperor Alexius surrendered to Bohemond because the Franks were invincible.[56] In any case, the anonymous author adds, incoherently, Bohemond would have captured Dyrracchium, had one of his brothers, Guy, corrupted by bribes from Alexius, not plotted against him.[57]

Another monk from the monastery of Fleury, named Rodulfus Tortarius, wrote a grand poem about the siege of Dyrracchium and likewise declared Bohemond the winner. It was another Trojan War, only this time the Greeks were the besieged. According to Rodulfus, a Byzantine general with the Homeric name Patroclus tried to rally his men against Bohemond with these words: "It is right to recall your ancestors, o powerful Danaans! Be mindful, warriors, of your origins...Troy perished, burned in Mycenean fires!"[58] One of the Norman leaders, Guy (the same Guy whom the chronicler from Fleury named as a traitor), exhorts his men to "remember the strength that Gaul has: it has tamed the world that once lay under

Roman rule."[59] If the Franks had replaced Rome on the historical stage, they could certainly replace the Greeks. Empires fall, and from the ruins new mountains rise.

Unlike these writers from Fleury, Orderic Vitalis, a Norman monk and a renowned twelfth-century historian did acknowledge Bohemond's failure, blaming it again on his brother Guy. At the same time, Orderic felt reservations about the whole basis for the campaign. To criticize it, he imagined a group of soldiers asking Bohemond a question that would have seemed self-evident in 1108, after the magic of his sermons had begun to fade: "No hereditary right drew us to this bold enterprise; no prophet sent from God roused us with a message from heaven; only lust to rule in the dominions of another caused you to undertake this difficult task and, on our side, greed of gain lured us on to suffer an intolerable burden of toil and peril."[60]

But this was a minority view. Despite his three-year imprisonment and subsequent military failures in the east against Saracens and despite the disastrous siege of Dyrracchium, Bohemond's reputation as hero and figure of prophecy survived him. He had led armies into battle against enemies whose roots stretched back to Nebuchadnezzar and had won. In doing so, he had forged himself into a weapon of God, a stone uncut by human hand. As the inscription on his tomb observes, "Because the world surrendered to him, I cannot call him 'man,' and would not call him 'god.'"[61]

Galeran would never have called him a god either, but he found the prophetic tenor of the giant's message compelling. A few years later, he wrote a new account of Bohemond's adventures, which he dedicated to Gertrude of Saxony, mother of the crusader Robert of Flanders. The world had not ended, but Galeran kept the sermon's apocalyptic vision front and center.[62] In recounting Bohemond's invocation of Nebuchadnezzar's dream, Galeran imagines the "chosen heroes" saying to one another, "Behold! The end of the world approaches. Nation rises up against nation and kingdom against kingdom, West against East, Europe against Asia, good angels oppose evil ones, Christ opposes the ancient dragon! Thanks be to God, Michael stands as victor in heaven, the ancient enemy falls, the savior strikes the dragon's head! Angels and archangels rejoice, every tribe and every tongue celebrates Christ's victory, since now salvation has arrived with the strength and power of Christ, and Christ will be all things in all people!"[63] It is an amalgamation of some of the most common apocalyptic imagery from the bible, combining language from the "Little Apocalypse" of the gospels, where Christ tells his disciples how to recognize the End Times, with the war for heaven described in the book of Revelation.[64] This general discussion of the Apocalypse led Bohemond and his band of heroes directly to Nebuchadnezzar's dream, and how the stone uncut by human hands was both Christ "and the army of Christ, falling like a storm and dispersing the wicked crowd through the might of God. It cast them down and scattered them like dust on the face of the earth."[65]

After Bohemond's carefully choreographed tour of Europe, it was not hard for many to believe that the Apocalypse was nigh. Bohemond himself may have failed to connect all the dots and to carry the story to a sulfurous conclusion, but other historians, theologians, and storytellers were ready to fill the intellectual breach and to preserve the idea of an apocalyptic First Crusade, even if they forgot to whom they owed their beliefs.

CHAPTER 3

Building Blocks of the Apocalypse

The Apocalypse: A Celebration

The man who best refined Bohemond's vision of the apocalyptic crusade was himself no great storyteller, and probably no great theologian either. But he had a vision of history, which he expressed not through narrative but through diagrams and pictures.

His name was Lambert, and he had heard Bohemond preach near the midpoint of his tour, on March 30, 1106, at the church of Saint-Omer in Flanders. So impressed was Lambert by Bohemond's performance that he made record of it in the church's calendar of feast days. He may have noticed, in doing so, how closely Bohemond's visit followed March 25—the most important day in history. It was, according to that same calendar, the anniversary of the creation of the earth and of Adam, the Annunciation of Christ's birth to the Virgin Mary, the Crucifixion, the crossing of the Red Sea, Abraham's sacrifice of Isaac, and the victory of St. Michael over the dragon, as foretold in Revelation and as mentioned by Bohemond in his battlefield oration against the Danishmend in 1100.[1] Key events in salvation history, all resonating across centuries, from Creation to Judgment, and then five days later, the most charismatic man alive came to Saint-Omer to tell stories of wars against Greeks and Saracens and to proclaim a new phase in humanity's journey.

This message from Bohemond helped inspire Lambert to write a book. Not a narrative history, as many of his contemporaries were doing. Instead, he constructed an encyclopedia, a massive one-volume work called the *Liber floridus*, or *Book of Flowers*, to reflect the diversity of its contents, gathered from "the heavenly meadow."[2] While it is not like a modern encyclopedia—Lambert did not arrange content alphabetically—the word does suggest the ambition of the project. He hoped to capture, describe, diagram, and often illustrate as many events, animals, geographic concepts, planets, and trees as possible. The event which most inspired this project was the First Crusade.

It was a topic to which he returned regularly in his book. In the liturgical calendar—in addition to Bohemond's visit—Lambert noted the date of Pope Urban II's sermon at Clermont in 1095, the day the crusaders departed for Jerusalem, and the dates of the campaign's most important battles. The longest text in the *Liber floridus* is a version of the *History of Jerusalem*, written by the priest and crusader Fulcher of Chartres. Lambert himself described the crusade, briefly, in a set of historical annals of his own composition.[3] The crusade also appears at the end of the very first page of the *Liber floridus*, a breathless one-page summary of everything that had ever happened in the history of the world, starting with Cain and then mentioning, among other topics, the discovery of music, metallurgy, and astronomy; the invention of the alphabet; the writing of the Ten Commandments; and the founding of Rome, before concluding with these two sentences: "Godfrey, son of Count Eustace of Bouillon, in the year of the Lord 1099, captured Jerusalem. Robert, the fourteenth count of Flanders, then established Godfrey as King of Jerusalem."[4]

It is not completely surprising that Lambert set the First Crusade at or near history's climax. Numerous passages in scripture predicted a great battle against an unbelieving enemy to be fought in and around Jerusalem. In 1099, it had happened. History had not unfurled exactly as expected, but prophetic language is always less ambiguous after the fact. Lambert's task, when he started writing around 1110—four years after Bohemond's tour—was to revisit old prophecies and to try to make sense out of them based on everything that had just occurred and perhaps catch a glimpse of what was yet to come.

To do so, Lambert did not study the crusade in isolation. He needed to put it in the grand sweep of history, beginning with Adam and Eve and looking forward to the Last Days. Certain building blocks lay ready to hand, including scripture, of course; St. Augustine of Hippo's massive work of theology and history, *The City of God*, composed in the early years of the fifth century; and *Histories against the Pagans*, written by Orosius, one of St. Augustine's contemporaries and disciples. These last two works are not explicitly prophetic. Augustine in particular has the reputation of being a rational man, one who used his considerable intellect to tamp down superstitions about the Last Days. History would end when God willed it. Christians had no business trying to predict it or hurry it along. And in any case, anything of any importance had already happened with the Crucifixion of Christ. After the death of Christ, in Augustine's view, God was just running out the clock. Orosius, by contrast, wrote history in a triumphal register. God's hand had guided the achievements of Rome; the Last Days were at worst a distant problem of little concern to modern Christians. Christians were too busy taking over the Roman Empire to bother wondering whether it all might end soon.

Whatever their differences, Augustine and Orosius did share some common ground. Both described a world divided geographically and historically between East and West, and it was this language that shaped Lambert's view of the First Crusade.

One other point about Lambert and his prophetic vision needs emphasis. Modern apocalyptic ideas, shaped by the threat of nuclear war and possibility of an all-too-literal rain of fire, allow only one rational response: terror. But Lambert and his contemporaries did not imagine the End of Time in this way. The Apocalypse was a drama in which Christians would play important roles, many of them heroic. It was not a cause for fear or resignation. It was a call to arms, an exciting tale, an adventure easily reconcilable to the prosperous urban world of Flanders where Lambert lived and which he celebrated in his encyclopedia, even as he drew diagrams to demonstrate why that history was reaching, if not its termination, its climax.

The Last Days as a Historical Problem

There was, however, an obstacle for anyone—historian or prophet—who wished to write about the end of the world. According to scripture it was impossible to say when it would happen. God the Father had sealed that information so tightly that even Christ claimed not to know. "Of that day and hour no one knows, neither the angels in heaven, nor the Son, but only the Father."[5] Outside of the Bible, there was no greater religious authority than St. Augustine, who had also condemned attempts at calculating the end of time.[6] Because of Augustine's reputation, historians have usually assumed that his word was final.

But the gospel offered a loophole for date counters. Just before declaring the Day of Judgment unknown and unknowable, Christ presented a parable: "From the fig tree learn this lesson. When its branch becomes tender and its leaves bud, you know that summer is near. So also when you see these things, know that [the Son of Man] is near, at the very gates. Amen, I say to you that this generation will not pass away before these things have come to pass."⁷ The signs of the Last Days form a familiar litany: war, rumor of war, persecution, false prophets, solar and lunar eclipses, stars falling from the sky. On the one hand, the end is unknowable. On the other, it is near, and clear signs will precede it. With a proper sense of history and current events, by watching fig trees, it might still be possible to decode God's secrets. To someone like Lambert, a Christian conquest of Jerusalem would seem to have portended an imminent abundance of figs. Lambert was at least willing to believe as much.

Augustine, by contrast, remained skeptical, despite the fact that during his later years, figs seemed to be sprouting everywhere, particularly after 410, when armies of Goths had sacked Rome. That was the well-nigh apocalyptic moment that forced him to write *The City of God.* For a thousand years, formidable walls and pagan gods had kept the city safe. Then, less than a century after Constantine's conversion, barbarian tribes had plundered it. Who was to blame? In the eyes of traditionally-minded fifth-century Roman aristocrats, it was the fault of Christianity. Christians, on the other hand, were tempted to read barbarian incursions as a sign of God's wrath and the imminence of the Last Days. Augustine's contemporary Jerome believed as much. It had been foretold in Nebuchadnezzar's dream. "As for [the statue's] feet and toes, partly of iron and partly of clay, it obviously is happening now: Just as in the beginning nothing was stronger or harder than the Roman Empire, so now at the end, nothing is weaker."⁸

To respond to both camps, Augustine fashioned a sophisticated, nuanced historical theory capable of explaining everything—past, present, and future. The central image, as the title of his great work implies, was the city or, more precisely, two cities: the City of Man and the City of God. The story of humanity and of each individual life is one of pilgrimage, a journey from the earthly city to its heavenly counterpart. Historically, the City of Man originated in the Bible when Cain murdered his brother Abel—not coincidentally the starting point for Lambert of Saint-Omer's one-page summary of world history in the *Liber floridus*. Driven away from the face of God, Cain built a city and called it Enoch, after his son. Humanity's journey to redemption began there. "It is written of Cain that he founded a city; Abel, however, as a pilgrim, did not found one. For the saints' city is in heaven. It produces citizens here, and through them it continues on its pilgrimage until the time of this kingdom shall end. Then the city will bring together all people, resurrected in their own bodies, and they will receive the kingdom promised to them and will reign with the prince and king of the ages in that place for all time."[9]

The most common earthly, historical avatars for these cities, the City of Man and the City of God, are Babylon and Jerusalem, with Rome somewhere in the middle. For Augustine, these three cities shadow and inhabit one another, just as they had for John of Patmos, author of the book of Revelation, and for Lambert of Saint-Omer, too. In Augustine's formula, "Babylon, as if the first Rome, moves in this world alongside the pilgrim City of God."[10]

When John of Patmos referred to Rome as "Babylon," his purpose was to encourage its destruction. Augustine, by contrast, did not wish to attack Rome, only to downplay its importance.[11] Rome, as a way station on the pilgrimage to heavenly Jerusalem, may suffer catastrophe, as it had in 410. It might even fall into oblivion. If so, its fate (like the fate of the earthly city of Jerusalem) would be of little import when set against God's plans for human salvation.[12]

As part of this program, Augustine created a new historical schema: the Six Ages of History.[13] It would prove to be one of his most enduring achievements. In brief, all of history paralleled the story of Creation: God labored for six days to create the earth and then rested on the seventh. In the same way, humanity would labor in the world for six ages until, with the seventh age, the elect would rest in heaven.

The six historical ages all parallel one another, too. Each begins with a moment of creation or renewal: (1) Adam and the Garden of Eden; (2) Noah's emergence from the ark after the flood; (3) God's covenant with Abraham; (4) the reign of King David in Israel; (5) the Israelites at rest in a foreign land; and (6) the Incarnation of Christ. Correspondingly, each age ends with a moment of crisis or destruction: (1) the flood; (2) the confusion of languages at the Tower of Babel; (3) the wickedness of King Saul; (4) Nebuchadnezzar's conquest of Jerusalem; (5) the destruction of Israel by the Romans; and (6) the terrors of Antichrist and the Last Judgment.

The significance of this model for historical theory in the Middle Ages and for writers like Lambert was threefold. First, it undercut the importance of political history, and especially Roman history. The rise and fall of empires and kingdoms, including Jerusalem, while engaging topics, were not the principles around which to compose history. Second, Augustine implicitly argued against the use of chronological calculation as a means for predicting the end of time.

The six ages parallel one another, but their lengths varied remarkably. One could not use the span of one age to predict the length of another. Third, and most importantly, Augustine argued that with the start of the Sixth Age, discrete events in human history (like, had he lived to see it, the First Crusade) had ceased to matter. Everything important that was going to happen had already happened. There were to be no more major turning points, no plot twists. From now until the end it would be only one thing after another, none of it particularly consequential.

Lambert of Saint-Omer did not get that part of the message. He was likely not a careful reader of Augustine. In the nearly six hundred manuscript pages of the *Liber floridus*, he quotes Augustine only six times. On three occasions he uses him to describe the mechanics of bodily resurrection. Another time he quotes *The City of God* as a source for Sibylline prophecies. In two other places he misattributes to Augustine quotations about heaven and hell. On the few occasions when Lambert turned to Augustine, he saw him as an apocalypticist.[14]

Lambert probably inherited whatever Augustinian theory he did possess indirectly, in large part through a prolific seventh-century writer, historian, and encyclopedist, Isidore of Seville. Of the numerous scribes who copied Isidore's chronicle of world history, many divided it according to Augustine's Six Ages (whether Isidore did so is uncertain). Events within these six ages, were carefully arranged according to the year of creation, or *anno mundi*. Isidore's history, as most medieval readers would have encountered it, encouraged readers to think about how long the world had lasted, how long it might endure, and how to connect all of this to the theory of the six ages of history—precisely the sort of chronological speculation that Augustine had advised against.[15]

The Politics of History

It was a common misreading, one made by Augustine's own student, Orosius, author of a book called *Histories against the Pagans*, which, for about seven hundred years after Orosius's death in 420 CE, remained the most influential history book in Europe. More copies of it survive from the early Middle Ages than of any other historical text, including one at the library at Saint-Omer with which Lambert worked, notes in his own hand occasionally scribbled in the margins.[16] In the *Liber floridus*, Lambert included one long excerpt from the *Histories against the Pagans* and made at least five other references to it—for geographic information; for supplemental biographical details on Alexander the Great; and for the history of the Roman Empire from Julius Caesar to Theodosius II.[17] More than Augustine, Orosius gave form to Lambert's sense of history.

The key difference between Augustine and Orosius is the latter's optimism. He believed that Rome could recover from the disaster of 410 and would continue to dominate the Mediterranean world and beyond, perhaps for all time—and it would do so because God willed it. Encouraged to write a Christian history imbued with Augustine's philosophy, according to one modern writer, he "wholly failed to understand his master's mind."[18]

That verdict is not entirely fair. At the time Orosius began his *Histories,* Augustine had finished only the first ten of the twenty-two books that would eventually comprise *The City of God.*[19] These early sections argue not so much that the sack of Rome did not matter, but that equally bad or worse things had happened in ancient Rome, when the pagan gods were supposedly keeping it safe. Only in the latter twelve books, written after Orosius had finished his *Histories*, did Augustine develop the image of the church as a "pilgrim city," a stranger in this world on its journey to Heaven.[20]

Orosius had in fact fully absorbed the first half of *The City of God.* The sack of 410, he argues in his *Histories*, was far less traumatic than what had happened when the Gauls devastated the city in 390 BCE. Gallic warriors had massacred the population of Rome and sought to destroy the city's very name; the Goths, by contrast, had allowed sanctuary to whoever entered a church. Hardly any senator survived the Gauls' attack; more recently, hardly any senator suffered at the hands of the Goths. "Behold, those past times to which we compare the present! Behold, the past times for which man's memory longs!"[21] It was the most important legacy Orosius left to Lambert (and other medieval writers) and one that left room for the portentous interpretation of the First Crusade—a sense that, despite what Augustine had argued, history still mattered. God's plan was continuing to reveal itself through the activities of men. And human institutions—imperial governments or armies emblazoned with the cross—were capable of advancing the work of salvation.

Chronology mattered too. The calculation of years contained secrets, if only one knew how to read them. For example, the first Christian Roman emperor, according to Orosius, was not Constantine but rather Philip the Arab, who reigned from 244 to 249 CE. A Christian needed to rule at this time "for this reason alone: so that the one-thousandth year of the city of Rome might be dedicated to Christ rather than to idols."[22] More august than his predecessors yet in typical

Roman fashion, Orosius says, Philip celebrated the millennium with magnificent spectacles. He did not, however, allow processions to the Capitoline Hill in Rome or sacrifices to be performed in the temples of the pagan gods as had once been customary—or at least no writer Orosius knew of reports that Philip did so.[23] Once again, for Orosius, God's secrets lurked in the shadows of political events.

For Lambert, seven centuries (and one crusade) later, the tension between sacred and secular history became something of a dilemma. Which one was the more important, which one more clearly revealed God's plan? His uncertainty on this point shows through most clearly in his treatment of a particular chronological question: whether the number of years between the Creation of Man and the Incarnation of Christ was 5,217 or 5,258. He arrived at these two sums by a variety of paths. To generalize, he usually preferred 5,217 when calculating the years of the world according to the Six Ages of History (see table 1), but he learned toward 5,258 when calculating according to three ages, a new schema developed around the foundations of the cities of Babylon and Rome (see table 2).

The question was not one of mathematics or even divergent sources. It was instead about theory. Did the Sixth Age of History, the Age of the Church, begin with the Incarnation, as Augustine had believed, or with the accession of Augustus Caesar to the imperial throne—which according to Orosius had happened forty-two years

Table 1: Lambert's Six Ages of History

Six Ages of History	Number of Years for Each Age
1. Adam to Noah	2,242 years
2. Noah to Abraham	942 years
3. Abraham to David	973 years
4. David to the Babylonian Captivity	512 years
5. Babylonian Captivity to Incarnation	548 years
6. Age of Church	Begins in year of the world 5217

Table 2: Lambert's Three Ages of History

Three Ages of History	Number of Years for Each Age
1. Creation to Founding of Babylon	3,342 years
2. Babylon to Founding of Rome	1,164 years
3. Rome to Incarnation	752 years
Age of Church	Begins in year of the world 5258

before Christ?[24] Lambert waffled between these two options. If he wished to emphasize Christ's place in history, he put Christ's birth and the beginning of the Sixth Age in *anno mundi* 5217. If he wished to emphasize the role of Augustus, he would start the Sixth Age of history with the emperor's accession to the throne and thus place the Incarnation forty-two years later, in *anno mundi* 5258.

At the very least the emperor played a major part in the story of salvation, as Lambert demonstrates through a portrait of Augustus Caesar (see fig. 2). He inserted it into a chronicle of world history, at a point immediately after the end of the Fifth Age and before the beginning of the Sixth. Below the emperor's feet is a note indicating that during his reign Augustus Caesar sealed the doors of the Temple of Janus—the tangible sign that the empire was at peace, because Janus, the two-faced god, hence a symbol of discord, was trapped inside. In a circle around the emperor, Lambert quotes Luke 2:1, which describes how Augustus ordered a census to be taken of the Roman world, leading indirectly to Christ's birth in Bethlehem. Lambert juxtaposes these points—peace in Rome and Christ's birth in Bethlehem—visually, just as Orosius notes them in his *Histories* one after the other, to show how unusually fruitful the reign of Augustus had been and why Christ chose to be born during it.[25] Empire and Incarnation, secular and spiritual history, inextricably linked, moved in tandem throughout the story of human salvation.

That was Lambert's conclusion, Augustinian caution be damned. History had mattered in the days of Caesar, and as the fall of Jerusalem in 1099 demonstrated, it still mattered. In the words of the prophet Daniel, God changed kingdoms and ages. At one time he had done so through heroes like Augustus Caesar; now he worked through Bohemond and his companions—men who built and ruled kingdoms that encompassed the lands where Christ lived.

Orosius the Prophet

Orosius was no prophet. He celebrated the past and present, but he never claimed to predict the future or to speak in the voice of God. That was Lambert's greatest challenge in using *Histories against the Pagans* as a guide to the Apocalypse. Orosius had believed that despite what had happened in 410, Rome was entering an era of renewed progress.[26] Antichrist would one day come, and it would be terrible, but those days were far removed and not really a fit subject for history.[27] Whatever Lambert learned from Orosius, it had little to do with the Apocalypse. Instead, and in connection with the First

Crusade, Orosius taught Lambert that there existed a fundamental division in the world between East and West, a historical truism most clearly illustrated through the fortunes of empires and cities.

To begin with empires, Orosius, like the prophet Daniel, believed that there had been four great world powers. But he did not base his model on Nebuchadnezzar's dream. He took his inspiration more from cartography and the four cardinal directions. Babylon was the great empire in the East; Macedon, in the North; Carthage, in the South; and Rome, in the West.[28]

The two most important of these empires were Babylon, the first, and Rome, the last. The other two lay somewhere in a murky chronological middle. "Between the first and the final of these," writes Orosius, "that is between Babylon and Rome, as if between an old father and his little son, came Africa and Macedon, briefly and in the middle, like a tutor and a guardian, elevated by the needs of the time rather than by right of inheritance."[29] Babylon had endured for 1,400 years. The middle kingdoms each lasted 700 years, though they overlapped chronologically with one another. Rome nearly followed the fates Carthage and Macedon and almost collapsed after 700 years, when a great fire came close to destroying the city. But it survived, and at the time Orosius was writing in the early fifth century, it had endured for about 1,170 years. Orosius never addresses what would have seemed an obvious question to a reader steeped in apocalyptic theory. Were the Last Days going to begin in another 230 years, to align Rome's fall with Babylon's?[30]

Whatever his admiration for Orosius, Lambert found this model defective. He preferred something closer (though not identical) to Jerome's traditional reading of Daniel. As was characteristic for Lambert, he explained his own system most clearly through a diagram, titled "The Order of the Principal Ruling Kingdoms."[31] The first kingdom was "the Assyrians," generally synonymous with "Babylonians" in medieval historical writing. They were succeeded by the Medians, among whom Lambert, like Orosius, numbered Nebuchadnezzar. The Persians, who conquered Nebuchadnezzar's Babylon, were the third great kingdom. And of course Rome was the fourth.[32] But in reality, Lambert's four great kingdoms are but two: Babylon and Rome, for the first three kingdoms are all in the East, each one connected to Babylon, and they stand in complementary opposition to Rome in the West. Babylon and Rome, like Babylon and Jerusalem, are archetypes—political, spiritual, historic, and geographic entities whose symbolic resonances are discernible only when placed alongside one another. In Orosius's words, "Babylon finally was overthrown by King Cyrus at the same time that Rome was freed from the domination of the Tarquinian kings. Indeed at the same moment one fell, and the other rose. The former [Babylon], for the first time in its history, became dominated by foreigners; the latter [Rome], for the first time in its history, cast down the arrogance of some of its own people [the Tarquinian tyrants]. The former [Babylon], as if dying, lost its inheritance; the latter [Rome], as if growing up, knew itself to be the heir. The empire of the East died, and the empire of the West was born."[33] It is one of the earliest, and probably the simplest, expressions in Christian thought of *translatio imperii*—the idea that legitimate political authority shifted from East to West.[34]

In Lambert's conception of history, *translatio imperii* was more of a leap to the west than a drift. On one of his world maps, he placed the kingdoms of Assyria, Media, and Persia one after the other roughly on a line from west to east (with Babylon lying between the first two kingdoms). In other words, during the first three eras of history, kingdoms moved steadily to the east before suddenly lunging dramatically back across Asia and half of Europe to land in Rome.[35] He makes the point more explicitly in another passage in the *Liber floridus* called "The Five Most Famous Cities." The list comprises the original Babylon in Assyria, the second Babylon in Egypt, Ecbatana (the Median capital), Nineveh, and finally Rome.[36] Again, urban history—for Lambert the city dweller, the only kind of history—lingered in the East and then shifted decisively to the West and to Rome, where the center of cultural and political power was to remain until King Godfrey, with the help of Robert of Flanders, reconciled geography and world history by conquering Jerusalem in 1099, establishing it as a new, or renewed, kingdom.

Orosius's model also provided a secular, political counterpoint to Augustine's *City of God*. All history is a journey from one city to another, from earthly Babylon to heavenly Jerusalem, with Rome as a way station along that path. In the case of Babylon and Rome, history and allegory were the same thing. Even Augustine thought so. He used the analogy three times in Book 18 of *The City of God*. There have been many great empires, he observes there, but two of them were longer and more famous than the rest—the Assyrians and then the Romans. Together they form a pattern: "the one is earlier, the other later; the one was only in the East, the other arose in the West; when the one ended, the other immediately began. I could call all other kingdoms and kings mere appendages of those two."[37] Babylon was the first Rome, and Rome, the second Babylon.[38] Just as the first conquered Asia, so the second would conquer the world, facing armies better trained and better equipped than the first Babylon had done. But they were both incarnations of the City of Man and shadows of the City of God, backdrops to be struck down when the divine city finally revealed itself.[39]

Orosius and Lambert's takeaway message was much simpler than Augustine's. Babylon and Jerusalem were at war. One city was filled with Persians or Saracens or demons; the other, with Romans or Franks or angels. The former would fall, the latter would triumph. It was thus Orosius who inspired Lambert to fill the *Liber floridus* with cityscapes. Orosius was also the source of Lambert's threefold division of history, arranged around the walls of Babylon and Rome and presented (among other places) as part of an illustration of Nebuchadnezzar's dream (see fig. 3). The statue from the dream stands on the left side of the picture. Nebuchadnezzar lies sleeping to the right. In the corner above him are the words: "From Adam to the founding of Old Babylon, which is in Persia, there were 3,342 years. It survived 1,164 years, and then Rome began. From there, it was 752 years to Christ."[40]

It is the same model cited in table 2 and also a variation on an older, threefold vision of Christian history: the time before Jewish law, the time of the law, and the time of grace, with an age of glory still to come.[41] The moments that Lambert emphasizes in his tripartite rendition of history—Adam to Abraham, and Abraham to Christ—are equally traditional (see table 3). Instead of putting an accent on spiritual history, however, Lambert based his divisions on changes in secular government. Ninus, the founding king of Assyria, seized power the same year that Abraham was born.[42] Later, Rome rose when Babylon fell.

Might another such transition occur at the end of the third age, the age of Rome (which would encompass the entire time of the Church)? Might there be a seventh age or a fifth empire, after the end of the era of Rome? Lambert never says so explicitly, but he did raise the possibility in the *Liber floridus* by juxtaposing two diagrams, two sixfold circles that each represented the entirety of world history. In the first diagram, the "Order of Kingdoms," he defines the six ages as the time before the flood, the Time of Labor after the flood, the Age of the Assyrians, then of the Medes, the Persians, and the Romans. In the second diagram, on the following page of the manuscript, he again illustrates the six ages, this time with an emphasis on spiritual events. And it all ends with the First Crusade. Lambert actually titled this second diagram, "The Ages of the World until King Godfrey."[43]

Table 3: Lambert's Kingdoms and Ages of the World

The Order of Kingdoms	The Ages of the World
1. Time before the Flood	1. Adam to Noah
2. Time of Labor after the Flood	2. Noah to Abraham
3. The Assyrians	3. Abraham to David
4. The Medes	4. David to Babylonian Captivity
5. Persia	5. Babylonian Captivity to Augustus/Christ
6. Rome	6. Augustus/Christ to Godfrey of Jerusalem

He sums up the Sixth Age with this list: "Octavius, Christ, apostles, evangelists, martyrs, confessors, virgins. In the year of the Lord 1099, in the seventh indiction, Duke Godfrey took Jerusalem." Lambert then adds, "In the Sixth Age to the capture of Jerusalem, 1099 years."[44]

The phrasing is careful. Lambert does not use the past tense and say, "In the sixth age there were 1099 years."[45] But the juxtaposition of these diagrams and the prominence given to recent events in Jerusalem is at least suggestive. As the prophet Daniel proclaimed, after he had found the correct interpretation for Nebuchadnezzar's dream, "God changes times and ages! He overthrows and builds up kingdoms!"[46]

That verse perfectly encapsulates Lambert's view of history. God reveals moments of profound spiritual transformation by creating new empires. He did so first in the East, and then in the West. And it was the experience of the First Crusade, channeled through the preaching of Bohemond, that led Lambert down this speculative path. The capture of Jerusalem in 1099 was another transformative moment in salvation history, an instance of spiritual and political renewal. Was it the opening act of the Last Days, with power lurching once more back to the East, stopping this time in Jerusalem? If Lambert believed so, he was not alone. His contemporary Guibert of Nogent said as much in his own crusade chronicle, addressing the city of Jerusalem in a song:

> O, city, by this blessed conquest,
> You deservedly ought to rule.
> You should draw to yourself Christian kingdoms,
> And you will see the glories of this world come here
> And give thanks to you, their mother.[47]

With hindsight, Guibert's suggestion that Christian Jerusalem might one day rule the world is naive. But it was a feeling shared by at least one higher-ranking, better informed church leader, Peter the Venerable, from 1122 to 1156 abbot of the monastery of Cluny, the largest monastic community in Europe. From such a high ecclesiastical perch, Peter was not immune to the crusade's spell. In a sermon called "In Praise of the Holy Sepulcher," he directly addresses an audience of First Crusaders and tells them that through their deeds they have fulfilled Old Testament prophecy, specifically Isaiah 66:19–20: "And I shall set a sign for them, and I shall send the ones who will be saved to the nations, armed with arrows, into Africa and Libya, into Italy and Greece, to islands far away, to men who have not heard of me and have not seen my glory, and they will proclaim my glory to the nations. And they will lead all your brothers from every nation as a gift to the LORD, on horses and chariots and litters, on mules and carts to the holy mountain Jerusalem, thus says the LORD."

God had foreknown Jerusalem's liberation, Peter explains, but he had kept it secret, set aside for the crusaders' triumph. The original spread of Christianity had been the first step toward fulfilling Isaiah's words. And yet, Peter adds, "it was more perfectly fulfilled by you, when for the love of Christ, the glorious sepulcher of your Lord and God was freed from the lordship of wicked men."[48] Africa, Libya, Italy, Greece, and the islands of the Mediterranean, all drawn together to offer tribute to the holy mountain of Jerusalem, an empire to fill the world after the crusaders (as if a stone uncut by hand?) struck down the Saracens.

Peter likely wrote this sermon with considerably more hindsight than either Lambert or Guibert had attained, yet he shared their optimism, imbibed from Bohemond and his entourage. All of them could imagine an exalted destiny for Christian Jerusalem, a kingdom atop the ruins of Rome, a bulwark against, in Guibert's words, "the oncoming madness of Antichrist."[49]

CHAPTER 4

The Oncoming Madness
of Antichrist

Antichrist, the Son of Perdition

Who was Antichrist? It is a difficult question, since the Bible says almost nothing about him. The Letters of John are the only parts of scripture to use the name "Antichrist," but they say only that his arrival is imminent, that he is a deceiver, and that there will be more than one of them. Christian exegetes assumed that Antichrist was the person whom Paul, in his Second Letter to the Thessalonians, called the "son of perdition." It also seemed likely that Antichrist was one of the beasts mentioned in Revelation.[1]

To fill in the gaps, Lambert and other prophetic thinkers turned to two additional sources, the *Revelations* of Pseudo-Methodius and the *Life of Antichrist* by Adso of Montier-en-Der. These two short books were wildly popular in the twelfth century—best sellers by contemporary standards—and scribes often bound one or both together with chronicles of the First Crusade, as if in recognition of an implicit connection between current battles with Saracens and future ones with Antichrist.[2]

Lambert seems to have felt this connection. In the *Liber floridus* he placed his copy of Fulcher of Chartres's history of the crusade immediately after a version of Adso's *Life of Antichrist* (attributing it, confusingly, to Methodius). The two works occupy the same sheet of parchment, on opposite sides, separated by a short text titled, "Fifteen Signs from the Days before Judgment Day."[3] Before reading about the Crusade, Lambert wanted his audience to think about

Antichrist and the End Times. And he returned to the subject of Antichrist much later in the book, adding a revised copy of the *Revelations* of Pseudo-Methodius, followed again by the list of the fifteen signs preceding the end of time.[4]

The earlier of these texts, *Revelations*, pretends to be the work of a fourth-century church father, but it was actually written near the end of the seventh century, first in Syriac and then translated into Greek and Latin. It is therefore an example of *vaticinium ex eventu*, a technical term meaning essentially "prophecy after the fact." The writer pretended to be working around the year 300, making his forecast of events from the fourth to the seventh centuries seem remarkably prescient.

Despite the four-hundred-year gap in time, it was Pseudo-Methodius who created the connection between crusade and apocalypse. For what mainly inspired him to write was the advent of Islam, whose adherents in the 690s seemed on the verge of conquering Constantinople, destroying the Roman Empire, and perhaps wiping out Christianity altogether. It was very much an End Times scenario, and Pseudo-Methodius responded by writing about it in those terms. His message was equal parts hope and caution. The Byzantine Empire was going to survive, he maintained. It would defeat Islam, but it would soon face greater battles still, first against the tribes of Gog and Magog, and then later, against Antichrist. As the Latin version of the text traveled west, and as history continued to unfold, scribes would revise its contents to better account for recent events. Prophecy thus evolved, and in 1100, Pseudo-Methodius's prediction of Islam's initial defeat would seem an accurate *vaticinium* of the First Crusade.

The other text, Adso's *Life of Antichrist*, originated at the Carolingian court in France, written in the mid-tenth century at the request of Gerberga of Saxony, wife of Louis IV of France and sister of Otto I of Germany. Gerberga apparently wished to learn more about the Last Days (a request that by itself indicates the existence among the wellborn, near the end of the millennium, of a healthy curiosity about the Apocalypse). She asked a monk named Adso to tell her especially about the future career of Antichrist. In his response, Adso drew heavily on Methodius, though he blended in some of his own speculations.

To summarize the two texts: Antichrist, the son of perdition, will be a Jew from the tribe of Dan, whose early life would be passed in small towns on the northern shores of the Sea of Galilee. Born in Chorazin, he will be raised in Bethsaida and rule in Capernaum, home of the Apostle Peter. Eventually, he will capture Jerusalem and sit in the temple of God as if he were a god. Many will fall under his spell, fooled by the numerous miracles he will perform, including the raising of the dead. After a short time (usually forty-two months), the Lord would appear and kill him with the breath of his mouth. And at some point during all of this activity, the Jews will convert to Christianity. Lambert did not imagine that they would do so in great numbers. Breaking from his sources, he claimed that only 144 representatives from each tribe would accept baptism.[5]

Would Antichrist be a Saracen? Obviously not, if he were born from the tribe of Dan. But Lambert held an unusual belief that caused him to doubt the continuing existence of any Jews in his world. After the Roman legions had destroyed Jerusalem in 70 CE, he says elsewhere in the *Liber floridus* that Titus, the army's commander and future emperor, wished to destroy the Jews altogether, so he ordered all Jewish men made into eunuchs. "The women who were in Judea saw this misfortune and took as husbands Vandals and Huns, who at that time happened to be attacking kingdoms in the East. From that time forward, [Jews] are thought to descend not from Abraham, but from the seed of Vandals."[6]

Perhaps in Lambert's imagination Antichrist was for some a hybrid figure, a product of borderland mixing between Saracen and Jew. Lambert gave his readers some clues that this might be the case. In a portrait of Antichrist (see fig. 4), Antichrist emerges from the sea, the picture of courtly elegance, framed by an undulating serpent's tail, his face soft, his hair arranged in long, flowing locks, looking for all the world like a parody of Botticelli's *Birth of Venus*—particularly with the words "Antichrist will be born" written to either side of his head. At the top of the page, a caption reads, "Antichrist, sitting atop the serpent Leviathan, symbol of the cruel beast of the End."[7]

In the context of the *Liber floridus*, the figure whom Antichrist most immediately resembles is not Venus—sadly Lambert never draws her—but Augustus Caesar. Both are crowned and seated in regal fashion, directly facing the viewer.[8] They both wear similarly fashioned draperies and cloaks. The scepter in Antichrist's right hand echoes the sword in Caesar's. Caesar holds a globe in his left hand; Antichrist gestures with his left hand toward the name of his birthplace, Chorazin, written near his head. Both men strike imperial poses, and as such recall Lambert's fascination with empire. A key, if subtle, difference between the two is that Antichrist is beardless. Perhaps Lambert wished to make him appear youthful.

More likely, though, he wanted Antichrist to seem effeminate, attractive. The smooth cheeks, long hair, and pointed shoes together create that impression. His shoes are especially striking—garish red stockings leading into the freakishly long, curled toes, vaguely resembling elephant tusks. Superficially, a strange choice in couture, but in reality this flamboyant footwear represented the height of courtly dress. According to the monk Orderic Vitalis, nobles in the late eleventh century everywhere favored this look, especially at the court of William Rufus of England. It had started with a certain Robert, "a worthless fellow, who first began to fill long 'pulley-toes' with stuffing and in this way bend them into the shape of a ram's horn. As a result he was nicknamed Horny. A large part of the nobility was soon imitating the frivolous fashion he had invented, as if it were some great and important achievement. At the time, effeminates were setting the fashion in many parts of the world: foul catamites, doomed to eternal fire, unrestrainedly pursued their revels and shamelessly gave themselves up to the filth of sodomy."[9]

Orderic's contemporary and fellow historian William of Malmesbury seconded this verdict: "Long flowing hair, luxurious garments, shoes with curved and pointed tips became the fashion. Softness of body rivaling the weaker sex, a mincing gait, effeminate gestures and a liberal display of the person as they went along, such was the fashion of the younger men."[10]

It was also the sort of behavior—an effeminate demeanor, sexual license, and the liberal practice of sodomy—that Christians associated with Islam. In his memoirs, Guibert of Nogent mentions this same style of footwear (though he associates it with women more than men) and attributes its origins to Spain, referring to "curled toes on shoes from Cordoba."[11] Thus Antichrist, Islam, and transgressions of gender all meet around one coiled foot. This effeminate stereotype spanned centuries of propaganda. A biography of the tenth-century Spanish martyr Pelagius of Córdoba turns on the failed attempt of a Caliph to seduce the Christian boy (not to convert him, as would have been typical of Classical martyrdom stories).[12] Closer to the First Crusade, Guibert of Nogent reports that Saracen men had raped a Christian bishop, which was common behavior for them. "By their own rules these wretched men can have any number of women, but it is not enough. They still need to soil their dignity by wallowing at the same filthy trough with men."[13]

In the prophecies of Pseudo-Methodius and Adso, Antichrist would prove especially attractive to Jews once he had established himself at the Temple. "Then all the Jews will flock to him, thinking that they will receive God, but in reality they receive the Devil."[14] Two witnesses for the faith then appear. Unnamed in Revelation, biblical commentators usually identified them as Enoch and Elijah, figures from the Old Testament who did not die but were instead taken directly to heaven. The witnesses would preach against Antichrist, expose his lies, and give strength and comfort to the elect. "These two great prophets and teachers will also covert to the faith the sons of Israel, whoever among them might still be found, and render for the remnant of the elect a grace unassailable, even in the face of such a storm."[15] Thus the Jews would abandon Antichrist and join Christianity in the final war against diabolical tyranny.

That was Adso's rendering of the story. Lambert saw things differently. In his revision, Jews stand by Antichrist to the bitter end, their devotion almost risible. "And so Antichrist was killed. But the Jews, fools yet again, guard him for three days so that he might arise from the dead. Finally, on the fourth day, they will sense that his corpse has begun to stink, that he is entirely dead and snuffed out and consigned to eternal fires and will lament that they have been wretchedly deceived, and beating their guilty breasts they will be converted to the Lord Jesus Christ and will abandon the Jewish sect."[16] According to scripture, Lambert notes, "If the children of Israel numbered as the sands of the sea, a remnant will be saved."[17] A small and foolish remnant indeed.

The war of the Last Days, then, in Lambert's eyes, would be an extension of the conflict between Christians and Jews, not Muslims. But maybe for Lambert there was no difference between Jews and Muslims. His contemporary Peter the Venerable, the abbot of Cluny, drew only the slightest distinction between them in his sermon on the Holy Sepulcher. The Jews were the successors to Cain, whose sacrifices God had rejected. The Saracens were the worshippers of Baal, whose sacrifices the prophet Elijah proved false and whose priests were subsequently massacred.[18] They were two religious traditions united in a shared history of failed sacrifice.

Some secular audiences, too, seemed to draw little distinction between Jews and Muslims. The earliest vernacular epic of the First Crusade, *The Song of Antioch*, probably composed toward the end of the twelfth century and aimed at a knightly audience, opens with a retelling of the Crucifixion. As Christ hangs on the cross, he attempts to comfort the good thief, Dimas, who is being executed just to his right. "Friend, there is a people, not yet born, who will come here to avenge me with sharpened spears. They will kill these devils' pagans, who have never kept my commandments. Then all of Christendom will be cleansed, my land will be conquered, and my country freed! After one-thousand years it will be baptized and raised high! And then the Holy Sepulcher shall be visited and venerated anew."[19] Crusade as revenge fantasy: Jews and Muslims lumped together, God's rejected stepchildren, to be killed at the same time by an army of the elect.[20]

Lambert may have never laid eyes on an actual Muslim, but as he imagined a long-haired, clean-shaven, exotically dressed Antichrist, born and nurtured in the East, he must have had some sense that what he was looking at was a Saracen, descended from Ishmael, the bastard son of Abraham. He also drew a connection between Antichrist and Babylon because whoever Antichrist might be in a historical sense, allegorically speaking, he was Nebuchadnezzar.

The Two Dreams of Nebuchadnezzar

The most basic evidence in the *Liber floridus* for this correspondence lies in pictures. Simply put, Antichrist and Nebuchadnezzar look alike. Nebuchadnezzar appears in the book's later pages, in a diagram of Nebuchadnezzar's dream—or rather, his dreams.[21] For the Babylonian king experienced a second vision later in the book of Daniel, after the dream of the statue. This second one concerned a tree that grew from the center of the earth and reached unto heaven. As Nebuchadnezzar watched from his bed, a heavenly "watchman" ordered it cut down and the stump bound with a ring of iron and bronze.

Lambert combines these dreams into a single image. The tree grows from a sleeping Nebuchadnezzar's loins. At the head of the king's bed stands a giant axe man, who also represents the statue from the first dream of Nebuchadnezzar. The watchman who orders the tree's destruction is depicted here as an enthroned man. His posture and form echo both Augustus and Antichrist but he is probably meant to be Christ, hovering above it all, guiding the action and choreographing the various allegories.

Visually, in the *Liber floridus*, the two men, Nebuchadnezzar and Antichrist, have the same soft features and similarly shaped crowns—noticeably different from either the statue's or Augustus's crown—and each man is beardless. The resemblance would have been all the more striking if Lambert's cycle of illustrations from the book of Revelation had survived. Based on the earliest copy of the *Liber floridus*, which preserves copies of some material lost from the original (see fig. 5), a similarly dressed, beardless, crowned Antichrist was active in and around the walls of Babylon-Jerusalem, drawing into tight association the visions of Daniel and John of Patmos.[22]

Lambert emphasized these connections verbally, too, through the commentary that he wrote in the empty spaces surrounding his picture of Nebuchadnezzar's dreams. Here for the first time in the *Liber floridus* all of the major elements of historical program come together—the six ages of political history, the four kingdoms, and the three eras of salvation history—to reveal the secrets of wars between Rome and Babylon, Christendom and Islam.[23]

First, the statue. On the left side of the page, Lambert lists the six ages of the world, associating each with one of the statue's body parts. The passage is clearly based on Nebuchadnezzar's first dream, but with a difference. Lambert has added an extra metal. "The world in its first age has a golden head; in its second a silver chest; in its third a bronze belly; in its fourth, iron thighs; in its fifth, lead shins; and in its sixth, mud feet."[24] Five metals plus mud, or clay—six elements in total, corresponding to the six ages of history.

But where did the lead come from? To alter scripture so brazenly, to add an entirely new element to one of the Bible's most famous stories, is unusual but not unheard of. Lambert's contemporary Hugh of Saint-Victor, for example, fiddled with the dimensions of Noah's ark in order to make them better match his own intricate vision of salvation history.[25] Lambert's tampering with scripture, however, was less subtle.

The simple explanation is that it was damn difficult to reconcile six ages with four kingdoms. Others besides Lambert would try. A slightly later commentator named Philip of Harveng managed to pull off the trick with a solution more elegant than Lambert's. The first four metals, in Philip's system, pertained to the first four ages. The "iron mixed with clay" pertained to the Fifth Age, and the stone uncut by human hand, to the Sixth.[26] Such a maneuver eluded Lambert, or else he knew from Bohemond that the stone symbolized the crusade—a moment in history rather than an entire age. It marked the end of history, not an era (Lambert's reading here is also closer to Daniel's than Philip's later one would be). Whatever the case, when Lambert wanted to reconcile the six ages and the four kingdoms, he had to cheat.

The purpose of the cheat was to create an effect more sophisticated than anything Philip of Harveng (and arguably more sophisticated than Daniel himself) had imagined—to illustrate the symbolic unity of Babylon and Rome. The real action, literal and figurative, occurs around the axe, which represents the Fourth Age. Along the length of the axe handle, Lambert has written a combination of two verses from Revelation: "Fallen is Babylon the great, with whom kings of the earth have fornicated!"[27] In striking down the tree, the statue was striking down Babylon. The gloss, however, does not actually match the meaning of Nebuchadnezzar's second dream, the dream of the tree. In Daniel 4, the destruction of the tree fore-tells a crisis in Nebuchadnezzar's own reign but does not signal his kingdom's end. Rather, Nebuchadnezzar would go temporarily mad. For a period of "seven times" he would live in the wilderness as an animal. Finally, reason would return to him, and he would recognize God's sovereignty over the world. The iron and bronze band placed around the stump of the tree symbolized the eventual restoration of both the king's mind and his monarchy.[28] For Lambert, however, the fall of the tree is the fall of Babylon, full stop.

It is also the fall of Rome. For here, around the axe and the tree, the Fourth and the Sixth Age meet. The gold and the iron king-doms fall at the same time. The golden empire of Nebuchadnezzar (which Lambert places in the Fourth Age) is cut down by an iron axe, iron being the usual symbol of Rome. What is left in place of the tree is a stump bound by an iron band. According to Daniel, the band is made of both iron and bronze, but Lambert has reduced to one element, probably to emphasize its Romanness. For Rome is, again, the iron kingdom, and it will (after the interlude of the Fifth Age) fill the void created by Babylon's fall.

Despite many interpretive challenges, Lambert managed with his diagram to explain the most important turning point of world history. Babylon's fall and Rome's ascent are linked, and hence the Fourth Age, which is Babylonian, and the Sixth Age, which is Roman, connect allegorically and chronologically.[29] Or as Lambert writes on the far right side of the page, just above the roots of Nebuchadnezzar's tree, in a paraphrase of Orosius, "At one and the same time, Babylon fell and Rome rose, in the year 752 before the advent of Christ." And above that passage, in the upper right-hand corner of page, he has written his three-part division of history: "From Adam to the founding of Old Babylon, which is in Persia, there were 3342 years; it stood for 1164 years; then Rome began. From there to Christ there were 752 years. This totals 5258 years."[30]

But as Daniel told Nebuchadnezzar in scripture, the dream of the statue revealed what would happen *in novissimis temporibus*—the last times. Or, as Lambert phrased it more simply, at the statue's feet, *finis mundi*, the end of the world. The aging statue, who cuts down the tree springing up from Nebuchadnezzar's loins, symbolizes all of earthly authority, from the first age to the last. As such, the statue might represent not just Rome striking a blow against Babylon but also the Franks striking Islam with a mortal wound, an event Lambert associated with the end of the Sixth Age. Thus with one swing of the axe, the statue brings to an end both the Fourth and Sixth Ages of history.

Lambert leaves unstated what will happen after the tree falls, perhaps because he has already discussed it in several other places in the *Liber floridus*. But he has given careful readers enough clues to guess just who the statue, depicted here as an aged king with an axe, might be. Not just any old king, he was the final one, a legendary figure of prophecy known as the Last World Emperor.

Antichrist and Emperor

The Bible does not mention a Last World Emperor. He is a product of postbiblical prophecy, folklore, and imagination. By Lambert's time in the twelfth century, however, the last emperor had achieved near canonical status, widely recognized as a crucial character in the drama of the End Times.

Most likely the inventor of the story was Pseudo-Methodius. At the end of his seventh-century prophetic history, he describes how the Sons of Ishmael will arise from the desert and spread their dominion throughout the world. It will happen "during the time of the seventh week," by which he meant the seventh millennium. At a moment when the destruction of Christendom appeared inevitable, a renewed energy would seize the emperor (presumably for Methodius, the emperor reigning in Constantinople). He would appear, with reference to Psalm 77:65, "like a man arising from a drunken sleep, one whom men had thought of as dead and good for nothing."[31]

Adso, in the *Life of Antichrist*, made one key change to this story. The bloodline of the Roman emperors in the West, he argued, had been preserved through the Carolingian Franks. The final world ruler, king of the Greeks and Romans, would be not a Greek but a Frank. He would lead his armies east and drive back the Ishmaelites. Peace would break out, but then other barbarian tribes from the north would swarm into Roman territory. The same ruler would again unite his armies and "strike them down in a single moment of time." And then, strangely, unaccountably, the Last World Emperor would go to Jerusalem where—either at the Mount of Olives or atop Golgotha, immediately adjoining the Holy Sepulcher—he would lay down his crown and bring the Roman Empire to an end. Because of his abdication, Antichrist could now arise, as Lambert imagined the scene, from the seas, seated atop a green dragon called Leviathan.[32]

Apocalyptically, this was the point of no return: Antichrist would appear when the Roman Empire ended. It was an old idea based on Paul's Second Letter to the Thessalonians, where the apostle writes, "the man of sin and son of perdition will not reveal himself unless there is a falling away."[33] The "falling away" was likely the collapse of Rome, foretold in Daniel and foreshadowed in the fall of Babylon.[34] As Pseudo-Methodius and Adso reconfigured things, Rome would not so much fall as recede. There would be a willing surrender of power, perhaps out of a sense of humility, perhaps out of a misguided belief that with the defeat of the last barbarian armies, history's work was done.

At first glance, this scenario does not look at all like what happened in 1099. The crusading armies, as contemporaries on occasion pointed out, had had no king. That was part of what made their victory miraculous. No single ruler, no Last Emperor, had emerged. Instead, somehow, loosely organized bands of fighters had set aside their differences just long enough to achieve one of the most improbable military victories in history. Upon conquering Jerusalem, they elected Godfrey of Bouillon to be either prince or king of the city; Godfrey accepted the office but refused to wear a crown in Jerusalem—a gesture of humility or perhaps a recognition of the awesome prophetic implications such an act would entail.[35] Whatever the case, neither he nor his heirs did what was expected of the Last World Emperor. In Adso's formula, "After happily ruling his kingdom, he will finally come to Jerusalem and there on the Mount of Olives lay down his scepter and crown. This will be the end and consummation of the Roman and Christian Empire."[36] Instead the kings of Jerusalem entered into a never-ending series of wars against the Turkish and Egyptian cities and civilizations that surrounded them, defending and seeking to expand their kingdom rather than abandoning the trappings of earthly rule.

Such a break with prophecy must have bothered Lambert—enough that, when copying this passage from Adso, he cut the offending lines out and added new ones in their place. The Last World Emperor, now, "after happily ruling his kingdom, will finally come to Jerusalem and there will gain a scepter and a crown and the empire of the Christians."[37] It is an audacious revision, but obviously no less so than changing the book of Daniel. The Last World Emperor would not lay down a crown in Jerusalem. He would receive one, just as Lambert believed Godfrey had done in 1099, when he had accepted the kingship from Lambert's own prince, Count Robert of Flanders, in anticipation of future battles against Antichrist and his minions.

Other scribes and chroniclers shared Lambert's prophetic concerns, though they adopted different strategies for integrating them into the crusade story. For example, one manuscript containing three crusade narratives includes an additional detail about the siege of Jerusalem, where, in the heat of the battle, an unknown rider on a white horse charged down from the Mount of Olives and led a contingent of Franks into the city. It was a scene right out of Revelation (specifically, Revelation 19:11–16). In a similar vein, one of the eyewitness chroniclers, Raymond of Aguilers, observed that, during this final battle, the blood in the city flowed as high as horses' bridles, a detail taken from Revelation 14:20.[38]

Two other unknown scribes added into their manuscripts substantial liturgical materials that are highly apocalyptic in tone. One of them, a hymn intended to celebrate the First Crusade, observes that Christ had struck down "the empires of demons." In another manuscript, an anonymous hymnist imaginatively splashes around in Jerusalem's rivers of blood on July 15, 1099:

> Rivers of blood flow
> In those hours
> While that race of error dies.
> Jerusalem, rejoice!
> And the pavement of the Temple
> Becomes bloody
> With the blood of the dying.
> Jerusalem, rejoice!

Both of these hymns likely originated from Jerusalem in the aftermath of the First Crusade.[39]

The latter one, in its manuscript context, follows a curious description of the battle for Jerusalem, written apparently by another anonymous participant in the battle.[40] Between the actual narrative and the liturgy, the writer included a sermon intended to contextualize the war, mainly by insulting the Jews. "But now, you pathetic people, why do you not come to your senses when you see the sepulcher of the Lord made glorious, just as you have read it prophesied, and when you see the faithful field workers divinely admitted into the vineyard, after your own disinheritance and after those foul pigs, the Saracens and Turks, have now been driven out too?"[41] As with Lambert, Muslims fade into the background. The success of the crusade was, among other things, an opportunity for the new Chosen People to ridicule their predecessors.

This anonymous preacher, however, is more traditional in his discussion of the Jews than Lambert. "A false messiah," Antichrist, will deceive the Jews with promises and lies. God, however, will send the previously mentioned witnesses, Enoch and Elijah, to preach against him and to open the Jews' eyes. To clarify the anti-Judaic lesson, the preacher turns to Nebuchadnezzar's dream: "At last the stone cut from the mountain without human hands will become the foundation stone and fill the earth, and finally you shall return, having penitently drunk the blood that you once poured forth in slavery, and he will guide you into the land of the living. In this way, the remnant of your people will be saved at the end of the world." The statue will fall. Earthly government will end. And the Jews, who used to make blood sacrifices at their altars, will learn to partake of the Eucharist—although when juxtaposed to images of sanguinary rivers purifying the Holy Land, this standard biblical language must have carried a threatening, nigh cannibalistic force. "Just think on the enmity of Antichrist and the amity of Christ!" the preacher concludes.[42]

Among actual crusaders, Godfrey of Bouillon had more occasion than most to think about prophecy, empire, and End Times. In making his case to be king of Jerusalem, he likely mentioned his descent from Charlemagne, and he may have added that at Constantinople Bohemond's nemesis, Emperor Alexius, had adopted him as a son, giving him something like a viable claim to be "King of the Greeks and Romans." An Armenian historian living in Edessa reported that Godfrey carried with him the sword of Vespasian—the emperor under whom Jerusalem had been conquered in 70 CE. A better sign of apocalyptic imperial grandeur is difficult to imagine. If Godfrey or his fellow crusaders took the Last Emperor legend seriously, moreover, it would explain why he was reluctant to wear a crown in Jerusalem. The two most likely outcomes of such hubris would have been to lay his crown down on the Mount Olives or else to become an Antichrist, one who wanted to sit in the Temple of God as if he were a god.[43]

Of the European chroniclers Guibert of Nogent expresses these ideas most directly. As he describes Urban II's sermon at the Council of Clermont in 1095, the pope drew upon the legend of the Last World Emperor, urging his audience to think on what might happen if the Franks retook Jerusalem and restored "eastern lands" to Christianity. "It is self-evident," his pope says, "that Antichrist is coming to make wars not against Jews, not against Gentiles, but as his name suggests, against Christians." According to Daniel and his interpreter Jerome, Antichrist will plant his tents on the Mount of Olives and set himself up in the Temple of God. "But this cannot at all happen unless Christianity first appears where now there is only paganism." If the Franks could strike a significant blow against the followers of Muhammad, if a Christian kingdom could be established in the East, the drama of the Last Days might finally begin. Guibert, writing in 1107–8, likely thought that those processes were already underway, with Bohemond playing the principal part.[44]

Guibert's fellow monk and crusade historian, Baldric of Bourgueil, actually began his crusade chronicle with a reference to Nebuchadnezzar's dream, noting there that God "changes ages and kingdoms." Near the end of the same book, on the eve of the battle for Jerusalem, an anonymous preacher, identified only as a "hero," preaches that the fate of the heavenly Jerusalem might rest on the outcome of the battle for its earthly counterpart.[45]

The other great early French historian of the crusade, Robert of Reims, does not make direct use of Pseudo-Methodius or Adso. He does, however, more than any other writer, emphasize the Frankishness of the crusaders, and in particular their connections to Charlemagne and hence to the ideal of world empire. Urban II, in Robert's version of the sermon at Clermont, urges his audience to consider the deeds of their ancestor Charlemagne and of his son Louis the Pious, both of whom had fought against unbelievers and had expanded the boundaries of Christendom.[46] A call to the nation of the Franks to rise up from internal confusion (like a man from a drunken sleep?) and reclaim the Carolingian mantle is at least resonant with Adso's conception of the Last World Emperor.

Robert's interest in Charlemagne is also indicative of more widespread ideas associated with the crusade. According to Ekkehard of Aura, around the year 1096 rumors circulated that Charlemagne himself had risen from the dead.[47] Ekkehard put little stock in the rumors (or, in retrospect, claimed that he had not), but he did perceive them as a motive driving some of the German pilgrims who took the cross.

At least one crusader, Emicho of Flonheim, actually professed to be the Last World Emperor. In the wake of sermons preached by Peter the Hermit, Emicho gathered together an army of knights and commoners and promised to lead them to Jerusalem by way of Constantinople, where Christ would descend from heaven and crown him king. The first step in Emicho's program was to eradicate

European Jews, since Jews and Saracens were, in his eyes, equally loathsome before the Lord.[48] Emicho thus shared Lambert of Saint-Omer's worldview, a vision of Jerusalem conquered by a figure of prophecy who would at the same time resolve Christendom's most difficult internal problem—the continued existence of Jews, whose treachery would endure to Antichrist and beyond.

Lambert's vision of history was therefore widely shared by contemporary historians and theologians and at least some crusaders. Not just a scene of military triumph, the First Crusade was a moment of spiritual transformation, an event that promised to remake the entire world, starting at Jerusalem and spreading out geographically to every place touched by a victorious Christendom.

CHAPTER 5

Sacred Geography

LAMBERT OF SAINT-OMER THUS had a theory about an apocalyptic crusade; to turn that theory into a story, he relied primarily on the *History of Jerusalem* written by the priest and crusader Fulcher of Chartres. Fulcher began the campaign in 1096 among the followers of Count Stephen of Blois, son-in-law of William the Conqueror and one of the expedition's leaders (who would infamously desert the crusade in 1098 at its moment of greatest crisis outside Antioch). A year after his departure from France, Fulcher transferred allegiance to Baldwin of Boulogne and followed him into Syria, where he soon established himself as count of Edessa. In 1100, when Baldwin was elected king of Jerusalem, succeeding his brother Godfrey, Fulcher went with him and for the next twenty years served at the Church of the Holy Sepulcher, all the time working assiduously on his *History*. He put at least three different versions into circulation—revising and expanding the text each time.

Lambert knew the earliest edition of Fulcher's book, which covered events up to 1106.[1] He probably found it in the library of Saint-Bertin, a monastic community directly outside the walls of Saint-Omer, a then-thriving Flemish city of which Lambert counted himself a proud member. At some point, probably around 1110, the scriptorium at Saint-Bertin had obtained a version of Fulcher's *History*, which they copied and abridged.[2] As one of the monks explained in the book's second chapter: "At God's direction we will try to set forth what Brother Fulcher collected and assembled into one book, based on what he saw with his own eyes or on the descriptions of deeds told to him by people who had actually performed them. Informed by careful consideration of his book and by the accounts of others, we have avoided wordiness in our own retelling. Focused only on those things that seem especially pertinent to us, we have conscientiously worked to revise his text."[3]

At some point, Lambert began making his own copy of the *History*, seemingly in consultation with the brethren Saint-Bertin. The product of their collaboration was one of the most beautiful images produced in all the Middle Ages: a circular map of the city (see fig. 6).[4] Maybe that is why Lambert became involved in copying Fulcher's book in the first place. Someone at Saint-Bertin may have asked him for advice about drawing the map. Based on the *Liber flori-dus*, it is likely Lambert would have been making some reputation for himself as a cartographer. Whatever the case, the image the monks of Saint-Bertin produced would prove to be a revelation, by itself transforming ideas about the shape of the world and of history, in ways that resonated far beyond the county of Flanders.

Jerusalem as Microcosm

The monks of Saint-Bertin situated their map within their copy of Fulcher's *History*, immediately adjacent to a description of the actual city, and Lambert did the same thing in the *Liber floridus*. Both the text and the map encouraged readers to use their imaginations and explore Jerusalem, before subsequently, as the story continued, visualizing what the city looked like drenched in Saracen blood.[5] The two items, history and map, are not just connected topically. One was based directly on the other—specifically, the cartographers used Fulcher's text to create their map. With only three exceptions, every site labeled on the map is mentioned in Fulcher's *History*. And the exceptions themselves are revealing, opening a window onto the scriptorium as Lambert and the monks created this masterpiece.

The first exception: In the lower left-hand corner of the page, just outside the city walls, the cartographers have drawn two circles to represent Mountjoy (or Mount Scopus, as it is known today). It was the vantage point from which pilgrims usually first saw Jerusalem and as such would have been important to anyone who had actually traveled there. Fulcher did not think to mention it, but if the designers of the map had asked crusaders what they most remembered about Jerusalem, they would likely have talked about Mountjoy.

Similarly with the second exception: Near the center of the map, just to the east of the Zion Road, is a marketplace. Surrounded

on all sides by small towers, it is likely intended to represent the
Byzantine Cardo Maximus, the place where pilgrims would have
stocked up on souvenirs and supplies. Part of the rhythms of everyday life in the city and not at all sacred, Fulcher did not bother talking about it. For pilgrims, however, it would have been one of the
streets they most frequented, and they would have likely told the
mapmakers about it, too.

Finally, and most surprisingly, the description in Fulcher's chronicle does not mention al-Aqsa mosque (or the "Temple of Solomon,"
as it was known in the Latin world). The mosque was in a state disrepair after the crusade—the roof had been stripped of its lead by King
Baldwin I—but it nonetheless would have dominated Jerusalem's
skyline.[6] Any visitor would have remembered it, particularly because
of its associations with the Old Testament, and would have insisted
it be included on the map. An attentive reader might have noticed
the Temple of Solomon mentioned later in Fulcher's *History* as the
place where the Franks killed so many of the enemy that they found
themselves wading through shin-deep pools of blood. A memorable
image, but firsthand guidance would have been necessary to locate
the Temple correctly to the south of the Dome of the Rock, as the
cartographers did.[7]

In all three cases, the mapmakers have added locations that
Fulcher did not mention but that would have been important to an
actual pilgrim. In other words, the mapmakers, including possibly
Lambert himself, must have talked with crusaders to learn more about
Jerusalem. The crusaders' advice would have also been crucial for getting minor details right. The travel guide, for example, notes only that
the Church of the Holy Sepulcher lay "a little to the left" of the Golden
Gate.[8] While technically true, the Church of the Holy Sepulcher is in
fact on the opposite side of the city, fairly close to where the cartographers have placed it. Indeed, it is one of the map's most overlooked
virtues—that while it idealizes Jerusalem, it still presents a roughly
accurate guide to where the most crucial sights in the city could be
seen. In spirit, it is similar to an amusement park map—not drawn
painstakingly to scale but useful for moving from place to place.

This quality—the map's underappreciated utility—gives one
other reason for thinking that Lambert was involved in its design.
It is an intangible and subjective judgment, to be sure, but arguably
the most compelling reason for thinking that he helped create it.[9]
That is, the map is a work of genius. Based on a sketchy description
combined with oral report, it presents a plan of Jerusalem that is at
once cartoonish, visually compelling, and roughly accurate. It became

one of the most enduring images of Jerusalem (or of anything else) from the entire Middle Ages, widely copied all over Europe throughout the twelfth century.[10]

More to the point, the map of Jerusalem encapsulates one of the key aspects of the imaginative program in Lambert's *Liber floridus*. Without explicitly making the point, the cartographer has depicted Jerusalem not only as an ideal city, a perfect circle, but also as a microcosm of the world—a visual echo of world maps then in circulation, commonly called "T/O" maps. Such maps appear occasionally in the *Liber floridus*; Augustus Caesar, for example, bears one in his hand as a way to demonstrate universal authority. The world he holds is round, with Asia at the top (in the east), and Europe and Africa at the bottom (in the west).

The same T/O shape is recognizable in the map of Jerusalem. The circular city itself is the "O." It has two major thoroughfares— the "road to the Temple of the Lord," running from the bottom of the circle to a point just above its center, and then a single thoroughfare running perpendicular to the first, comprising "St. Stephen's Gate Road," and the "Mount Zion Gate Road." There are a handful of smaller streets, but the two grand boulevards of the "T" give shape to the city, dividing it up into three major neighborhoods and echoing the three continents on world maps.

A hundred years later, in the thirteenth century, cartographers would make yet another imaginative leap, placing Jerusalem at the center of the world, at the point where the two lines of the T meet. In doing so, they made the relationship between Jerusalem and world, between microcosm and macrocosm, all the more striking.[11] That visual tick was in fact unknown in the twelfth century. In geographic treatises, however, "Jerusalem as the center of the earth" was a well-established concept that bled over into theological speculation. The abbot of Cluny, Peter the Venerable, for example, in his sermon on the Holy Sepulcher, described Jerusalem as the heart of the world, adding that just as the heart lies at the center of the body, so must Jerusalem lie at the center of the earth. It was also useful for building a religious empire. For God intended to spread Christianity not just to a handful of places but "to the farthest reaches of India, the utmost ends of Gaul, the burning south and the freezing north." Salvation therefore had to begin "not in a corner of the globe but in the middle of the globe, not in a part of the earth but in the middle of the earth, equidistant from all places."[12]

This dreamlike, near hallucinatory, conception of Jerusalem probably intensified Lambert's fascination with geography writ large.

If Jerusalem was a microcosm of the world, then the world itself became something that demanded study. Its contours and land-scapes, biological and geological oddities all revealed God's designs for salvation. Crusade and travel narrative blended together into a single project aimed at uncovering mysteries and bringing the activity of man more into concert with the designs of God.

Lambert's contemporaries shared this sensibility, even if they could not express it with his visual, encyclopedic bravado. On a basic level, they did not think it possible to appreciate the crusade without engaging with the physical city. The compiler of *The Deeds of the Franks*, the text circulated by Bohemond's entourage in 1106, added a description of Jerusalem to the end of his narrative. It is, admittedly, a dull, workmanlike list of biblical locations and characters, much of it badly out of date by 1099, but it opens with one impressive rhetorical flourish: "If anyone from Western lands wishes to go to Jerusalem, let him always follow the rising sun, and he will find there around Jerusalem places to pray."[13] To reach Jerusalem, leave the West and go east. Follow the sun. No other instructions were needed—which was also Lambert's fundamental message about the crusade, drawn from Orosius. In 1099, empire in the West had gone back to the East, and in doing so had written salvation history anew.

In general, travel guides to the Holy Land proliferated in the twelfth century, often circulating in manuscripts that contained crusade narratives.[14] The specific chronicle did not matter. Scribes just seemed to sense the need to describe Jerusalem when writing about the crusade.[15] Fulcher of Chartres never lost this impulse. As he grew older and revised his text, he added further details about the city and the Holy Land's topography and wildlife. Some of his material came from classical sources, but he also drew on firsthand experience: what the water of the Dead Sea tasted like and how easily everything floated in it; why the water of the Red Sea appears red from distance, even though it is in fact clear; what a literal plague of locusts looks like.[16] It is a small step from crusade texts like Fulcher's to the "wonders of the East" literature that would proliferate in the later Middle Ages.[17]

And the East imagined in these texts is truly wondrous, often veering close to myth. Crocodiles were especially fascinating (see fig. 7). As Lambert imagined them, they were Nile-dwelling, elongated, saffron-colored, leonine creatures, with immense claws, obdurate skin, and mustachioed human faces. Unlike men, Lambert says, the crocodile can move its upper jaw—an anatomic peculiarity made all the more remarkable by its anthropoid skull.[18] Another crusade-era travel guide specifies that crocodiles are "terrifying serpents," who "hate man above every other animal." Originally they had lived only in the Nile. In more recent times, they migrated to Caesarea, the port city built by Herod the Great and named in honor of Augustus. The crocodiles had been brought there by a king who wished to use them as weapons to assassinate his brother.[19] Lambert's crocodile would have looked especially menacing to readers of the *Liber floridus*, set side by side as it was with a picture of a sallow devil mounted atop a blue beast called Behemoth.

Less striking but more unnerving, one of the manuscripts of *The Deeds of the Franks* includes on its final page a simple image based on information from the Holy Land: two lines of unequal length, with a brief explanation attached. One of the lines, if multiplied fifteen times, would reveal the height of Christ. The other, if multiplied nine times, would give his breadth. If a person gazed on both these lines in the manuscript even for a moment, he was guaranteed not to die for the rest of the day.[20] Points of meditation charged with magic, these lines faintly echoed Jerusalem's music, resonating as it did from microcosm to macrocosm.

The Travels of Alexander the Great

Lambert also explored the East through storytelling—particularly through the legends of Alexander the Great, who was for Lambert an especially difficult figure. As already noted, most exegetes (Lambert is one of the few exceptions) believed Alexander's kingdom to be one of the four empires dreamed by Nebuchadnezzar. Alexander's rule was usually associated with bronze, the eloquence of the Greeks comparable to the tones of bells. More to the point, Daniel 8 all but identifies Alexander by name as the goat who shattered the horns of the ram, symbolizing Persia. "And the he goat is the king of the Greeks, and the great horn that was between his eyes is the first King."[21]

Lambert did not connect Alexander to Nebuchadnezzar, but he did acknowledge his prophetic significance, mainly through cartography. In the latter stages of Alexander's journeys, he sealed Gog and Magog (shadow figures of prophecy from both Old and New Testaments) and twenty other barbarian tribes behind the Caspian Gates. Lambert marks the location of their prison, with Alexander given full credit, on two of his world maps.[22] The story was common knowledge in the Middle Ages, discussed in detail in the *Revelations* of Pseudo-Methodius. In Lambert's own rendition of Methodius, however, he skipped over Alexander altogether, passing directly from the early wars between the Israelites and Ishmaelites to the rise of the Saracens at the time of the crusades.[23]

Instead of being a leader of one of the four great empires, the Alexander that Lambert gives readers is an adventurer plain and simple, a heroic knight of romance, albeit a few years before the invention of knightly romances.[24] To create this character, Lambert uses four texts and one picture. The first of the written sources is the Latin biography by Valerius, a fourth-century Roman patrician and scholar.[25] The second, a version of a letter by Alexander supposedly written to his teacher Aristotle. It details Alexander's adventures in India, particularly his encounter with two talking, oracular trees that foretold his destiny in a bizarre nocturnal ceremony.[26] The third is an epistolary exchange on moral philosophy between Alexander and Dandamis the Brahmin, one of the "gymnosophists," or "nude wise men," whom Alexander encountered upon entering India. Though the gymnosophists practiced asceticism and lived in isolation, Dandamis is identified in these letters as a king.[27] Finally, typically for Lambert, he adds a description of the sites where Alexander founded twelve cities, all of them named Alexandria.[28] Together this material comprises not a coherent biographical account but rather a fragmentary character study, decorated with adventure stories, exotic beasts, and mythical landscapes.

Given the intrinsic excitement of his presentation, Lambert's drawing of Alexander is a disappointment—more a sketch than a portrait (see fig. 8). A crowned king, seated atop Bucephalus, depicted here as a dappled red horse (without any apparent apocalyptic connotations), Alexander wears a green cloak and holds a sword in his right hand and a shield and bridle in his left. Like Antichrist, he is beardless, wears red stockings, and has long flowing hair. These details make him seem a bit Eastern. His crown, however, pulls him back westward; decorated with three fleurs-de-lis, it is more like the crowns worn by Augustus and the axe man in Nebuchadnezzar's dream than the exotic diadems of Antichrist and Nebuchadnezzar.

Alexander's overall demeanor is thus something of a hybrid, a mixture of the characteristics of Western and Eastern world rulers. But he does not belong to either group. Seated on a horse instead of a throne, depicted in profile rather than facing the reader, he is less a king and more a knight errant.[29] The figure he most resembled, perhaps, is Bohemond—a charismatic leader who dreamed of world conquest but whose fortunes collapsed in the East beneath the weight of his own ambitions.

If so, like Bohemond, Alexander has a bit of uncanny charisma about him, and just a hint of divinity. Indeed in Lambert's fragmentary treatment, he is a forerunner of Christ. Consider Alexander's parents. His mother, Olympias, while not a virgin, was a young woman unable to conceive a child for her husband, Philip of Macedon. She eventually became pregnant, but not by Philip. Instead, Olympias had sex with a man she believed to be the god Ammon of Egypt. Thus, Alexander is, potentially, a god-man, like Christ.[30]

Rather than a god, however, her lover was the former pharaoh of Egypt, Nectanebo, also a magician. Nectanebo, according to Lambert, had learned that an army from Persia was about to invade Egypt, so he fled across the sea, eventually landing in Macedonia. There he lived in anonymity for a time until becoming smitten with Olympias. A cunning and unscrupulous man, Nectanebo decided to take advantage of her barren womb. While Philip was away on campaign, he disguised himself as the god "Ammon of Lybia," and lay with her. Alexander was the product of this liaison. Happily for Olympias, Nectanebo used his dark arts to deceive Philip into believing that his son really was half-god.[31]

Born of a sullied woman who had lain with a false god, the figure Alexander more closely approximates is Antichrist, whose conception Adso of Montier-en-Der described thus: "Just as the Holy Spirit came into the mother of our Lord Jesus Christ and overshadowed her with its power and filled her with divinity so that she might conceive from the Holy Spirit and so that what was born would be divine and holy, so also the devil will descend onto the mother of Antichrist and will fill her up and wholly surround her and wholly possess her inside and out, so that through the devil's activity she will conceive through man and what will be born will be wholly wicked, wholly evil, and wholly lost."[32] The circumstances of Alexander's birth make him a prophetic hybrid (between Christ and Antichrist) as much as a historical one (between Western king and Eastern tyrant), perhaps in hindsight a viable prism through which to evaluate the crusade.

For despite the ambivalence and ambiguity characteristic of Lambert's treatment of Alexander, he did recognize some connection between him and the crusaders.[33] One of the key additions he makes to Valerius's *Life* is a description of Alexander's visit to Jerusalem, drawn on information from the *Jewish Wars* of Josephus, the renowned first-century Jewish historian. After Alexander had defeated King Darius of Persia and recovered his body, according to Lambert, he decided to travel to Jerusalem. According to Josephus, though, the visit happened much earlier. Lambert's revision is slight but consequential. By placing the visit to Jerusalem where he does, Alexander arrived there as rightful king over Greece, Egypt, and Persia.

Jaddus, the Jewish high priest—or "pontiff," in Lambert's words—met Alexander outside the city. The other priests of the Temple accompanied Jaddus, all clad in white stoles and carrying a gold plate inscribed with the name of God. One of Alexander's captains, "Duke Parmenio," asked the Greek king why he would show veneration to a barbarian priest. Alexander replied that he did not venerate the man but rather the God who had elevated him. (He added that he had seen Jaddus previously in a vision and was therefore inclined to respect him.) Together Alexander and Jaddus entered the city and made sacrifices at the Temple. Instead of claiming plunder, which was his right, Alexander gave gifts to the priests and remitted to them seven years of tribute. He then went into Persia to claim Babylon as his capital, before marching to India.[34]

Josephus adds—but Lambert does not—that, after the sacrifices, the priests showed Alexander a copy of the book of Daniel and told him that according to the prophet, a Greek ruler would one day destroy the empire of the Persians. Alexander, naturally, believed himself to be the one. If Lambert had included this anecdote, he would have needed to face up to the obvious interpretation of Nebuchadnezzar's dream—that the Greeks were one of the great empires. And that was an argument that for any number of reasons he did not wish to make.[35] His Alexander instead left Jerusalem unenlightened, on the literal and figurative road to Babylon.

Neither good nor evil, son of a false god's priest and yet worshipper of the true God, a figure of prophecy who somehow remains on the margins of the Apocalypse, Alexander was for Lambert what he appears to be in his portrait—a daredevil, an explorer, someone who, like Bohemond, was ever "a restless man, living amidst great labors and enduring many troubles."[36] Long before Ferdinand Magellan, Alexander wished "to circumnavigate the globe and the ocean," as the formula appears in the *Liber floridus*.[37]

These vices of curiosity and delight were shared by Lambert. He surely felt a sense of spiritual kinship as he transcribed Alexander's letter to Aristotle: "I wanted to describe to you the country of India and the character of its skies and the countless sorts of snakes and savages, because I knew that you had dedicated yourself to philosophy. In this way I might offer some useful knowledge for your consideration and genius." Lambert likewise compiled the *Liber floridus* by gathering together curiosities so that "we might devour with the mouth's heart rare dishes set before us from the table of the great king."[38]

In life, a swashbuckling hero whose exploits set off sparks of empire and apocalypse, Alexander's deeds remained nothing more than tall tales, opportunities for the display of zoological and geological marvels, separate from the grand movements of history about which Nebuchadnezzar had dreamed and whose contours Lambert plotted, a fine guide to the East, the scourge of Gog and Magog, but not a founder of Empire.

Legends and Last Days

Other legendary figures in the *Liber floridus* similarly lurk at the edges of prophecy. Their exploits flicker with images of the divine plan. And if properly interpreted, they can open windows onto heaven while establishing relationships with the crusade on the planes of history and myth.

Consider King Arthur. Early in the manuscript, in a section dealing with the "Wonders of Britain," Lambert inserted a lengthy description of a palace later generations would call "Camelot." "There is in Britain in the land of the Picts the palace of the knight Arthur, built with astonishing skill and embellishment. Sculpted there are all his deeds and wars." Specifically, Arthur fought the Saxons in twelve battles, of which Lambert provides a list. Lambert likely intended the sculptures to recall the twelve towers of heaven—since he placed the list immediately opposite a drawing of the heavenly Jerusalem, where those twelve towers are depicted and named.[39] In this way Camelot too became a signpost to the City of God and the Celestial Jerusalem.

Lambert also probably intended Arthur's battles to recall the crusade. Of the eighth battle, he writes, "Arthur carried an image of Holy Mary above his shoulders and turned the pagans to flight. On that day there was a great slaughter of pagans because of the strength of our Lord Jesus Christ and of his holy virgin mother." The material for this story was drawn, almost verbatim, from the ninth-century *History of the Britons* by Nennius.[40] But because of the way in which the crusade had charged the interactions of history and allegory, Lambert's retelling gave an obscure tale fresh symbolic import.

The city of Troy had similar eschatological implications. One of the last texts that Lambert added to the *Liber floridus* was an abridged history of the Trojan War attributed to a mythical historian named

Darius Phrygius. In part, Lambert included it because he had learned
that the Franks were descended from Faramund, a refugee from
Troy.[41] The news was exciting enough to cause him to revise an earlier historical annal so that it contained this information. "During
the reign of Valentinian, in the year of the Lord 366, the Trojans
were in Germany. From them the Kings of Gaul are descended."[42]
On his one-page summary of world history, Lambert draws a still
tighter connection: "Faramund, the nephew of Duke Priam of Troy,
was the first king of all the Franks."[43] How Priam might have produced a nephew ruling in Europe twelve hundred years after the
Trojan War defies explanation.[44] The crucial point for Lambert was
simply that the Franks and Trojans shared a lineage—a family tree
whose limbs touched all the crusaders. Pure fantasy, but not confined to Flanders. Around the year 1100 a poet writing in Cologne
described its citizens as "Trojan Franks."[45]

The story of the Trojan War, like the biographies of Alexander
and Bohemond, told of a war between East and West—a war for control of a city in which gods became directly involved. And the city of
Troy fell in Lambert's version not because of a wooden horse but
because of treachery within its walls. As would happen at Antioch two
thousand years later when one of the guards of Antioch secretly
agreed to turn his city over to Bohemond, traitors within Troy struck
a deal with the Greek general Agamemnon and allowed his men to
pass through the gates in the middle of the night. And the next
morning, in the Temple of Minerva, Agamemnon announced that
he would share the spoils of Troy equally with his men, a scene that
could have been lifted directly from a crusade narrative.[46]

Chronologically, finally, events at Troy, like the histories of
Babylon and Jerusalem, resonated in sympathy with other key moments
of history.[47] Founded in the year of creation 3244, it came into existence at almost the same time as Babylon. About 950 years later, Troy
fell, and twenty years after that, just after Troy's destruction, King
David founded Jerusalem.[48] Was Troy a precursor to Jerusalem, an
imperfect historical type more fully realized one thousand years after
the fact in Rome? Were the Greeks, like Alexander, imperfect incarnations of the Franks, their great war, however dazzling in its detail,
a muted prelude to the battles fought during Lambert's life? It is
impossible to know. These revelations came late during the composition of the *Liber floridus*, meaning that Lambert never fully developed them. As he was finishing his book, however, images of
Jerusalem were popping up everywhere, all over his historical and
symbolic maps.

As with so many of his speculations, Lambert was not alone among crusade historians in being fascinated with Troy. Guibert of Nogent compared the number of Franks who departed on crusade to the number of Greeks who left to fight at Troy, and he argued elsewhere in his chronicle that the Franks were worthier than the Trojans because their motives had been purer.[49] Baldric of Bourgueil likewise felt that the Franks had put Troy and Greece to shame: "Such beautiful camps, such imperial tents! Who has ever seen tents like these? Let cease that beloved tale of Troy! Let the tents of the Achaeans be struck! Let the names and deeds of their nobles evermore grow dark! There Ulysses employed his cunning; Ajax showed his bravery; Achilles made plain his strength. Here Christians showed a dove-like simplicity, while at war they deployed a virtuous and glorious knighthood."[50]

The Franks had surpassed Troy, or perhaps they had actually become Trojans—a more perfect incarnation of what Troy had tried to embody. Such would explain the rather awkward formula used by Ralph of Caen, the biographer of Bohemond's nephew Tancred, to explain what happened when Bohemond became prince of Antioch. "Ilium regained Troy," effectively saying, "Troy conquered Troy."[51] Troy would have been on the minds of many Frankish pilgrims to the Holy Land for another more tangible reason; the city's ruins on the shores of Anatolia offered a possible rest stop for pilgrims and soldiers on their way to Jerusalem.[52]

In still another sense was Troy foundational to the crusade story. Both the Franks and the Turks, according to the best medieval historical traditions, were descended from Trojans. Centuries earlier, as the peoples who one day became the Franks traveled across Europe looking for a home, a Promised Land, a faction broke away under the leadership of a man named Torquatus. From him his followers took the name, "Turks." Based on an entry in a seventh-century chronicle, this tradition is not only pre-crusade but also pre-Islam.[53]

The anonymous eyewitness in *The Deeds of the Franks* echoes this belief, though without mentioning Troy. The Turks, he claims, had a saying, "that they are of common stock with the Franks, and no men, except the Franks and themselves, are naturally born to be knights. This is true, and nobody can deny it."[54] The Turks, of course, had no such tradition. Nonetheless, about eighty years later, the historian and bishop William of Tyre, who lived in Jerusalem and was himself an authority on Islam, elaborated these points. Turks, like Franks, were descended from Trojans who had barely escaped the destruction of their city. The two races were brothers, refugees from the same disaster. They had traveled different directions, some east and some west, but were evenly matched as soldiers.[55] Perhaps climate was destiny since, as Guibert of Nogent argues, the lighter, hotter air in the East makes men there more prone to heresy, presumably incapable of sticking to one belief, however self-evident its theology.[56]

Twelfth-century scribes and copyists also sensed these connections. When they or their patrons wished to celebrate the crusade in a manuscript, and to do more than just transcribe one or two chronicles, they used similar building blocks: a chronicle of the crusade (any one of them would do), a description or two of the Holy Land, and stories about Alexander, Troy, and King Arthur. To this list one might add legendary materials related to the deeds of Charlemagne, who died in 814 and by the early twelfth century was as much a figure of legend as of history.[57] To contemplate the conquest of Jerusalem was to take a stroll through Europe's mythic and historic imagination.[58]

Out of this mix of chronicle, fable, prophecy, magical beasts, and miracles, one collection of manuscripts deserves special emphasis.[59] All of its representatives originate from Flanders, thus were produced in the same intellectual circles through which Lambert of Saint-Omer moved. When combined with the various copies of the *Liber floridus*, they comprise a remarkable and largely unrecognized contribution to European thought, what might be described as "a Flemish school of crusade history." There is significant overlap in the material that these manuscripts contain, though no one manuscript precisely duplicates another. All of them include the *History* of Robert the Monk. Two of them also contain the *History* of Fulcher of Chartres, while another includes the poetic crusade narrative by the twelfth-century monk and later Cardinal Gilo of Paris. They also incorporate travel guides to the Holy Land, lists of rulers in both Europe and the Latin East, and some materials of special interest to Flemish readers. Two contain a fictionalized and deliberately scurrilous biography of Muhammad. One of them includes, appropriately, a list of the Seven Wonders of the World.[60] For the scribes who assembled, copied, and rearranged these various texts, the task of explaining the First Crusade demanded not just a record of events but a presentation of the whole world, its marvels laid bare, with an accent on how the crusade had remade, and was continuing to remake, everything.

Perhaps the most revealing text included in these manuscripts is one that seems at first to have no connection to crusading: a short description of the Church of the Lateran in Rome. It is a travel guide similar in spirit to the ones about Jerusalem. The canons of the Lateran likely composed it in the aftermath of the crusade, perhaps in rivalry with the Vatican, perhaps to meet the demands of an increasing number of pilgrims and sightseers to their church.[61] Copies of the guide survive in the Lateran archives, but the earliest versions of it appear in these Flemish crusade manuscripts.

Why were crusade historians in Flanders so intrigued with one particular church in Rome? Obviously, the city of Rome and the Lateran were luminous sites in the Christian imagination. Lambert included a drawing of Rome, surrounding an enthroned St. Peter, in his *Liber floridus*.[62] The relic collection of the Lateran, moreover, contained many precious items brought from Jerusalem by the Empress Helena, mother of Constantine. Several narrative passages in the text, therefore, relate to Jerusalem.[63]

Within this collection, however, one item stands out, particularly for historians or churchmen or tourists intrigued by the Holy Land: "In the Church of the Lateran, which is the head of the world and is the patriarchal and imperial see, and the apostolic, pontifical cathedral, the principal altar of that very church is the Ark of the Covenant."[64] Built by Moses, carried by the Israelites into battle, plundered by Nebuchadnezzar, the Ark had made its way to Rome. Within the Ark were the candelabrum from the original tabernacle, the flowering rod of Aaron, the tablets of the law, the staff of Moses, and a variety of Christian relics, including, for example, remnants of Christ's cradle and the seamless tunic made for the infant Jesus by Mary. So important was this altar that no one save the pope was allowed to celebrate mass on it, and when he did, seven bishops and twenty-seven cardinals necessarily attended.[65]

It was an extraordinary claim, to possess the Ark, and the writers of the text admitted that not everyone believed them. The prophet Jeremiah, doubters argued, had hidden the Ark when Nebuchadnezzar had destroyed Jerusalem, and it would not be revealed again "until God shall gather together his people and show them his mercy, and then the Lord will reveal things and the Majesty of God will appear."[66] But, the defenders of the Lateran Church countered, all of these conditions had been met by the birth of Christ. The Incarnation had been the revelation of God's majesty. One might therefore infer that the Jews had, during Christ's life, recovered the Ark, taken it to Jerusalem, and kept it hidden until 70 CE. At that time Titus sacked the city and brought its treasures, including the Ark, back to Rome. Anyone whose wished see evidence for this claim, the travel guide observes, could simply step out into the city and look at the relief sculptures on the Arch of Titus.[67]

The Lateran's possession of the Ark of the Covenant also made manifest the ways in which the First Crusade had reconfigured the world. The Franks had become the new Israel. Allegorically, Christians had always claimed this title.[68] The conquest of Jerusalem had made that claim something akin to historical reality and had invested it with an ethnic, Frankish specificity. Allegory had become history. In a similar way, in the first millennium of Christianity, followers of Christ had viewed Jerusalem as a symbol which they had sought to locate in their hearts or in their churches. A baptistery was the Jordan River, the altar was Calvary, a saint's shrine was the Holy Sepulcher. Constantine may have rebuilt the city of Jerusalem, but its more potent, meaningful level of existence was spiritual. When Jerusalem became a Christian capital again in 1099 and a cultural outpost for the Frankish European world, the allegory necessarily ceded place to a less elegant, more cumbersome reality.

For observers like Lambert, however, the physical city offered those magical charms that the allegorized Jerusalem had once possessed. It was a microcosm of the world, onto which the divine plan—the journey from the City of Man to the City of God—had been imprinted. Rome possessed, at the Lateran, arguably the most powerful physical relic of the Old Testament city, but aspects of Jerusalem could be found in cities throughout the Christian world and throughout historical memory, too—be it Saint-Omer, Troy, the many versions of Alexandria, or the court of King Arthur. The truth that Lambert's book repeatedly communicates—in its depictions of heavenly and earthly cityscapes, in its world maps, in its reiterations of the movements of empire, in its explorations of legend and myth, in its prophecies, in its one-page world history that opens with the city of Cain near the beginning of time and ends with the conquest of Jerusalem in 1099, in its reading of Nebuchadnezzar's dream—is that after the First Crusade, the outlines of heavenly Jerusalem were clearer, sharper, and always within imaginative reach. The world was transforming. Or better still, in the trendy, technical vocabulary of the day, the world was transubstantiating. Not the shape, but the substance was new. That is why the First Crusade seemed like an apocalyptic event, the opening act of the End Times so long desired.

A Babylonian king had dreamed it. A Jewish prophet had recorded it. And now Christian knights and historians were making it real.

PART II

Warning Signs

CHAPTER 6

Crusaders Behaving Badly

D ESPITE WIDESPREAD CONFIDENCE THAT the conquest of Jerusalem in 1099 had advanced salvation history, it was possible, almost from the moment of conquest itself, to see things differently. In the 1120s, William of Malmesbury, one of the Middle Ages' greatest historians, argued that the crusade happened not because Christians in the East were in danger, nor because of devotional love for the city of Jerusalem. Rather, it began with a secret pact between Pope Urban II and the future failed Duke of Antioch, Bohemond. The former, because of ongoing wars with German king Henry IV, could not live in Rome and wished to return, while the latter wanted to set up a kingdom for himself in Illyria and possibly beyond. The two men agreed that if they could recruit enough soldiers and convince them that they were fighting for Jerusalem, they could both get what they wanted.[1]

William's is a stunningly pragmatic and cynical take on the crusade and likely a product of his familiarity with classical history. He thought less about prophecy and salvation history than did, say, Lambert of Saint-Omer. But William's outlook also indicates the existence of a worldview more widespread than is apparent in medieval sources. For there were more than enough reasons to feel skeptical about the crusade. Amid the celebrations of military victory and prophecy fulfilled lurked other stories of lives ruined or ideals betrayed—stories that at the very least would have raised questions about the value of the expedition and the integrity of its heroes.

Penitential Warriors

The call to crusade had always been, among other things, a way to teach knights how to behave. In Guibert of Nogent's concise formula, European warriors "had found a new way to attain salvation." Its name was "holy war."[2] Thanks to this single oxymoronic expression, the First Crusade had resolved one of Christianity's most intractable problems: how to reconcile a soldier's life with religion, how to harmonize regular combat with the gospel injunction to turn the other cheek, and how to combine the drive to plunder with the instruction to give a beggar twice as much as he asks for.[3]

Before the crusade, theologians wrestling with this problem would probably have turned to St. Augustine. Pragmatic as always, Augustine managed to transform the phrase "turn the other cheek" into a lesson on the best way to kill. Christ's words, Augustine preached, were never meant to be taken literally. The Gospel of Matthew specifies that if someone strikes you first on the right cheek, then you should allow him to hit you on the left cheek too. Why did Christ specify the right cheek? He did so to encourage followers to dig deeper. Most people are right-handed. Therefore, an attacker would in all probability hit someone first on the left cheek. If Christ had meant his words literally, he would have begun, "if someone strikes you on the left cheek" or else he would have identified no cheek at all. His words communicate a symbolic truth only, an exhortation to all Christians to change their internal dispositions, to turn their allegorical cheeks. Soldiers, when they are attacked or in combat, need not become pacifists; they need only fight with the right combination of dispassion and love.[4]

For an actual knight this argument probably would have been of little value. Soldiers going into battle did not need theological hair-splitting. They needed something like a free pass or a preemptive pardon for what they were about to do. And once Bohemond's nephew, the First Crusader Tancred, heard that Urban II had offered something like that in exchange for service in Jerusalem, in the words of his biographer, "his strength returned, his eyes opened, his boldness grew twofold."[5] A professional fighter such as he could find redemption not in spite of bloodshed but because of it. Most scholars have come to believe this penitential revolution is by itself powerful enough to explain why Urban's call to crusade was successful.[6]

The terms of the papal indulgence, however, were not as straightforward as they seem. The main difficulty concerns the meaning of "holy war." Then, as now, holy war had no definition. Like pornography, you knew it when you saw it—when, for example, in the eighth-century epic poem *Song of Roland,* angels carry dead Christian warriors to heaven, demons drag dead Saracen souls to hell, and the archangel Gabriel helps Charlemagne strike death blows against a Babylonian king, you know you're looking at "holy war."

To win God's help, warriors like Roland, Charlemagne's chief lieutenant in the poem, needed to be imbued with righteousness and justice. In an ordinary war, soldiers could be reprobates and not endanger the outcome of battle, which depended on strategy or which side God favored. Holy warriors, by contrast, needed to be pure. If they were not, if they did not perform enough penance to redeem their transgressions, they were slaves to sin and hence fatally flawed instruments in the war for salvation. Their simple presence on the battlefield undermined their cause, no matter how righteous that cause might be. These ideas gave shape to stories about the First Crusade and helped to explain its success. As evidenced by their suffering and victories, crusaders had attained that necessary level of cleansing and redemption. They had forged themselves into weapons of a vengeful God. How these processes worked, though, remained unclear in 1099 and later, leaving a difficult moral legacy for survivors and for their lords, kinsmen, and spiritual advisers.

The Fruits of Penance

Urban II apparently did consider these questions at the 1095 Council of Clermont. Each version of his sermon proclaiming the crusade— there are four, all with significant differences—note that knights needed to stop killing Christians and start killing Muslims: "you devour one another and struggle against and wound and kill each other. Let your hatred cease! Let your quarrels be calmed, your battles settled, and all your fractious disputes ended."[7] "Let those who were once accustomed to exert themselves brutally in private war against believers now fight honorably against unbelievers and claim victory. You who were once thieves have become soldiers of Christ. You who once clashed with your brothers and kinsmen now fight rightly against barbarians."[8] "You oppressors of orphans, predators against widows, murderers, blasphemers, robbers of others' birthrights! You await a thief's wages for spilling Christian blood. Like vultures smelling corpses, you sense distant battles and pursue them. This path you are on is the worst possible."[9] The benefits of the crusade were obvious, and the transformation from one damnation to salvation, apparently, simple.

Urban's formal indulgence, however, contained stipulations. Not everyone could "substitute" going to Jerusalem for "all penance." Penance would not be guaranteed to all crusaders—rather, only to those who left with pure motives: for love of God and Jerusalem, not for fame or treasure. Yet fame and treasure would have been difficult to avoid, since they were all part of the same package. One version of the pope's sermon, for example, stresses that Palestine is a land flowing with milk and honey, with economic opportunities far beyond what warriors could find in the overworked fields of France.[10]

To avoid these pitfalls would require a soldier to seek a sophisticated spiritual counselor, the kind of pastor few would have known. The best available teachers would have kept their message simple, relying on easily understandable analogies, such as this one attributed to an abbot named Thierry. Thierry used to tell of a sinful monk who was nonetheless an excellent scribe. Of his own volition he had written one particularly large theological tome. Upon death, he found himself before a tribunal, where demons cataloged his faults. To reach a verdict, "letters in the huge book were carefully weighed one by one against his sins. In the end one letter alone remained in excess of all the sins; and the demons tried in vain to find any fault to weigh against it." The monk returned to life, performed further penance, and presumably reached heaven.[11] A crusader doubtless had more and far worse sins and needed a correspondingly thick book, full of letters, some illuminated with gold leaf—beautiful enough to tip the scales of justice toward salvation.

But how to gain such a book, particularly through the mechanism of crusade? The idea of "armed penitential pilgrimage"—of "pilgrim warriors of the Holy Sepulcher"[12]—was an oxymoron. Pilgrims traveled in peace. They did not carry weapons. Chroniclers who celebrated the First Crusade recognized this sticky problem, even if they did not admit it directly. According to the monk Baldric of Bourgueil, who wrote in the wake of Bohemond's 1106 preaching tour, certain Greek Christians, on seeing the Franks marching to Jerusalem, thought them not pilgrims or Christians but "gladiators and tyrants."[13] During the siege of Antioch, in February 1098, as Baldric's contemporary Robert the Monk tells it, Egyptian ambassadors to the Frankish camp raised similar concerns, asking, "why do you carry weapons while seeking the tomb of your Lord, driving people from lands they have held for so long—no, more truly, slaughtering them at the edge of the sword, a wicked thing for pilgrims to do?"[14] It is likely that these historians wrote in this way in

1107/8 not to record Greek or Egyptian concerns but to address lingering doubts among Christian readers who after the First Crusade continued to see "warrior" and "pilgrim" as mutually exclusive categories.

Urban's promise of indulgence raised yet another problem, more fundamental and potentially more dangerous. Namely, to borrow from Abbot Thierry, how weighty a book had the First Crusaders actually received because of their efforts? Had they won enough letters to foil demons on Judgment Day, no matter how numerous their crimes, or only a few prodigious tokens that they might later bring into play to try to redeem their souls? The formula ironed out at Clermont notes that the journey served as a substitute for "all penance."[15] But was that "all" limited to sins confessed before (or during) the campaign? Might it embrace later sins, too?

Urban II likely recognized the potential confusion. In a letter written in 1096, a year after Clermont, he specified that the indulgence covered only past sins: "We remit all penance for sin, for which [crusaders] make full and true confession."[16] But it is doubtful that everyone got the message. Tancred's conception of penance and crusade, according to his biographer Ralph of Caen, who wrote around 1115, thus with twenty years' hindsight, not only did this promise not impose a limit on the indulgence it actually removed any and all stipulations, including the need for confession. The indulgence, Ralph says, gave "to every Christian about to battle against the Gentiles remission of all sins."[17]

To suggest that the crusade guaranteed a soldier's entry into heaven, no matter what he did during the rest of his life, seems at best unrealistic. Similar ideas, however, had long circulated about other pilgrimages, and far less challenging ones at that.[18] Around 1020, decades before the First Crusade, the famous church lawyer Burchard of Worms denounced laymen who believed that pilgrimages to Tours or Rome allowed them "to sin, or to have sinned, with impunity." About one hundred years later, in the immediate aftermath of the First Crusade, another lawyer, Ivo of Chartres, would copy the same passage into his own book.[19] Both Burchard and Ivo conclude their case with the citation of a popular epithet from St. Jerome, writing at the end of the fourth century: "It is praiseworthy not to have seen Jerusalem, but to have lived well in Jerusalem."[20] For Burchard this maxim would have been symbolic, with Jerusalem representing life in the church. For Ivo, writing a century later and sometimes considering cases that involved actual crusaders, the same words offered commentary on current events.

Guibert of Nogent similarly, around 1108, attacked veteran crusaders who believed that Urban's indulgence had won them lifelong
get-out-of-hell-free cards. He describes them while defending the
reputations of two of the campaign's most notorious deserters,
Stephen of Blois and Hugh the Great, both of whom had abandoned
the campaign early at Antioch in 1098, a year before Jerusalem's fall.
Stephen and Hugh each tried to make amends by going back to the
Holy Land in 1101, and both had died on that march. The men who
captured Jerusalem take pride in what they did, but in terms of
"crimes, treachery, and lies," not one of them seems to want to be
outdone by any of the others. They ridicule Stephen and Hugh,
whose deaths carry "the sure scent of nobility," while they themselves
"stink of every possible outrage."[21] It is impossible to know how many
people Guibert had in mind when he wrote this, but one of them was
a man named Thomas of Marle, who, according to Guibert and one
other contemporary observer, was the worst man ever to live.[22]

As Guibert describes Thomas, writing around 1115, he was a
sadist and psychopath, torturing and killing those with whom he
came in contact. When he held captives for ransom, as was a common
if frowned upon practice among knights, he would "hang them,
sometimes with his own hand, by their testicles, and when these were
torn away from their bodies, as happened frequently, their vital
organs would burst out at almost the same time." Others he would
"hang by their thumbs or genitals, then place a stone over their
shoulders to weigh them down, while he walked back and forth
underneath them, and when he could not force out of them a possession that they could not possibly own, in a frenzy he beat them
over their entire bodies with a stick until they promised anything
that would satisfy him, or else died from their torture."[23] He imprisoned lepers, stabbed hermits, cut the feet off captives and ordered
them to march, all for the sake of his own amusement.[24] To a man
such as Thomas, the need to reckon between virtue and vice had
no meaning.

But if Thomas was psychotic at home, at Jerusalem he was
heroic. As Albert of Aachen reports in his history of the First Crusade,
begun probably around 1110, Thomas set off with the followers of
Emicho of Flonheim, famous for leading pogroms against Jews and
claiming to be Last World Emperor. Emicho abandoned the crusade
in Hungary, but Thomas changed course and pressed on, first jour-
neying to Italy where he joined the armies of Hugh the Great. Unlike
Hugh, he continued all the way to Jerusalem and apparently fought
magnificently, later becoming a main character in two epic poems,

The Song of Antioch and *The Song of Jerusalem,* written down around the turn of the thirteenth century (though likely based on earlier traditions) and aimed at secular audiences. When actual knights heard stories of the crusade, one of the heroes they celebrated was Thomas of Marle.[25]

If Guibert's complaint about misguided crusaders does indeed apply to Thomas—if Thomas believed the crusade had absolved him of all past and future sins because he had seen Jerusalem—then he not only felt no qualms about his behavior after 1099, he believed that he could sin with impunity with no spiritual consequence.

It is an astonishing irony. The pope had called the crusade in part to channel the violent impulses of men like Thomas of Marle toward salvific ends. Instead, in the case of Thomas, the crusade gave him a sense of entitlement, a confidence that he could dismiss ordinary moral restraint. Such were the fruits of penance. He could declare early victory at Judgment Day. Maybe Thomas was a uniquely awful person. Or perhaps he was only unusual in that he had in Guibert of Nogent an uncommonly talented observer to chronicle his misdeeds.

For other veterans, the First Crusade left similar, if fainter, traces in the historical record of comparable patterns of behavior. For example, Gerard of Quierzy, whose heroics at the battle of Dorylaeum and the siege of Jerusalem were celebrated, had a checkered career after returning to France. At the time of his death in 1111 he was under excommunication for kidnapping and ransoming two German boys. Before that date he had taken as a lover Sibyl of Porcien, the wife of the nobleman Enguerrand of Coucy—as such, she was Thomas of Marle's stepmother. Sibyl conspired with a bishop to have Gerard assassinated while praying in a cathedral. As he died, Gerard looked up at his killers with one eye—the other eye was lost, probably during battles in the Holy Land—and said "Get away from here, you filthy lech!" And then, as they began to hack at him, "Blessed Mary, help me!"[26]

Rotrou of Perche is another such case. On returning from the Holy Land, Rotrou entered into formal friendship, or "confraternity," with the monastery of Cluny, where Peter the Venerable would one day become abbot. Rotrou also entered into a series of disputes with local rivals over land tenure. During one of them, according to the contemporary monk and historian Orderic Vitalis, Rotrou and an adversary "fought each other ferociously, looting and burning in one another's territories and adding crime to crime. They plundered poor and helpless people, constantly made them suffer losses or

made them live in fear of losses, bringing distress to their depen-
dents, knights and peasants alike."[27] Not beyond the pale of preda-
tory knightly behavior in the early eleventh century, but surely
discordant with Rotrou's reputation as a pious soldier of Christ.

Drogo of Mouchy-le-Châtel departed for Jerusalem in the army
of Hugh the Great. Shortly upon his return, in 1101, the cathedral
chapter at Beauvais asked King Philip I to intervene against him.
The reasons are unclear, but presumably they involved the harass-
ment of clerics or the confiscation of property. Philip sent his son,
the future Louis VI, to fight for the cathedral. His retaliation left
Drogo a broken man.[28]

Rebellions against the king often counted First Crusade veterans among their leaders. Among them was Guy of Rochefort, who
returned from Jerusalem renowned and rich and then later joined a
revolt in 1104 against Philip of France. Ralph of Beaugency sided
with Count Theobald of Blois in one of his periodic insurrections
against the king. Abbot Suger, the biographer of Louis VI and champion of royal prerogatives, held a dim opinion of another crusader,
Evrard III of Le Puiset, whom he depicts as a wretched man made
rich only by virtue of tyranny. Probably Evrard was guilty of the same
sort of crimes as his son Hugh—tyrannizing churches, brutalizing
the poor, and disrespecting the king's authority.[29]

It is not surprising that crusaders were prone to lèse-majesté.
Under normal circumstances, as Guibert observed, they would not
have given the king three days' service. After the crusade, in light of
their proven bravery and virtue, bordering on saintliness, they had
still less reason to show deference to the monarchy.[30]

Still more intriguing is the case of Raimbold Croton, one of the
first knights to scale Jerusalem's walls, an act of valor that cost him a
hand. Later, shortly after returning home around 1101, he became
involved in a dispute with a monk-priest at Bonnevalle. Some of
Raimbold's men, apparently, had stolen hay from the church there,
and in retaliation the monk-priest had ordered the thieves beaten.
Raimbold, "driven by a diabolical impulse and moved by rage," captured the monk and castrated him. Ivo of Chartres (the canon lawyer
who had discussed just how much or how little forgiveness pilgrims
were entitled to) heard the case and considered it unprecedented—
perhaps because of the violence involved, perhaps because of
Raimbold's status as a crusader, of which Ivo took note. He imposed
on Raimbold an unusually harsh penance. For fourteen years, the
one-handed Raimbold would be forbidden from carrying weapons.
Raimbold appealed the judgment, arguing that it left him vulnerable

to attack. But Ivo refused to reduce the sentence, lest through clemency he create a dangerous precedent.[31]

These are a handful of such examples—not enough from which to advance a general theory of post-traumatic stress disorder among crusaders, perhaps, but enough to suggest that a behavioral problem existed. The heroes of the First Crusade were, of theoretical or ideological necessity, close to living saints, men fearless on the battlefield who had also engaged in warfare against their own worst impulses. A few prominent, countervailing examples like Thomas of Marle and Raimbold Croton could undercut this sense of prophetic virtue.

One cannot, however, blame Thomas, Raimbold, or any of the other veterans who mistook sociopathy for sanctity. They had scaled Jerusalem's walls and smashed its gates. They had advanced God's plan for history and in the process acquired indulgence for their sins. Why should they not feel entitled to rebel against a king, plunder a neighbor, torture a peasant, or castrate a monk?[32]

Templars

A long-term solution for a later generation of knights was to instill in them a higher code of conduct. (The small but notable generation of disturbed veterans of 1099 was probably a lost cause.) The nascent cult of chivalry played a part of this story. Tales of romance, quest, and adventure gave warriors fictional models of how they might productively direct their murderous impulses while not surrendering the trappings of aristocracy. As for the stories of the First Crusade, with their emphasis on superhuman sacrifices and impossible suffering, coupled with enforced celibacy and poverty—European knights might find much to admire, but not much worth emulating.

But then a compromise appeared. In January 1129, in the city of Troyes—Troy reborn in the land of France—a council of ecclesiastical dignitaries and secular notables gathered. Not as big an affair as what happened at Clermont in 1095, the Council of Troyes nonetheless included some genuine celebrities: Cardinal Matthew of Albano; Count Theobald of Chartres; Count William of Nevers; two archbishops; ten bishops, and eight abbots. This last group included Bernard of Clairvaux, the most famous preacher alive and one the most important political actors of the twelfth century, too.[33] This mostly French group had gathered to meet with six knights who had traveled from Jerusalem, all of them members of a newly founded order called the Knights of the Temple of Solomon.

The Templars, as they became known, had been established in Jerusalem around 1119. One of the founders, Hugh of Payns, was from the region of Champagne, just a few miles from Troyes, whose most famous poet, Chrétien, would write the first fully realized adventure stories of King Arthur and his knights. The other founder was Godfrey of Saint-Omer, the same city where Lambert had recently completed his *Liber floridus*. Romance and Apocalypse—the Templars embodied both halves of this cultural inheritance. They were virtuous warriors fighting for Christ and standing guard at the threshold of the Last Days. Originally, though, they served a very practical function. In the frontier world of Frankish Jerusalem, they protected the hundreds and possibly thousands of pilgrims to the Holy Land. This prosaic duty transformed into poetry when Hugh traveled to France on a recruitment drive ten years later, leading him to Troyes in 1129.

Ideally, Templars lived as monks—following a rule of prayer, abstinence, and formal poverty. But they also fought as knights. Monks, of course, had always considered themselves warriors. Together they formed the *militia Dei*, God's militia. The Templars took this allegory and made it literal—real warriors who were also real monks. To make the concept succeed, they needed a written rule, and it was the goal of the Council of Troyes to produce one. The churchmen who gathered there composed a seventy-two-point guide to delineate, among other things, how the monk-knights should pray, how they should eat, how they should dress. On this last topic, the rule specified that all Templars absolutely, positively had to avoid wearing pointy-toed shoes—equally characteristic, as Lambert had made clear, of lascivious knights and Antichrist.[34]

To accompany the technical rule, Bernard of Clairvaux composed something akin to an anthem: a short pamphlet titled, *In Praise of the New Knighthood*. A mission statement for the new order, it was filled with a nostalgia for the recent past as it attempted to revive—or perhaps for the first time to realize—the ideals of the crusade.[35]

In Praise of the New Knighthood divides all soldiers into two groups: worldly knights and "new knights." The former group Bernard hesitates even to describe as "a knighthood." Theirs is a passion for wickedness, not honor—to use Bernard's Latin pun, they form *malitia* instead of *militia*, "malice" instead of "militia."[36] They fight for earthly, carnal goals. For them, to win in battle is to lose, since they dishonor themselves through sin. To die is a double loss: destruction of life and damnation of soul. Vanity fills these knights. They cover their horses, Bernard says, with silk and their own armor with ridiculous finery. Their spurs and bridles are bedecked with gold, silver, and precious stones, their hair, their sleeves, their tunics all long and flowing in womanish fashion—again, like Lambert of Saint-Omer's Antichrist. As they ride into battle in this extravagant and impractical attire, they feel only greed, anger, or hunger for praise.[37] They are, in short, epitomes of the erratic blood-soaked men whom Urban II recruited in 1095 for the First Crusade, men in need of redemption that only a new kind of war, a holy war, could provide.

This is the sort of battle at which Bernard's knights excelled. For them, to win is victory on earth; to die, victory in Christ. The cause is just; their conscience and their penitential ledgers, clear. Combat for them is twofold, waged against enemies physical and spiritual, against Saracens and sins.[38] They shun the aristocratic pleasures to which they are entitled, not just sex and marriage but indeed every sign of wealth and status. "They foreswear dice and chess, they abhor the hunt; they take no delight, as is customary, in the ridiculous cruelty of falconry. Jesters, wizards, bards, bawdy minstrels and jousters, they despise and reject as so many vanities and deceitful follies." They keep their hair cut short and their clothing modest, ordinary. They are fierce in battle but unmoved by hatred. They enter combat with great deliberation and as "men of peace."[39]

They are "an astounding and unique" hybrid, combining the callings of the warrior and the monk. "I do not know," Bernard concludes, "if it would be more appropriate to refer to them as monks or as soldiers, or whether it would perhaps be better to recognize them as being both, for they lack neither monastic meekness nor military might."[40] Their headquarters is, appropriately, the Temple of Jerusalem (al-Aqsa Mosque). It is not, Bernard specifies, the Temple of Solomon, nor is it as splendid as that earlier temple was. Then again, the Temple of Solomon's glory lay in gold and silver—in a fashion typical of biblical commentary, the Jewish Temple depends on tangible, physical glory, whereas the Christian temple derives honor from its residents. Cleansed of pagan impurity, the new knights "honor the temple of God earnestly with fervent and sincere worship, in their devotion offering, not the flesh of animals according to the ancient rites, but true peace, brotherly love, devoted obedience, and voluntary poverty."[41]

Bernard's rhetoric contains faint echoes of Lambert of Saint-Omer's apocalyptic vision—"events in Jerusalem have shaken the world," he writes. But in 1129 he was mainly interested in moral conversions. Soldiers, once brutal despoilers of their own people, had become servants of Christ. Their homelands could rejoice in the peace created by their absence, while pilgrims in Jerusalem could celebrate the protection they now enjoyed against Christ's foes: "This is the revenge Christ has contrived against his enemies, to triumph powerfully and gloriously over them by their own means. Surely it is both happy and fitting that those who have so long fought against him should at last begin to fight for him."[42]

Bernard's rhetoric is distinctive, yet his ideas are familiar. Most obviously they recall Guibert's description of the crusaders as "a new knighthood of God" who had found a new way of achieving salvation. Like monks, the original crusaders had abandoned worldly possessions, even though they did not adopt a monastic vocation.[43] Still, even with no formal rule, they lived together as equals, again like monks, feeling no greed and sharing in physical hardship. According to Baldric of Bourgueil and Albert of Aachen, each writing about twenty years before Bernard, the crusaders had shared possessions equally.[44] Their camps were "a school of moral discipline"—discipline being the main virtue of both Templars and monks.[45] Unlike monks, but, like Templars, the crusaders' struggles were twofold, repressing their own vices with spiritual weapons while wielding actual swords against Saracens.[46] Even in the desperate battle against Kerbogha, the atabeg of Mosul, in 1098 fought outside Antioch, the Franks marched forth with equanimity, on the outside showing military ferocity while on the inside blithely preparing for martyrdom.[47]

Bernard in 1129 and crusade historians in 1108 also shared concerns about the behavior of worldly knights. Without the crusade, soldiers were plunderers of the poor, men who fought only out of a "lust for rule," in Guibert of Nogent's terms. The crusaders, by contrast, fought for God, not to expand territory, not for money, and not for "foolish glory"—language, again, reminiscent of Bernard's description of the Templars.[48] Both Baldric and Robert the Monk made the same Latin pun as Bernard, comparing knighthood and wickedness, *militia* and *malitia.* "The holy church has reserved for herself a militia to protect her own," Baldric's version of Urban II's speech says. Knights who had not yet joined the crusade, by contrast, were "dragging her down into malice."[49] Peter the Hermit, as a character in Robert's *Historia*, insults Kerbogha and his Saracen followers by saying: "Oh, you princes, not of a militia, but of malice!"[50]

The concept of the Templars as monkish knights or knightly monks, therefore, did not spring entirely from the imagination of Hugh of Payns or from the genius of Bernard of Clairvaux. It grew instead out of the history of the First Crusade. "In terms of austerity and piety, these men led not a military but a monastic life," wrote

Guibert in 1108.[51] The only distinction between the two types of Christian soldier is that while the First Crusaders lived "like monks," abandoning the company of women, sharing their possessions, and fighting only for the love of God, the Templars took formal vows and actually became monks. At the same time, they functioned as living letters of the First Crusade, their calling a testimony to the reality (or at least the possibility) of honorable, monkish soldiers described by Guibert, Baldric, Robert, and others, whose books were rapidly filling church libraries across Europe. One contemporary observer, occasional historian, and friend of Bernard of Clairvaux, named Anselm of Havelberg, embraced such a connection between crusaders and Templars. The idea for the Templars, he argues, was invented when Pope Urban II first preached the crusade.[52]

Seen from this angle, the Templars were part of the celebratory, prophetic atmosphere that characterized the years after the First Crusade—a time of unprecedented public jubilation. Christianity had reclaimed its birthplace; world maps were being redrawn and world histories rewritten. From another perspective, the Templars were a response to a later crisis, born of the conflict of idealized memory and lived realities, between the memory of the paragons who had stormed Jerusalem's walls in 1099 and the later careers of sadists like Thomas of Marle and the one-handed, castrating Raimbold Croton. From this vantage, the Templars were less a continuation of the First Crusade and more an attempt to save it, to keep its history authentic even as so many veterans stubbornly refused to follow the script that fawning historians had written for them.

As a sort of coda for the Council of Troyes, in 1130, a year after it had taken place and probably as Bernard was finishing *In Praise of the New Knighthood*, the most notorious of crusading heroes, Thomas of Marle, lay dying. In a rare display of piety, according to Abbot Suger, biographer of Louis VI of France, he consented to receive the Eucharist. Thomas may have believed in his own salvation, based on what had happened at Jerusalem, but in the face of death he still took precautions. He raised his head from the bed to receive of the host. Before he could do so, Suger notes with satisfaction, his neck snapped. He died instantly. Whatever had happened at Jerusalem, whatever heroic songs Thomas had earned, Christ rejected him at death.[53]

The Templars were a stopgap between the memory of Thomas of Marle in song and legend and the brutal truth. The question of how to commemorate the First Crusade, of how to keep retelling the story, and of deciding what it meant for the future, remained a problem for a later day.

CHAPTER 7

Troubling News from the East

A LARMS SOUNDED FROM THE EAST, too—stories of military failure and moral compromise. Of course, not all the news was bad. Indeed, the history of the early crusader states was one of steady territorial expansion. Seen from another perspective, however, the rot began setting in almost as soon as Jerusalem fell to the Franks and calls for a new campaign went out.[1]

The Crusade of 1101

Those calls began barely a year after Jerusalem's conquest. There was no single proclamation, no Council of Clermont, no Peter the Hermit, and as of yet, no warrior figure like Bohemond to enthuse crowds. Nor was there any specific goal. According to the monk Orderic Vitalis, people were excited about what had happened in 1099 and wanted to celebrate in person. Some did leave under compulsion. Pope Paschal II ordered everyone who had earlier taken the cross and promised to go to Jerusalem to fulfill their vow now or face damnation.[2] As a result, the army included two notorious deserters, Hugh the Great and Stephen of Blois, to whose defense Guibert of Nogent rose in response to the ridicule of men like Thomas of Marle.

Not everyone was as charitable as Guibert in their judgments of Stephen and Hugh. Orderic Vitalis, for one, describes how Stephen's wife, Adele, "amidst sweet words of conjugal affection," reminded him that people across France were laughing about his cowardice and that once upon a time he used to be brave. "For the salvation of many thousands of people, take up the weapons of that admirable army, so that Christians throughout the world might celebrate and so that pagans might know fear and witness the public destruction of their accursed law." Stephen was still reluctant. He quaked at the thought of new hardships. But he eventually—out of sexual frustration, Orderic implies—recognized the wisdom of her words and returned to the Levant, accompanied by thousands of Franks, a dazzling array of men from Germany, Lombardy, France, and Burgundy, among them bishops, counts, commoners, poor pilgrims, wives, and children.[3]

The motives of this new army were as varied as those of the original crusaders: desire to see the Holy Land, hope for salvation, the chance to improve one's lot in life, and a sincere belief that the campaign would advance God's plan for history. To these well-worn notions must be added an entirely new one: They wished to equal or surpass the heroism of the original crusaders. According to Guibert, they were "expecting that they would do new and greater things than their predecessors."[4] It would become a familiar theme.[5] Twelfth-century knights wished to match or exceed the "exertions of their forebears"—in Latin, the *stenuitas patrum*.

As in 1096, the new crusaders departed in waves.[6] The first group left from Lombardy in September 1100, under the leadership of Archbishop Anselm IV of Milan. They crossed Hungary without incident. On entering Bulgaria, the leaders negotiated for and received market privileges from Emperor Alexius. From there, things went badly. Some of the army started plundering cattle—worse still, the twelfth-century chronicler Albert of Aachen notes, they did so during Lent, when they were supposed to be fasting. Some crusaders heard that the locals were hiding their possessions inside churches, so they broke into the emperor's chapel and tore it to pieces. "And what is terrible to hear, one of the army's hangers-on hacked off a woman's breasts because she was defending her possessions."[7]

Alexius hurried the Franks along to Constantinople and pressured them to cross the Bosporus quickly, just as he had done with the First Crusaders five years earlier. But the Lombards resisted. Instead of leaving, they attacked Constantinople, dispatched one of Alexius's young relatives, and—somehow most galling of all, Albert recorded—"killed a tame lion who had been welcome in the emperor's palace."[8] The Lombard leaders managed to calm their followers and, almost as tricky, to assuage the emperor. They received help in these endeavors from the unexpected arrival of Count Raymond of Saint-Gilles, the leader of the Provençals during the First Crusade, who acted as a mediator between the two sides.

A truce ironed out, the Lombards finally crossed the Bosporus but only after receiving generous imperial gifts. In the eyes of Albert of Aachen, these were straightforward bribes, intended to hurry them along. Orderic Vitalis, who had access to some of the same information as Albert, saw a more nefarious motive. Alexius, he says, distributed a coin to each of the crusaders as a way to get an accurate head count and then passed on that intelligence to the Turkish leader Kilij-Arslan, who might then better prepare an ambush.[9]

Reinforcements followed—a German contingent, led by Conrad, constable to Emperor Henry IV, and a French contingent led by the aforementioned Stephen of Blois. But the shocking news of Bohemond's capture in northern Anatolia reached the army. Rather than continue to the Holy Land, they headed toward the Danishmend's kingdom on a rescue mission. Alexius and Raymond both counseled against the decision—or else they surreptitiously encouraged the crusaders to go to Niksar, intending to lead them into a massacre, according to conspiracy-minded French observers.[10]

Whatever the cause, Greek trickery or Frankish incompetence, the outcome was disastrous. While crossing mountains, the Franks were subject to severe hunger and frequent ambush from followers of Kilij-Arslan and the Danishmend. Anyone who strayed too far in search of food was captured and decapitated. The wealthy lived off their own supplies; the poor depended on roots and unripe grain. When the final battle came, Archbishop Anselm of Milan rallied his followers by parading the arm of St. Ambrose (or else the saint's golden cloak, according to Guibert). Raymond of Saint-Gilles similarly had the Holy Lance of Antioch put on display. But even with all this spiritual matériel, Frankish lines collapsed. Raymond of Saint-Gilles clambered up the side of a cliff in an attempt to escape. He would have died had Stephen of Blois not sent men to rescue him. Raymond fled the camps that evening, though, taking with him a contingent of Turkish mercenaries that Alexius had provided.[11] Alexius himself, according to Orderic, received a substantial gift from grateful Turks. In thanks for the advanced warning the emperor had provided, Kilij-Arslan returned all of the coins that the emperor had distributed to the Franks under the guise of generosity and which the Turkish soldiers had recovered from their bodies.[12]

For the poor pilgrims, women, and children who had accompanied the crusaders, there was no Stephen of Blois to save them. Instead, according to Albert of Aachen, the Turks "cruelly seized the noblest women and outstanding matrons, as many Gauls as Lombards, wickedly raped them, and held them in chains." The others, more than a thousand, Albert says, were "sent to barbarous peoples who spoke an unknown tongue, as if they were plundered livestock, to endure perpetual exile in the land of Khurasan, like animals locked in cages. The rest, who were a little older, they put to the sword."[13] These details are necessarily speculative, since Albert could have had no direct knowledge of the prisoners' fates. What he wished to communicate was disbelief at how callously the Franks had abandoned their women.

The scene would occur two more times during the 1101 campaign. While the Lombards were still crossing the mountains of Anatolia, Count William of Nevers (who would later attend the Council of Troyes) reached Constantinople from eastern Francia with additional reinforcements. Albert says that there were fifteen thousand—a number that probably ought to be understood as meaning "a lot." They entered Constantinople without incident and crossed the Bosporus peacefully. They had hoped to catch up with the Lombards, but instead Turks ambushed them and "filled up an entire expansive valley with their blood." Again, the Christian knights fled, the stragglers were slaughtered, and "around a thousand wives of the knights of Christ" were taken captive and led into slavery.[14]

Among the survivors, William of Nevers retreated to the imperial town of Germanicopolis. There he hired twelve Turkish soldiers to accompany him and a few of his men to a castle dedicated to St. Andrew, just inside the territory of the Frankish county of Antioch. The Turcopoles, Turkish mercenaries in Byzantine employ, proved treacherous. They robbed the count of his possessions and left him and his men alone in the desert. Exhausted, hungry, and dressed in rags, William reached Antioch looking more like a proper pilgrim than the leader of crusading soldiers.[15]

One final contingent, partly from southern France and partly from Bavaria, arrived at Constantinople and again enjoyed relatively amicable relations with Alexius. Its most famous leader was Count William IX of Aquitaine, celebrated as a troubadour—in Orderic's words, "wise and so droll, able to vanquish the cleverest jongleur with his endless witticisms."[16] Perhaps it was this urbane if not frivolous reputation that led Guibert to say of William that, "in addition to a mass of soldiers, he brought along with him crowds of girls."[17] His other followers included Hugh the Great, Welf I of Bavaria, and Countess Ida of Austria (presumably not numbered among Guibert's "girls"). Less prominent but still remarkable was Odo Arpin, a noble who financed his crusade by selling his family inheritance of Bourges to King Philip of France.[18]

Despite Constantinople's warm reception, a few of the Germans grew uneasy, disturbed by rumors of Alexius's treachery against the first waves of pilgrims. Some broke with the army and arranged to travel by sea directly to Jaffa, among them the chronicler Ekkehard of Aura.[19]

The remainder continued into Anatolia in late summer 1101. It was a difficult march, predictably. The Turks had burned supplies along the route and blocked wells. The army's poor grew so hungry that they prayed for combat so that they might die and end their misery. Ordinary pilgrims were dropping dead along the road. The knights were greatly annoyed by the stench given off by their corpses. Finally in September, near Heraclea, their fortunes took a turn for the better. They reached a river where the soldiers, women, and pilgrims could at last refresh themselves.

But Kilij-Arslan lay in wait. Caught off guard and exhausted, the Franks retreated. Hugh the Great was hit in the knee with an arrow and died a few days later. Countess Ida disappeared. Presumably many of the Aquitanian girls did too. Some of the Franks found shelter with local Christians. Others were taken off as slaves to Eastern capitals— the beginning of a new Babylonian Captivity, wrote Orderic Vitalis.[20]

Among the women who disappeared in Heraclea was Corba of Thoringé. No crusade chronicler mentions Corba, but her story appears, sketchily and episodically, in a local history of the county of Anjou. For Corba, the battle of Heraclea represented the end of a long, sad association with the crusade movement, one most chroniclers would have found impossible to reconcile with their celebratory stories. She was the orphaned heir to a ruined castle in Amboise, inherited after her uncle, Sulpice of Amboise, ordered her father, Fulk of Thorigné, beheaded. The uncle later denied responsibility for the death, saying that the execution happened because of miscommunication among his followers. Afterward, but still before the First Crusade, Corba married Aimery of Courron, of the household of Count Fulk of Anjou. She did so over the objections of Hugh, who had recently succeeded his father Sulpice to become count of Amboise. Whatever their differences, both Hugh and Aimery joined the First Crusade in 1096. Hugh survived, but Corba's husband Aimery died at the siege of Nicaea. On learning of his death back in Anjou, Count Fulk had Corba married again, this time to "a very old man" named Archard of Saintes, who kept Corba imprisoned in his house.[21]

Eventually, news of the victory at Jerusalem reached France, and the elderly Archard feared that Hugh of Amboise would confiscate his wife (or, from Corba's perspective, would rescue her), so he sent her to his brother, who oversaw the food and wine supplies at the cathedral of St. Martin of Tours. A servant of Hugh of Amboise named Auger managed to make contact with Corba and arranged for her to escape from what was obviously a miserable marriage. Accompanied by twenty other servants, Auger boldly entered the cathedral during matins, seized Corba, gave her a horse, and led her to the house of a blacksmith, where she hid until her cousin Hugh could lead her to safety.

Corba's story would seem to end happily—a life turned upside down by the First Crusade made right again when her lord returned, especially so when the aging Achard died of "sickness and grief at the loss of his wife." She was able to marry a third time, now to Geoffrey of Bourel. Geoffrey, however, decided to accompany William of Aquitaine on the crusade of 1101 and to take his new wife with him. Luckily for Geoffrey, he escaped the carnage at Heraclea. But like so many of his brothers-in-arms, he abandoned his wife. "The Turks seized whatever they found in the tents and led away Corba and many other Frankish wives with them."[22]

Among the tens of thousands of lives wrecked by crusading movement, it is hard to imagine any as thoroughly demolished as Corba's. Perhaps she had had some say in the early stages of the drama. In theory, a husband had to obtain his wife's permission before making a vow to go on crusade.[23] In practice, however, such protocols may have gotten overlooked. In any case, Corba's tale, for anyone who heard it, would have served as a counterpoint to the prophetic jubilation the crusade otherwise inspired.

For all intents and purposes, the adventure of 1101 ended with Corba's disappearance and with the destruction and dispersal of the followers of the droll William of Aquitaine. Bereft of its supporting cast, the army's glitterati continued on to Antioch and then Jerusalem, but in an impoverished state. At Jerusalem, they prayed at the Holy Sepulcher, collected palm fronds along the Jordan River, and prepared to return home. Count William and William of Nevers reached France safely. Welf of Bavaria died during a stopover at Cyprus. A few of the nobles—possibly delayed by unfavorable winds, perhaps anxious to burnish their reputations—stayed a bit longer to fight alongside King Baldwin I of Jerusalem. Among them was Stephen of Blois, who disappeared at the Battle of Ramla and was presumed dead. The German constable Conrad and Odo Arpin of Bourges were taken prisoner at the same battle. Both spent three years in prison in Cairo, until ransomed by Emperor Alexius, once again willing to support the cause.[24]

At Constantinople, Alexius welcomed both Conrad and Odo Arpin and gave them lavish presents to carry home, even though, Albert of Aachen notes resentfully, Conrad was worth more "than gold or silver, than purple dyes or precious stones."[25] En route to

France, Odo Arpin visited Paschal II at the papal court. As Orderic Vitalis imagines the scene, Paschal assured Odo that he had fulfilled the elusive bargain of penance offered to crusaders: "You have been purified through confession and penance. Through the toils of pilgrims and the struggles of martyrdom you have gained the laurels of virtue." But lest there be any confusion, Pope Paschal warned Odo to stay on his guard, and never again to bear arms against Christians. "Beware that you don't become like the dog returning to its own vomit or the washed sow wallowing in filth." Only by adhering to Christ's precepts could he hope for an "eternal reward" and "joyfully win the prize of a heavenly summons to the bosom of Abraham!"[26] In the spirit of the pope's admonishment, Odo retired from secular care and became a monk at the church of Cluny. Then again, he may have had little say in the decision, since he had no home to return to. He had sold his inheritance to King Philip to finance the mission that had redeemed his soul but ruined his life.

What else might Paschal II, or any empathetic pastor, have said to comfort Odo Arpin or Conrad or, had he had the chance, Corba of Thorigné? The standard explanation for their sufferings was that the armies of 1101 had not been virtuous enough. They had not set about their task in a serious frame of mind. They had also brought too much money and thus relied on riches rather than prayers. As evidence, after the Lombards had been defeated in northern Anatolia, they left the ground covered in pennies and gold and silver coins. As the Turks pursued them, they seemed to be wading for three miles through "gold, gems, silver vessels, wonderful and costly purple cloth, delicate garments and silks."[27] The story of the relic of St. Ambrose, in Guibert of Nogent's eyes, made a similar point. The loss of such a valuable cloak (or arm) was God's way of punishing the madness "of such a foolish bishop who brought so sacred an object into barbarian lands."[28]

Similarly, the reports of abandoned women and children are not just laments at cruel fate but evidence that the new crusaders, unlike their predecessors, were too weak, unable to leave their wives and families at home. Corba was less a casualty of the crusading movement than an explanation for its failure. "But God punished the sinful Crusaders who could not do without their wives," the great twentieth-century French historian Georges Duby observed. The "attractive, bubbling nature of William of Aquitaine" made the whole enterprise more akin to knight-errantry "than to the dogged pertinacity of the First Crusaders," notes the British historian Jonathan Riley-Smith.[29]

In short, the 1101 crusaders had failed because of sins: avarice, lust, and pride.[30] Their campaign was the inverse of what had gone before, according to Guibert: "There occurred such a slaughter of men and women from the Christian world, such a loss of money, of vestments, of gold and silver that the victory seemed to the Turks to serve as an adequate payback for the losses caused by that first expedition."[31] A few years later, William of Malmesbury (whose reading of the First Crusade, as noted, was so profoundly cynical) made the same point about 1101, with slightly more of a poetic flourish (using the type of Homeric imagery that other writers were still applying to the First Crusade): "thus Suleiman [Kilij-Arslan] from the spoils of the Franks was able to make splendid tributes for his fallen soldiers and avenge the loss of Nicaea."[32]

Such interpretations would have provided cold comfort to Corba of Thorigné, whom the First Crusade had left vulnerable to abduction, and for whom the crusade of 1101 had led to enslavement, rape, or death, and likely all three. In a different way, Odo Arpin of Bourges, who had mortgaged his future to join the cause, must have been mystified to learn that it had taken three years of imprisonment in Cairo to teach him to take his duty seriously.

One might wonder also what impression Odo's plight had made on Paschal II in 1105, when the two men met. Did it cause the pope at all to rethink the wisdom of a new crusade?

Apparently not. A few weeks later he was meeting with Bruno of Segni and Bohemond of Antioch to plan yet another expedition, the similarly disastrous crusade of 1107.

The Trouble with Baldwin

After the twin failures of 1101 and 1107, nearly fifteen years would pass before a pope would sanction a new holy war in the East. In the meantime, news from Jerusalem was relatively positive. Despite everything that went wrong in 1101, King Baldwin captured the cities of Caesarea and Arsuf by working in concert with mercenaries from Genoa. Jerusalem and the Genoese next conquered Jubayl and the crucial port city of Acre in 1104. In 1109, due in part, again, to Genoese help, a Provençal army originally put in the field by Raymond of Saint-Gilles (who had died four years earlier) finally captured Tripoli and thus founded a fourth crusader state to complement Edessa, Antioch, and Jerusalem. King Baldwin also proved adept at recruiting pilgrims to his cause. In 1110, for instance, he enlisted a band of Norwegians, led by King Sigurd, to help conquer

Sidon. Earlier that same year Baldwin captured Beirut. It is an astonishing record of success, especially for a monarch in so precarious a
position.[33]

Against these victories, however, Baldwin displayed certain character traits that were troubling to Western eyes—most notably, a tendency to go native. As a small example, Albert of Aachen had heard
that Baldwin named his horse "Gazelle," a word borrowed from "the
Saracen tongue."[34] In his monastery in France, Guibert learned other
curious details about Baldwin's style of rule at Edessa. "Wherever he
went, he had a golden shield carried before him with an eagle carved
into it, after the fashion of the Greeks. Following the custom of the
Gentiles, he walked about here and there clad in a toga, let his beard
grow long, received bows from those who reverenced him, dined on
carpets spread on the ground, and when about to enter any town or
city under his authority, two knights sounded identical trumpets at
his chariot's approach."[35] There was probably a bit of Islamic influence here, but mainly Baldwin seems to have conducted himself as a
Greek tyrant—less the serious, imperial Augustus Caesar pictured in
the *Liber floridus* and more the heroic, frivolous Alexander—perhaps
somewhere between Godfrey of Bouillon and William of Aquitaine.

Guibert was willing to accept these personality quirks, since
when he was writing, Baldwin was alive and still might reconcile
Western virtue with Eastern pomp. But time was wasting, and one of
Guibert's readers or copyists grew concerned. Apparently dissatisfied
with the end to *God's Deeds Through the Franks*, he attached a post-
script—a brief and wholly imaginary story about Egyptian-Frankish
relations in Jerusalem. It was intended as a bit of newsy entertain-
ment, but like all good fairy tales, it had a moral.[36]

In 1 1 1 2, the story goes, the emir of Ascalon asked for a two-year
truce with the kingdom of Jerusalem. Impressed by all of the building
projects going on in the Holy City, he proposed that Egyptian merchants be allowed to set up shop within the walls. The Christians did
not entirely trust the emir, so they sent a spy into the Egyptian camp, a
Saracen youth named Mathomos—Guibert's spelling of Muhammad—
whom they had raised from childhood and baptized. Mathomos ingra-
tiated himself to the merchants and discovered that they had filled
their sacks not with wares but weapons. Upon entering the city, they
intended to massacre all Christians and reclaim it.

The Franks responded aggressively. They ambushed the merchants, captured the armaments, used them to kill Saracens, and
gained masses of plunder in the process. The story concludes, "Christ
sent confusion to his enemies and victory to his followers, because he

wished to cast the former into the trap they had set themselves, and to save the latter from the dangers they had not deserved."[37] It is a simple fable about a prosperous kingdom employing cunning tricks, normally frowned upon but acceptable if done in response to an enemy's treachery; and it tells of a Jerusalem that is pure in its Frankishness—its citizens tempted by the riches of the East but ultimately able to shun them.

A fine tale, but not really one indicative of Baldwin's personality as described by the writer who knew him best, Fulcher of Chartres. Fulcher's attitude toward Baldwin grew progressively colder the older both men became, the disdain apparent through a comparison of the earliest (ca. 1106) draft of his chronicle with its later revisions (ca. 1118 and 1128). To take one example, in the first rendition, when discussing Godfrey of Bouillon's death in Jerusalem in 1100, Fulcher describes the actions of Godfrey's brother Baldwin thus: "After Baldwin heard the news, without delay he granted the land that he held to a relative named Baldwin and set out for Jerusalem, taking with him an army of around two hundred knights and seven hundred infantry."[38]

Ten years later, as Fulcher expanded his chronicle, he changed this passage substantially, making it less neutral. This sentence, originally in the middle of a chapter, now became the opening words of Book 2, thereby taking on a new narrative and structural significance. "When rumor reached Lord Baldwin that all the people of Jerusalem awaited him as heir and to assume his place as prince of the kingdom, he grieved a little for his brother, but he rejoiced more about his own inheritance."[39]

The key revision obviously concerns motive. After a decade of observation, Fulcher had learned to question Baldwin's intentions and more fundamentally his character. Among the king's flaws, and related to his having "gone native" in the eyes of some contemporaries, was an unhealthy fondness for Saracens. Albert of Aachen for one had heard rumor that Baldwin once campaigned alongside a Turkish leader named, predictably, Muhammad. This Muhammad had fallen into difficulties in Damascus and abandoned it to offer his services instead to Christian Jerusalem.[40] Albert, as is his custom, offers no judgment on this relationship. Muhammad was simply an ally who had pledged prompt and loyal service whenever needed, and based on Albert's testimony he seems to have been true to his word.

A few decades later, around 1180, the historian William of Tyre describes a similar figure, a Turkish man in whom Baldwin placed great trust. But there were differences. Instead of "Muhammad," this man's name was Baldwin. Born a Turk, "a former Gentile," as William puts it, he had converted to Christianity, with Baldwin standing as godfather—hence why he took his name. He rose in the king's service to become not just a confidant but a chamberlain—literally, privy to the king's bedroom. Is this a different Turkish follower from the "Muhammad" described decades earlier by Albert, or is he a garbled historical memory, a character around whom legends have accrued? Unlike Albert, William does emphasize the consequences of Baldwin's friendship. When the king was laying siege to the city of Sidon in 1110, helped by those Norwegian pilgrims, the chamberlain Baldwin conspired with the city's defenders to poison him. Christians in Sidon learned of the plot in time to send out a warning, and the Christian Baldwin ordered his godson, the former Saracen Baldwin, hanged.[41]

Beyond questions of misplaced trust, William of Tyre encouraged his readers to draw further conclusions about this relationship and what it revealed of King Baldwin's personality. Writing again of the chamberlain, he says, "This same person was so close and dear to the lord King that he was often the only one to accompany the King to the secluded places where one goes who wishes to satisfy the requirements of nature, to purge himself."[42] Practical concerns underlie the contorted prose here. In a society on constant war footing, a king would need to be well protected when relieving himself. For comparison, a Muslim writer in the tenth century, who visited Scandinavia, says of Vikings that they "never go off alone to relieve themselves, but always with three companions to guard them, sword in hand, for they have little trust in one another."[43] William of Tyre thus criticized Baldwin on two counts: for taking only one person to guard him when he probably needed two or three, and for trusting this one guardian in particular.

Perhaps that is all William wished to communicate—that Baldwin did not take his safety seriously. And yet William had access to any number of anecdotes to make this point. The notion that a king and a young Turkish man in charge of his bedchamber periodically withdrew together alone to secluded places, because the king needed to purge himself, does seem more than a little suggestive. A twelfth-century monastic reader would have caught the implications. According to well-established tradition, if two brothers went off to the lavatory together, especially at night, it was cause for scandal. To avoid calumny and temptation, it was best to void one's bowels in groups of three.[44]

Putting this detail from William's history together with Baldwin's failure to produce offspring, despite three marriages, modern historians—like gossipy monks—have suggested that Jerusalem's first king lived in a chainmail closet.[45] William of Tyre, of course, would not have seen the situation in those terms. His purpose was not to out a long-dead ruler. But he does seem to have committed to historical memory whispered rumors of the king's proclivities and the possibly related problem of unduly close friendships with Turks, converted or otherwise.

In the eyes of William's readers, these two points were linked. Sodomy, they believed, was a vice with an Eastern veneer, visible in the *Liber floridus* in the accoutrement and flowing locks of Antichrist. Baldwin was a successful king, and in truth much of that success depended on a willingness to adapt to local customs and to accept into his circle advisors and confidants born in the East and familiar with its languages, conventions, and commerce. He would not have survived, let alone prospered, without them. But in Western eyes, such concessions to practicality came with a price—the undermining of Frankish virtue and a possible slide into Babylonian decadence.[46]

What William thus conveys is gossip, but it is culturally revealing gossip. Rumors of Baldwin's dalliances may or may not have been true, and indeed his Turkish friend named Baldwin or Muhammad may not have even existed. But the chamberlain's presence as a historical memory is a sign of the anxiety triggered by the first Frankish king who unapologetically sought to meld the apocalyptic fantasy of crusader Jerusalem with the realities of twelfth-century life and politics in the Levant, anxieties that spread quickly from East to West.

The Field of Blood

The worst news from the period between the First and Second Crusades was the Battle of the Field of Blood in 1119. Its story traveled to Europe through a variety of channels—letters and narratives—but most spectacularly through a curious, incendiary, and arguably brilliant book called *The Antiochene Wars*, by an otherwise unknown writer called Walter the Chancellor. His title of office indicates that he was responsible for all the legal and financial business of the county of Antioch. His narrative indicates that he was an eyewitness to the Field of Blood and likely a prisoner of war afterward.

The main character in Walter's story is Roger of Salerno, prince of Antioch, the son of Richard of the Principate. Richard is the same man who, in 1104, in Niksar, had discussed Nebuchadnezzar's dream with Bohemond. His son Roger assumed the leadership of Antioch after the death of Tancred, acting as theoretical regent for Bohemond II, child of Bohemond and Constance, living then in Puglia in the south of Italy. As Roger's chancellor, Walter was something like chief minister for the Antiochene government. Walter, by virtue of his office, would have been one of Roger's closest councilors and thus directly implicated in the events in his history.

He opens his book with some apocalyptic scene-setting—or perhaps more accurately, with a vision of an Old Testament God angry and active in the world. "First, there were hordes of locusts, a metaphor for our enemies, scattered far and wide, who carried away all of the food needed to support the people of Syria."[47] The locusts were metaphorical only because it is God who spoke through them, and his figures of speech can be deadly. What had made him so angry? Not the Franks but the Syrians and Armenians, who were behaving just as prevailing stereotype would suggest. They were "haters of fasts, followers of feasts." Gluttony in turn led to a love of other pleasures, notably brothels.

The citizens of Antioch spent lavishly, of course, and when they ran out of money, they stole. They fashioned their Arabian gold with Solomonic artistry into elaborate, jeweled clothing for their wives, "carefully designed to cover their shameful parts." They did so, however, "not for the sake of hiding their shapely sources of shame or of controlling the fires of their own lust, but so that they who did not wish for what was permitted, might burn more hotly over what was prohibited."[48] Effectively, God started a war to punish Eastern Christians because women were wearing sexy and expensive lingerie. The wives, meanwhile grew bored with their husbands and sought work at brothels, or else they displayed themselves on streets and in crossroads, hoping to attract customers. Their activities were less about desire for money than about simple lust.

The Byzantine Empire and later the Turks had been unable to tame the Antiochenes. And now the crusaders had failed, too. Whether any of the Franks stepped over the line and sampled Syrian pleasures, Walter does not say. He only observes that God decided to hit the land hard, on the model of Sodom and Gomorrah. He struck Syria with an earthquake unlike any in living memory, and it affected everyone equally. "Latin, Greek, Syrian, Armenian, foreigner and pilgrim, all together professed that it had occurred because of their sins."[49] Antioch was damaged; the city of Marash was completely destroyed. The buildings in another city, Cerep, became so unstable that its people moved into tent shelters and lived with animals.

But all was not lost. Just as Nineveh repented because the preaching of Jonah, so Antioch followed the advice of its patriarch, Bernard, and performed a three-day fast in sackcloth and ashes.

Nineveh had been indefinitely saved, but the Antiochenes managed to buy themselves only a five-month reprieve before far worse locusts—armies from Baghdad—arrived.[50]

The events surrounding the Syrian Turks' attack on Antioch form the bulk of the first part of Walter's book. In brief, because of the effects of earthquake, Bursuq, the sultan of Baghdad, or "Persia," as Walter calls it, decided that the time was right to invade Syria. Roger of Antioch prepared defenses and sent a plea for help to Jerusalem. More surprising, he struck an alliance with local Turks. Two Muslim leaders, Tughtegin of Damascus and Il-Ghazi of Mardin, apparently preferred the chaos of a frontier society to direct rule from Baghdad. Walter disapproved of this coalition. He refers to it as "a false peace," one that Tughtegin embraced only because he knew that "the Parthians" were crueler in peace than were the Christians, his new pretended friends.[51]

The Antiochenes and the Syrian Turks passed the summer in this alliance and kept the armies from Baghdad at bay. Once further reinforcements arrived from Jerusalem and Tripoli, the enemy dispersed. All of Antioch's allies, according to Walter, decided to return home at that same time. Bursuq of Baghdad, however, was a "leader of deceitful cunning." His retreat was a feint. As the Syrian and Frankish armies dispersed, his soldiers regrouped and plundered the lands around Antioch. Roger had to recall his men quickly and lead them into the field, this time with no support from either Jerusalem or Damascus. The desperate situation allowed Walter to draw the moral to his story: "I recognize that it did not happen by the power of these men but was undoubtedly because of Him, who wished to separate our men from the company of Belial"—Belial being a common Christian name for the devil, or possibly Antichrist.[52]

Normally, in comparable situations, God oversaw miraculous victories for Christians in order to demonstrate how a smaller army might prevail against a larger one. Not in this case. Here God simply wanted to teach the Franks a lesson: don't mix with Muslims. New setting, new characters, but the same story as the one about Muslim merchants in Jerusalem tacked onto the end of *God's Deeds Through the Franks.*

The remainder of Book 1 is a sort of reenactment of the First Crusade. The armies of Antioch gathered together to hear a sermon from their patriarch, who several months earlier had enjoined a three-day fast in response to the earthquake. Again, Bernard spoke "clearly and distinctly words more pleasing to God than men," and the soldiers themselves "did not blush to confess their sins." In place of an indulgence, Bernard ordered them to go into battle, assuring them that whoever died would gain absolution for their sins. Survivors were to meet again on November 1 to sort out quarrels and differences.[53]

When the battle began, the Turks of Baghdad were astonished by the enemy. Sunlight reflected off the Franks' weapons in such a way that their armor shimmered white and the earth seemed covered in Frankish banners.[54] Walter, of course, would not have known what the Turks saw, but he would have read enough about similar engagements in the First Crusade to fill in the gaps.[55] The Franks were victorious. They drove the Turks from the field, massacred them ruthlessly, and refrained from plunder until the issue was settled. Roger of Antioch then led a triumphal procession to his capital. Having narrowly escaped the sin of allying with Turks, he had confirmed through battle the practices and purity of the First Crusade, and his people could sing to him in triumph, "The enemies of God fear you! Let there be endless peace for you, salvation and victory, forever and ever! Amen!"[56]

Four years later, in 1119, Roger's victory would be reversed at the hands of his two erstwhile allies—Tughtegin of Damascus and Il-Ghazi, now lord of Aleppo. In the summer of 1119, Il-Ghazi's army besieged the town of Cerep, probably barely restored from the earthquake four years earlier. Against the advice of Patriarch Bernard and many other pious men but (according to Walter) in line with his own bold, knightly spirit, Roger decided not to wait for help from Jerusalem but to attack immediately. There were signs that the battle might not go well. Namely, "a madwoman" appeared from nowhere and cried, "Do it! Do it! Don't wait! For tomorrow when the enemy prevails and when heads roll, you will give me the due that up to now you have refused!"[57] In hindsight, Walter admits, there was something to her warning.

Preparations went forward nonetheless. Following models from the First Crusade, soldiers gathered in a tent chapel to make public confession—probably a formulaic pronouncement of communal guilt—and to receive the Eucharist. Roger made private confession to the archbishop of the Syrian city of Apamea and then performed public penance by distributing gold coins to the poor. Walter does not specify what the prince's sins were but does note that Roger decided to renounce pleasures of the flesh, past, present, and future. His sexual dalliances were apparently an open secret. His own wife later complained of his many adulteries. Perhaps Roger had been too weak in face of exotically clad local women.[58] In any case, opportunities for martyrdom and heroism awaited, but, as Walter reports, Prince Roger was guarded in his pre-battle oration: "Ay!

Knights of Christ, do not be frightened at this many-sided front! Let us follow our knightly duty and prosper as we might, so that after today's result, we, who have up till now fought for the world, living or dead, may fight for God!"[59]

The battle went badly. There was endless speculation about why. Roger did not wait for help, or the Turkish mercenaries in Roger's army retreated too quickly, or perhaps authentic penance had come too late for Roger and his men.[60] Whatever the reasons, the Antiochenes retreated. A Turkish knight caught up to Roger and slashed a sword through his nose and into his brain. A priest carrying a relic of the True Cross was killed. Much plunder was captured. Hundreds of Franks were taken prisoner. Walter was probably among them, for he fills the end of his chronicle with some of the most vivid accounts of torture ever committed to writing.

First, Il-Ghazi ordered any wounded Frankish prisoners to be executed. But the Turks did not just decapitate them. Rather, they peeled skin off their skulls to prolong agonies, before finally chopping off their heads, now barely adhering to their necks—the pornographic scourging of martyrdom stories revisited, only now without the miracles that those torments used to produce.[61] For sheer pleasure, Il-Ghazi had healthy prisoners tied together by a rope and marched naked in the desert heat, the pitiable Franks willing (literally) to give an arm or a leg for a drink. They passed a vineyard and fought over a handful of grapes, some prisoners biting their tongues in excitement or trying to suck juice out of other men's beards. Many of them drank urine for the first time, Walter concludes, indicating that it happened regularly thereafter. Finally, Il-Ghazi set a little bit of muddy water out for the prisoners to fight over and encouraged his own men to stab, spear, and stone them to death as they struggled against one another to relieve their thirst. Il-Ghazi probably would have killed them all if one of his counselors had not encouraged him to set aside the wealthier captives for ransom, or else force them to undergo still more creative tortures later. Presumably, this intervention saved Walter's life.[62]

The poor were slaughtered, so thoroughly chopped up that the guards could not find "intact parts of parts of their captives." But even this level of gore could not satisfy the Turks. They wallowed in it like pigs at a trough—a level of cruelty that Thomas of Marle would have appreciated. This kind of comparison was not lost on Walter. He preferred not to reveal all of the detail of the tortures, "lest Christians do similar things to Christians and turn such actions into habit."[63]

Walter did say enough to inspire readers with genuine horror and hatred for the Turks. At drunken parties, Il-Ghazi would have Frankish prisoners brought into the midst of the revelers, hung upside down by their feet and beaten with clubs and shot with arrows. Thirty-seven prisoners were executed at once in front of the entry to his palace in Aleppo, and (in a scene deliberately reminiscent of the conquest of Jerusalem in 1099) "a wave of blood flowed out and splattered on the pavement around the portico of the royal palace." Later, drunker, Il-Ghazi ordered prisoners marched to him one at a time and then demanded that they apostatize Christianity. After all of them refused, he began cutting off their heads with his own hand, "because driven by drunkenness he wished to destroy them all." And he probably would have done so except, miraculously, at that moment, he received an unexpected gift from "the King of the Arabs of Dubai"—a wondrously beautiful horse that caused him, now beaming with joy, to throw aside his blade and forget the prisoners.[64]

Il-Ghazi's partner Tughtegin, "the servant of Antichrist," joined in the mayhem. He sent envoys to Il-Ghazi, Walter claims, asking if he might enter the Franks' prison and decapitate them all himself. Then, in lieu of a bath, he might be cleansed in their fresh blood and thus emerge from their dungeon "rejuvenated like a young eagle." Il-Ghazi declined, thinking again of the possibility of ransoms.[65]

More emblematically, Tughtegin and Il-Ghazi took turns tormenting a prisoner named Robert fitz Fulk. At one point, as they sent him back and forth between Aleppo and Damascus, Tughtegin reminded Robert that "you recently paid tribute to me from your possessions, and so for this reason I cannot find it in me to kill you." Perhaps because of this friendship as much as for any other reason, Robert found himself caught in a cruel, debauched game. Inevitably, Tughtegin broke his word and cut off Robert's head with his own sword. The skull he ordered fashioned into a jewel-encrusted goblet, which he used for drinking on solemn occasions, and he intended for his heirs to continue to drink from it long after his death. By the time Walter finished his book, Il-Ghazi had died—he literally shat out his soul while being carried on a litter, according to Walter—but Tughtegin lived on, probably quaffing wine from Robert fitz Fulk's head, the image Walter most wanted readers to carry away from his tale.[66]

Walter's Book

Walter's book soon reached Europe. It may have formed part of a recruiting campaign undertaken by Pope Calixtus II, who sought to promote a crusade in the aftermath of the Field of Blood, in 1120.[67] Or perhaps the book simply traveled home with pilgrims. Whatever the case, it did not travel alone.[68]

Rather, the earliest copy of Walter's book, and the one from which all later medieval copies were made, arrived first at the cathedral of Sainte-Marie-du-Puy-en-Velay—the church of Bishop Adhémar, spiritual leader of the First Crusade—bound together with two other texts: the earliest revised copy of Fulcher of Chartres's *History* (which is to say, the 1118 draft) and the chronicle of Raymond of Aguilers. They survive as a sort of trilogy, these three histories—bound together in six surviving manuscripts, other copies no doubt lost to time, fire, and flood. It is a fairly logical collection—two very different versions of the story of the First Crusade paired with an account of more recent events. The person who bound them together, however, placed *The Antiochene Wars*, the sequel to the first two books, in the middle of the manuscript. If one imagines a medieval reader sitting down to peruse the collection, interested in learning about the First Crusade, he or she would be forced to wade through the Field of Blood and to gaze into the maniacal, drunken eyes of Il-Ghazi.

The copy at Le Puy was an impressively large presentation manuscript. It had a few decorated initials, some gold leaf, and a pair of attractive illustrations. It probably originated in the crusader states, where all three of its authors had written their books and likely died, and perhaps from the Church of the Holy Sepulcher itself. As such, this book would have made a near priceless addition to the cathedral's library, or else it could serve as an impressive gift, should the proper occasion arise.

And the proper occasion did, in 1137, appropriately enough on Christmas Day. That year, the recently crowned king of France, Louis VII, and his new bride, Eleanor of Aquitaine, held their first Christmas court at Bourges (the city that Philip I, Louis's grandfather, had acquired in 1101 when Odo Arpin sold it to finance his expedition to the East). A brilliant assembly of counts, bishops, and other notables gathered together to pay respects to their king, to offer service to him, and no doubt to win his favor through gifts. One of them was a knight named William Grassegals, who acted as a goodwill ambassador for the church of Le Puy-en-Velay. He carried with him the cathedral's original copy of the three crusading histories (the canons there had had a new version made to keep in their library before giving away the precious original). William himself had fought in the First Crusade and had witnessed with his own eyes the conquest of Jerusalem. Like the book itself, the act of offering such a gift was charged with the energy of the Holy Land.

To preserve memory of the moment, the canons of Le Puy had inserted an introductory page, written in Latin and in a clerical hand but in the name and voice of William Grassegals. It is possible, and even likely, given the circumstances, that the manuscript contains something of William's actual thoughts concerning the crusade and what he hoped to accomplish by giving the king a written record of events in the East. In any case, the dedication ends with a striking invocation, bordering on conjuration:

> Thus with the eye of reason, you might look in this book at the images of your ancestors—Hugh the Great, Robert the count of Flanders, and others—as if you were looking into a mirror, and you might follow their footsteps on the path of virtue. If only you might learn how necessary it is not to appear to wish to fall short of them in physical exertion and in the use of the earthly sword! May you ponder how you have merited to rule upon this throne, so that you might remain ever vigilant in the service of the Lord, by whose permission you have risen to such high honor. In all other respects I beseech you by humble prayer that the book be not removed from your presence or from your heirs', so that you might always have these signposts to lead you to an ideal of similar goodness.[69]

It is an exhortation to remember the First Crusade, to recall that the king's own relatives had participated in it, and to follow their examples. At a time when the interpretation of the crusade remained in flux, when the actions of its veterans and of their successors in Jerusalem threatened to undermine its celebration, William gave Louis this book as a call to do like the Templars—to act, or reenact, the First Crusade. Read this book, study its meaning, and follow in the paths that its stories and characters have cleared for you.

Did Louis, who probably could in fact read, actually follow William's advice? Did he take time to study this book and learn its lessons, ill-defined and elusive though they might be? It is impossible to know. But there is at least some reason to think that he did. Eight years later, in 1145, again at a Christmas court in Bourges, Louis made an unexpected announcement. The time for a new crusade had come. He was going to Jerusalem, the latest dreamer to follow the path laid out by Nebuchadnezzar.

PART III

Prophecy Revised (1144–1187)

CHAPTER 8

The Second Crusade's
Miraculous Failure

Your "L" Will Then Become a "C"

What led Louis VII to take the cross? The most immediate cause was the fall of Edessa. The first of the crusader states, established in early 1098, was also the first lost to the Turks. In December 1144, Zengi, the ruler of Mosul and Aleppo, besieged the city and conquered it on Christmas Eve. Hugh, bishop of Jabala, or Jableh, in Syria, was sent to Rome to plead for aid, and by December 1, 1145, nearly a year after the Fall of Edessa, Pope Eugenius III proclaimed a new expedition to the East in the papal bull *Quantum praedecessores*, roughly translated as "How Much Our Predecessors" (papal bulls are titled by their opening words). Before news of the pope's decision even reached France, however, Louis VII had made up his mind.[1]

A number of personal concerns drove the king's decision. According to the German historian Bishop Otto of Freising (also a participant in the Second Crusade and, as we shall see, something of a crusade theorist), Louis's older brother Philip, had promised to go to Jerusalem, but died before he could fulfill the vow. His soul had thus incurred a spiritual debt, possibly keeping him from heaven. As his oldest surviving relative and heir to his legacy, Louis was probably the only one who could pay it off.[2] The king was also concerned about his own salvation. In January 1143, during a siege of Vitry-le-François, a city in the Champagne region of France, the king's troops set fire to a church and killed everyone, as many as fifteen hundred people, who had sought shelter inside. A spectacular penitential gesture was needed to make good on their deaths. The possible liberation of Edessa, family duty, personal guilt, and perhaps the book of histories that he had received eight Christmases earlier from William Grassegals inspired the twenty-five-year-old king to "reveal his heart's secret for the first time to the realm's bishops and nobles whom he had called together to his crown-wearing from farther afield than usual."[3]

Otto of Freising suggests still another motive. On the eve of the Second Crusade, a prophecy was circulating around France. Some thought it came from ancient Roman prophecies; some thought that an Armenian had spread it. In elliptical language typical of the genre, it spoke of "the spirit of the pilgrim God" coming to "L, the shepherd of bodies" and sending him to the place "which the angel or son of your mother promised to visit and did not visit." Louis, as king, was obviously a shepherd of bodies, and the reference to Philip's failed journey also spoke directly to his situation. The pilgrim God further urged L to plant a red standard (the color of the Oriflamme, the banner of the church of Saint-Denis, first carried into battle by Louis VII's father) at the limits of the labors of Hercules. At that point, the gates of "B" would open to him. "Your L will then become a C and you will spread afar the river's waters until those who had busied themselves in the care of their sons might cross over it."[4]

The city here is Babylon (in this case the "Baghdad" version of Babylon rather than the "Cairo" version).[5] The "C" most immediately refers to Cyrus, the Persian king who centuries earlier had conquered Babylon and allowed the enslaved Jews ("those who had busied themselves in the care of their sons") to return to Jerusalem.[6] Louis, the new Cyrus, not only would march to Jerusalem but also lead an army of Franks (who were, in their own eyes, the new Israel) to Babylon and overturn Muslim rule once and for all.

Otto probably had in mind two other meanings for "C." First, it could refer to Charlemagne, whom some amateur prophets believed had come back to life on the eve of the First Crusade, nearly three centuries after his death in 816, and whose name, because the pope had crowned him with the imperial diadem in 800, was synonymous with the word "empire." Louis VII, who bore the name of Charlemagne's hapless son Louis the Pious, might improve his own fortunes through the crusade—cease to be an L(ouis) by becoming a C(harles). Second, Louis might elevate his status mathematically. In a joke more apparent to readers trained in Roman numerals, the king would double his worth, from 50 (L) to 100 (C)—that is, transform from a king to an emperor. In this connection, there was yet another prophecy that circulated in the twelfth century, which said that the Last World

Emperor's name would begin with a C—in origin a reference to Constantine, the first Christian Emperor, and also to Charlemagne.[7] Backed by such apocalyptic expectations, Louis could finish what Godfrey had begun fifty years earlier—smash the forces of Antichrist, lead Christian armies through the gates of Babylon, and sit on the throne in Jerusalem as an agent of the pilgrim God.

At the time when Otto was actually recording these prophetic traditions, the Second Crusade had ended, and he knew very well that Louis failed. The story for him was a learned joke, a take-down of the reigning French monarch, intended to glorify his own lord, the emperor Frederick Barbarossa, elected king of the Germans in 1152. But ironic though Otto's presentation might have been, he nonetheless cast light on some of the dreams that surrounded the Second Crusade. Otto, himself a crusader, is cagey about how seriously he took the expedition's prophetic character. His intellectual trajectory may very well have been like that of Abbot Bernard of Clairvaux, spiritual godfather of the Knights Templar, who seems in 1146 to have surrendered to the crusade's vatic allure. Bernard would aggressively promote the expedition, and though, unlike Otto, he did not participate in it, its outcome would all but destroy him.[8]

Crusade as Reenactment

According to Otto, Bernard initially felt reluctant to involve himself in the new campaign. King Louis consulted the abbot as if he were a "divine oracle," in Otto's words, but Bernard still demurred. Such a great business pertained only to the pope. So Louis sent a delegation to Eugenius III, and Eugenius, "turning over in his mind the examples of his predecessors," decided to charge Bernard with recruiting an army to reenact the First Crusade.[9]

"Reenact" is not too strong a word. The idea infuses the pope's official proclamation, *Quantum praedecessores*, which begins, "We have heard from our elders and have learned based on what has been said about their achievements how much our predecessors as Roman popes strove for the freedom of the Eastern Church." Urban II had been "the heavenly trumpet" who fired with love armies of all peoples, but especially the Franks, to "liberate Jerusalem from pagan filth."[10]

The problem with this reenactment was the goal: Edessa. It was simply not as compelling as Jerusalem had been. Eugenius nonetheless framed the situation in terms similar to the ones used in earlier chronicles in their descriptions of Urban. Edessa, long the sole beacon of (Armenian) Christianity in the East, had fallen. The enemies of Christ's cross had taken it and had occupied many nearby castles. "The archbishop of that city along with his clerics and many other Christians were killed there, and saints' relics surrendered for pagan feet to trample and scatter. We think and believe that you, in your prudence, will recognize how great a new danger threatens God's church and all Christendom." The solution: Frankish warriors, led by Louis VII, needed to follow the example of their forebears, who had freed the Eastern Church fifty years earlier. The reward promised was the same: "By the authority God has granted us, we concede and confirm the remission of sins instituted by our aforesaid predecessor, Pope Urban."[11]

Fortified by papal mandate, Bernard of Clairvaux proclaimed the new crusade on Easter Sunday 1146 in the city of Vézelay in Burgundy, in the presence of Louis VII and near the bones of Christ's friend Mary Magdalene. As at Clermont, such a tremendous crowd had traveled to hear the speech that Bernard had to deliver it on a wooden platform specially set up in a field outside the church.

According to the monk Odo of Deuil, the only contemporary writer and actual participant who composed a chronicle of the Second Crusade, Louis VII stood alongside Bernard on the platform at Vézelay and wore a cross sent from the pope. The abbot's voice, when he preached, sounded as if from the heavenly choir. No one recorded his words, but in response soldiers everywhere demanded crosses like the one the king wore. Bernard was ready for them; he had arranged for satchels of ready-to-sew cloth crosses to be distributed. Supplies ran short, though, so like Bohemond of Antioch on the eve of the First Crusade in 1096, he ordered his own cloak cut into crosses and passed out to lucky pilgrims.[12] So close was Bernard's gesture that he surely copied it directly from Bohemond after reading about it in a crusade chronicle—or else maybe great showmen just think alike.

Bernard was not ashamed to boast of his successes at Vézelay. As he wrote to Pope Eugenius, "I declaimed and I spoke, and they multiplied beyond number! Cities and castles are empty. You can hardly find one man whom seven women are not laying hold of, so many wives are everywhere made widows while their husbands still live."[13]

So many hearts conquered in France, Bernard was now free to work on Germany. At the top of his recruitment wish list was King Conrad III. It would be a real coup—"the miracle of miracles," as one of Bernard's biographers deemed it.[14] With a second king, who could command an even larger army than Louis's, the success of the crusade seemed assured. Conrad's command over his own barons, however, was tenuous; his lands in northern Italy were in turmoil; and the possibility of wars against Hungary and Sicily loomed. It would require a spectacular performance on Bernard's part, or many such performances, to create a secure enough peace at home to allow for a crusade abroad.[15]

But there was another problem in Germany. Just as Bernard had reprised Urban II's role in France, a Cistercian monk named Ralph was reviving the message of Peter the Hermit and Emicho of Flonhcim, whose words had led to the pogroms of 1096, in Germany. Why travel so far to fight Christ's enemies, Ralph asked, when there were so many local Jews ready to be killed? A contemporary Jewish writer named Ephraim of Bonn describes that message thus: "Avenge the crucified one upon his enemies who stand before you; then go to war against the Ishmaelites." The similarity to what had happened a half century earlier, when Peter's fans and Emicho's followers murdered Jews up and down the Rhine, was not lost on Ephraim. "Alas, Lord God, not even fifty years, the number of years of a jubilee, have passed since our blood was shed in witness to the Oneness of Your Reverend Name on the day of the great slaughter. Will you forsake us eternally, O Lord?"[16]

The violence was less sustained than in 1096, when Jewish communities in Speyer, Mainz, and Worms were killed, committed suicide, or accepted forced conversion—but the 1146 attacks were, occasionally, spectacular. To take a few examples: A group of Christians ordered a Jew named Simon of Trier to accept baptism. When he refused, they crushed his head in a winepress—a crime redolent of prophecy.[17] A Jewish woman named Mina of Speyer died after Christians attacked her and cut off her ears and thumbs. A little later, a Jewish woman named Gutalda escaped baptism by drowning herself in a river.[18] Some Jews, including Ephraim of Bonn, then thirteen years old, escaped persecution by hiding in bishops' castles, protection offered partly from sympathy, partly for money. A few months later in Würzburg, Jews were accused of murdering a Christian man and throwing the body in a river. The locals proclaimed him a martyr and in retaliation dragged a Jewish woman into a church to baptize her. She refused and instead spat on a crucifix. After being tortured, she faked her own death and later escaped with the help of a sympathetic Christian laundress. Other Jews were killed and dismembered, their body parts collected in a wagon the next day at the order of the local bishop.[19]

Bernard recognized the similarities between 1096 and 1146, too, and concluded one of his letters about the crusade with a general warning to stop the pogroms. He cautioned German Christians in a letter against following the example of "a man called Peter," Peter the Hermit, who had led so many men and women to their deaths. The implication was obvious. If the Germans treated Ralph similarly to how the predecessors had treated Peter, they would meet a similar end.[20] He followed up this warning with a letter to Archbishop Henry of Mainz—in whose city Ralph was rumored to be living in comfort. Here Bernard accused Ralph of "noising it about that he is a monk or a hermit." A monk, however, does not have a license to preach. For a monk, life in town is a prison, whereas solitude is heaven. "This man, by contrast, sees solitude as a prison and town as paradise."[21] In 1095, the sermons of Peter the Hermit had caused the crusade nearly to go off the rails. Bernard wanted to make sure that in this respect at least, there was no reenactment.

On a grander level, Ralph's message was misguided, even dangerous, because it ran counter to Bernard's sense of salvation history. As such, it provides rare insight into the abbot's own apocalyptic reading of the Second Crusade. Christians were responsible for protecting the Jews. However wicked they might be, Jews were not to be killed. Christians were to pray for their redemption, to ask the Lord "to lift the veil from their hearts so that they might be plucked out of the shadows and led into the light of truth."[22] Until then, the Jews were to live in miserable captivity, their existence a witness to the truth of Christianity. If the Christians could only subdue "Gentiles," by whom Bernard meant Muslims, in a similar fashion, then their lives too might be spared in anticipation of future judgment. "Until that time, because (Muslims) bear violence to us, it is proper that the ones who justly carry swords fight force with force."[23]

Would the Muslims ever convert? In truth, Bernard does not seem to care. As for the Jews, "They shall be converted in the evening, and at that time they will be accepted."[24] Working with the language of the Apostle Paul, Bernard reminds the Archbishop of Mainz that, "When the fullness of peoples shall enter, then all of Israel will be saved." Bernard had quoted this same passage in another letter written to all the archbishops of Eastern Francia and Bavaria.[25] Everyone in Germany needed to know that not just the lives of the Jews but the fundamental outcome of salvation history was at stake.

What remains unclear about Bernard's message is whether he believed the "evening" of the Jews' conversion was near—that is to say, how closely intertwined were the Second Crusade and the Last Days? Had the moment anticipated by Lambert of Saint-Omer, Guibert of Nogent, and the followers of Bohemond in 1106—the destruction of Nebuchadnezzar's statue—finally begun to manifest itself in human events? Was the mountain of the kingdom of God to grow from the stone cast by the First Crusade and fill the world?

Bernard of Clairvaux and Prophecy

Bernard does not directly answer this question and indeed never discusses the Apocalypse at length in any of his writings. The general contours of salvation history are important to him; the specifics of the end of time, less so. It is possible that he mentioned the Last Days in 1146, as he preached the crusade, but almost nothing of those sermons survives. The traces of prophetic thought that appear in his other writings, however, do at least give a hint of how the Last Days might have fit into his crusade message.[26]

Bernard's earliest direct mention of apocalyptic expectation appears in a letter he wrote in 1124 to Bishop Geoffrey of Chartres. Geoffrey had earlier asked Bernard whether one of their mutual acquaintances, a religious reformer and contemplative named Norbert of Xanten, intended to visit Jerusalem. Bernard answered that he had recently spoken to Norbert but heard nothing about a pilgrimage. He then adds that he did ask Norbert about Antichrist—by itself, a noteworthy associative leap: Geoffrey had asked Bernard about Jerusalem, and Bernard responded with a remark about Antichrist. As for Norbert's reply, that saintly man "was sure that [Antichrist] would appear during the time of this present generation."[27]

Only fifteen years later, in 1139, did Bernard present his own ideas on an apocalyptic timetable. It was part of a lengthy a verse-by-verse commentary on that awkwardly erotic Old Testament book, the Song of Songs. Bernard worked hard to make its sexual imagery applicable—and presumably less arousing—to an audience of monks. He did not rush the process. By Sermon 33 he had only reached chapter 1, verse 6, and was focusing only on the first half of that verse: "Tell me, you whom my soul loves, where you pasture your flock, where you make it lie down in the noonday sun."[28]

The reference to "the noonday sun" causes Bernard to consider eschatological themes. The noon hour represents "the whole day, and it knows no evening."[29] For Bernard it is equivalent to the Seventh Age of history, the time when toil will end, and Christ will live with his elect in heaven. As is often the case with Bernard's exegeses, he then began to fill in what he perceived as scriptural gaps. Earlier in the same commentary, for example, when considering Song of Songs 1:2— "Let him kiss me with the kiss of his mouth"—Bernard felt that something was missing. The kiss of the mouth must be preceded by at least two others, the kiss of the foot and the hand. He then went on to consider what each of those kisses, biblical and extrabiblical, symbolized. Likewise with Song of Songs 1:6. Not content with one hour, Bernard added three more: the first light of dawn, sunrise, and the spreading of light in anticipation of noonday splendor. Each moment represented both a temptation and a particular era in human history.[30]

Drawing from Psalm 90/91:5–6, Bernard connects the first moments of dawn to the beginning of a monk's conversion. The early rays of redemption have begun to shine, but a novice will experience the lingering terrors of the night. The rigors of his new calling seem insuperable. Historically, this period is Christ's mission, when he walked the world in flesh but went largely unrecognized by his own people. Had the light of day shone more brightly, the Jews might not have killed him.[31] This age also includes the early days of the church, characterized by Apostles and Martyrs, when Christians suffered persecution at the hands of some so blind that they actually believed they were doing good works.[32]

The increasing radiance of the second hour happily dispels this confusion. The world appears in "a light more serene than usual." But it is also the time when, according to the psalmist, "the arrow flies in the day." Having conquered his first temptation, a monk risks vainglory. Rumor of his virtue flies like an arrow on the wind and must be dodged. Historically, this era of brighter but still hazy illumination was also a time of heresy, a time when "vain men arose, greedy for fame, and wishing to make a name for themselves. They came out of their mother the Church but tormented her for a long time with various perverse teachings."[33]

Bernard's own era was the third hour of morning, a period free of the evils of persecution and the overt profession of heresy. And yet it was arguably the most dangerous time ever. Using the language of the psalmist, Bernard lived an age "soiled *by business that moves in the shadows.*" Hypocrisy, "the yeast of the Pharisees," had corrupted everything. Dangers now lurked within the church itself. "All are friends and all are enemies; all are allies and all are adversaries; all share one household but no one is at peace; all are neighbors, but each seeks his own good. They are servants of Christ, and they serve Antichrist."[34] In Bernard's description, the ecclesiastical embodiments of Antichrist—bishops, abbots, and other high-ranking churchmen—sound very much like the secular knights against whom he railed in his praise of the Templars. "Their bridles, saddles, and spurs embossed with gold—their heels shine more than do their altars." Given over to drunken feasts, they live lives of Bacchanalian delight, because Christianity has created for them a world of security and peace. In the church, "it is peace, but it is not peace. Peace from pagans, peace from heretics, but she has no peace from her own sons."[35]

These dangers lead into the fourth hour of the day, the noonday sun of the Song of Songs, whose light is fulsome and shall never fail. But to reach that point, a historical moment that is in fact beyond history, Christians must pass a final test. According to the psalmist it is "the noonday demon," a figure Bernard identifies more precisely as "Antichrist, who deceitfully calls himself not only the day but the noonday, worshipped above what is called or cultivated as God."[36] Christ will destroy him with the breath of his mouth and extinguish his false light with true brilliance, inaugurating the final age when all shall know God directly: "Your face is the midday sun."[37]

More to the point, Bernard believed himself, in his own spiritual journey, to have begun living through "the fourth watch of the night." The reference is to Mark 6:48–50, when the Apostles saw Jesus walking on water at the time of the fourth watch and mistook him for "a phantasm." This image applied to processes both moral and prophetic. As monastic conversion and historical time reached their respective endpoints, one might see Antichrist but believe him to be Christ. "In the fourth stage, which is the last stage, then, let us fear this temptation. Whoever thinks himself to have attained great heights must guard more vigilantly still against the attacks of the noonday demon."[38]

The sermon's final jeremiad draws these themes together. "All that is left now is for the midday demon to appear in our midst and seduce whoever still dwells in Christ's simplicity. He has drunk the rivers of the wise and the torrents of the powerful, and he thinks that the Jordan River—the humble and simple folk of the Church—will flow into his mouth."[39] Bernard would sound this same note on at least two other occasions—once, in a commentary on Psalm 90, and again in a short lesson where he compared the four stages of history to the four horsemen of the Apocalypse (see table 4). He observes in that latter passage, "The attack of the noonday demon, the time of Antichrist, is now near."[40] One of his disciples in turn grafted this model onto the vision of the four beasts in Daniel 7, thus drawing Bernard's ideas closer to Nebuchadnezzar's dream.[41]

Christian history thus fell into four parts for Bernard, as it would do for later thinkers as well. As a young man, Bernard believed the church to be in the third age of history, when evil lurked in the shadows. Near the end of his life, Bernard would personally enter into

Table 4: Bernard's Model of the Hours, Temptations, and the Apocalypse

Hours of Day	Temptations	Historical Eras	4 Horsemen of the Apocalypse	Beasts from Daniel 7
1. First Light	Initial Terrors	Early Church	White Horse	Winged Lion
2. Sunrise	Vainglory	Heresy	Red Horse	Bear with Tusks
3. Spreading Light	Hypocrisy	Business in Shadows	Black Horse	Winged Leopard
4. Noonday	Apostasy or Brilliant Light	Antichrist	Pale Horse	Beast Unlike Any Other

the fourth stage of monastic conversion, when he would have to face his personal noonday demon. Was the Christian world more broadly making a similar transition in 1146? Based on what little evidence survives—a handful of letters—Bernard seems to have thought so. At the very least, he was bandying about prophetic ideas in his crusade sermons.

The case for an apocalyptic Second Crusade was not at all an obvious one. Bernard does not emphasize, for example, the actual catalyst for the expedition—the loss of Edessa. It is the Holy Land more broadly that is in danger—"God's land," where God lived in the flesh for more than thirty years, filling it with miracles and consecrating it with blood. "But now, because of our sins, enemies of the cross have raised their sacrilegious heads and are laying low at sword point this blessed land, this promised land."[42]

Jerusalem obviously still occupied the preeminent place in the spiritual imagination, particularly for Bernard. As he aged, he saw his community at Clairvaux not just as a symbol for heavenly Jerusalem, but as the very gateway to it.[43] And events in the East represented an imminent, intimate threat. As Bernard imagines the psychology of Muslims, the physical, demonic adversary to both the heavenly and earthly Jerusalem, they were leering rapists about to invade a Christian bed. "Oh, alas! They are drooling from their sacrilegious mouths over the shrines of the Christian religion, they are trying to intrude and tread on the bed where our Life slept in death for us."[44]

The destruction of the Holy Sepulcher remained the enemy's goal, or at least so Bernard imagined it. Ever since 1099, the devil had been grinding his teeth in malice, looking for ways to reverse the Franks' salvific gains. Admittedly, God, if he wanted, could accomplish the work alone. He did not need soldiers. He could dispatch twelve legions of angels to reclaim his inheritance. But instead he had taken pity on an otherwise lost generation. "You now have the chance, powerful knight, brutal man, to fight without danger, in a place where conquest is glorious and death is gain. If you are a sensible merchant, a shrewd man of affairs, let me point out to you the profits to be made. Pay attention, lest it pass you by!" If soldiers seized this occasion and took up the sign of the cross, they would receive an indulgence for all the faults they confessed "with a contrite heart."[45] In another letter, Bernard claims that this blessing is unprecedented, unlike anything that has ever occurred—though in fact he is essentially repeating the warnings and promises attributed to Urban II half a century earlier, his language slightly updated for a commercially savvy audience.[46]

Bernard adopts a more apocalyptic tone in another crusade letter, in which he stops talking about Islam. As momentum for the Second Crusade grew, some churchmen—Bernard and Eugenius among them—started to define it as a three-front war against all of Christendom's enemies: Muslims in the Holy Land, Muslims in Spain, and pagans in northern Europe, whose presence "Christian strength has tolerated far too long."[47] Bernard promised any German soldier who fought against this last foe the same indulgence available in the Holy Land. The goal was "to wipe out those nations completely, or at least convert them."[48] No truces were to be allowed. The devil would gnash his teeth and live his worst nightmare "about the conversion of the Gentiles, since he has heard that the plentitude of them will enter and all Israel will be saved."[49]

The hope for the destruction of conversion of all Christ's enemies echoed language about the Last World Emperor, taken from a prophecy attributed to the Tiburtine Sibyl. This text pretended to be from pre-Christian Rome, an oracular pronouncement given by a pagan priestess, though it was obviously written much later and by a Christian. Like other prophetic texts, it spoke of an eventual Last World Emperor, to whom the Sibyl gave the name Constans. As such, it was part of the same literary tradition that had inspired Lambert, Guibert, Ekkehard, and other early interpreters of the First Crusade.[50] It also is a message that had sunk in with actual soldiers. According to Odo of Deuil, the army wished to visit Christ's tomb and "at the command of the highest pontiff, to wipe out their sins either with the blood of the pagans or else through their conversion."[51]

It is difficult to remember, given the Second Crusade's outcome, that this goal—the eradication of non-Christians—seemed plausible. And Bernard would have been very aware of the apocalyptic aspects of his message. His plan was to reenact the First Crusade, but also to improve upon it, to complete its mission through an all-out war, fought with weapons and baptismal fonts, against Saracens and pagans.

The message, however, would have been difficult to sell, in no small part because (as Bernard's silence on this point indicates) the loss of Edessa would not have seemed especially earthshaking. However much verbal distraction created by talk of the Jerusalem, demons, and Christ's enemies, the cause that Bernard and Eugenius were promoting was this liberation of an unfamiliar city, a place likely more significant to Muslims than Christians. To recruit followers, words were not enough. Bernard needed signs from heaven. He needed miracles. And he made them happen in abundance.

Bernard's Miracles, or God Goes All In

It was not the first time that Bernard had used marvels to bolster rhetoric. In the late 1130s, when preaching on behalf of Pope Innocent II (whose election many prominent Roman families opposed), several in attendance experienced miraculous cures, which seemed to provide evidence in favor of Bernard's cause. Arnold of Bonneval, one of Bernard's biographers, stresses the saint's facility at casting out demons during that tour.[52] In 1145, when campaigning against the heretic Henry of Le Mans, a shoddily dressed, charismatic, heretical preacher, Bernard once more supplemented words with miracles. In a particularly memorable instance at Toulouse, where Henry would spend the final years of his life in prison, Bernard healed a paralytic who had seemed all but dead. Later, a local witness saw the man walking and fled in terror, thinking that he surely must be a ghost.[53]

A year later, Bernard brought his razzle-dazzle to Vézelay. Odo of Deuil does not describe the cures performed there, observing only, "If I write about only a few of them, the many more that occurred would not seem credible. If I described many of them, I would seem to have lost sight of my theme."[54] The twelfth century was, arguably, the golden age of miracles, when pilgrims by the dozen and sometimes the hundreds would journey to saints' tombs in hope of divine favor. In such a context, what would constitute such an incredible number of miracles?

Other monks, who followed Bernard into Germany in 1146, help answer that question. In a text usually called "Book Six" of *The First Life of Bernard of Clairvaux*, he performed at least four hundred miracles in five short months while in Germany, although the actual number would have been even higher.[55] On certain days, the writers say, they could not keep track of everyone who received cures, over whom he made the sign of the cross, or else anointed with his own saliva. One extraordinary day, he healed at least thirty-six people.[56]

Sometimes the crowds were large and unruly enough to be dangerous, making accurate recordkeeping impossible.[57]

Miracle stories usually follow well-worn patterns, mostly drawn from the New Testament. The writer, or collector, introduces details about a sick person, including name, social status, village or city of origin, and a detailed description of the ailment. The sick person has often consulted doctors and wasted money on ineffectual treatments. Then, led by a vision or the counsel of friends, he or she would journey to a saint's shrine, there to pray for a night or a week or a month. With luck or patience or piety, a miracle might happen. The restored pilgrim proclaimed his cure to an enthusiastic crowd and then returned home. At a slightly later date, shrine keepers would send someone to seek out the pilgrim and to confirm both the details of the illness and effectiveness of the cure.[58]

The collection of Bernard's miracles follows none of these points, mainly because of the mode of presentation. There is no single narrator. Rather, two-thirds of the collection is in dialogue form with multiple participants. The different voices do not tell stories so much as jog one another's memory:

> THE BISHOP [Herman of Constance]: On Friday, in Basel, after the sermon was given and crosses distributed, a mute woman was presented to the man of the Lord. Immediately after he touched her tongue, the chain on her mouth came loose, and she started speaking correctly. I saw it, and I talked to her. But didn't he also welcome a formerly lame man who had already regained the ability to walk, whom the people acclaimed—who among you saw him?
>
> OTTO [a cleric]: We all saw him.
>
> EBERHARD [Herman's chaplain]: On that day, that is Friday, the knights of my lord and I together saw a blind boy whom his mother had led to the hospice where the saintly man was staying, and she took him away able to see.
>
> GERHARD [a monk]: So many things happened on that day that we couldn't find out about because of the great tumult. I heard him say that on that day he touched some blind people whose sight he believed had been restored, or at least it was restored a little later.[59]

The purpose of the collection is not to elicit sympathy for the sick or to inspire wonder at Bernard's ability to impart grace. It is, rather, to overwhelm with numbers.

The same can be said of how the miracles were choreographed. They were grand spectacles intended to overawe viewers and convince them of the righteousness of Bernard's cause. They created such a frenzy that men and women would clamor to receive a cross from Bernard or one of his companions.

This unerring sense of stagecraft reached an apex when Bernard met King Conrad in November 1146. Even as the king was approaching, "a lame boy regained his ability to walk right in front of him and we saw it, and so did his knights."[60] Later, at the Christmas court in Speyer, when Conrad, Frederick Barbarossa, and "countless princes" took the cross, another paralytic boy regained his mobility.[61] After yet another paralytic was healed before the king and his entourage, Bernard explained to him, "This was done for your sake, that you might know that God truly is with you and that he approves what you have begun."[62]

It has become somewhat de rigueur for historians to treat miracle stories empathetically, to acknowledge them as essential elements of medieval spirituality, and to write about them as if they were authentic, genuine experiences, joyfully received by the men and women who witnessed them. This approach, however, obscures another important aspect of medieval religious life—namely, that monks were very good fakers. It is not something they liked to acknowledge, for obvious reasons. One observer, Guibert of Nogent, complained at length that phony saints and false relics were being venerated all over Europe. He described specifically how canons from the cathedral church in the French city of Laon had staged miracles while parading relics near and far. "Feigned cases of deafness, pretended bouts of madness, fingers cunningly bent back to the palm, or feet contorted underneath buttocks can capture the avaricious hearts of the common mob," he observed of that tour, adding that he himself has heard otherwise honorable men discussing in hushed tones precisely how to fool an audience.[63]

Ordinary Christians in the Middle Ages were not entirely credulous. They would have known that some, if not most, public miracles were staged. But there must have existed an unspoken pact (comparable to that between modern magician and audience) that the miracles would be performed with a nod of complicity. The monks would put on a good show, and the pious would suspend disbelief. The sloppiness of Bernard's miracles violated this pact. One of his companions, Geoffrey of Auxerre, recognized a specific problem connected to the healing of deaf-mutes.

PHILIP [a cleric]: And I saw a boy, deaf and mute from birth, whom you heard right away speaking correctly and hearing clearly.

BISHOP [Herman]: After the boy was signed with the cross, I spoke with him, and he immediately answered freely, and all of you heard the people shouting.

GEOFFREY: Where did he learn words, if he had never heard them spoken before?

BISHOP: From the one who makes the tongues of babes wise.[64]

As presented in this retelling, Bishop Herman's answered satisfied Geoffrey. But when Geoffrey himself assumed sole responsibility for writing the collection's final chapters, he treated stories about deaf-mutes more scrupulously. One such boy, after a miracle, is asked, "Can you hear me?" And the boy responds, "Can you hear me?" Geoffrey explains, "Because he was deaf from the womb, he could only repeat whatever he had just heard from the mouth of his interrogator."[65] It was an important enough detail to Geoffrey—or perhaps the earlier goof was serious enough—that he included two other examples of this type of healing and interrogation.[66]

At least one of the miracle recipients, an archer in the service of Conrad, initially accused Bernard of shenanigans. He "belittled the name of the cross and blasphemed against the saintly lord, saying, 'That man can no more make wonders than I!'" The archer then tried to interfere with Bernard as he continued to lay hands on the sick, but right away fell to the ground, apparently dead. Bernard dropped beside the body to pray, and after a long time, the wicked man was helped to his feet, alive. Like Christ, Bernard apparently had raised the dead. So moving was the experience that the archer took the cross and joined the crusade—the happy denouement undermined somewhat by the fact that it was Bernard himself who had struck the man dead in the first place.[67]

Doubts aside, Bernard accomplished his goal. Conrad took the cross, and with the help of Bernard's visual performances—more than his preaching, since the French-speaking Bernard did not know German—a huge army joined the campaign.

But a successful preaching campaign was not enough. Bernard had staked his considerable reputation not just on raising an army but also on the eventual success of the mission. More problematically, he had staked God's reputation on it. A favorable conclusion had been foretold by an unprecedented display of miracles, on average at least one hundred a month. It was a calculated risk to fire up monastic thaumaturgic machinery so. But Bernard and Pope Eugenius had faith in both their cause and their armies, as well as confidence that they and Christendom alike never need know the experience of defeat.

The Experience of Defeat

The monk Odo of Deuil drew assurance from Bernard's miracles. Because of them, he wrote, the expedition "seemed to have pleased the Lord."[68] But God was not pleased. Indeed, so discouraging did the expedition prove, that Odo stopped writing about it just as Louis VII arrived by ship at Antioch in March 1148. Turkish armies had massacred most of the French and German armies as they crossed Asia Minor. The decision to follow the sea route from Adalia (modern Anatalya, Turkey) rather than the five-hundred-mile land route had been a painful choice for Louis, who was always thinking in terms of reenactment: "Let us follow the path of our fathers," he had urged his advisers, as he argued on behalf on the land route. "Their matchless integrity resulted in worldly fame and heavenly glory."[69] His followers responded that while they did not wish to "deprecate the praise due to our fathers," their predecessors had had an easier time because they had only had to fight Turks, rather than "deceitful Greeks," who, based on all available evidence, were not really Christians.[70] Exhausted, and with almost no horses left for battle, the knights convinced Louis to make haste by sea to Antioch.

Their host there, Duke Roger of Antioch, was Louis's relative by marriage—uncle of Queen Eleanor of Aquitaine. During the two months that the French spent at his capital, recovering from their long journey, Roger tried to convince Louis to delay his march to Jerusalem and instead to concentrate on shoring up Antioch's borders. But Louis was too eager to see the Holy Land. He departed in May, impelled by religious fervor and by the rumor that his wife Eleanor was having an affair with her uncle. The gossip traveled all the way back to France and inspired Louis's chief advisor, Suger of Saint-Denis, to send a letter congratulating the king on how well he had controlled his anger against his wife, adding, "God willing when you return to your kingdom you can attend to these and other matters."[71]

When Louis reached Jerusalem in June 1148, he found that Conrad had gotten there first with a remnant of the German army. The two princes, together with the nobility of Jerusalem, then faced what would have seemed two years earlier an unthinkable problem. What were they doing there in the first place? Edessa, the original cause of the Crusade, was more or less forgotten, and in any case the Turks had left so little of it intact that there was nothing there to liberate. After some discussion, they agreed to attack Damascus, a plan whose wisdom continues to inspire argument among historians.[72] The siege of Damascus began on July 24, 1148. Four days later, the Frankish

armies withdrew because of the imminent arrival of Turkish reinforcements and an implacable desert sun. What had begun with
Bernard's miraculous showmanship at Vézelay ended in near comi-
cal failure.[73]

There were many explanations (and accusations) about what
went wrong, besides the obvious one—that the leaders had realized
it was impossible to take Damascus and decided to cut their losses.
Most of the blame fell on local Christians. Conrad thought that the
Franks of Jerusalem had scuttled the siege deliberately by convincing
the army to relocate its camps from orchards near the walls of
Damascus to a far less amenable desert location. Some suspected that
Bernard of Clairvaux's special charges, the Templars, had been conspiring with the Turks to undermine the campaign. It does seem
likely that the Second Crusade got caught up in the politics of the
Frankish Levant, where the spiritual if not lineal heirs of Baldwin I
followed his example of alternating between aggression and accommodation with Muslims.[74]

Recriminations for this failure would shape the crusading movement for the remainder of the twelfth century and would affect the
rest of Bernard of Clairvaux's life, too. He addressed the outcome of
the Second Crusade directly, albeit briefly, in his treatise *Five Books on
Consideration*, originally conceived as an advice manual for Pope
Eugenius III. Bernard composed the first book while the crusade was
in progress, its outcome unknown but presumably never in doubt.
The second book began with tone drastically changed, as Bernard
finds himself again courting apocalyptic themes: "We have entered,
as you know, a difficult time, such that it almost seems for the living
that the end of their existence is near, not to mention the end of
their hopes; for the Lord, angered by our sins, would seem, as it
were, to have judged the world before its time, remembering justice
but forgetful of mercy."[75] It was a deeply troubling turn of events, one
that allowed the nations—that is, the Muslims, though perhaps Jews,
too—to ask (quoting the Psalms), "Where is their God?"[76]

At first glance, failure seems to have caused Bernard to engage
in genuine soul-searching. "We said, 'peace,' and there is no peace.
We promised a good outcome, but behold, turmoil. It is as if we
entered into this project rashly or foolishly."[77] He is quick, though, to
place the blame where he felt it belonged—with other people. The
original leaders, Eugenius and himself, were not at fault, any more
than Moses had been responsible for the Israelites' pigheadedness.
Responsibility lay solely with the crusaders. "Just ask [the soldiers].
Why do I need to say anything when they admit it themselves? How

could they ever have arrived when they were always walking back-ward?"[78] Bernard may have had in mind the halting progress of the armies in Anatolia, when they met with adversity and withdrew, or the march on Damascus followed by a near instantaneous retreat. Probably he was thinking in spiritual terms, too, that the crusaders confessed their sins and vowed to focus on heavenly things, only to backtrack and embrace earthly distractions. Faltering piety had led to a meandering, failed pilgrimage.

To make it right the crusaders needed to go back. The safety of Jerusalem was too important. Nothing suggested that such a course was advisable or necessary, so to make his case Bernard turned to the Old Testament, focusing on a story of war between Benjamin and the other tribes of Israel. He begins with wild understatement—the tribe of Benjamin sinned. In the story, a Jewish man was traveling from Bethlehem to "the hill country of Ephraim." He bypassed the city of Jebus (which, significantly, would become Jerusalem) because it was full of foreigners and stopped instead at Gibeah, home to the Benjamites. He and his concubine found shelter with a man there. As they shared a pleasant dinner, a mob surrounded the host's house and pounded on the door. Some of the Benjamites had seen the stranger and wanted to rape him. Instead, the host allowed them to rape his guest's concubine, for hours. They left her for dead. The next morning, her master returned home with her body, which he cut up into twelve pieces, sending one portion to each of the twelve tribes. "Never has such a thing happened in Israel since the day our peoples came out of Egypt up until today: Pass sentence and decide in common what must be done."[79] The Israelites decided on war against the Benjamites, their endeavor blessed by God. And they were, unac-countably, utterly defeated.

What had happened to the concubine in Gibeah was what Bernard feared was happening to Jerusalem—the same argument he made in 1146, when he had imagined Saracens as rapists in search of Christian prey. He did so again, frantically, in 1150, in a letter to his sometime ally Peter the Venerable, the abbot of the great church at Cluny, who also occasionally preached the virtues of crusading. Bernard, his mind ever in the heavenly boudoir, wrote to Peter: "The flowering and splendid bed where the virginal flower Mary was laid, festooned with linen and spices, is about to be carried from the earth, so that the Lord's Sepulcher is not glorious now but is disgraced to the eternal shame of the Christian faith."[80]

Like the Israelites, the Franks had gone to war and suffered an unexpected defeat, with no explanation from God. In the Old

Testament, the Lord sent the Israelites once more into battle against the Benjamites, and for a second consecutive time they suffered defeat. On the third day, again at God's command, they returned to the field, and this time won. "What do you think they would say about me," Bernard asked Eugenius in *On Consideration*, "if at my entreaty they rose again and were defeated again? When they heard me urge them to take that road a third time, to try yet again, on which once and a second time they had been checked, what would they do?"[81]

But the Franks needed to return, and quickly. Bernard spent most of 1150 saying so. At least three councils were held.[82] At the second one, in Chartres on May 7, the secular and ecclesiastical leaders gathered there made a surprising suggestion. As Bernard described events in a letter to Eugenius, the abbot himself had been invited to take command of the next army. He assured the pope that he had not sought the distinction. "Who am I to arrange divisions of soldiers, to march in front of armed men? How far removed from my profession would this be, even if I had the necessary strength or did not lack the skill for it?"[83]

Bernard was speaking truthfully. His poor health, particularly stomach problems, were well known. On the other hand, Godfrey, one of his monastic protégés who had become archbishop of Langres, had helped lead the Second Crusade and had been an outspoken advocate of attacking the Greeks before going on to the Holy Land.[84] So the idea of a bellicose monk acting as general was not entirely implausible.

Bernard likely did not consider another explanation for why the council offered him the post. The survivors of the Second Crusade, some of whom were still returning from prisons in the East—some missing eyes, hands, or feet—along with the relatives of the dead, may have wanted Bernard to take responsibility for the disaster he had created and whose consequences he now wanted to compound.[85] If Bernard wished to organize yet another campaign, it should be his enterprise, his nightmare.[86]

The plans came to nothing, and Bernard never did take responsibility for the Second Crusade. In the face of withering criticism, he saw himself as "God's shield." It was better for critics to attack him, he reasoned, than for them to blaspheme against the Almighty.[87] Despite his public confidence, some churchmen did try to console Bernard. One of them, a Cistercian abbot from Italy, John of Casamari, wrote him a letter because, he said with understatement, "this thing (I'm speaking about the pilgrimage to Jerusalem) has not been as successful as you might have hoped."[88] Adopting the usual rhetoric of the crusade, John assured Bernard that the dead had been purged of their sins on the march, thanks to the persecutions and afflictions with which God had smote them. Many of them (based on accounts of survivors, John claimed) had wanted to die, lest they return home and fall back into degenerate habits.[89]

Assuming for himself the oracular role usually played by Bernard, Abbot John claimed that he had had a vision. The apostles John and Paul appeared to him, "and they said that the multitude of places left vacant by fallen angels had been restored because of the ones who had died there."[90] It is a statement rife with apocalyptic implications. Humanity's purpose on earth was to replace the angels who had joined Satan's rebellion and followed him into hell. If John's words were to be taken seriously, this journey could now end. The idea finds its way into Bernard's first official biography. "The eastern church did not gain its liberty as a result of that journey, but the heavenly church was filled and gladdened by it."[91]

John had one other bit of good news that he had learned from his visions. The apostles still thought highly of Bernard, so much so that he would soon die.[92] This prediction proved accurate. Bernard passed away in 1153, having lived long enough to know that the Franks would not do as the Israelites and return to battle.

This failed reenactment of the First Crusade proved to be the event in Bernard's life most difficult to harmonize with his legend. He had invested so much of his energy and prestige into it that its failure could not be ignored. Geoffrey of Auxerre, who oversaw the composition of Bernard's biography, struck a tone at once apologetic and defensive. "I cannot keep silent about how certain men, either from malice or simplemindedness, raised a cry against him, because the outcome proved so lamentable."[93] Geoffrey goes on to remind his readers (and apparently they needed reminding) that Bernard had not called for the crusade on his own. He had entered the campaign reluctantly, because of the enthusiasm of Louis VII and at the command of Pope Eugenius III.

Mainly, though, Geoffrey uses the same defense Bernard had. He excused the saint by focusing on miracles. At the same moment news reached Europe of the disasters in the East, the saint healed a blind boy in public. Everyone cheered and felt encouraged.[94] Not everyone, however, was willing to fall again under Bernard's spell. A German historian in Würzburg, remembering the events of 1146 to 1148, lamented how the Western Church was then suffering at the hands of the"sons of Belial, witnesses of Antichrist." The Würzburg chronicler used these terms not to describe Muslims but rather preachers of the crusade, Bernard and Eugenius among them, who had misled

Christians with their "mad words" and convinced them "willingly to give themselves over to a shared destruction."[95]

The criticism of Bernard could be savage. The English courtier Walter Map, for one, tells of a conversation held at the dinner table of a future saint, Archbishop Thomas Becket. Two abbots, Walter says, were extolling Bernard's remarkable healing powers. Presuming that the dinner occurred in the early, more serene days of Becket's archiepiscopacy, it would have been around 1163, when the Cistercian order was making its first official push to have Bernard canonized. His miracles were extraordinary, one abbot says, but the saint's powers did fail on at least one occasion. Perhaps with a nod to the most show-stopping miracle on the German tour—the raising of the dead man, the archer—the unnamed abbot describes how he had once seen someone stop Bernard on the road and ask him to heal his dead son. "Lord Bernard ordered his body to be carried into a private room, turned everyone out, threw himself upon the boy, prayed, and got up again: but the boy did not get up; he lay there dead." Walter then replied to the man, "Then he was the most unlucky of monks. I have heard previously of a monk throwing himself on a boy, but always, when the monk got up, the boy promptly got up too."[96]

Most, however, like Geoffrey of Auxerre, continued to celebrate the saint's miracles, while trying to distract from his connection to the crusade. Geoffrey included in Bernard's biography a selection of the miracles performed while preaching in Germany but did not give any indication of why Bernard was there. He even notes the miracles that Bernard performed in front of Conrad III but does not state their effect—that they confirmed the king in his decision to join the Second Crusade.[97]

The expurgation of official memory of Bernard's crusading activity was more systematic still in his letter collections. Despite the enormous effort that had gone into the campaign, despite the dominant place that crusading held in Bernard's imagination in the later years of his life, and despite the great care with which Bernard and his scribes kept record of his official correspondence, barely a trace of the crusade survives in it. Later scholars had to track down Bernard's crusading letters in the libraries of churches other than Clairvaux.[98] Simple embarrassment over the crusade's failure might account for this decision. Similarly, Cistercian archivists might have wished to cover up the apocalyptic language Bernard used in promoting the failed campaign.

Whatever the motive behind this scrubbing of the record, it has dulled the prophetic colors of Bernard's crusade preaching.

He definitely drew on the apocalyptic imagery that shaped historical readings of the First Crusade, but how stridently he voiced those ideas is unclear. Was he, in modern scholarly parlance, eschatological— that is, concerned with the end of time but not committed to a belief in its imminence? Or did he take a truly apocalyptic stance— convinced that Antichrist was at work and the Last Days at hand? In his final word on the subject, one of the very last things he wrote, a *Life of St. Malachy*, an Irish archbishop who happened to die at Clairvaux, Bernard sounds a gloomy note about humanity's circumstances. The need for biographies of men such as Malachy was great, Bernard observes, because there were so few comparable figures left: "We see this lack clearly in our own age, such that no one can doubt we have been struck by this sentence: *Because wickedness abounds, the charity of many grows cold.* [Matthew 24:12] And I think that he is here now, or soon will be, about whom it is written, *A great lack precedes his face.* [Job 41:13] Unless I am mistaken, these words refer to Antichrist, whom hunger and the withering of all good accompanies and precedes."[99]

Whatever Bernard had once thought as a young man full of confidence and godly charisma, at the end of his life he thought that Antichrist, the Son of Perdition, was loose in the world, called forth after the failure of the Second Crusade and the inevitable destruction of Christian Jerusalem that would soon follow. It would be left to later historical thinkers, to rethink the fundamental questions of history and prophecy that Bernard's miracle-laden proclamation of a new age had raised.

Fig. 1. St. Michael slaying the dragon, from Lambert of Saint-Omer's illustrated Apocalypse. Herzog August Bibliothek Wolfenbüttel, Cod. Guelf 1 Gud. lat., fol. 15r.

Fig. 2. Augustus enthroned, from the *Liber floridus*. Ghent, Universiteitsbibliotheek, MS 92, fol. 138r.

Fig. 3. Two dreams of Nebuchadnezzar, combined, from the *Liber floridus*. Ghent, Universiteitsbibliotheek, MS 92, fol. 232v.

Fig. 4. Antichrist enthroned on a dragon, from the *Liber floridus*. Ghent, Universiteitsbibliotheek, MS 92, fol. 62v.

Fig. 5. Antichrist slays the two witnesses in Jerusalem, from Lambert of Saint-Omer's illustrated Apocalypse. Herzog August Bibliothek Wolfenbüttel, Cod. Guelf 1 Gud. lat., fol. 14r.

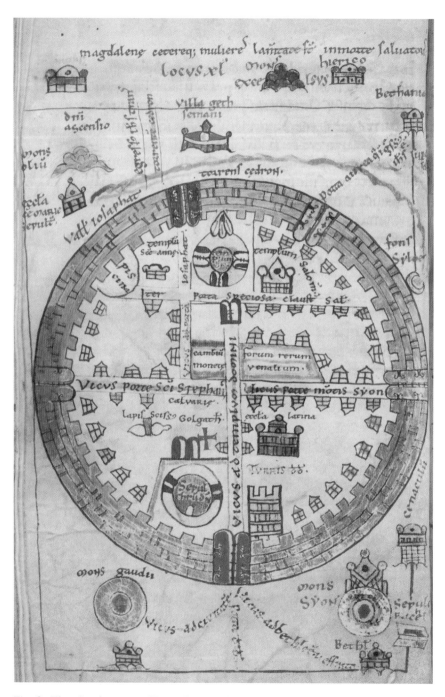

Fig. 6. The circular map of Jerusalem made at the monastery of Saint-Bertin. Saint-Omer, Bibliothèque d'agglomeration de Saint-Omer, MS 776, fol. 50v.

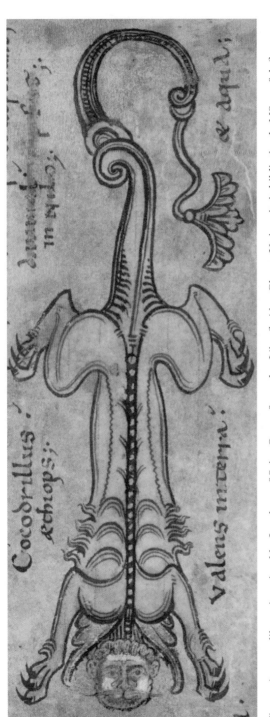

Fig. 7. A crocodile, as imagined by Lambert of Saint-Omer, from the *Liber floridus*. Ghent, Universiteitsbibliotheek, MS 92, fol. 61v.

Fig. 8. Alexander the Great, as depicted in the *Liber floridus*. Ghent, Universiteitsbibliotheek, MS 92, fol. 155v.

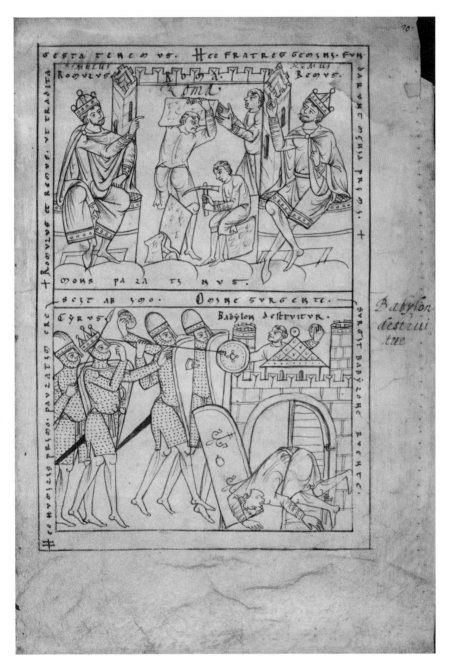

Fig. 9. The building of Rome (above) and the storming of Babylon (below), from Otto of Freising's *Two Cities*. Friedrich-Schiller-Universität Jene, Thüringer Universitäts- und Landesbibliothek, MS Bos. q. 6, fol. 20r.

Fig. 10. Augustus Caesar enthroned, from Otto of Freising's *Two Cities*. Friedrich-Schiller-Universität Jene, Thüringer Universitäts- und Landesbibliothek, MS Bos. q. 6, fol. 38v.

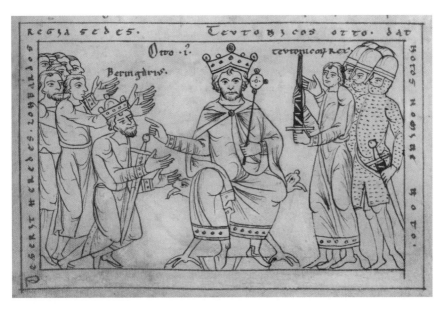

Fig. 11. Emperor Otto I enthroned from Otto of Freising's *Two Cities*. Friedrich-Schiller-Universität Jene, Thüringer Universitäts- und Landesbibliothek, MS Bos. q. 6, fol. 78v.

Fig. 12. Armies of Henry IV and Henry V face off at the river Regen, from Otto of Freising's *Two Cities*. Friedrich-Schiller-Universität Jene, Thüringer Universitäts- und Landesbibliothek, MS Bos. q. 6, fol. 91v.

Fig. 13. Hildegard of Bingen's vision of Antichrist emerging from the loins of the church. Erich Lessing/Art Resource, NY.

Fig. 14. Frederick Barbarossa preparing to leave on Crusade, as depicted in Vatican, Biblioteca Apostolica, Vat. lat. 2001, fol. 1r. Album/Art Resource, NY.

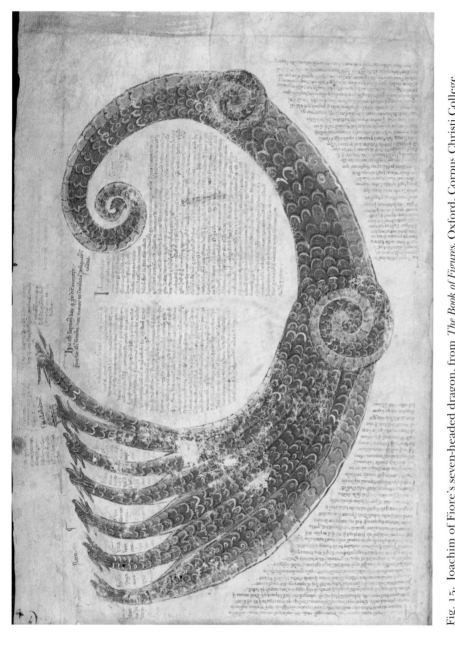

Fig. 15. Joachim of Fiore's seven-headed dragon, from *The Book of Figures*. Oxford, Corpus Christi College, MS 255a, fol. 7r.

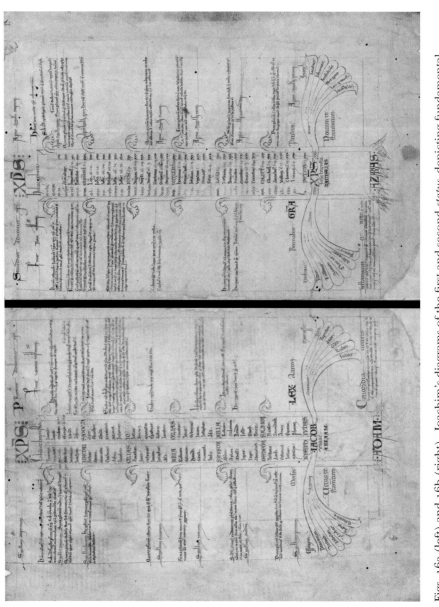

Figs. 16a (left) and 16b (right). Joachim's diagrams of the first and second *status*, depicting fundamental parallels in history, from *The Book of Figures*. Oxford, Corpus Christi College, MS 255a, fols. 5v and 6r.

CHAPTER 9

Translatio imperii

Leaving Jerusalem

I N 1147, ON THE EVE of the Second Crusade, one of Bernard's
contemporaries, the German bishop Otto of Freising, was already
rearranging history's building blocks. Like Bernard, Otto was a
Cistercian monk and had deep respect for Bernard as the founding
spirit (if not the actual founder) of their order. Otto described
Bernard as "revered in life and bearing, renowned within his religious order, wise in learning and gifted with knowledge, famous for
signs and miracles."[1] But according to Otto, Bernard was also a bit
naïve and unreasonably hostile to teachers.[2] These last complaints
carried particular weight, since, unlike Bernard, Otto had studied at
Paris and used what he had learned there liberally in his writing.

Otto was also of a high social status—half-brother of King
Conrad III of Germany and uncle of the next ruler, Frederick
Barbarossa. These connections put Otto's career as a churchman on
the fast track. He joined the Cistercian monastery of Morimond in
the Champagne region of France around 1133 at the age of eight-
een, and five years later he was promoted to the bishopric of Freising
in Bavaria. As an admirer of Bernard and a member of the German
aristocracy, his decision to join the Second Crusade was, in retrospect, almost predictable.[3]

The experience, however, was not one he wished to dwell on. In
his biography of Frederick Barbarossa, Otto mentions his nephew's
decision to take the cross, alongside two other bishops, a duke, and
many other noble and famous men. He adds that brigands and
freebooters took the cross as well—a widespread change of heart so

wondrous as to appear a miracle.[4] God himself seemed to have spoken in favor of the plan: "the whole West grew quiet, such that not only did war appear wicked, but carrying weapons in public did, too."[5] The wondrous peace at home promised the possibility of renewed, virtuous bloodletting abroad.

When it came time to describe the events of this new crusade, however, Otto punted. What happened had happened simply *peccatis nostris exigentibus*—"because our sins demanded it," a stock phrase in Second Crusade literature. At the time Otto was writing about the crusade, in the mid-1150s, everyone knew the outcome, and "since I have proposed to write a pleasant history and not a tragedy, I will leave it to another place or another person to describe it."[6]

It is easy to see why Otto felt this way. In one of the few details he does give about the journey, as the army neared Constantinople, soldiers set camp in what seemed a pleasant meadow near a refreshing stream. "I must say that for the entire journey we never had a happier camp, our tents never spread out in so wide a space." Only Frederick camped a bit higher on the slopes of a mountain. It proved a fortuitous decision. The next morning, such a fierce storm struck that it seemed "a divine judgment rather than a natural downpour." The field flooded; the stream became a rapid and deep river. Men drowned trying to cross it, and supplies and horses were washed away.[7]

Otto and a few others reached Frederick's tent, which alone had escaped danger. There they heard mass, and as they listened to the sounds of their companions crying, screaming, and drowning, they sang together, "Let us rejoice!" The liturgical song, performed bitterly no doubt, draws on Revelation 19:7, from a passage just before Christ, as a rider on a white horse, appears with a sword in his mouth and kills the beast, the symbol of Antichrist. It was the victory anticipated for the Second Crusade, and one whose failure to materialize Otto expects his readers to infer from this scene. "You could see the next day clearer than light, when the waters receded and the face of the land appeared, all of us scattered here and there, our tents looking as miserable as they had so recently looked happy, how great was the power of heaven and how swift and unstable is anything of human happiness." His coda: "But enough of that."[8]

Otto then abandoned talk of crusading for the comparably rough-and-tumble world of academic theology. Specifically, he describes how Bernard of Clairvaux and other churchmen in 1148 at the Council of Reims prosecuted Gilbert of Poitiers on charges of heresy. Gilbert was a master under whom Otto had likely studied and for whom he had great sympathy and respect. In this case, Bernard failed to win a conviction.[9]

Despite his early protestations, Otto then resumed his story of the crusade. After passing Constantinople and Nicea, Conrad, he recounts, divided his army into two parts. The knights and better armed soldiers went with the German king on what was considered to be the more direct but also the more dangerous route into Syria. The foot soldiers and the poor, according to a chronicler at Würzburg, took a road closer to the coast longer, but reportedly safer—under Otto's leadership. These men, Otto tells us, suffered such deprivations that they killed their pack animals, ate their flesh, and drank their blood. But it was not enough. "Almost all of the people became desiccated, many withered away from hunger, thirst, disease, and daily struggles, until news of their sorry state reached the enemy. Seizing their opportunity, the Turks made a sudden attack on Otto and his followers. Meeting no resistance, the Saracens savaged them, scattered them, killed the old, and led the young as slaves into a dismal captivity."[10] Years later, the Würzburg annalist noted that he was still running into maimed and dismembered soldiers making sad returns home.

Hungry and cold, his shoes and feet equally worn down, Otto led a remnant of the soldiers and poor pilgrims to an unnamed Byzantine coastal town. There he was able to book passage for himself and a few of his companions to Jerusalem, entrusting others to the generosity and pity of the locals.[11]

Otto's observation that he wished "to write a pleasant history and not a tragedy" was a good line. It was learned and witty. It served to distinguish between his first great book (a grand universal history, which was a story of steady decline) and his second (the biography of Frederick, presumed to be a tale of rebirth and triumph). But it was also an observation born of genuine trauma, misery, and failure.[12]

When Conrad later arrived in Jerusalem, the Templars welcomed him. It was then that the barons decided to attack Damascus rather than other potential targets like Edessa or Ascalon. But Otto's story once more ends abruptly, this time for good: "What the course and outcome of this expedition to Damascus was, must be told elsewhere, and perhaps by others."[13]

Otto's is a very brief retelling of events, for all of the obvious reasons and possibly for another that Otto leaves unmentioned. An English clerk named Ralph the Black, who like Otto had studied at Paris and had connections at the German court, attributed Conrad's enthusiasm for the crusade less to Bernard and Eugenius and more to Otto. It was Otto who encouraged Conrad not only to take the cross but also to hurry east, lest Louis VII arrive there first. If Ralph's observation is true, then Otto was more responsible for the catastrophe than he wished to admit.[14]

At the end of his tale, Otto ruminates on whether the expedition was in any way a good thing. He concludes that it depends on what the meaning of the word "good" is. Generally speaking, the crusade could never be described as good. It had neither saved lives nor expanded Christendom.[15] It was good, however, in terms of utility, in that it had led to the salvation of many souls. For all the technical vocabulary of genus, species, difference, and accident that he had learned in the schools of Paris, Otto is left with the cold comfort that John, the Cistercian abbot Casamari, had offered Bernard, minus the talk of angels. The Second Crusade was good because it had allowed Christians to die in a penitential state and thus reach heaven.[16]

But Otto was not satisfied with this explanation. Nor was he completely convinced that the armies, including the one he had led, had died because of their sins. Writing specifically about Bernard, he says, "We could say that the spirit of God had inspired that saintly abbot to rouse us, but that we, because of our pride and licentiousness, did not observe his salvific commands and thus deserved to lose both our lives and possessions." Maybe the soldiers deserved to die. On the other hand, maybe Bernard and Eugenius, in proclaiming the crusade, hadn't known what they were doing. Or as Otto sums up his story, "even the spirit of prophecy does not always reside with the prophets."[17]

Otto of Freising's Theory of History

Otto's reaction to the crusade was thus one of disillusionment born of horror and failure. He might not have even written as much about his experiences in the East as he did were it not for the optimism he felt at the accession of Frederick Barbarossa. After so many storms, an unprecedented calm had settled over the land—all due to Frederick's virtue. A time of weeping had become one of laughter; a time of war had become one of peace.[18] The Second Crusade was either a deviation from the normal course of events or else a final catastrophe before a long-awaited peace, depending on one's view of the direction of history.

And Otto had devoted considerable energy to figuring out history's general direction. Before departing for the East, he had completed a massive universal history, usually called *On the Two Cities*. There he wrestled with topics such as crusade, empire, and Nebuchadnezzar's dream, ultimately crafting one of the most endur- ing political theories of the Middle Ages—*translatio imperii*, the belief that the empire and imperial authority had moved steadily from East to West.[19]

He developed this theory working with the same source materi- als as Lambert of Saint-Omer: Augustine's *City of God*, Orosius, and a variety of prophetic texts. Like Lambert, Otto saw parallels between the historical and natural worlds, explicable through the perfection of God's plan.[20] Augustine's influence is plain enough in Otto's title. It is a history of the travels of God's children, "shackled as if in a Babylonian captivity," to a heavenly Jerusalem, just as Augustine's was a theological rendition of the same journey. "For there are two cities, one temporal, the other eternal; one of this world, the other of heaven; one of the devil, the other of Christ. Catholic writers have described the former as Babylon, the latter as Jerusalem."[21] In avoid- ing the celebratory tone of Orosius, Otto arguably produced some- thing closer to the narrative Augustine had wanted from his pupil seven centuries earlier.

Nonetheless, like both Orosius and Lambert of Saint-Omer, Otto viewed the patterns of human history, and particularly the sym- biotic relationship between Babylon and Rome, as more than acci- dents. In his narrative, for example, he juxtaposes the elevation of Brutus as the first consul of Rome with Cyrus's conquest of Babylon. Again, Rome rose as Babylon fell. The prophetic significance of this coincidence would have been still more apparent in the early manu- scripts of *The Two Cities*, which included a cycle of illustrations, among them a page that deliberately contrasts the fates of the two cities (fig. 9).[22] The top register shows Romulus and Remus, presented as enthroned kings, overseeing the construction of Rome. In the lower register the armies of Cyrus, the king himself fighting alongside them, storm the gates of Babylon. Chronologically, Persia and Greece would come between the two great kingdoms, but the message Otto sends is the same as that of Lambert. History moves from East to West, chiefly from Babylon to Rome.

The most famous moment of *translatio imperii* in Otto's narra- tive occurs in the year 800, when Pope Leo III crowned Charlemagne at Rome, as the people voiced their acclamation: "Life and victory to Charles Augustus, crowned by God, great and peaceful emperor of the Romans." Charlemagne was propitiously (numerologically speaking) the seventieth emperor, the sixty-ninth in succession from the original Augustus. Thus, Otto observes, the capital of the Roman Empire, which since the time of Constantine had been in Constantinople, returned to the Western world.[23] More crucially for Otto, it was through Charlemagne that the rulers of his own day (and Otto's own relatives) could claim the title of "Augustus." Otto made the point, again, not just through words but also with images. His picture of the Saxon emperor Otto the Great is indistinguishable from his portrait of Augustus Caesar (see figs. 10 and 11). Only the sartorial sensibilities of the courtiers reveal any significant change.[24]

This transfer of authority to Charlemagne was the final stage in a historical process written into the world's DNA. Humanity, like the sun, moved from east to west. To explain this concept, Otto opens his chronicle with geography, describing how the world is divided into three continents, with Europe in the North, Africa in the South, and Asia in the East. Paradise, the starting point for this story, "is believed to have been created in the land of Eden, to the east, as much as can be construed from the words of Genesis."[25] Lambert and previous mapmakers (notably the illustrator of the *Beatus Apocalypse*) had given this same idea cartographic precision by tucking Eden away in the far eastern corners of their world maps.[26]

This mention of Eden leads Otto to discuss briefly the Fall of Man, but as a student of Augustine, he knew the real drama began with Cain and Abel. The brothers belonged to different cities yet to be founded—Cain to Babylon, the City of Man, and Abel to Jerusalem, the City of God. Cain, after killing his brother Abel, was "the first man to build a city in this vale of tears." Abel left no abiding city, his soul transported to Heaven. Adam and Eve, meanwhile had another child, Seth, "from whom the people of God were descended. The sixth in this line was Enoch, a great citizen of the city of God, who pleased God so much that he was delivered out of his time and set aside alive in a place unknown to all mortals, there to await the last days of the church."[27] Thus in a short paragraph Otto outlines the essential drama of his story: a westward march along a trail of tears, murderous brothers from rival cities, and a hero hidden away until a battle in the Last Days.

This path is similar to the one that Lambert had traced in the *Liber floridus*. And like Lambert, Otto had trouble deciding, when formulating his story, which kingdoms to cast in starring roles. Because of Nebuchadnezzar's dream, there had to be four. But from Otto's dedicatory letter to Frederick Barbarossa (presumably, the last words he wrote in his world history, *The Two Cities*), it is impossible to say what the four kingdoms were. Directly after mentioning

Daniel, Otto observes, "I have written about the princes of these kingdoms chronologically—first the Assyrians, then, skipping over the Chaldeans, whom historians disdain to include among the others, the Medes and the Persians, and finally the Greeks and the Romans." That, of course, makes fives kingdoms, not four. It was probably less important to Otto what the four kingdoms were than that there be at least four, and that the first be Babylon and the last, Rome.

Otto speaks with greater clarity on the topic when, in Book 2 of *The Two Cities*, he directly interprets Nebuchadnezzar's dream. The first and the fourth kingdoms, Otto explains, were Babylon and Rome, "of which, as one fell in the East, the other rose in the West. The two in the middle were the Persians and the Greeks, each of which, as I have now often said, rose to the West." There is another model, he acknowledges, perhaps explaining why he was confused on this point in his introduction, that of Orosius, based on the four cardinal directions. "Some people," Otto notes, lump the Medians, the Chaldeans, and the Persians all together under the label "Babylon," and make Africa (specifically, Orosius would have said, Carthage) into the second kingdom, thus affixing the four kingdoms to the four directions. Otto does not pass judgment on this model, but given his preference for westward political movement it is clear where his sympathies lie.[28]

Drift and decay—it is the theme that pervades *The Two Cities*, and all of creation, for that matter. It is enacted allegorically every day with the rising and setting sun. "As is shown in what follows, all human power and knowledge began in the East and ends in the West; thus the mutability and decline of all things is demonstrated."[29] Unaware of the renaissance that his nephew Frederick Barbarossa would inaugurate, Otto saw in the 1140s only a diminished empire, limping on feet of iron and clay toward the Last Days. As such, the Second Crusade would have made an ideal coda to his story.

But in *The Two Cities*, Otto does not discuss the Second Crusade at all. And a reader must doubt whether the gloomy stance he later strikes about it in *The Deeds of Frederick* accurately reflects his state of mind in 1146, on the eve of his departure. It is entirely possible that when he first heard of the prophecy about a ruler named "C" conquering Babylon (which Louis VII believed applied to himself), he would have concluded that his own king fit the bill. Conrad, after all, did not need to double his value from an L to a C, either literally or numerically.[30] The related prophecy, attributed to the Tiburtine Sibyl, gave further support to this interpretation. In its earliest rendition, the Sibyl gave the Last Emperor the name of Constans. By Otto's time, in revised copies of the text, the Last Emperor was identified only by the letter "C," symbolically another Charlemagne, literally perhaps Conrad himself. All in all, Otto had every reason to enter Second Crusade with real apocalyptic hopes.[31]

And more than Bernard, Otto of Freising states plainly in *The Two Cities* that by 1146, the Last Days were at hand. To conclude his analysis of Nebuchadnezzar's dream, on the destruction of the statue and the rise of the mountain of the Lord in its place, he writes, "We who stand at the end, which he predicted, are now experiencing it and fearfully await what is to come next."[32]

In Otto's system, however, the Last Days had begun not because of the crusades but because of the Investiture Controversy—the war between popes and emperors launched in the 1070s by Gregory VII (r. 1073–85) and Henry IV (r. 1056–1106). The issue at the heart of that war seems anodyne enough. Gregory and Henry disputed whether kings or churchmen had the right to invest bishops with their offices. But it proved intractable, and the war continued until well after the death of each man and was settled finally, though imperfectly, in 1122 with an agreement known as the Concordat of Worms.

The connection between an ancient Babylonian king and the contemporary war between secular and ecclesiastical powers might appear tenuous, but for Otto it was crucial. Indeed, he places it at one of the most structurally significant points in his history, the end of Book 6—six being the number of humanity's allotted days on earth. Gregory's church, Otto says at that point, is the stone, uncut by human hand, the one that Nebuchadnezzar saw. This stone, or the church, struck the feet of the statue—the statue symbolizing empire and the feet, as the end of the body, symbolizing the end of imperial history. When Gregory smote the German/Roman Empire with his sword of anathema, its authority collapsed, and its place grew the church, "once small and humble, now grown into a great mountain, as anyone can see."[33]

In simpler language, the church had won the Investiture Controversy. It was growing into the great mountain foretold by Daniel but doing so at a price: the destruction of Roman authority. So great was the ensuing chaos that Otto found it wearisome to recount. "In sum, this perfect storm has fomented so many evils, schisms, and dangers to soul and body that it alone suffices to prove the misery of the human condition, brought on by persecutions immense and regular."[34] The sixth age was drawing to a close, and the terrors of the Last Days were beginning, brought on, ironically, by a triumphant church.

The world's condition reached its nadir in the early years of the twelfth century. Byzantium was ruled by Alexius Comnenus, whom Otto considered "utterly duplicitous," and Germany by Henry IV, at war with the pope and his own son. "Lo, the dangerous times! Two emperors, one in the East, the other in the West, each an enemy of God!"[35] When Otto describes an 1105 standoff between the armies of Henry IV and his son, separated by the Regen River—a scene whose significance Otto chooses to indicate through another illustration (fig. 12)—he reads it as one more sign of the End Times. "These are what Paul calls *the Last Days*....Know that our times are believed to be the final ones, since they are going to put an end to previous crimes, threatening to bring an end to the world because of the enormity of wicked deeds, while proclaiming on the other hand that Christ's kingdom is about to rise."[36] The final revelation was not yet visible but was at hand, as close as the lance points of knights facing one another on opposite side of a river.

Crusading did fit into this story, but only as a sideshow. For what could honorable men do in such a time? In 1096, as civil war divided Germany, a few men followed their consciences and "took on the belt of knighthood and went to Jerusalem. There they practiced a new kind of warfare, taking up arms against the enemies of Christ's cross, so that they might carry the death of the cross on their bodies. They seemed in life and manner not knights but monks."[37] It was the solution later perfected by the Templars: to live as bloodied warriors in a flawed world. The fate of Jerusalem might have no direct connection with the Last Days, but it did at least give knights the opportunity to prepare for their own personal Judgment Days.[38]

Going to Jerusalem

To fit Jerusalem into this tragic tale of westward decline was, for Otto, awkward. The City of God, the heavenly Jerusalem, provided half of the organizational principle for his chronicle, but Otto showed only mild interest in its earthly counterpart, or in the politics and history that drove the crusade.

The rise of Islam merits only one sentence in *The Two Cities*: "Around this time Muhammad, whom the Saracens worship today, is said to have been born from a gentile father of the stock of Ishmael and from a Jewish mother."[39] Otto tells readers only this much so as to give context to a story about the Emperor Heraclius, whose reign

would end with devastating losses to Arab armies. Otto had a rudi-
mentary knowledge of Islamic practice. He knew, for example, that
Muslims worshipped one God, condemned idols, practiced circum-
cision, and followed a code of written law, whose precepts included
regular washing (which Otto found particularly offensive). He knew
that Muhammad was a prophet but also accused him of pretending
to be the Son of God.[40] Like many contemporaries, he knew enough to
be interested in Islam but did not care enough to get it right.

The First Crusade itself earns a little more attention, serving as
the opening act of Book 7 of *The Two Cities*. It is a celebratory account,
particularly in the context of a chronicle dedicated to crisis. To
describe the crusade, Otto makes heavy use of Ekkehard of Aura, a
German writer who filled his narrative with apocalyptic signs and
portents, but Otto by and large avoided such prophetic flourishes.
"About the signs and auguries seen on heaven and earth at that time,
portending the breakup of the empire and the march on Jerusalem,
others have said enough."[41]

The origins of the expedition were earthly. Christians in Jerusalem
together with Emperor Alexius, according to Otto, wrote to Urban II
and asked for help against "pagans," who were abusing the city and
its people. Otto adds that those same Christians were partly to blame
in that they had not shown sufficient respect for the Holy Sepulcher.
Moved by their plight, Urban went into Gaul and preached at
Clermont. Peter the Hermit played no part in Otto's story. Otto does,
however, mention Emicho of Flonheim, who led the massacres of
Jews along the Rhine (just as the monk Ralph would do during Otto's
life). Emicho was, for Otto, nothing more than a false Christian who
accomplished little except to incite murder and fictive baptisms.[42]

With dispassion, Otto describes the travails and compromises of
the First Crusade. Unlike most of the early chroniclers, he acknowledges that the leaders actively negotiated with Egypt, and that Egypt
offered (deceitfully) to form an alliance against the Turks.[43] He mentions that at Antioch scarcity was such a problem that the Franks
barely kept themselves from eating human flesh, and that they did
eat human flesh, even rotting corpses, after capturing the city of
Ma'arra. Otto accepts without question the authenticity of the Holy
Lance of Antioch. He describes the procession performed by the
crusaders around Jerusalem's walls in imitation of the Israelites at
Jericho and adds that the Franks took the city on the octave of that
ceremony, thus demonstrating, through the number eight, that
Jewish law and the Sabbath had been abolished. When the city fell,
blood flowed as high as the horses' knees (an impossible level, but

about average for crusade histories). "Henceforth Jerusalem and the Lord's sepulcher are possessed by us."[44]

Finally, the Franks elected Godfrey as their king. It was a practical decision. As someone raised on the borderlands of the Franks, Romans, and Germans, Godfrey was the only one who could speak all the languages necessary to mediate among the different peoples. Otto is likely being autobiographical here, since he too would have spent most of his life crossing these same linguistic frontiers. It was a hard job, Otto observes. The soldiers often made cruel jokes at one another's expense, sometimes leading to bloody reprisals.[45] Meanwhile, back in Europe, Urban II took advantage of the situation to reclaim Rome and declare victory in the Investiture Controversy.

Otto's account of the First Crusade is thus traditional, if a little earthbound (like that of William of Malmesbury, who attributed the whole enterprise to a conspiracy hatched between Urban II and Bohemond of Antioch). It adds nothing of substance to the earlier chronicles and is ultimately notable more for what it does not do— emphasize signs, miracles, and divine intervention—than for what it does.[46]

The crusade also provided Otto with the opportunity to meditate further on themes raised by Augustine and Orosius and to engage with the world both geographically and historically—again like Lambert of Saint-Omer. The most salient of these themes is a clear division between East and West. Easterners, Otto believed, call all Westerners *Franks*, in recognition of Frankish superiority, "because, I think, of the ancient dignity of that people, and its virtue." When the Egyptians welcomed Frankish ambassadors to their capital, "The barbarians marveled at the strength, nobility, dress, gait, and beauty of the men and declared them to be not human beings but gods."[47]

Presuming that Otto was writing the seventh book of his history in 1146, the crusade and eastern geography would have been very much on his mind. A year earlier, he had been in attendance at the court of Eugenius III in the city of Viterbo, about fifty miles north of Rome, when a delegation arrived from the Holy Land.[48] Its leader was Bishop Hugh of Jabala, whom Raymond of Antioch had sent to ask for help in the light of Edessa's fall. (He also wanted the pope to endorse his claim to possess 10 percent of any plunder taken from Saracens; even in crisis, it was business as usual in the Holy Land.)[49] Otto thus learned firsthand about turmoil in the Frankish settlements and no doubt would have had the opportunity to interrogate Hugh and his entourage at some length before returning home.

He also would have had the chance to assess Eugenius's mind-set, and he certainly would have known, as he was finishing up Book 7 of *The Two Cities,* that another crusade was in the offing.

Accompanying Hugh were legates for the "metropolitan" (an office somewhere between "archbishop" and "pope") of the Armenian church. At some point when talking to members of this delegation— Otto identifies Bishop Hugh of Jabala as his source, but surely the Armenians made some contribution as well—he learned electrifying news. A Christian king in the East named Prester John, a direct descendant of the Magi who had visited Christ in Bethlehem, was planning to come to Jerusalem's aid. His realm lay beyond Armenia and even Persia, in the farthest East, and he ruled it as both king and priest. Thus with one stroke, Prester John had cut the knot of the Investiture Controversy, the war between Roman popes and German emperors, and had joined together into a single office kingdom and priesthood. Prester John also possessed tremendous wealth. His royal scepter was made of emerald. But such riches were not at all surprising. Had not the Magi brought exotic treasure to honor the newly born Savior?

More to the point, Prester John had defeated a combined army of Persians, Medes, and Assyrians—the most ancient kingdoms from the early pages of Otto's history, also perhaps coincidentally the first three world empires in Lambert of Saint-Omer's model of history. The priest-king wanted to follow his victory over the Saracens by marching to Jerusalem, partly as a pilgrim and partly as an ally to the Franks, but unable to cross the Tigris he had returned home. The moral of the story is clear. If Western leaders would send aid to the East, help would arrive soon. And there would be treasure, too.[50]

It was not the first time rumor of an eastern Christian king had reached the pope. In 1122, in the aftermath of the Field of Blood and the last time that the papacy had tried to start a crusade, a man named John, claiming to be patriarch of India, spoke before Calixtus II. He described his home city, which he named "Hulna," as the largest and wealthiest in the world, one whose population was entirely Christian. Its walls were so thick that two chariots could ride on them side by side. A river of Paradise flowed through the city, leaving deposits of gold and jewels behind. And a church on a nearby mountain contained the incorrupt body of the Apostle Thomas, who was the evangelist to India and whose supposed burial place Nestorian Christians maintained in a church near the city of Chennai on the Bengal Bay. Once a year Thomas's body came to life to administer the Eucharist—and to kill unworthy communicants.[51]

A learned, innately skeptical observer like Otto had every reason to discount the more fabulous elements associated with Prester John, and indeed he included few of them in his chronicle. But he did expect his readers to take the news seriously. It was one of the last things reported in *The Two Cities*—the existence of a powerful and wealthy Christian kingdom in the East, preparing in 1145 to aid Jerusalem, even as kings of the West were doing the same. The direction of history, so long migrating toward the setting sun, might be set to do an about-face, with everyone heading to the world's center, toward Jerusalem, for a final confrontation against Saracens and to prepare for the Last Days, which Otto believed at hand.

It would have made a fine conclusion to *The Two Cities*, especially since, as Otto had announced at the beginning of his project, he had hoped to give Book 7 a happy ending. In that dedicatory letter to Frederick Barbarossa he explains how each of the first six books, in the manner of tragedy, "end in misery." The final two books, by contrast, symbolized "the repose of souls and the double vestment of resurrection."[52] A famed miracle-working preacher whose message spread a blanket of peace over Germany would have been an appropriate note on which to conclude Book 7. Better still would have been a triumphal military campaign in the East.

That was not to be. Instead, Otto, avoiding the Second Crusade altogether, devotes the last pages of the historical section of his chronicle to descriptions of monastic orders, "by reason of whose sanctity the most merciful judge is able to bear with the world's wickedness."[53] And then, in Book 8, he writes about the Apocalypse.

Otto's Apocalypse

Otto's description of the Last Days has been characterized as a "relatively standard presentation of Antichrist," and from a certain perspective it is.[54] He acknowledges a debt to the still popular Pseudo-Methodius, inventor of the Last World Emperor legend, in a dedicatory letter, where he writes that Rome "will endure until the end of time, according to Methodius, when the stone cut from a mountain will bring it down completely."[55] He also writes that his own forecast of the Last Days is no different from Augustine's in *The City of God*.[56]

The reign of Antichrist, Otto continues, represents the last of the four great persecutions experienced by the City of God. To fill out this picture, Otto may have relied on Bernard's theory of the prophetic "four hours of the watch." First, tyrants had inflicted violence on the early church. Second came the fraudulent deceits of heretics.

Third, oppressions grew out of the secret, subtle, mendacious activity of the hypocrites who worked within the church. Finally, Antichrist would employ all of these strategies at once: violence, fraud, and deceit.[57]

More specifically, Otto follows paths cut by Pseudo-Methodius and Adso of Montier-en-Der, the author of the ninth-century *Life of Antichrist*, both of whom were important sources of inspiration for Lambert of Saint-Omer. As Christ humbled himself, Antichrist will exalt himself. Christ hid his divine nature, whereas Antichrist will proclaim himself God. Christ renounced the pomp of the world, but Antichrist will teach his followers to delight in pleasure. In a more original (and perhaps autobiographical) observation, Otto says that schoolmen will prove especially vulnerable to Antichrist, particularly because of his attacks against difficult doctrines of the church, which seem to contradict Reason—the Virgin Birth, the Eucharist, and the Incarnation. "For as you read in Job, the food of [Antichrist] is the elect. Truly it is easier to use reason and argument to lead men who follow human reason and philosophize about the causes of things into denying their faith than it is to frighten them into apostasy through threats or else to entice them into it using the pleasures of the world."[58]

Antichrist is, moreover, a subtle, cunning villain. He is not a savage tyrant but an attractive false prophet capable of winning adherents by words and force. And he works in tandem with the devil, whom Otto identifies as the dragon from Revelation.[59] A handsome man in league with a dragon, an image reminiscent of the picture of Antichrist in the *Liber floridus*—suggesting that Otto may have at some point thumbed through its pages and internalized some of its lessons.

Sticking close to Pseudo-Methodius's script, Otto says that Antichrist will arise from the tribe of Dan, based on an oft-cited passage from Genesis 49:17: "Let Dan be a serpent in the way, a viper in the path." This prophecy, or rather its interpretation, led most commentators to conclude that Antichrist would be Jewish and especially adept at deceiving other Jews. But Otto makes a break with tradition, giving the prophecy an allegoric spin. Dan represents servitude. Therefore, Antichrist will be "from a servile state," his ethnic and religious backgrounds unknown and unknowable.[60] Without fanfare, he has eliminated the necessity of Antichrist being Jewish.

Otto, however, is no apologist for the Jews. He believed that they would be especially receptive to Antichrist's message. To give them a chance to repent, God would send two Jewish witnesses, Enoch and

Elijah, to preach against him. Antichrist, however, will kill the two prophets, and then Christ will descend from heaven to slay him with the breath of his mouth. Then, finally, the Jews would recognize their error, that Antichrist was not the Messiah and that he has deceived them. At long last, they will accept the truth of Christianity.[61] Not exactly heroic, the Jews in the Last Days as Otto depicts them, were relatively neutral players.

This presentation of the Jews was Otto's own creation. To make it, he departed from both of his most immediate sources, Pseudo-Methodius and Adso. The former portrays Antichrist as deceiving people in general with his message, with no emphasis on the Jews at all. The latter says that the Jews will be enthusiastic about Antichrist's preaching, in no small part because he will have himself enthroned in the Temple in Jerusalem. Despite their initial devotion, Adso continues, the Jews will abandon Antichrist after he kills Enoch and Elijah.[62] Several copyists rewrote Adso's *Life of Antichrist* and introduced changes into in his story but with only one exception, no one altered the basic narrative of the Jews at the end of time. Initially dupes of Satan, they learned to repent upon seeing Antichrist's true character.

In the one exception to this trend, the Jews are presented not just as dupes but as malevolent fools. This version of the story appears in the *Liber floridus* and was likely the work of Lambert of Saint-Omer. In Lambert's rendition, Antichrist will haul the corpses of Enoch and Elijah to the top of Mount Golgotha, where Christ was crucified. After three days, the witnesses will rise up to heaven. The Jews, however, despite this transparent act of murder and God's miraculous rejection of it, stay loyal to Antichrist, and Antichrist himself begins to devise ways to shore up his reputation. Drawing on his knowledge of the dark arts, he creates an illusion, a magic trick, whereby he transforms a living ram into a perfect likeness of himself. Hiding off-stage, Antichrist has the ram's body sliced open "in the sight of all," making it appear that he was dead. Then, after three days, he reappears, crowned and dressed in royal garb decorated with precious stones—a resurrected messiah, a bizarre parody of Christ as the sacrificial lamb. By this method, "this most evil deceiver filled the hearts of the Jews." Finally, the Lord descended from heaven and struck Antichrist dead on the Mount of Olives. The Jews, however, "stupid to the end, guarded him for three days so that he might rise from the dead. On the fourth day his body started to stink, and they admitted that he was dead, extinguished, consigned to eternal flames, and beating their criminal breasts, they converted to the Lord Jesus

Christ, and gave up their Jewish cult."[63] Otto removed the vitriol from this story, but he followed its timeline—in his version, too, the Jews stuck by Antichrist until Christ killed him.

Lambert of Saint-Omer is the only writer to use this version of the *Life of Antichrist*. Otto's familiarity with it leads to at least three important conclusions. First, he must have seen the *Liber floridus*, which was composed in the 1120s in the same border regions where Otto lived and studied and would have been of great interest to him and his intellectual circle. So when Otto imaginatively drew lines through history and across maps, connecting dynasties to biblical prophecy and God's plan, he likely had Lambert's work in mind. Second, when he acknowledged "Methodius" as an important source for his prophetic thought, he was likely thinking of Adso's *Life of Antichrist* as it appears in the *Liber floridus*, and which Lambert had mistakenly attributed to Methodius. Finally, Otto did not use his source slavishly. Rather (probably as someone who had seen the effects of Ralph's anti-Jewish preaching and who admired the effectiveness with which Bernard of Clairvaux had shut it down),[64] he elected to remove all of the most abhorrent anti-Jewish imagery from the text and ultimately restored the neutral and indeed largely positive role attributed to the Jews in Adso's original rendering.

This familiarity with the thought world of the *Liber floridus* is suggestive on still another level. If Otto looked at Lambert's work as something like an authoritative text, he would have absorbed its apocalyptic reading of the crusade and perhaps, before 1148, found in it hope that he might give his chronicle, *The Two Cities*, a thunderously happy ending, where Conrad would reveal himself as the "C" of prophecy.

After 1148, though, he necessarily rejected that vision. Most strikingly in Book 8 of *The Two Cities*, there is no Last World Emperor, who is the key dramatic figure in the *Revelations* of Pseudo-Methodius and easily the second most important character in Adso's *Life of Antichrist*. Otto would not have made this editorial decision lightly, especially given his family connections to Conrad and Frederick. But it is likely that his devastating experience in the East would have made him want to disown all aspects of the Last Emperor prophecies connected to the Holy Land.

Equally surprising, the only prophetic role that Otto does suggest for a Roman emperor is negative. At first, in his final and prophetic book in *The Two Cities*, he speculates that in the Last Days, the Roman emperor might become so dejected at the state of the world that he would simply give up trying to govern his realm effectively.[65]

Later, he offers a darker possibility. The devil would not appear on earth physically during the Last Days but rather would work spiritually through a powerful ally—maybe an emperor. "If anyone maintains that [the devil] will associate himself for this purpose with a powerful man like a Roman Emperor and that this figure is the one called 'the beast,' I won't disagree."[66] In either case the role of the emperor in the Last Days—villain or apathetic failure—has declined significantly from what it had been in earlier prophecies. In particular, there is no indication at all that a Western emperor will lead attacks on Constantinople and Jerusalem, where he would stand guard at the Mount of Olives against the oncoming madness of Antichrist.

There is, in fact, no mention at all of the Mount of Olives in Otto's apocalyptic speculations, nor of the Temple Mount where Antichrist would claim his throne, nor of Jerusalem. Apart from a single reference to Golgotha, the apocalyptic events have become divorced from their original geographic settings.[67] Similarly, Antichrist (who, again, might not be Jewish) would not be born in the earthly city of Babylon. As surely as the monks of Clairvaux excised material about the Second Crusade from Bernard's official letter collection, so Otto of Freising has excised the earthly Jerusalem from his vision of the Last Days.

The Apocalypse as Otto imagined it was instead a moral one. Satan had been imprisoned for one thousand years (a symbolic number, Otto stresses) not bound in hell but in men's minds, in a psychological abyss. At the time of Antichrist, he will be released, "that is, he will burst forth in his full iniquity, ready to let flow all his great power." Rather than the destruction of Rome, the "falling away" or "rebellion" foretold in 2 Thessalonians, there would be an abandonment of Truth.[68]

The questions that most fascinated Otto thus had less to do with the events of the Last Days and the mechanics of persecution Antichrist would unleash, but rather their theological and intellectual implications. How could God allow such evil to occur? Otto parses meanings as much as possible but can offer only this consolation: "We must believe that it happens not cruelly, but rather because of the foresight of the Creator, for we now find ourselves always fearful about the advent of the judge, always prepared to render account."[69] As someone who lived through the darkness of the crusade after hearing the greatest preacher of his age sound the trumpet for war in the East, Otto used the final book of his *Two Cities* to diffuse these ideas, to erase the lines that ran from Babylon to

Jerusalem, from Nebuchadnezzar to Godfrey of Bouillon, or to "L" or "C," or whoever might wish to be Last World Emperor.

Keeping the Nightmare Alive

It was not a doctrinaire statement, since Otto made it through silences—editorial decisions about what to cut rather than what to add to prophecy. And not everyone chose to follow his lead. To take one prominent example, around the time of Otto's death in 1158, an anonymous author at the German monastery of Tegernsee composed a play about the Last Days, the *Ludus Antichristi,* or "Play of Antichrist."[70] It is doubtful Otto had any direct input into the script, but the monks at Tegernsee would have been familiar with his work. Their community, located about fifty miles south of Freising, was an imperial church and had an active literary culture. More particularly in 1150, Eugenius III placed it formally under the bishop of Freising's— which is to say Otto's—protection.[71]

They also were familiar with a version of history similar to the Flemish school of crusade thought. Their library at Tegernsee included a twelfth-century manuscript that contained Robert the Monk's chronicle alongside many of the texts that had shaped Lambert of Saint-Omer's worldview—Orosius's history, Josephus's *Jewish Wars,* lives of Charlemagne and Alexander the Great, supplemented by a letter from Prester John.[72] Historically and prophetically minded monks at Tegernsee thus had the opportunity to reflect at length on the place of the crusade and the East in God's plans for salvation.

These influences come together in the "Play of Antichrist." Its story falls roughly into two halves. The first is a celebration of the might of German emperors. Otto would likely have approved of this section. Action occurs on a stage decorated mainly with thrones. To the east sat the Temple of the Lord, flanked by the (Crusader) king of Jerusalem and the Synagogue, which represented all Jews. On the opposite side of the stage, to the west, sat the Roman emperor, flanked by the king of the Franks and a throne for the king of the Germans—empty because during the reign of Frederick Barbarossa, when the play was written, emperor and king were the same person. To the south was the king of the Greeks, sitting between the king of Babylon and *Gentilitas,* or "Gentile-dom." The Muslim figures are portrayed as polytheistic idol worshippers.

When the action begins, the emperor of the Romans has announced his intention to restore the fullness of imperial power by collecting tribute from around the world: "The writings of historians tell us that all the world was once Roman property. The strength of our forebears brought this about, but the weakness of their heirs squandered it. Under them collapsed the empire's power, which the majesty of our might seeks to renew."[73]

One by one, the kings of the Franks, the Greeks, and Jerusalem all accepted the emperor's authority. The unification of the Christians foretold in Pseudo-Methodius and Adso had thus come to pass.[74] The king of Babylon, however, feared the resurgent Christian world and decided to strike at its heart, Jerusalem. The emperor vowed to intervene and in fact scored an astonishing victory. The "Play of Antichrist" thus maintains the part of the Antichrist legend that Otto had suppressed in *The Two Cities*: the Last Emperor marched to Jerusalem and made war on Babylon.

More troubling to Otto would have been this battle's outcome. Victorious and yet overcome by humility, the Roman emperor enters the Temple of the Lord to worship and just as Methodius, Adso, and the Tiburtine Sibyl had predicted, he lays down his crown. "Take what I offer, for with a goodly heart I resign to you, King of Kings, my empire. Kings govern throughout it, but you alone are and are able to be called Emperor and Governor of all."[75] Humility, a willingness to give up high office and its trappings, was central to political theory in the Middle Ages, perhaps in the Western Roman Empire above all others.[76] From that perspective, the Last Emperor's gesture made a certain amount of sense. By descending the ladder of humility, he might attain a throne in heaven.

The remainder of the play concerns the advent of Antichrist. Otto would have found this part of the story entirely unacceptable. As soon as the emperor abandons the Temple, hypocrites draw the king of Jerusalem into their counsel. Next comes Antichrist himself, accompanied by figures representing Heresy and Hypocrisy. With ease they depose the Crusader King and take the throne of Jerusalem. The fallen king flees to Germany and tells the emperor what would seem to be the real takeaway lesson in the play: "Now it is clear that your abdication was wrong. The law of deadly superstition is growing strong."[77]

Meanwhile, the Greek and Frankish kings send embassies to acknowledge Antichrist's rule. The German king (his imperial title now downgraded) refuses Antichrist's promises and bribes and prepares to make war in the East. Antichrist responds, with no little irony, by declaring a crusade. He sends messengers to proclaim that he has assembled a host of martyrs in order to tame Teutonic madness.[78] Despite his bluster, the German king prevails in battle. Antichrist, however, reestablishes his credentials using a familiar method: he performs miracles. In fact, exactly as Bernard of Clairvaux had done in recruiting Conrad, Antichrist in the play stands before the King of the Germans and heals a lame boy. When that marvel fails to move the king, Antichrist (again, following Bernard's script while preaching the crusade) raises a man from the dead. Overcome by these miracles, the German king relents and pledges his allegiance to the abomination of desolation.

Both the monks of Tegernsee and Otto of Freising composed their retellings of Adso's *Life of Antichrist* in the aftermath of the Second Crusade, and in each case their work carries the scars of that disastrous expedition. Otto may have completed *The Two Cities* before he left for the crusade in 1147, although the only version of the work that survives was not put into circulation until 1157, a year before his death. Even if he had completed a draft of the chronicle before going east, he would have had ample opportunity to revise it according to his experiences there.[79] And even though Otto believed that Frederick had restored peace to his empire, he nonetheless chose in that year to circulate a universal history that argued that Nebuchadnezzar's dream had already been fulfilled—some eighty years earlier, when Gregory VII had struck down Henry IV with the sword of excommunication, launching the war between empire and papacy, laying low the statue of secular rule and turning the Church into a great mountain that had filled the earth. What his nephew Frederick Barbarossa might ultimately accomplish (or destroy) by the end of his reign, Otto did not live to see, let alone write about.

If Otto's view prevailed, the ground rules of prophecy and history would need to change. The Apocalypse had begun in the West with the Investiture Controversy, not the East with the Crusade. That expedition, with fifty years hindsight, had been foolhardy, even self-destructive. Bernard of Clairvaux's performance of miracles in front of Conrad had been the work of at best a misled mystic, at worst a false prophet.[80] The key events of the Last Days might occur anywhere, and the key player, the one who could bring peace or scuttle it, was the Roman emperor. The Last Days had come unmoored from the Middle East. Like the *Play of Antichrist*, it had become a story that could be performed at any church, in any town square. Apocalypse begins at home.

CHAPTER 10

Apocalypse Begins at Home

I N THE AFTERMATH OF OTTO'S work, it was time to rethink the Apocalypse, and Gerhoh of Reichersberg, a cantankerous and brilliant theologian who traveled in the same circles as Otto and occasionally corresponded with him, was ready to take up the challenge.[1] By the time of his death in 1169, he had moved his own historical thought further than Otto could have ever imagined— certainly more boldly than Otto ever would have done. He did not abandon traditional historical and prophetic models, but he did eliminate the Last World Emperor from the story, and he did so because of his own bitter disillusionment with the entire enterprise of crusading. Along with a few of his contemporaries, such as the German mystic Hildegard of Bingen and the English cleric Ralph the Black, he created a worldview that consigned the crusades to near irrelevance.

Gerhoh of Reichersberg's Dream of Jerusalem

Admittedly, the crusade was never Gerhoh's main concern. Instead, he spent most of his life wrestling with the same issues that had driven the Investiture Controversy—especially the sin of simony. A compromise had been reached in 1122 over how to divide up questions of investiture—bishops would invest other bishops with the signs of their office, where the king or emperor would invest them with temporal landholdings. But the same fight seemed to start again in 1159, because of a new papal schism. A majority of the College of

Cardinals elected Alexander III as pope. A separate faction, supported by the people of Rome, refused to accept the result and elected instead Victor IV, whom the emperor Frederick Barbarossa and most of the secular leaders of Europe supported.[2] This latest fight, Gerhoh believed, was unique. Schisms had been relatively common during the previous hundred years, but in all earlier cases it had been obvious which pope had had the better claim (Gerhoh writes here, of course, with complete obliviousness to the power of hindsight). With Alexander III and Victor IV, by contrast, both sides could make a persuasive case. Alexander's party said that their candidate had been lawfully elected and that Victor had usurped the trappings of office.[3] Victor's supporters retorted that Alexander had won his election through simony and an anti-imperial plot hatched with King William of Sicily. So poisonous did the situation become that near the end of his life, in the late 1160s, Gerhoh claimed that he had to write in secret, lest he offend one side or the other.[4]

Against this backdrop, crusades were of little account. But Gerhoh did nonetheless return to the topic from time to time. His local church maintained a healthy interest in crusading—the oldest German manuscript of Robert the Monk's *Historia* was produced at Reichersberg.[5] Over time, as a result of historical study, conversation, and bitter personal experience, Gerhoh became one of the crusade's fiercest critics. Indeed, by the time of his death in 1169, he had systematically condemned the entire enterprise.

He still could marvel at the First Crusaders' achievements. Like his contemporaries, Gerhoh saw the fall of Jerusalem in 1099 as a high-water mark in Christian history, but not because of the military victory. Rather, Gerhoh celebrated the First Crusade for what it demonstrated about church reform. Priests and princes had worked in concord, exactly as they should. Bishop Adhémar of Le Puy "with other religious men watched over the divine offices, and strong knights conducted themselves wisely according to his teaching."[6] Gerhoh wrote these words around 1142, well before the fall of Edessa. Just a few years later, when the Second Crusade began, he was still celebrating 1099, finding prophetic evidence for it in the Song of Songs, just as Bernard of Clairvaux had done (albeit working from a different passage): *You are beautiful, my love, sweet like Jerusalem, terrible as armies ordered into camps.* "The beautiful sight of such an army shone in our days when Pope Urban of blessed memory, roused Christian knights with urbane words so that, visibly marked by the cross of Christ, they set out to liberate the holy city Jerusalem from pagan hands."[7]

Gerhoh drew these images directly from early chronicles, particularly Robert the Monk and Raymond of Aguilers.[8] But he did not always use them accurately. Consider his account of the discovery of the Holy Lance. He writes that when Peter Bartholomew found the Lance, some people did not believe him. Peter, "however, drew comfort in the Lord and asked that a massive fire be lit in front of the people. If he carried the Lance through it without injury, its authenticity would be plain. It was so done, and the monk emerged unharmed. Not even one tiny thread from his cloak was singed."[9] Peter Bartholomew, in fact, did not undergo an ordeal by fire until almost nine months after the Lance's discovery, and he died shortly thereafter, having suffered severe burns. Either Gerhoh's memory was faulty or else he was being deliberately misleading in the name of effective storytelling.[10]

Whatever the case, Gerhoh memorialized the First Crusade as a triumphant, miracle-laden event. It was a crucial moment in history but not so much in salvation history. Rather, it offered Gerhoh a chance to revel in some of his deepest fantasies about how the world ought to work. Three fantasies in particular:

First, Jerusalem was a place where Frenchmen and Germans fought and prayed together in harmony. After the Franks defeated Egyptian armies at Ascalon in August 1099 and thereby secured their recent conquest Jerusalem, "Germans sang according to their custom, and the Franks yelled after their own fashion, raising such a ruckus unto heaven that its echo reverberated from the mountains to the valleys." Gerhoh saw this as fulfilling a prophecy buried in Christian liturgy, that mountains and hills "will sing a song before God, and all the trees of the forest shall clap their hands."[11] During the many papal schisms, France and Germany invariably backed different popes. It was a recurring, dissonant motif in Gerhoh's life. In 1099, for an instant at least, the two linguistic groups managed to sing together. Their harmonies may not have been perfect—the German language, Gerhoh believed, was apt for singing; the French language, not so much—but it was the best one could hope for.[12] That historical moment of peace was one that Gerhoh clearly wished to transfer to his own age two generations later and to his own western quarter of the globe.

Second, Jerusalem provided an example of Gerhoh's particular vision of how churchmen ought to live. For Gerhoh was a canon who followed the rule of St. Augustine. His way of life blended monastic discipline with pastoral care and study. It would prove one of the dominant ideals in twelfth-century Europe, and it also thrived in Jerusalem.[13] "There are in the same city four great houses of canons regular, men who follow the common life blessed by the holy apostles and professed according to the rule of holy Augustine."[14]

Third and most important, the crusade demonstrated the cooperative relationship that ought to exist between secular and ecclesiastical leaders. The latter group prayed according to the Augustinian fashion, in the manner of the Apostles, and the former drew swords to fight as needed. "For to protect those [Augustinian] congregations and many others, who worship and fear God in that city, *the angel of the Lord has set camps around the ones who fear God*, carefully ordered divisions of knights, who are always on hand and ready to fight pagans."[15]

Such was crusader Jerusalem, a land where different Western peoples lived in harmony, some of them following the rule of Augustine, others protecting them in their calling. The political and spiritual factions that dominated Gerhoh's life—the schisms and the jostling for power—had no place in the city of Christ and in the shadows of Babylon, where pagans worshipped a god called Muhammad.[16] It was a unique setting, for God had set watchmen there both visible (knights) and invisible (angels), as well as religious men, followers of the apostolic example, who, "because they are the poor of Christ, it is not to be doubted that their angels always see the face of the Father, and"—at the risk of repetition—"*the angel of the Lord has set camps around those who fear God.*"[17]

Gerhoh's Disillusionment

Like Otto, Bernard, and others, Gerhoh felt no early doubt about the righteousness of the Second Crusade or about the probability of its success. In 1148, while writing a commentary on Psalm 39, he took a moment to celebrate the crusaders' departure and their anticipated victory.[18] The psalmist says that he had been waiting for God, and that the Lord heard him. "As often as [the psalmist] speaks, he knows that God hears him, because Israel receives some consolation. So now in the year of the Lord 1148, great consolation has come to Israel." Recently, Gerhoh continues, there had been real desolation in that land, because "kings and princes" had come together against it—a reference to the fall of Edessa.[19] Now, however, other "kings and princes are coming together as one to inflict vengeance against the nations that devastated God's church and attacked the city of Jerusalem, where the tomb of the Lord lies."[20]

Gerhoh's description of the scene is familiar. Silver trumpets sounded and crowds assembled, called by Pope Eugenius III and

Abbot Bernard of Clairvaux. Sermons thundered, miracles coruscated, and an earthquake shook the land.²¹ Knights readily settled disputes before departure. Following Christ's example, they offered enemies the kiss of peace and then set out for battle, ready to become human sacrifices for the Lord. Not all soldiers were of equal virtue, but Gerhoh prefers to emphasize the positive. "Who can doubt that they should be counted as saints? By fighting and winning they make gains for Christ and by dying they will gain Christ for themselves!"²²

As with the First Crusade, prophets seemed to have foretold victory. Levels of meaning—the literal, allegorical, moral, and apocalyptic—were merging together, just as Guibert of Nogent had believed them to have done forty years earlier. The key text for Gerhoh was, again, the Song of Songs, where sixty of Israel's strongest men surround the bed of Solomon, armed with swords, "just as they are now armed to protect and defend the tomb of Christ!" Their swords would defend them against "the fears of the night," according to scripture, which Gerhoh interprets as sexual temptation. A Christian army must remain continent, as the crusaders most certainly would do. "Hence it is a delight for me or any faithful Catholic how this song commemorates times long past and mixes them with current events."²³

It was probably no coincidence that this latest outburst of enthusiasm was happening at the same time (or so it seemed, without benefit of hindsight) as Henry IV's war with the papacy was winding down. Gerhoh's language on this point was near Shakespearian. "After the long winter of simony, the holy vine of sweet springtime flowers anew."²⁴

Of course, the Second Crusade did not go as planned, and disillusionment hit Gerhoh harder than most. Unlike Otto of Freising, he did not obscure his dismay with literary tropes and elisions. Gerhoh was simply bitter, his shame at the crusade's failure dovetailing with the interminable schism between Alexander and Victor. He wrestled with these questions directly in his book *On the Investigation of Antichrist*. In 1161, as he recalled how the expedition had started fourteen years earlier, Gerhoh does not even mention Edessa. The crusade happened because of Jerusalemite Christians. Messengers from the East had complained at the courts of kings and princes, at the councils of bishops, and at the feet of Pope Eugenius, and before "that column, that shining light of the church, the abbot of Clairvaux" about Jerusalem's troubles. Hordes of enemy nations were attacking Christians in the Holy Land, subjecting it to plunder and fire. If help from across the sea did not come soon, Saracens would conquer

Jerusalem, kill its citizens, and claim the holy city and the Lord's Sepulcher for themselves. The response was overwhelming. "I would judge that such a multitude of men, knights and infantry both, had never before assembled," Gerhoh concludes.[25]

But Gerhoh acknowledges the usual problems. Too many poor folk joined the army. They may have hoped that God would feed them manna from heaven in the desert, but instead they starved or drowned during floods (the same floods witnessed by Otto of Freising). The enemy constantly harassed Conrad's armies, although it did not directly engage them until late into their march through Anatolia. German soldiers set a camp where they thought themselves safe, and the Turks ambushed them, all but wiped them out—left the desert road covered in corpses.[26] Gerhoh also describes the sufferings of the French, how Louis VII endured still worse humiliation at Antioch when "the princes of the city violently robbed him of his wife's company." She later returned to his side, but not to his intimacy or trust. Later still, Gerhoh says, they divorced but "for other reasons."[27]

At last, when the armies reached Jerusalem, they learned shocking news. Gerhoh alone reports it, though he claims to have heard the story from King Conrad.[28] Namely, Jerusalem had never been in danger. There had been occasional raids, but nothing beyond ordinary skirmishes. The entire justification for the crusade—again, Gerhoh does not bring up Edessa—was a fake. The Jerusalemites had stirred up the entire earth to this expedition, which resulted in so many Christian deaths, "not for the sake of peace, which they enjoyed already and completely, but because they wished to increase the gold and silver in their treasuries."[29] They thought they had succeeded, too. After forcing the crusade to abandon the siege of Damascus, they collected massive bribes from the Damascenes. God, however, did not long permit them to celebrate. Their gold turned out to be burnt copper. So much Christian blood for so little money. Or as Gerhoh concluded, "What an ending!"[30]

Gerhoh's vitriolic rhetoric against the Jerusalemites is remarkable. He even conflates them with Jews, the gold standard of twelfth-century abuse.

> Jerusalem! Jerusalem! You once killed the prophets who had been sent to you—you stoned them to death! Why have you decided to add new murders of Christians to old ones, unless you thought that by doing so you might top off with Christian blood your father's half-full measuring cup? Or what counsel convinced you to do so, to sell so much blood at such a small price, unless

driven by the same avarice that persuaded Judas to sell our master, the Lord of all, for thirty pieces of silver?[31]

Not just an expression of disillusionment, Gerhoh sees Jerusalem—despite all its redemptive and salvific allure—as a source of corruption. The Holy Land was the place of Christ's ministry, but it was also the home of Simon Magus, the Samarian conjuror who gave his name to simony, the selling of church offices, the sin that reformers like Gerhoh saw as the source for the worst spiritual infections of the age, the root of papal schism under Frederick Barbarossa.[32]

In short, Gerhoh's diatribe against Jerusalem goes beyond the Second Crusade and the leadership of the Frankish East. It is a devaluing of Jerusalem itself, an argument that Western Christians need not travel there anymore and indeed probably should not have gone there in the first place. Gerhoh did not merely reject the Second Crusade. He rejected crusading, or at least the goal of crusading, the need to protect and defend the city where Christ's tomb lay, the purported center of the world.

Putting the Last Emperor to Bed

Disillusionment need not necessarily lead to despair. In Gerhoh's case it became a spark for creativity, even genius. It forced him to rethink fundamental questions of history, and in the end, he did not content himself with tearing down old dreams. He built new ones, starting with a set of rules about how to read prophecy.

Such guidelines were necessary. The Apocalypse had proven equivocal. Signs and miracles could mislead. "I have seen with my own eyes honestly false miracles that I do not know how to explain." Specifically, Gerhoh saw some of the supposed recipients of miracles who later returned to their former conditions—the lame walking on crutches, the blind being led by guides. Whether the healing had been ephemeral or the illnesses never genuine in the first place or whether the sick had faked their own cures for the sake of attention, Gerhoh does not say. He also does not give names or dates, but he almost certainly had in mind Bernard of Clairvaux's tour of Germany. Not only does he place his observation about deceptive miracles near the end of a long discussion of the Second Crusade, but he locates it immediately after an excerpt from Bernard's self-exculpatory treatise *On Consideration*.[33] The miracles had seemed authentic at the time. In retrospect, however, their interpretation required caution and even a healthy dose of skepticism.

The same might be said of the signs that had preceded the crusade. A great and terrible wind had blown through Germany in 1145 or 1146. "Coming from Western kingdoms and lasting almost eight hours it crossed the same lands which afterwards we saw the army cross." The meaning of the storm seemed transparent. Indeed, there were precedents. Great movements in the skies portended great movements of peoples. In the context of the First Crusade, meteor showers had foretold the march to the East. In Gerhoh's day, a comet crossed the heavens and suffused the skies with crimson—a sanguinary warning to the Saracens.[34]

But what had the signs of 1146 actually presaged? In retrospect, the wind referred to the "terrors of Heaven" described in the Little Apocalypse, a warning about the "sterile and baleful" outcome of the campaign. As for the comet, it did foretell blood, just not Saracen blood. Gerhoh also describes how carrion meat fell from heaven, perhaps God's parody of the manna that the army's poor were hoping to find in Middle Eastern deserts. The physical world had spoken with the voice of God, but it had provided no usable information.[35]

Prophetic signs in scripture presented similar difficulties. Gerhoh describes the book of Revelation (borrowing from Jerome) as "full of as many secrets as words—no, truly, in each of its words many senses lie hidden."[36] Any claim to have unlocked its meaning—as if there were only one meaning—demanded skepticism.

Bearing in mind these caveats, Gerhoh does offer a few interpretive guidelines. Prophetic readings fall into two categories: type and trope. According to type, prophecies point to specific events at particular moments and places. God's language, however, is always multivalent. He speaks not just to one audience at one time but to all peoples at all times. "Typic" prophecies therefore recur on the level of trope, of similitude or likeness—which is an elaborate way of saying that the same words predict multiple events. But with a difference. The secondary, "tropic" meanings do not occur with the specificity of their original ones. Language is looser, more charged with allegory than it was the first time.[37]

Gerhoh brings this methodology to bear on Antichrist. Consider first Antichrist's purported origins. Pseudo-Methodius and Adso held that he would be a Jew born from the tribe of Dan, based on Genesis 49:17: "Dan is a snake on the road, a viper on the path." Gerhoh refers to this verse and expands on it significantly, drawing together several biblical passages about Dan that point to that tribe's malefic destiny. Dan shall produce a destructive force, and the most likely identity of that force is Antichrist.

Yet these words are prophetic, obscure by design. They do not necessarily refer to Antichrist, especially "since some argue that this prophecy [about Dan] has been fulfilled through Samson." A member of the tribe of Dan famous for his strength and coiffure, Samson used serpentine cunning and leonine might in his wars against the Philistines. Antichrist will no doubt be snakelike, but none of these passages need connect him literally to Dan. The serpentine, destructive Danite has already lived and died to the letter. His tropic successors were free to be of any tribal or ethnic identity. It is a radical argument, an attack against a thousand-year-old tradition. Otto of Freising had undermined it, but only elliptically. With one bold stroke, Gerhoh invalidated Antichrist's Jewish origins.[38]

According to the same traditions, Antichrist would be born in Babylon. No passage in scripture specifically makes this point, although Gerhoh sees some interpretive potential in Jeremiah 1:14: "Then the Lord said to me, 'From the north evil shall rain down on all the world's inhabitants.'" Gerhoh correctly notes that the verse refers to wars between Jerusalem and Babylon, which lay to the northeast of Jerusalem. Antichrist will rain down evil on the world; therefore, Antichrist might be Babylonian.

The prophecy, however, had already been fulfilled to the letter, and by Nebuchadnezzar, no less. It might be fulfilled again, but if so "north" need not refer to a particular city, Babylon or otherwise. "North" in the Bible can symbolize the devil, "the destructive provost of death," as Gerhoh, "provost of Reichersberg," titles him. Even if that passage from Jeremiah did pertain to Babylon and to Antichrist, Babylon could be, exegetically, Rome. Writing in the midst of a papal schism that was, in Gerhoh's analysis, the fault of Roman citizens, this reading of Antichrist's origins would have seemed compelling. Then again, "Babylon" can refer to worldly confusion, such as the confusion that had long plagued Gerhoh about which pope to support in the schism, a schism that seemed a harbinger of Antichrist's reign.[39]

More importantly in terms of crusading, Antichrist was expected to establish his kingdom in Jerusalem. According to 2 Thessalonians 2:4, "he will sit upon his throne in the Temple of God and declare himself to be a god." Based on Daniel, Antichrist will set up "an abomination of desolation" in the same temple, and his followers will make sacrifices to it. Christ confirmed the general tenor of this prophecy by saying, "When you see the abomination of desolation standing where it ought not to be (let he who reads this understand), then whoever is in Jerusalem should flee to the mountains."[40] The meaning, again, seems clear. Antichrist will establish his rule from Jerusalem, erect a statue of himself in the temple, and demand that his followers make sacrifices to it.

The enthronement in the temple was such a dramatic, cherished aspect of medieval prophecy that Gerhoh felt reluctant to discard it; he recognized at least that his readers might not want to give it up. "I will not deny the possibility that Antichrist might sit in a temple made by hand, but I do not think it is necessary for him to do so to fulfill this prophecy."[41] First, the word "temple" is equivocal. It can refer either to the Temple in Jerusalem or to the "spiritual temple," which is to say, the church. As Paul wrote in another letter, "Do you not know that your bodies are the temple of the Holy Spirit?"[42] Given how shaky Gerhoh's spiritual temple, the church of Alexander III, appeared to be during the long schism, this allegorical reading likely sounded persuasive.

But more importantly, this prophecy about the abomination in the temple, like some of the earlier ones, had already been fulfilled to the letter—not once but many times. The original "abominator" was Antiochus IV Epiphanes, who in 167 BCE had erected idols in the Temple of Jerusalem that stood there for three years.[43] Two centuries later, in 44 CE, Herod Agrippa, who had killed the apostle James, had himself publicly enthroned wearing a shimmering golden cloak. The people proclaimed him a god. When he did not correct them, an angel of the Lord struck him dead, and worms ate his body. At about the same time (Gerhoh's chronology is confused), the Roman emperor Caligula ordered statues of himself erected in Jewish places of worship, most notably in Jerusalem. In doing so, he sparked the rebellion that led to the pillaging of Jerusalem and destruction of the Herodian Temple in 70 CE. Gerhoh interprets all these events according to his rule of prophetic types. Daniel's prophecy about the establishment of the abomination of desolation had been fulfilled literally, according to type, in the times of Tiberius and Caligula. It was not necessary to fulfill it again to the letter in the time of Antichrist. There need be no material throne set up in the literal temple. Allegory would suffice.[44]

Gerhoh then imagines an immediate objection to his argument (a sign of just how attached he expected readers to be to the idea of an apocalyptic war in Jerusalem). Revelation refers specifically to a beast of the earth who will force men to venerate statues of another beast. There would be literal idols, not allegorical ones. John of Patmos, the author of Revelation, thus appears to confirm at least part of the literal reading of Daniel.

In devising a response, Gerhoh offered a third, especially damning objection to this interpretive tradition. Namely, the beast, or Antichrist, is known to be a creature of great cunning. Such an astute character would not be so stupid as to think he could trick Christians into idolatry. Nor could he expect other idolaters (Gerhoh probably imagines Muslims) to give up the statues with which they were comfortable in order to venerate a new, unfamiliar image. No—prophecy in this case reveals only how deceit spreads under the guise of truth. The beast, or Antichrist, will be a vessel of heresy and schism, in Gerhoh's view two of the greatest threats to Christianity. "To set up an idol in a holy place is to set up a falsehood in opposition to Catholic truth, or else it is a sect opposed to Catholic unity."[45]

In short, what Gerhoh imagined was a new, homegrown Apocalypse. He was not alone. His thought echoes, for example, in the prophetic writings of his contemporary Hildegard of Bingen. The nun Hildegard was a polymath, known as much for her writings on medicine and her musical compositions as for her theology. Hildegard was also a brilliant allegorist. She expressed ideas more visually and viscerally than Gerhoh.[46] In one of her visions, for example, she saw Antichrist ripping his way, literally, out of the body of the church (see fig. 13).

Described and illustrated in her book *Scivias*, the church appears as an elegant crowned woman but with sores on her genitalia, bruises on her legs, and blood on her shins. From her loins— gnawing and tearing with teeth of iron, like the fourth beast in Daniel 7—emerges Antichrist, a monstrous, fiery-eyed, black head covered in shit.[47] Near the woman stands a mountain, which represents, as in Nebuchadnezzar's dream, the kingdom of God. According to Hildegard's text, Antichrist will try to climb that mountain, but God shall strike him dead with a thunderbolt and the whole mountain will stink of the excrement (the works of Satan) that had covered the creature's head.[48]

Hildegard's images have a power Gerhoh could not equal, yet their conclusions were nearly identical. The ultimate enemy would come from within the church, from the West—Hildegard in her vision pointedly envisions her disemboweled church standing to the West, in the heart of Christendom, not in the Holy Land of the East. For Gerhoh, the "abomination of desolation in the temple" is corruption within the church, especially the sin of simony. As Otto of Freising concluded, too, the Apocalypse will begin at home.

To reach this point in salvation history, Gerhoh traveled a long, meandering route. Like Otto, he focused on key moments in the relationship between empire and church—the reign of Constantine, the crowning of Charlemagne, the wars between Henry IV and Gregory VII, the crusades, the ongoing papal schism—with frequent pauses to meditate on the symbolic resonances that connect these various moments. He concludes with a return to his original point about the abomination of desolation, to argue that his own time is the most apocalyptically charged in history. "However abominable was the desolation when an image of Caesar was set up in that holy place in the Temple of Jerusalem (or any other handmade statue), I honestly think that avarice—which is slavery to idols—placed in the see of blessed Peter is something more abominable still."[49] The end might be nigh, but it will have nothing to do with Jerusalem and nothing to do with crusading.

Gerhoh's Apocalyptic Vision of History

In developing his own historical models, Gerhoh drew inspiration especially from Bernard of Clairvaux, with whom he had discussed face-to-face the politics of reform.[50] Bernard, as described earlier, divided church history into four periods, onto which he grafted a number of images, notably the four horsemen of the Apocalypse and the reference in the Gospel to the fourth hour of the watch. The defining events of these four periods are: the martyrs of the early church; the later battle against heresy; the long era of peace that concealed sinful business conducted in the shadows; and the appearance of Antichrist, the noonday demon, who would usher in the Last Judgment and the end of days. Bernard, as we have seen, wavered on the question of whether he was living through the Last Days, but by the end of his life, especially in the aftermath of the Second Crusade, an imminent apocalypse seemed more likely than not.

Gerhoh tinkered with similar models throughout his life.[51] In the *Investigation of Antichrist*, written in 1162, he applied Bernard's thought, with some minor revision, to the history of the Temple in Jerusalem. Its initial construction corresponded to the work of the early church. David, who began it, is a type of Christ, and Solomon, who completed it, is a type of the Holy Spirit.[52]

The Temple's destruction under Nebuchadnezzar corresponded to the second age, of persecution and martyrdom. Gerhoh draws particular inspiration from Daniel 3, where the three Hebrew men, Shadrach, Meshach, and Abednego, are forced into a fiery furnace for refusing to worship a gold statue of Nebuchadnezzar. (Nebuchadnezzar had apparently learned the wrong lesson from his

earlier dream, where Daniel compared his reign to a statue's splendid golden head.) The Babylonian king was a type of Roman emperor.
His persecution of Jewish wise men made him a forerunner of Nero,
killer of Christians.[53] Still, Nebuchadnezzar was a pliant symbol.
His friendship with Daniel made him forerunner to the Emperor
Constantine. In this reading, Daniel was a type of Pope Sylvester, who
legendarily cured Constantine of leprosy in the baptismal font. In
gratitude, Constantine invested Sylvester with the city of Rome and
gave him authority over all bishops and princes of the world, an idea
immortalized in the Middle Ages' most famous forgery, the Donation
of Constantine. Likewise, in Gerhoh's imagination, Nebuchadnezzar
and Daniel divvied up earthly and spiritual responsibilities amicably,
setting an example for political and spiritual harmony that Christian
Europe seldom achieved.[54]

The rebuilding of the Temple under Cyrus of Persia in Gerhoh's
system points to the outbreaks of heresy in the third age. Heretics
began their malicious work under Constantine's immediate successors, his son Constantius and later Julian the Apostate (r. 361–63 CE).
This connection to heresy grew not out of the Temple itself (though
Gerhoh spent considerable time meditating on why the Second Temple
was only half as tall as the original). Rather, the Israelites faced a
series of obstacles and enemies, described in the book of Nehemiah,
most notably Sanballat the Samaritan, Tobias the Ammonite, and
Geshem the Arab. Together they represent the advent of heretics,
particularly the Arians, who corrupted Christian learning and who
achieved great victories with the help of Gothic kings. For a long
time, Arians hindered the construction of Christianity's spiritual
temple, but church fathers, such as Hilary, Ambrose, Augustine, and
Gregory the Great exposed their lies.[55]

The fourth and final phase in the Temple's history, according
to Gerhoh, concerned its desecration by the Macedonian ruler
Antiochus. "As for the evils which the Jewish people suffered under
the kingdom of Greeks—the profanation of the Temple, the building of a gymnasium under the citadel, the prostitution of boys, the
placing of an abominable idol in the Temple along with a brothel,
the selling of the priesthood, coercion to follow the Gentile rite, acts
of mass murder"—these things, Gerhoh says, pertained directly to
his own lifetime. Simoniacal princes and libidinous priests alike were
robbing Christ of his rightful possessions.[56] Had Gerhoh been writing a generation earlier and in the wake of Bohemond's preaching
tour of 1106, for example, he would likely have drawn comparisons
between Jerusalem under Antiochus and Jerusalem under the

Turks. But after the Second Crusade, Gerhoh preferred to focus on the allegorical Jerusalem in Europe, not the literal city in the East.

When Gerhoh returned to this theme in his final book, *On the Fourth Watch of the Night*, the debt to Bernard becomes more obvious, starting with the title. Gerhoh likely would not have thought much about the "four watches" had Bernard not led the way. The source material is the story of Christ walking on water. The apostles were crossing the Sea of Galilee in a small boat. The skies were clear at first, but the weather worsened. By the fourth watch of the night (late in the night, near dawn), the winds had so turned against them that they feared drowning. Then Christ appeared, walking on water. It seemed that he was going to pass them by. At any rate, the apostles were terrified because they thought him a ghost. Christ turned to reassure them, and Peter responded, "Lord, if it is you, command me to walk to you on the water." Christ did so, and Peter stepped onto the waves. But the winds terrified him, and he slipped suddenly beneath the water. Christ pulled him to safety inside the boat, disappointed at his lack of faith.[57]

For Gerhoh, the critic and reformer, the story offered a nice lesson, beyond the obvious ones. Currently, tempests of greed and pride threatened to destroy the church, symbolized by the boat in which the apostles sat. Charity had grown so cold that it seemed Christ would walk by without extending a hand. When Christ took notice of his followers, Peter (allegorically, and later literally, the pope) lost faith and nearly drowned, but the Lord pulled him to safety.[58]

Like Bernard, Gerhoh does not confine himself to the fourth watch, the only one mentioned in scripture, but instead talks about the first three watches as well (see table 4, chap. 8). Again, the four hours symbolize four ages of church history. Gerhoh begins with the persecution of martyrs, followed by the advent of heresy, and then, for the third watch, the general corruption of morals. This third watch he dates with precision. It started with the pontificate of Gregory the Great (d. 604), the last of the church fathers and the man who had laid down the decisive arguments against heresy. It ended with Gregory VII (d. 1085), the implacable defender of church liberty and unyielding enemy of Henry IV. Gregory had "struck the head from the house of the wicked when he condemned King Henry," who had elevated a wicked and schismatic Antipope, Clement III, thus empowering a small army of simoniacal bishops.[59]

Gerhoh then departs slightly from Bernard, who had associated the fourth watch with the noonday demon, Antichrist (see table 5). Gerhoh's reading was actually grimmer. It was the age of avarice, "the

Table 5: Bernard's and Gerhoh's Fourfold Models of History

Bernard's Model of Four Hours	Gerhoh's First Model of Four Hours, from *On Antichrist*	Gerhoh's Second Model of Four Hours, from *On the Fourth Hour*
1. Persecution/Martyrs	1. Work of Christ	1. Persecution/Martyrs
2. Heretics/Doctors	2. Persecution/Martyrs	2. Heretics/Doctors
3. "Business in Shadows"	3. Heretics/Doctors	3. Corruption of Morals
4. Noonday Demon	4. Simony	4. Avarice

contrary wind that threatens the disciples in their boat."[60] In some ways a continuation of the third watch, the corruption of the final age had become omnipresent, reaching its nadir with the papal schism in 1159. Knights were no longer content with their stipends. Priests were no longer satisfied with the income provided by a single altar. With avarice unchecked, "sound and true doctrine is detested, as if a phantasm," in the same way that the apostles had thought Christ a ghost, walking a stormy sea at the fourth watch of the night.[61]

In sum, Gerhoh's fourfold model, particularly his second version, closely follows Bernard's. The three key periods in Christian history concern battles against persecutors, heretics, and internal enemies. In Gerhoh's reading, the fourth age had begun. Did he also believe, like the aging Bernard of Clairvaux, that the time of Antichrist was at hand? Gerhoh hesitated. In the *Investigation of Antichrist*, he made the near obligatory disclaimer, drawn from the Gospel. "It is not ours to know the day of judgment, the time of the final correction of all, which God has kept in his own power."[62] And he makes the point throughout his work that prophetic imagery is polyvalent—no image more so than the figure of Antichrist. Besides the obvious historical prototypes (Nebuchadnezzar, Antiochus, Herod, and Nero), there were arguably as many Antichrists as there were sinners. Following the church fathers, "every Christian who does not live according to the rule of his profession or teaches something contrary to it is an Antichrist."[63] The fourth watch "would seem to threaten," but Gerhoh could not say definitively that it had begun.[64]

On the other hand, just as Gerhoh believed that his schism (1159–77) was different from all the ones that had come before, so he seems to have believed that the apocalyptic signs of his time were different from earlier ones. In his *Investigation of Antichrist*, he had said that the schism under Henry IV (1080–1101) corresponded to the release of Satan foretold in Revelation 20: the inauguration of the final conflict with Gog and Magog before Christ finally would return to earth. "For at that time, through the previously mentioned and still to be mentioned King Henry, the devil was seemingly released—no, truly, he was released and began to act as a tyrant. A thousand years had passed since the Lord's passion, and during that time the devil, as just said, had been confined to a prison and locked away there."[65]

It is a radical indictment of Henry IV, but Gerhoh's perspective was shared by others, Hildegard of Bingen among them. Based on visions she experienced in 1163, Hildegard compared Henry's disastrous reign to the great flood of Noah. After the flood, Hildegard wrote, humanity began to ascend in virtues, especially during the age of the prophets, whose work announced the advent of Christ. Progress continued through the times of the apostles and early church fathers, who preserved and spread Christ's doctrine, but then stopped with the birth of "a secular judge, a philanderer," "of royal name," who ruled like another Nero until God struck him down, as he had done other tyrants. Starting with the years of that tyrant's life, the fertility of the earth began to dry up and all things turned to the worse, just as it had done from the time of the flood to the prophets.[66] In brief, by appointing an antipope and starting the Investiture Controversy, Henry IV had wrecked the world and opened the door for Antichrist.

Gerhoh makes an equally provocative, if understated, comparison in *On the Fourth Watch of the Night*, when he describes the two popes most famous for opposing Henry—Gregory VII and Urban II—as "two witnesses, two lamps, two candelabra standing against that great Antichrist."[67] The reference is to Revelation 11:3–4, where the two witnesses, usually identified as Enoch and Elijah, were sent to preach in the Last Days. In most interpretations of prophecy (though not in Lambert of Saint-Omer's or Otto of Freising's), their message would lead to the conversion of the Jews. An enraged Antichrist then would strike them dead.

In the *Investigation of Antichrist*, Gerhoh briefly dealt with these ideas and admitted that they confounded him. He was unsure whether Enoch and Elijah (or Elijah and Moses—he wasn't sure of their precise identities) would return in their own flesh or would spiritually possess others. Similarly, he did not know whether their killing would be "material or spiritual."[68] This early cautious and confused reading is not incompatible with the later radical idea Gerhoh had suggested in *On the Fourth Watch of the Night*. Henry had made war on Gregory and Urban, but he hadn't killed either of them, as Revelation foretold of Antichrist and the two witnesses. He had, however, outlived both popes. That fact alone may have given Gerhoh enough allegorical rope to tie together current events and apocalyptic prophecy. As Gerhoh entered his own last days (he died in 1169), apocalyptic signs seemed more and more to line up with recent happenings in Europe and to connect little if at all with wars in the Holy Land.

In terms of imaginative geography, however, Gerhoh ends up in the same place as the crusaders—the center of the earth. "Come, Jesus our Savior, work salvation in the middle of the earth, that is, in the middle of the church, make peace between kingdom and priesthood."[69] The passage refers to Psalm 73:12 (74:12, NRSV), the verse most commonly used to locate Jerusalem in the world's center: "God our King before the ages worked salvation in the middle of the earth." No longer a city, the center of the earth had become that elusive place between popes and emperors where Gerhoh might find peace.

The Death of Crusading

It is difficult to know how widely Gerhoh's ideas circulated in the twelfth century. He had few disciples. He did, however, have some attitudinal heirs—people who, even if they did not know him, moved in the same circles and were subject to the same influences. One of the most extraordinary among them was an English cleric known as Ralph the Black.[70]

As with Gerhoh, much of Ralph's career was caught up in aftershocks from the Investiture Controversy—in Ralph's case, the conflict between King Henry II of England and Archbishop Thomas Becket of Canterbury. Famously, the two men had been friends before Henry appointed Thomas archbishop in 1162. From that point forward, their relationship turned rancorous, largely over whether kings could tax churches or act as judges over clerics convicted of secular crimes. Under threat of imprisonment or murder, Becket went into exile in 1164 and was unable to return to England until 1170, though his conflict with the king remained unresolved. Finally, on December 29 of that year, after Henry had pronounced some intemperate words at dinner, four knights decided to settle the dispute permanently. As the sun set over Canterbury and while Becket performed the vespers liturgy, they chopped off the top of his skull and stirred up his brains for good measure. Blood, brains, and bones alike became miracle-working relics. Henry and the now-dead Thomas were only reconciled in 1174, when the king performed public penance at Canterbury.

For the most part, Ralph the Black was a bit player in this drama. He probably studied in Paris at the same time as Becket, but he kept a low profile during most of the later conflict. Just before Becket's murder in 1170, he threw in his lot with the archbishop, a political misstep he compounded by siding with Henry II's sons during a failed rebellion against their father in 1173–74. As a result, Ralph spent most of his mature years in exile, able to return to England as a canon at Lincoln Cathedral only after Henry II's death in 1189.

In one of his books composed in the later years of his life, a chronicle of world history, Ralph used the model of the Six Ages as an organizing principle. He was a little inconsistent with it. At one point, he said that the fourth age began with David and the fifth with the Babylonian Captivity. Later, he started the fourth age with Moses and the fifth with Solomon's construction of the Temple. Like Lambert of Saint-Omer, Ralph also was keenly aware of the importance of the four kingdoms from Nebuchadnezzar's dream. Rather than adopt the westward drift of *translatio imperii*, he preferred the geographic model of Orosius: Babylon in the East, Carthage in the South, Macedonia in the North, and Rome in the West.[71] Also, like Orosius and Lambert, Ralph noted the convergence of Babylon's fall and Rome's rise. It is difficult to tell if Ralph saw in this correspondence anything other than happy accident. "Certainly the empire in the East declined as the empire in the West rose," he observes simply.[72]

In sum, Ralph was aware of all the important prophetic structures and used them in his own writing. He did not give pride of place to apocalyptic readings of current events, but he did have the nagging sense that the world might be ending. Charity, he noted, was growing cold, even as history entered into its final winter months, a reference to Christ's words in the Little Apocalypse.[73] But it could also have been a straightforward meteorological observation. Around 1190, when Ralph was writing, average temperatures in Europe had dropped a full degree.[74]

As for the crusades, they barely receive notice. In his universal history, Ralph mentions the First Crusade twice, but only in passing. The first time was to give context to the rise of Robert Guiscard, Bohemond's father, in southern Italy; the second time, to discuss the precipitous fall of Robert of Normandy, who spent the last twenty-eight years of his life (1106–34) in prison. This latter instance is especially noteworthy for its inaccuracy. During the Easter liturgy at the Holy Sepulcher, Ralph claims, the famous holy fire descended from heaven and illuminated Robert's candle first—a sign that he ought to be king. The assembled crowd offered him the crown, but he refused it and instead rushed home in hopes of claiming the throne of England. But in fact Robert never attended the Easter liturgy in Jerusalem—he had long before headed back west—and the election of a king had nothing to do with the appearance of the Holy Fire.[75]

As for the Second Crusade, Ralph treated it only as a disaster "brought about by our sins." The reputations of the French king and German emperor suffered equally, and were redeemed—only partly by the honor associated with such a pilgrimage.[76] In another book, also written around 1190, he observes that the disasters of the Second Crusade were so well known and so often discussed that it was pointless to describe them.[77] Based on such a scattered, haphazard, and perfunctory treatment, it would appear that crusading held little interest for him.

But crusading is in fact central to Ralph's most ambitious work. Titled *On the Threefold Path of Pilgrimage to Jerusalem*, it examines the tensions between the Christian life and the military calling, as well as the place of crusading in history and spirituality. The central image of the work is familiar. A virtuous life is like a pilgrimage from the City of Man to the City God. The City of God is always Jerusalem. The City of Man has several guises. Ralph focuses on three biblical examples of this pilgrimage: the exodus of the Israelites from Egypt to the Promised Land; their later return from Babylon back to Jerusalem; and Peter's miraculous escape from prison into the city of Jerusalem. From unfavorable starting points—Egypt, Babylon, and prison—the Christian finally arrives at the same destination, not the geographic city of Jerusalem but rather its spiritual expression as a soul at peace.[78]

Alongside these allegorical paths, Ralph considers their literal counterpart, crusading. He does not dismiss crusading out of hand. Jerusalem remains important as a site of memory and a storehouse of relics.[79] But one does not need to go there literally—not ever. The interior pilgrimage is enough. A cross ought to be worn on the heart rather than on a soldier's cloak. To go to Jerusalem can be a useful exercise in penance. "Nevertheless, the labor and the journey do little good unless, as they say, the mystical pilgrimage has not first nurtured the man. Only then will the exercise benefit the soul more than the body."[80] This description of earthly pilgrimage is disparaging but within the bounds of tradition, even enshrined in crusading doctrine. According to the terms of the papal indulgences offered before the First and Second Crusades, knights needed to examine their souls and confess their sins before departure, if they wished to receive the full benefit of penance. One had to complete the inner quest first (which might very well prove to be a lifetime's work) before attempting the geographic one.[81]

In Ralph's interpretation, however, the crusader's vow to fight for Jerusalem was not just a morally neutral decision. It could be dangerous, for reasons that might be described as the "Thomas of Marle Syndrome." A pilgrim might believe that because he was traveling to the earthly Jerusalem, he would automatically attain the heavenly one. In practice, the mind might remain mired in the same vices that had caused a pilgrim to make his vow in the first place. The body in Jerusalem, the mind in Babylon. "The mistake is to place one's hope in pilgrimage alone, for *we all make many mistakes,* and so we require many medicines to treat our various ailments."[82] The key movement in pilgrimage is to depart from sin, not home.

Again, the language is traditional, going back to St. Jerome in the fourth century. More recently, twelfth-century theologians like Anselm of Bec and Bernard of Clairvaux had urged monks to seek Jerusalem in the monastery rather than in the Levant. Ralph, however, gives everyone, layman and cleric alike, the same advice: Find Jerusalem at home, and not only in churches. It could be anywhere. "Happy and wise, therefore, is he who makes a Jerusalem in his soul and his household and his kingdom and moves forward by this better method. In truth, he who makes a Jerusalem for himself derives no less merit from it than does he who goes all the way to Judea as a pilgrim."[83] A century earlier Guibert of Nogent had enthused that the crusade gave laymen a new road to salvation, a literal equivalent to the monks' spiritual journey. Ralph the Black believed that the spiritual path to Jerusalem, once the prerogative of monks, was now open to everyone, regardless of profession.

There was still another reason for knights to stay home. The most serious threat to Christendom was not Islam but heresy. Like the preachers of the so-called Albigensian Crusade in the early thirteenth century, Ralph saw heretics everywhere—the Manichees against whom Augustine had once battled were now invading Europe, tearing apart Christendom like the black head Hildegard had seen ripping through Lady Church's loins. "What is the benefit if an earthly Jerusalem is built, while the Zion that is our mother church is broken apart? If Palestine is liberated from the Saracens while the wickedness of unbelief runs riot at home? If unbelief is fought abroad while the purity of faith is trampled and ridiculed at home?"[84]

Ironically, Ralph frames this argument in terms of the East-West dichotomy characteristic of crusade rhetoric. War against Islam had made Christian Europe proud of its Western identity. The result, in

Ralph's mind, was not an increasing contempt or hatred for the East but a detachment from it. "What is the benefit for [our princes] if their land is emptied of men and wealth to consume men and wealth in the East, while evil makes the West perish?"[85]

Like Gerhoh and Otto, Ralph was not totally disinterested in Islam. He had a good grasp of its history, both in the grand sense (Muslims were descended from the children of Ishmael) and in particulars (the Islamic kingdom had split apart into factions after the seventh century Muslim conquest of Jerusalem).[86] Saracens also functioned as symbols for vice and sin in Ralph's allegorical system.[87] But whereas the conquest of vice was a moral necessity, the conquest of Saracens was a dicey spiritual proposition. A penitent sinner must make appropriate satisfaction to God, and "bloodshed of any sort is never appropriate satisfaction."[88] Warfare is justified when it is defensive, aimed at repelling an aggressor and thus creating peace, but arms cannot be taken up in aggression, even against Saracens. "Whoever seeks to spread the faith through violence has exceeded the discipline of the faith."[89]

Ralph is arguing here against the practice of forced conversions of Muslims, a problem which had never really arisen during the crusades. Muslims were simply the enemy, a dimly understood—or perhaps a deliberately misunderstood—villain, limbs of Antichrist, enemies of the Last Days, doomed to hell and loving that fact. Ralph believed otherwise. "They are men of the same condition and nature as we are."[90] For Ralph, Saracens participated in a shared humanity. In popular academic parlance, for Ralph, Muslims had ceased to be the Other.

The same could not be said of the Jerusalemite Franks. Their kingdom was "more dissolute than any other land; it has no reverence for God and excels all other places in terms of lasciviousness and gluttony."[91] Apart from Templars and Hospitallers, the immigrants to the East were criminals and exiles.[92] It was a land fully deserving of whatever punishment God might mete out against it.

And Ralph was not describing a Frank he did not know or had not seen. Rather, in 1185, probably in Paris, he had met a delegation from Jerusalem led by the patriarch Heraclius, traveling in Europe in hopes of calling attention to crises in Jerusalem. Ralph was unmoved.

> I saw the patriarch of Jerusalem come into western parts seeking aid, pomp-ously, ensconced in silver and gold accoutrement. His presentation was tire-some to hear on account of all the clatter his clothing made. I almost choked on the smoke from the various types of incense, which caused everyone's

clothes to reek and their brains to grow disturbed. I saw his cloak and have never seen another like it, or one so costly. In sum, no patriarch in the Western world has similar appurtenances. If we are to presume that the other extravagances of their land are like the ones I have seen, then I may conclude that God holds them in contempt.[93]

Pompous, effeminate, perfumed, garishly dressed—the Franks had gone native. They were Easterners; they were Other. They looked like Antichrist. And they were not worth saving.

Beyond the particular arguments, the most extraordinary aspect of Ralph's presentation is its date. He was writing around 1190, three years after Jerusalem and most of the Frankish East (not to mention the True Cross) had fallen to Saladin. French and English kings were preparing a new crusade, and Frederick Barbarossa had already departed for the Holy Land. At a time when Europeans were rallying together for the grandest crusading adventure of them all, Ralph was urging everyone to stay home, specifically King Philip Augustus of France.[94] Even the loss of Jerusalem could not shake Ralph's certainty. The important wars were the ones to be fought at home, against enemies spiritual and physical. If Empire had, according to Otto of Freising's formula, shifted to the West, it should stay there. Crusading was dead. Or, Ralph believed, it ought to be.

PART IV

The New Iron Kingdom

CHAPTER 11

Jerusalem Lost

WHAT HAPPENED IN 1187 is straightforward enough. Frankish settlers in the kingdom had seen it coming for some years. The purpose of the European tour by the odiferous Patriarch Heraclius in 1185 was to try to raise awareness about the situation there.[1] The kingdom of Jerusalem had survived for so long (and the First Crusade had succeeded) in part because of Muslim disunity—political, tribal, and credal. The First Crusaders and their heirs in the Holy Land had exploited divisions among the Seljuk Turks in the north, tribal groups nominally united under the Sunni Abbasid Caliphate in Baghdad, and between the Turks and Shi'i Fatimid Caliphate in the south to carve out a narrow space of survival in and around Jerusalem. In the 1150s and 1160s, however, the Turkish leader Nur ad-Din began to unite the various Syrian principalities. Then in 1169, one of his generals, Saladin, established himself as ruler of Egypt. Five years later, Nur ad-Din died unexpectedly, leaving a ten-year-old son, as-Salih, as heir. Saladin declared his loyalty to the ruling family, but by 1185, the year of Heraclius's tour, he was governing both Egypt and Syria in his own name. A united collection of Sunni states now surrounded the Frankish settlements. Barring significant aid from the West, the kingdom's survival was unlikely.

And it lasted only two more years. On July 4, 1187, Saladin's soldiers routed the armies of Jerusalem at the Battle of Hattin. The Frankish king, Guy of Lusignan, was captured along with several hundred followers. The relic of the True Cross was taken as loot. Two days later, all captured Templars and Hospitallers were beheaded, while a grimly satisfied Saladin looked on. King Guy was later freed in exchange for ransom and a vow never to fight against Muslims again (a vow from which Guy quickly obtained release). Over the next several weeks Saladin's armies took possession of nearly all the Franks' cities and castles until finally, on October 2, Jerusalem itself surrendered. Only Tripoli and Antioch remained under Frankish control. To all appearances, in the space of just four months, Saladin had obliterated the achievements of the First Crusade, which for nearly a century had seemed to be the pivotal event in human history.

Calls for a new crusade went out immediately. Barely a week after he became pope, Gregory VIII issued a bull called *Audita tremendi*, roughly translatable as "Shocking News." Dire prophecies had been fulfilled, notably Psalm 78: "God, the heathen have gone into your inheritance. They have polluted your holy Temple. They have made Jerusalem into a place to store apples. They have given the bodies of your saints to beasts of the earth, their flesh to birds of the air." Eighty years earlier, the chronicler Baldric of Bourgueil had put this same verse into the mouth of Urban II at Clermont as a way to describe what the Seljuk Turks had been doing in and around the Holy Sepulcher. Same enemy, same battleground, same response from the West.[2]

Although working from the usual playbook, Gregory made no reference to the First Crusade. It is a stark contrast to Eugenius III, who in 1145 had urged Christians to meditate on their forefathers' travails and achievements. Gregory did recycle some of the fundamentals of the First Crusade; he just did not mention that any of it had happened before. He talks, for example, about the heroism of the Maccabees. He offers an indulgence to anyone who departs with the right motives and who has properly confessed his sins. He exhorts soldiers to give up their aristocratic finery, including hunting dogs and falcons. In terms of recent events, he discusses only the Second Crusade, which he sees as a lost opportunity. "It was possible to attend to these things when Edessa and other land fell under the rule of the pagans. This outcome could have easily been prevented if the people who stayed there had renewed their penance and if, after offending God through their transgressions, they had placated him through conversion."[3] Rather than saying with Eugenius, "Think on the deeds of your forefathers," Gregory essentially said, "Don't mess up like the last bunch did." In the heat of the moment, the First Crusade had been written out of crusading history, the Second Crusade preserved only as a shaming device.

Put another way, Gregory was shocked at Jerusalem's fall because it undercut historical and prophetic expectation. Recalling its charged cartographic location, he writes, "He who worked salvation in the middle of the earth consented to carry out this work himself, such that tongue cannot say nor reason grasp how much we and all Christians must grieve. For that land has suffered again what it is read to have endured under the people of old."[4] The prose is contorted because the thought is unwelcome. Christianity was the perfect fulfillment of the promise of Judaism. Any student of the New Testament recognized that fact. And the First Crusade was the final righting and realization of Old Testament history. The Jews had lost Jerusalem repeatedly—the last time in 70 CE, when Roman legions destroyed their Temple. Judaism foundered, but, because of the Incarnation, Christianity had laid claim to its spiritual legacy. And in 1099, Christians had taken over its geographic inheritance too. The victory would be permanent, the ruler of Egypt sulking back to Cairo after his loss at Ascalon realizing that he would never defeat the Christians. But like the Jews of Old, the Franks had lost Jerusalem. Not a more perfect realization of the Old Covenant, the Franks were now simply new Jews whom God punished as he saw fit. It was a sobering realization.

In this context, the First Crusade was an inconvenient memory, bordering on a historical and mathematical impossibility. Consider a mid-twelfth-century manuscript containing the history of Robert the Monk.[5] It comprises ninety-two folios, of which Robert's chronicle occupies ninety-one. On the last two pages, a scribe has written a short, celebratory history called, "On the Ten Conquests of Jerusalem." It consists of a list, beginning with the story of David and ending with the First Crusade. It could have contained many more items, as it notes, but the point was not to present an accurate summary of Jerusalem's history but rather to associate the First Crusade with the number ten, a figure charged with spiritual meaning. It symbolized divine law through the Ten Commandments; the number of the Trinity added to the seven gifts of the Holy Spirit; not to mention in its Roman form, "X," the sign of the Cross and of Christ. And coming at the end of this copy of Robert the Monk's narrative it was the number for the First Crusade, a symbol for completion, a sign that the earthly battles for Jerusalem had come to an end.

A few years after the list's composition, probably with no small dismay, another scribe filled in blank space on the last page with these words: "In the year of our Lord 1187, on July 4, the land of Jerusalem was captured by King Saladin of Damascus and Babylon."

The same hand then noted laconically in the margin, "The Eleventh Time."[6] Ten symbolized perfection. Eleven, according to St. Augustine, meant sin because it meant going beyond the law. It meant transgression.[7] The story of Jerusalem now went to eleven.

The Lost Ark of Christ

Gregory VIII had no doubt about whom to blame for Jerusalem's fall. It was Frankish settlers in the East. The crusader settlements had always teetered on the edge of extinction, but as the pope imagined their world, it was one of endless harems and hashish. Fears that they might go native had finally born fruit. But Gregory also acknowledged that there were problems in Europe, with "not only the sins of the inhabitants of that land, but also with our sins and the sins of all Christian peoples." On the one hand, it is an admission of shared guilt; on the other hand, an implicit acknowledgment that the Eastern and Western Franks had become two different cultures, two entirely different breeds.[8]

At least some in the West, though, were especially culpable. Most likely Gregory had in mind the princes and knights who had pledged to go to Jerusalem then postponed their departures, in some cases interminably. Most notorious among them was Henry II of England. In 1172, two years after the murder of Archbishop Thomas Becket, Henry negotiated a sort of penitential truce with Pope Alexander III. Part of the agreement required him to travel to Jerusalem as a pilgrim, but he continually deferred his vow through monies sent east and through the foundation of churches at home.[9] With Henry as Europe's best-known procrastinator, it is no wonder that his court produced one of the fiercest and most original advocates for the Third Crusade, a cleric and courtier named Peter of Blois.

Like Ralph the Black, who saw Heraclius speak and nearly choked on the patriarch's perfume, Peter lived, wrote, and worked in the shadow cast by Becket's murder. He was a cleric torn between loyalty to his king and veneration for a saint. Unlike Ralph, he maintained a balance in his career, keeping one foot planted at the king's court and the other in the households of Becket's successors.[10] Indeed, when news of Hattin reached Europe in late 1187, Peter was at the papal court at Ferrara representing Archbishop Baldwin of Canterbury. He therefore found himself at ground zero for the papal response and even participated in its formulation.[11] For in the months following Hattin, he wrote two tracts. One was a lament on the interminable delays that were keeping knights from going to the Holy Land. The other was a sort of saint's life called *The Passion of Prince Reynald.*

Reynald was an unlikely candidate for sanctity, but Peter worked wonders with unpromising material.[12] A Burgundian knight of modest means, Reynald had traveled east as a crusader (perhaps with Louis VII in 1147). In doing so, according to Peter, he gave up a promising marriage in his homeland to help Jerusalem, an early sign of his sanctity. He was thus not unlike Moses, who similarly abandoned his place in pharaoh's household to suffer with his people.[13]

But Reynald was not opposed to marriage or social advancement per se. In 1153, he married the widowed Constance of Antioch, daughter and heir to Bohemond II, making himself ruler of the duchy. His most notable achievements during his rule involved making wars against other Christians and inventing creative punishments for his own subjects. Memorably, he once ordered the city's old and sickly patriarch to be imprisoned in Antioch's great citadel and then exposed to the hot summer sun, forcing him to sit outside (possibly on top of the fortress) with his head uncovered and smeared with honey so as to attract flies. A theatrical act of violence carried out with great panache, it shocked and angered everyone who heard of it, including the king of Jerusalem.[14]

In 1161, followers of Nur ad-Din captured Reynald and imprisoned him in the city of Aleppo, where he remained for fifteen years. Nur ad-Din must have thought him especially dangerous, or loathsome, for he kept him locked away longer than any of his other Christian prisoners—indeed for the rest of Nur ad-Din's life. Peter of Blois believed it to have been a harsh confinement, too. During those years, he writes, Reynald was "purged like silver and emerged from the furnace of imprisonment as finest gold." He returned to Jerusalem, finally, in 1176, hair prematurely white and mind perhaps a bit unhinged.[15] Baldwin IV rewarded his endurance with marriage to a new heiress and lordship over the Transjordan, the frontier region between Egypt and Palestine.

Reynald apparently viewed the chief duty of his new office as making mischief against Saladin, a task at which he excelled. During his captivity he probably learned how to hit Muslims where it hurt the most, psychologically if not strategically.[16] Notably in 1182, he ordered five ships carried on camelback across the desert and dispatched onto the Red Sea. From there they harassed, raided, and plundered Egyptian and Arabian ports. The holy cities of Mecca and Medina seemed at risk. Ships from Saladin's own navy eventually drove the Franks from the sea, and all the sailors were captured and killed, many in spectacular public executions. But Reynald had taught Muslims to believe their most sacred places vulnerable.

Less theatrically but more effectively, he conducted occasional raids against Arab caravans crossing his lands, going from Saladin's Egyptian holdings to Syria. One of these raids, in the winter of 1186, occurred at a time of truce between Jerusalem and Saladin, but Reynald did not believe that this peace agreement applied to him, or else he thought that Saladin himself had violated the truce by providing the caravan with an armed escort.[17] Through this attack, inadvertently or deliberately, he gave Saladin diplomatic cause to renew his campaign against Jerusalem, leading to Hattin and the expulsion of nearly all the Franks from the East.[18]

In Peter of Blois's narrative, Reynald looks decidedly different—a well-spoken preacher and a willing martyr. He stands in the midst of captured Templars and Hospitallers—King Guy is nowhere to be seen—while Saladin demands that he and the other prisoners renounce Christ. To impress upon the Franks the totality of his victory, Saladin has the True Cross brought before the captives. It is a psychological misstep. Instead of provoking despair, the sight of the Cross fills Reynald's heart with love and inspires him to deliver an off-the-cuff sermon on the Crucifixion. He concludes: "Behold! the fruit of our labors, whose love inspires us to delight in death and to hold this present, sad, arduous life in contempt! For today the Lord shall gather us together in his kingdom as saintly martyrs." In the face of such resolve, Templars and Hospitallers alike are ready to die.[19]

The choreography of this scene is wholly conventional, a reenactment of the martyr legends of old. Saladin is like a wicked Roman emperor and Reynald, an early Christian convert. Peter adds a few contemporary details to the traditional framework. Saladin, for example, mocks Reynald in Arabic. "Your Christ has deceived you, and if you do not deny him today, he will not be able to free you from my hand!" Reynald, who had picked up some Arabic during his captivity, responds in kind. "Christ deceives no one; rather, he who does not believe in him is himself deceived!"[20] A classic confrontation: Saladin, "the hammer of the faithful," vs. Reynald, "the Lord's Champion."[21] Rhetorically, Reynald gets the better of his opponent. Saladin can only answer with violence: "This man dared to blaspheme against my own glorious majesty! My own hand will kill him! Take the others away and execute everyone who will not deny Christ!" Reynald falls before the Cross and looks toward heaven. Patiently, he accepts death.[22]

In terms of crusade writing, Peter of Blois's story is almost unprecedented. For despite widespread associations between crusading and martyrdom, earlier chroniclers had almost never presented crusaders in these terms. Guibert of Nogent is a rare exception—he described the death of a childhood friend named Matthew in the style of an early saint's life. Otherwise, "the new path to salvation," which had served to fill the empty choirs of heaven, had never successfully promoted any of its participants as actual martyrs worthy of veneration.

While Peter's treatise did not succeed in creating a cult of St. Reynald, the possibility did at least gain currency. The skeptical Ralph the Black referred in his universal history to the capture and death of "blessed Reynald."[23] Peter's description of his martyrdom, moreover, was not entirely fanciful. Saladin really had vowed to kill Reynald with his own hand, not because Reynald insulted his majesty but because of his earlier raids on Muslim caravans. Even so, just as in *The Passion of Prince Reynald*, Saladin gave his prisoner the chance to profess Islam and save his life.[24] When Reynald refused, Saladin, according to his biographer Bahā' al-Dīn Ibn Shaddād, chopped off Reynald's arm and then let his men finish him off, the body no doubt convulsing and twitching, blood gushing out of its shoulder. Standing near the brutalized corpse, Saladin explained his actions to King Guy: "It has not been customary for princes to kill princes, but this man transgressed his limits, so he has suffered what he suffered."[25]

The Arabic version of the death scene and its depiction of Reynald of Châtillon's character likely would have seemed authentic to anyone who had actually known the man, more so than Peter of Blois's stylized account of a monkish soldier who had embraced poverty and never uttered a boastful word.[26]

But Peter was not writing for warriors. His target audience consisted of fans of old-fashioned martyr stories—which is to say clerics like himself. It was these listeners and readers, potential preachers of the crusade, whose enthusiasms he needed to set ablaze. At the end of the *Passion* Peter directly addresses one of his audience, a preacher reluctant to answer Jerusalem's call. "What business with knights have I," Peter wonders, imagining a skeptical listener, "a cleric, defenseless among the armed, a peaceable fellow amid the bellicose?"[27] Obviously Peter's purpose, and the cleric's, was to preach, to motivate, to explain the stakes, and to excite soldiers about the possibility of dying for Christ.

Even in aftermath of an event as eye-catching as Jerusalem's fall, however, a new crusade was not an easy sell, either to preachers or to warriors. Its promoters, like the Patriarch Heraclius two years before them, were still paying for the failures of the Second Crusade and the disastrous misfire of Bernard's miracle campaign. More fundamentally, the legend of the First Crusade had rested on the idea that salvation history had changed forever after 1099. Saladin had exposed that victory for what it was: one of God's protean mood swings.

For this reason, Peter begins his treatise with a long mediation on why bad things happen to good people, be they Jews or Franks. God scourges the ones he loves just as a doctor uses harsh treatments to purge illness. He strikes the just to test them, the evil to punish them. Christians can expect their reward, for Peter announces at the end of his treatise that God will restore Jerusalem to them before he, Peter, dies. He will live to see "my Joseph, nay rather my Jesus, ruling Jacob in the land of Egypt and to the ends of the earth."[28]

Besides the vagaries of God's plans, clerics were also troubled by questions of conscience, the same ones that had bothered Ralph the Black. Peter's imaginary, skeptical listener says, "Whoever kills unbelievers is a murderer. I do not wish to incur the crime of homicide, for the Lord despises men of blood."[29] The objection could come from the lips of a knight or of a preacher, reluctant to encourage others to commit bloodshed, lest their sins redound back to him.[30] Why now, in 1187, did these concerns arise? Partly because the fall of Jerusalem itself had undercut the crusade's claim to divine sanction. Partly because church law and academic ideas about what constituted just warfare had received a more thorough vetting during the twelfth century than in the eleventh. And partly because Europe had become an increasingly cosmopolitan and wealthy land, in part due to the crusades themselves. Increased travel, open trade routes, and more regular contact with Muslims had opened all sorts of avenues of wisdom and wealth. It would have become correspondingly difficult to find an audience so thoroughly ignorant of Islam that it would dismiss that religion's adherents as limbs of Satan and servants of Antichrist.

Yet Peter did make such a case. First, falling back on traditional language, he observes that it is acceptable for Christians to kill Muslims provided that they do so while "enflamed with the ardor of charity"—provided that they hate the Muslims for the right reasons. Saracens blaspheme Christ, pollute the sanctuary of the Lord by their very presence, and humiliate and abuse the glory of Christ the redeemer. Peter concludes with that passage from Leviticus: "Kill blasphemers and do not suffer witches to live."[31] Muslims are "most foul dogs," ministers of Satan who, not content with decapitating

Templars, use their swords to scoop out eyeballs and whip up innards.[32] As for Saladin, he is "the Babylonian dog, the son of perdition," his name so foul that Peter hates to contaminate his story by writing it out.[33] A bit more creatively, Saladin is the Whore of Babylon, drunk on the blood of saints.[34]

And of course, he is Antichrist. When Saladin first appears in Peter's story, he is enthroned in the entry to his tent, "a cruel beast." Saracen guards parade Templars and Hospitallers before the eyes of "that Antichrist."[35] And when Reynald grows impatient at Saladin's tyrannical dawdling, he demands, "You foul, wicked, and cruel Antichrist, why are you dragging this out? Why are you postponing our vows of martyrdom?"[36]

"Antichrist" was a normal enough medieval insult. Peter may have adopted it here as a way to communicate or inspire emotional distress.[37] But it was also an expression of apocalyptic crisis. The loss of the True Cross was comparable only to the Israelites' loss of the Ark of the Covenant (now ensconced in the Roman Church of the Lateran, of course). How wrathful must God have been to strike Christians with so grave a blow?

> The cross was for us the ark of the New Testament, it was the path of our reconciliation, the banner of salvation, the marker of sanctity, the hope of victory, the pledge and covenant of divine grace, the symbol of Christian knighthood, the foundation of faith, the upheaval of the enemy, the despoiling of hell, the ladder of heaven, the gates of paradise, the uplifting of the fallen, the opening of whatever is closed, the protection of bodies, the weapon of souls, the salvation of the living, life for the dead, liberation of captives, exaltation of the humble, and the downfall of the proud.[38]

Such was the prize that had been lost, and Peter hoped it would spur his co-religionists to action. He promised that God's wrath would abate. He floated the possibility that the Last Days were at hand, but he did not engage in the kind of detailed speculations characteristic of earlier writers. He also did not indulge in the recollection of Christian victories past. Really, all he could do was marvel at how improbable the situation appeared. The Lord was punishing his people, in a way that humiliated them, his Son, and God himself. God, he writes incredulously, had cut off his nose to spite his face.[39]

A Gift to Barbarossa

Gregory VIII, Peter of Blois, and others need not have worried. The call to crusade was wildly successful. Western Christians were shocked at the loss of Jerusalem—a ballpark figure of fifty thousand soldiers taking the cross in Germany, France, England, Italy, and elsewhere would not be unreasonable. Even if they did not take the cross, they might engage in extravagant acts of piety. In the city of Assisi, for example, home to a seven-year-old future St. Francis, people wore sackcloth and wept publicly as priests intoned a litany often cited during previous crusades, "God, the gentiles have come into your inheritance."[40] The reactions were in part spontaneous, in part carefully cultivated acts of public theater. Frankish princes in the East played a role in inciting these reactions, too. Conrad of Montferrat, lord of Tyre, commissioned paintings of a Muslim knight trampling the Holy Sepulcher and of Muhammad punching a bloodied Christ in the face. The propaganda was striking enough that two Arab chroniclers in the Middle East made note of it in their histories.[41]

Equally important was the enthusiasm of western princes. In the end, a full two years were needed, most of the principal leaders in Europe settled their differences and united behind the cause of retaking Jerusalem. Leading the way was Richard of Poitou, the future King Richard the Lionheart. In November 1187, he took the cross at Tours. His father, Henry II, who by this point had deferred his crusading vow for fifteen years, went into shock at his son's decision. Nevertheless, that January, Henry and his rival, the French king Philip Augustus, vowed to go to Jerusalem too.[42] Frederick Barbarossa likewise accepted the cross at the behest of Cardinal Henry of Albano, the pope's chief spokesman in Germany. Like Peter of Blois, Henry had been at Ferrara when news of Hattin reached Europe. When Urban III died in October 1187, Henry was considered a leading candidate to succeed him, but apparently he felt that his talents would be better used as preacher rather than pontiff. Urban's actual successor, Gregory VIII, therefore, sent him to Germany.

The precise terms of Henry's sermons are unknown, but he did at least avoid the mistake of his most immediate predecessor, Bernard of Clairvaux. Henry performed no miracles. In a theological treatise on Jerusalem, he all but boasts about their absence. "Today is not like the beginning of the Church, when the blind saw, the lame walked, lepers were cleansed, the deaf heard, the dead rose. Now there are no signs like that." The miracles that were occurring were invisible. Hearts were changing. Those who were blind to truth, lame and thus unable to perform good works, leprous in character, deaf to teachings of the spirit, and dead to charity—they were changing.[43] But there would be no external miracles for this crusade, no phony dumb show as with Bernard.

Henry's message was otherwise broadly similar to his predecessors' and to that of Peter of Blois. Like Peter, he describes the True Cross as "the ark of the New Testament."[44] Also like Peter, he makes use of the language of martyrdom, comparing the crusaders to the Maccabees and St. Stephen.[45] He frets about crusaders delaying their vows and uses shaming language to hurry them along—soldiers who had vowed to fight for Christ only to return home to their own vomit needed to go back at once to fight there anew.[46] Like the visual propaganda, he frames the conflict as a personal battle between Christ and Muhammad: "the wood of the life-giving cross, consecrated by his body, his limbs decorating it like pearls, has not only been captured, mocked, and befouled by its enemies' filth, but it is being offered to Muhammad, so that through Christ's disgrace, Muhammad might be glorified; and Muhammad's followers might proclaim him the victor not just over all Christians, but over Christ, too."[47]

Despite the stereotypically contemptuous language about Muhammad, Henry's treatment of Islam, or at least of Saladin, was surprisingly nuanced. Crusade literature usually elided Saracens and demons, and Peter of Blois accused Saladin of being Antichrist. Henry was more measured. Saladin was a tool of evil, but his motives were comprehensible and distinct from Satan's. Saladin opposed Christians so that he might lay claim to their lands; the devil used Saladin to persecute Christians and hoped through him to eradicate the name of Christ.[48] For the Franks, the crusade was a holy war. The ultimate enemy was Satan, whose unwitting tool Saladin was. For Henry, Islam was a collection of misguided men who wished to increase their wealth. Christians could understand the apocalyptic stakes of the battle, Saracens not so much.

As Henry puts this picture together, he tries to imagine the devil's actual psychology. Like many Christians, the devil was wondering if the Apocalypse had begun. Current conditions seemed like "what the crucified man had predicted," when he said that there would be a tribulation unlike any other, or like what Daniel had prophesied when he spoke of the "abomination of desolation standing in the Temple." But Satan, again like many Christians, simply did not know. All he could do was prepare stumbling blocks for any soldier preparing to make war against him.[49]

Remarkably, Henry only mentions the First Crusade when he imagines how it looked in the devil's eyes. Satan, as he envisions him, directly addresses the Cross and places the current crisis, as well as the First Crusade, in a long continuum of triumphs and setbacks in the Holy Land—including the discovery of the True Cross, its capture by the Persian king Chosroes, and more recent and more mythical events as well:

> As often as I have raised up warriors against you, you have found strong defenders. Judas buried [the Cross] at my behest, but Helena uncovered it and Constantine wondrously raised it up. With my help, Chosroes captured it, but Heraclius elevated it to yet greater glory. Our Gentile people [Islam] occupied that whole land, hateful to me, through my assistance, but then Charlemagne came from the West and reached out with a strong hand and arm to free it from his enemies. The Christians were expelled once more, but again Westerners conquered our people and drove them out, despite the fact that ours were stronger and more numerous. What can I hope for now? What can be done?[50]

Satan comes off as a bit foolish. The comic tone of this passage, however, would not have had a long shelf life.

Setting aside questions of hindsight, Henry was ultimately successful with his German mission. In March 1188 in the city of Mainz, Frederick Barbarossa took the cross, and he was the first of the great Europeans rulers to depart—an event which Henry celebrates in his treatise, fully expecting Barbarossa to follow in the proud tradition of imperial conquerors of Jerusalem, from Constantine to Heraclius to Charlemagne.[51]

Another churchman named Henry, this one provost of the church of Schäftlarn about fifteen miles south of Munich, felt similar confidence in Frederick. As a sign of faith, he commissioned a small book to be presented to the emperor, on the model of what William Grassegals had done for King Louis VII fifty years earlier. Whereas Grassegals had given Louis a grand book with three texts related to the crusade, Henry of Schäftlarn presented only a single text, the *History of Jerusalem* by Robert the Monk, the most frequently copied crusade history in twelfth-century Germany.[52]

Henry's manuscript is best known for an image, the frontispiece, depicting Frederick Barbarossa, his red beard and hair turned to white. His head is crowned; his left hand holds an orb, symbolizing worldly rule, and crosses are emblazoned on both his shield and his chest. He is a self-assured crusader, ready to destroy Saladin, if not eradicate Islam itself from the earth. Just to the emperor's left, Henry of Schäftlarn appears as an older, tonsured man, his miniaturized frame emphasizing Frederick's grandeur. Compensating for Henry's frame is his ethereal presentation. He seems to float by the emperor's side, having swooped through the air on the eve of Frederick's departure to offer him a book, which Henry holds in his hands—in fact, the very copy of Robert the Monk in which this illustration appears. Like a mirror, when Frederick held this book in his hand, he would have seen a picture of himself holding that very book in his hand (see fig. 14).

On the last page of the manuscript, in red letters, Henry has inserted a poem to commemorate the gift. He begins the inscription with an apology. The manuscript was prepared in haste and is "not adorned in a way suitable to a king's court, let alone an emperor's."[53] He nonetheless urges Frederick to take it with him, as he prepares with confidence (he was *securus*—secure, safe) to face the Saracens. "Prospering according to the pattern of dauntless Duke Godfrey, may he never fail. May peace and glory be his!"[54] The sentiment is close to the one expressed by William Grassegals five decades earlier—that Louis VII should study the stories of the First Crusade and find therein images of himself. Given the uncertain political fortunes of King Guy in the Holy Land, Frederick may also have aspired to claim the throne of Jerusalem, as prophecy had long led Western Christians to expect one of their rulers to do.

There is at least one subtle but noticeable difference between Grassegals's and Henry's books—size. Grassegals's was a large presentation manuscript, one appropriate for a royal or monastic library, whereas Henry's is quite small. At eight by five-and-a-half inches, it could conceivably have been carried in a saddlebag. Henry hoped Frederick would do so, as indicated in another inscription, this one written into the archway that surrounds the portrait of the king on the manuscript's opening page. It reads, "May this book lead Frederick, peaceful to no Saracen, to a place free from all destruction."[55] The words have a near talismanic quality, particularly when set alongside the image of Provost Henry hovering imp-like beside the emperor. As such, they are also reminiscent of those lines drawn into manuscripts of the *Gesta Francorum*. Whoever looked upon those lines, based on measurements of the Holy Sepulcher, would be free for the rest of that day from the threat of sudden death.

If Frederick did take this book with him as instructed, it did not lead him to such a place of safety. He departed for the East in the spring of 1189, following the land route of the first two crusades. On the march he convinced the king of Hungary to join him, forced terms on Byzantium, and scored significant victories over the Seljuk Turks of Anatolia in the spring of 1190. And then, on June 10, 1190, while crossing the Saleph River, Frederick Barbarossa drowned.[56] It was an event stunning not only for its suddenness but also for its irony. Otto of Freising's most vivid memory of Frederick during the

Second Crusade had been of the moment when the young prince had offered Otto and others a safe haven during a flood, ensconced in a tent on the side of a mountain, a place free from destruction. About forty years later, in his sixty-ninth year of life, Frederick's turn came to drown on crusade.

Perhaps Barbarossa had left Henry's book at home or had failed to take it with him as he approached the Saleph River. If he did carry it (and even if he did not) the lesson is clear: The First Crusade had lost its magic.

CHAPTER 12

The Crusade of Joachim of Fiore

A FEW MONTHS AFTER Frederick Barbarossa drowned, the crusade's other two royal leaders, Richard the Lionheart and Philip Augustus, were wintering in Sicily. Unlike Frederick, Richard and Philip had decided on the sea route to Jerusalem. Richard in particular had a full plate of activity in front of him. His sister Joan had been married to the previous king of Sicily. After her husband's death, the new king, Tancred of Lecce, ordered her placed in confinement. Richard thus needed to free his sister, lay claim to money and military equipment to which he felt she was entitled, construct siege engines for use in the Holy Land, and, in his spare moments, conquer Messina. All of which he managed to do relatively quickly.[1]

At some point during a winter respite, Richard also found time to listen to a sermon by a Calabrian holy man named Joachim of Fiore.[2] Joachim was a monk, biblical commentator, and an occasional presence at the papal court. He had also developed a reputation as a prophet. Through close study of scripture, and through a few well-timed visions, he had unlocked a biblical code that revealed not only the meaning of past events and recent history but, if used judiciously, could also unlock the secrets of the near future.[3] Joachim often found it difficult to express himself in mere words, so he supplemented his texts with heavily annotated diagrams and pictures.

When Joachim spoke before Richard, he showed the king at least one of these images—a striking picture of a red dragon with seven heads and ten horns (see fig. 15).[4] Perhaps Joachim carried it in a book or else had had it sketched onto a large sheet of parchment, or else painted onto a larger placard or signboard so that a small audience of students or clerics or knights could examine it together. The dragon's message spoke directly to Richard. To explain how this was so, Joachim might have pointed to the left side of the sixth head and said something like, "The First Crusade was here," and then moving his finger a little to the right, "and you are here."

A Newly Modeled History

Joachim of Fiore has been described as having, as the historian R. W. Southern put it, "the most powerfully imaginative and comprehensive historical mind of the Middle Ages."[5] He did not entirely discard the old rules. One finds, for example, scattered references to Augustine's six ages of history.[6] Alongside traditional models, however, Joachim crafted a new prophetic system based not on six or seven ages, or even on the four kingdoms, but instead on the Trinity, a system at once precise and bewildering. After a thousand years of apocalyptic algebra, Joachim invented calculus.

The details of Joachim's life are sketchy. Modern devotees have found in him a sympathetic personality—a historical worldview communicating something like ecumenicalism, his ideas an example of "paths not taken," a hopeful alternative to the bleak persecuting mentality that increasingly dominated medieval culture. Joachim foresaw a day when schismatic Christians, most notably the Greeks, would be reintegrated into the Roman Church. He anticipated a reconciliation between Christians and Jews at the "apotheosis of history wherein a merged populace would be endowed with the fullest spiritual understanding."[7] There has even been some suggestion that Joachim predicted reconciliation between Christianity and Islam.[8] At the very least, he preferred preaching, not warfare, as the best way to engage Muslims.[9] Spiritually, he was thus closer to Ralph the Black than to the more belligerent Peter of Blois.

Joachim was also a reactive thinker, inconsistent in many of his ideas and interpretations. Current events forced him to rework his models, none more so than the battle at Hattin and the fall of Jerusalem.[10] Afterward, Joachim could not envision a future free of wars between Christians and Saracens. Hattin and the fall of Jerusalem may have affected him so strongly because his first prophetic epiphany had occurred when he was a pilgrim to the Holy Land, probably in the late 1160s. It happened atop Mount Tabor, the traditional site of Christ's Transfiguration, where, according to the Synoptic Gospels,

Peter, James, and John saw the Lord's body transformed, the sun shining from his face, his clothes made dazzlingly white. At the same moment, Moses and Elijah seemed to stand beside Christ and to engage him in conversation.

When Joachim's biographer described the abbot's vision at Mount Tabor, Moses was very much on his mind. "Our Moses came down from the mountain where he had received the revelation of the law of doubles."[11] The "law of doubles"—literally, "the twin law"—refers to the most elementary aspect of Joachim's thought, that figures and events from the Old Testament exist in perfect chronological parallel with figures and events from the New Testament, continuing into the modern history of the church. Such parallels Joachim labeled "concordances." It was not an entirely new concept. Each of the six ages of history roughly paralleled all of the others. Joachim, however, brought to his system a mathematical precision unlike anything previously attempted. Joachim himself described his thought as "spiritual arithmetic."[12]

Only one other anecdote from Joachim's time in the Holy Land survives, included in a slightly later biography written by his secretary, Luke of Cosenza. Joachim had once told Luke how when he was still a youth and had just adopted a religious habit, a widow in Syria had tried to seduce him. Because he was staying in her home and it was nighttime, he could not safely run away. So he stayed up all night and prayed, forcing his hostess to go to bed frustrated.[13] By Joachim's standards, the story is a bit jejune, though it might help to explain why he left the Holy Land confident that God's wrath was about to fall on it.[14]

He returned to Europe, first to the kingdom of Sicily, where he lived for a time as a hermit on Mount Etna. Later, he joined the monastery of Corazzo in Calabria, where he became abbot around 1176. Corazzo was a traditional Benedictine house. Joachim hoped to join it to the network of Cistercian monasteries, whose practices he deeply admired and whose most famous representative, Bernard of Clairvaux, he believed to have been another Moses.[15] Specifically, he tried to affiliate Corazzo with the Cistercian abbey of Casamari. The attempt failed. Corazzo was too small to interest the larger, more established community.[16] Joachim spent more than a year there pleading his case, probably from early 1183 to the fall of 1184. During this time he would have had the chance to work with its library's holdings, which were more extensive than those of Corazzo.[17] He also met Luke, his secretary and future biographer. Finally, he claimed to have experienced at Casamari two additional visions, one on Easter and the other on Pentecost.[18] The first reaffirmed his understanding of concordances between the Old and New Testaments. The second opened up the workings of the Trinity in all their fullness.[19]

Because of these visions (and because he was relatively free from his duties as abbot), Joachim began writing simultaneously the three books that would define his legacy. They are *The Book of Concord Between the Old and New Testament*, a sort of introduction to his thought system; *The Ten-Stringed Psaltery*, a lengthy meditation on the Trinity built around the image of the titular musical instrument; and most importantly for the crusade, *The Exposition of the Apocalypse*, a massive exegetical reading of the book of Revelation.[20] These three works pretend to offer a coherent system of thought, but they remain, to some degree, works-in-progress. The core ideas are more or less consistent; the details are in a constant state of flux or metamorphosis.[21] Some rules, however, do emerge.

Fundamentally, Joachim divided history into three phases, or *status*, as he calls them in Latin.[22] Each *status* relates to one of the three persons of the Trinity, with the *status* of the Father corresponding to the Old Testament, that of the Son to the New Testament and the church, and that of the Holy Spirit to a third age yet to bear fruit. This third *status* has proved to be Joachim's most abiding contribution to prophetic thought since it represented a revival of millennialism in Christian history. Adherents to this belief, called "millennialists" or "millenarians," argued that the thousand-year reign of Christ foretold in Revelation 20 was not a symbol for the era of the church, as Augustine had decreed. It was instead an earthly kingdom, one that would occur during a historical era that had not yet begun. It might not last a thousand years, but it would be a real age of peace, the world governed by saintly judges, or, as Joachim called them, Spiritual Men.

In the early stages of his intellectual development, Joachim expected these Spiritual Men to be Cistercian monks. As time passed, and as he grew less enamored with the Cistercian order, he felt correspondingly less confident in that judgment. Instead, he saw Cistercians as the forerunners of an entirely new order. And in 1188 or 1189, probably not coincidentally, he abandoned Corazzo and founded a new monastic order in the region of the Sila Plateau in Calabria. Here was a new spirituality and a new home, where, from a great altitude, he might contemplate the implications of his threefold view of history.

Joachim probably needed both the distance and the quiet to do so, so elaborate was his system. It differed from the older model of

six ages not just in terms of number but also in terms of organiza-
tion. According to the traditional sixfold division of history, one age
began as soon as another ended, at a specific moment. To take two
examples, the first of the six ages ended with the Flood, and the
second began when Noah emerged from the ark; the sixth and final
age usually began with the birth of Christ and would end with Christ's
Second Coming. Joachim's three ages, by contrast, overlapped with
one another. The second *status* began about two-thirds of the way
through the first one and reached its flowering at the time of Christ.
The third *status* began similarly two-thirds of the way through the
second, and Joachim believed that it was about to commence its flowering during his life. He used various images, including trees and
interlocking circles, to illustrate this system (see table 6). Boiled
down to its basics, it would look something like these arrows.

A variety of resonances and harmonies helped both unite and
differentiate the three *status*. For example, a different order of religious men would dominate each of them. The first had been the
time of the married. Its initiator was Adam and it reached its flowering with the patriarchs Abraham, Isaac, and Jacob. The second *status*
was the time of celibate priests. It began with the reign of Uzziah,
king of Judah, during whose life the prophet Isaiah was active. It was
during his reign too that the Roman Empire was founded.[23] The
second *status* reached its flowering, naturally, with Christ, when the
first *status* concluded. The third *status*, which began with St. Benedict,
about two-thirds of the way through the second *status*, was the age of
virgin monks. It had not yet fully blossomed, but for Joachim the
transformation seemed imminent.

And dateable, too. The most probable year for the end of the
second *status* and the beginning of the third, the start of a paradisal
era of Spiritual Men, was 1260—an unusually precise prediction and
an unusual number to fixate on as well. Joachim arrived at it in part
through symbolic reading of scripture and of recent history, but

Table 6: Joachim's Trinitarian Model of History

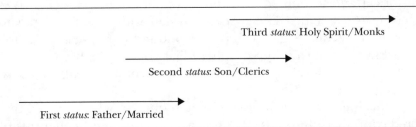

Third *status*: Holy Spirit/Monks

Second *status*: Son/Clerics

First *status*: Father/Married

mainly through mathematics. In brief, he had discovered the answer to the question of life, prophecy, and history, and that answer was forty-two—forty-two generations.[24]

Older would-be prophets had tried to calculate the end of the world by simply counting years, usually focusing on the numbers one thousand and six thousand. If the six ages of history reflected the six days of creation, and if a single day for God was as one thousand years, then human history would likely end in the year of the world 6000, or else (if one took Revelation 20 literally), the year 6000 would be followed by a millennial Sabbath of peace on earth, and then everything would end for good in the year 7000. The problem was that no amount of chronological hocus-pocus could make the events of the six ages, as recorded in the Bible, fall neatly into slices of one thousand years each. The fact that a sturdy man of the first age could be expected to live a good nine centuries made nonsense of any attempt to reconcile millennia and ages.

Joachim cut through this confusion by focusing not on years but on generations. And with a few literary and interpretive contortions, he was able to argue that each of the first two *status* had lasted, or would last, sixty-three generations—twenty-one generations before its flowering, and forty-two after it. Concretely, the first *status* began with Adam and reached its flowering with the patriarch Jacob (the twenty-second generation, in Joachim's reckoning). It continued then for a total of forty-two generations to Christ. The second *status* began with Uzziah, and continued for twenty-one generations to Joseph, Christ's father, reaching its flowering with Christ himself.

All of this information could be gleaned from scripture. To move beyond the New Testament and into recent history, Joachim abandoned specific events and focused instead on numbers and years. The life of Christ, he argued, had established the length of a generation—thirty years, Christ's age when John the Baptist baptized him and when his ministry began. Using simple math ($30 \times 42 = 1260$), Joachim could therefore calculate that the second *status* would end in or around the year 1260.[25] He illustrated these connections, both historical and arithmetical, through (among other devices) trees charting each status. The first tree began with Adam and ran to Christ; the second began with Uzziah and ran to the year 1260, followed by the return of the prophet Elijah, one of the two witnesses, as foretold in Revelation, and then the second coming of Christ (see fig. 16).

Joachim did allow himself wiggle room. He acknowledged that predicting the future was not an exact science. The final events of the second *status* could last a little longer or happen a little more quickly than his calculations indicated. And he never claimed to know how long the third *status* might endure. It would not be a thousand years, and it would not be nearly as long as either of the previous two ages. But he could say with some confidence the third *status* of the Holy Spirit was set to flower soon, near if not precisely in the year 1260.

Joachim's system, however, is more circuitous than even this already complicated summary suggests. The third *status*, for example, had its beginning not just in the second *status*, with the figure of St. Benedict, but in the first *status*, too, with the prophet Elisha. Theology as much history drove this interpretation. According to Latin tradition, the Holy Spirit proceeds from both the Father and the Son; it was fitting therefore that the third *status*, of the Holy Spirit, would also have a similar dual procession from each of the first two *status*, of the Father and of the Son.

Another complication: The lists of forty-two generations did not stack up quite as neatly as Joachim would have liked, forcing him to resort to exegetical sleight of hand. One of his tricks for making them cohere involved a story about King Hezekiah of Judah. In 2 Kings 20, Hezekiah fell sick unto death but the Lord cured him, added fifteen years to his life, and gave him a certain sign of the miracle by turning the shadow of a sundial back ten degrees. Exploiting the symbolism of the sun backtracking, Joachim allowed himself in one reckoning to count ten generations twice.[26]

Joachim's elaborate system of reading history nonetheless holds together, if barely. Human activity continued to follow the necessary patterns of God's storytelling even after the Crucifixion. It was not, as Augustine had argued, one random event after another, with no true progress, until the Second Coming. And there was to be a third age of human history, too, a time yet to come, one foretold in Revelation as lasting, allegorically, one thousand years. Joachim also—in contrast to earlier beliefs about the Last World Emperor and more in line with the ideas of writers like Otto of Freising and Gerhoh of Reichersberg—saw the final events in salvation history occurring within the boundaries of Christendom, usually with a resurgent papacy, represented by the angelic figure of Michael in Daniel 12, shaping events.[27]

Much of this thinking at first blush sounds revolutionary, but it is equally an outgrowth of prophetic beliefs developed earlier and in response to the First Crusade, beginning with Bohemond of Antioch and worked out, at first sketchily, by monastic historians and then in detail by Lambert of Saint-Omer in the *Liber floridus*. The resonances between Lambert and Joachim are particularly strong. Both men expressed their ideas most effectively through diagrams. More concretely, they wrestled with the problem of overlapping historical ages and with the inherent problems of reconciling seven eras and three ages of history (Father, Son, and Holy Ghost for Joachim; pre-Babylon, Babylon, and Rome for Lambert—not to mention four empires for Lambert and forty-two generations for Joachim). Both men also tried to syncretize classical history and Christian scripture, both placing the foundation of Rome at key moments in their systems. Also, though in different ways, each became fixated on challenges contained within the number forty-two (for Joachim, the number for calculating generations; for Lambert, the number of the year of Augustus's reign when Christ was born).

Had Joachim read Lambert? Very possibly. He would have had access to a variety of books during his sojourns at the papal court. In any case, Joachim is the final link in an intellectual chain, beginning with Lambert (or with Bohemond), running thence to Otto of Freising and Gerhoh of Reichersberg, with important influences along the way from other writers, crusaders, and preachers—notably Bernard of Clairvaux.[28]

Joachim's focus on events within Christendom likewise makes him less a revolutionary and more a part of this post-crusade tradition of prophetic speculation. The enthusiasm generated by the First Crusade, the belief that Western princes were staking anew claims to the lands in the East that in the divine plan needed to be Christianized, gradually gave way to disillusionment with the whole project—a process that began slowly in the aftermath of Jerusalem's fall, as observers were forced to recognize what flawed vessels the First Crusaders had been, and as increasingly troublesome news from the East undercut the triumphalism of 1099. The failure of the Second Crusade, made all the worse by Bernard of Clairvaux's flamboyant claims to divine sanction, intensified these trends. Joachim's Western, papal-centered apocalyptic prophecies would thus seem the natural conclusion to the increasingly skeptical outlooks of Otto, Gerhoh, and Ralph the Black about the centrality of the earthly Jerusalem in prophetic history. The crusade, according to this new worldview, was appropriate only for people who could not see past literal truths. Real Christians meditated on the heavenly Jerusalem. Jews dreamed about the earthly one.[29] So indifferent was Joachim to the project of crusading that he suggested in one of his earlier treatises that the Saracens might one day convert on their own, as the Jews would do.[30]

Such at least were Joachim's feelings in 1184, before the fall of Jerusalem.[31] In 1187, Islam returned to a place of menace in his imagination, and the crusade regained a crucial role in the apocalyptic narrative. According to Joachim's earliest biographer, the year 1187 was important in another way, too. For in the days before Hattin, Joachim had journeyed to Veroli, where Pope Lucius III was residing, to seek approval for his writing. The pope was reluctant to grant the request, so Joachim added: "'In order that you might believe what I am saying, let this be a sign unto you: Know that in the near future, the Saracens will capture Jerusalem.' The man of God had not yet left Veroli (he stayed there many days) before a messenger came to the lord Pope Lucius and said that Saracens had captured Jerusalem."[32]

It is a dramatic bit of storytelling and strictly speaking a chronological impossibility. Joachim did seek Lucius III's blessing for his writing, but Lucius died in 1185, two years before the battle of Hattin. It is possible that the biographer confused Joachim's audience with Lucius with a later one before Urban III.[33] Whatever the case, Joachim's followers remembered his theology of history as being intertwined with the fate of Jerusalem and, perhaps more crucially, that Joachim had predicted Saladin's victory before it happened.

That last point is likely true. Writing in 1187, before news of Jerusalem's fall had reached the West, Joachim commented on Revelation 17:17—"God put it into their hearts to do what pleased him, and they will hand their kingdom to the beast until the words of God are fulfilled." The passage reminded him of the current condition of the Holy Land. "We see this being fulfilled today. We watch pagan kings uniting as one at the same time as our kings divide against one another and to their own loss."[34] The unifying work of Saladin vs. the petty-minded politics of the crusade princes: modern historians have done no better in defining why the Frankish settlements collapsed. There can be a fine line between being a prophet and simply keeping up with the news.

As Joachim began his mature works, he sensed that his reading of scripture and his predictions about the future were better than those of anyone who had come before him. To explain why, he turned to Augustine who centuries before had compared life to a pilgrimage to a city. It was one thing, Joachim explained, to see that city, your destination, from a distance, as earlier prophets had done. It was another thing to stand in front of that city near the end of the journey and look at the gates. "We are at the gates. We can talk about many things that once lay hidden, wholly or in part."[35] While he declined to call himself a prophet, Joachim nonetheless believed that the Last Days were before him and that, as a result, he could interpret them with exactitude.[36]

Saladin, the Seven Seals, and the First Crusade

By 1187, or else in the immediate aftermath of Hattin, Islam and the crusades became central to this vision. The mechanics of the change, the prophetic evolution, appear most clearly in Joachim's various readings of the Seven Seals and of the number seven more generally.[37] The chapters of Revelation unfold in a spiraling pattern of sevens: seven churches, seven seals, seven trumpets, seven plagues, seven bowls of God's wrath, to name a few. Joachim likewise intended to divide his greatest work, *The Exposition of the Apocalypse*, into seven parts (although he decided at the last moment to go with eight, the final section examining the new Jerusalem and the heavenly age beyond history).[38] This pattern of sevens undergirds much of his other writing, too. Indeed, the secret of the seven seals is arguably the fundamental concordance between the first and second *status*, between the Old Testament and the age of the church.

Joachim's treatment of the seven seals, however, is not at all consistent—even within *The Exposition of the Apocalypse*. He spent nearly twenty years composing that book and thus had time to go back and revise his vocabulary as new ideas occurred to him or as unfolding events forced him to reconsider what he had previously believed. As a source of further confusion, Joachim wrote two similar introductions to the *Exposition*, one of them titled *The Enchiridion* and the other simply *The Introductory Book*.[39] Whichever one came first, neither was likely completed before the whole *Exposition*. It is therefore not possible to speak with precision about the development of Joachim's thought—only about a pool of competing ideas that he found useful or appropriate at various points in his career.

But there are some definite rules. Each seal has a twofold meaning. The seal itself refers to an Old Testament event, usually a war fought by the Israelites. Then there is the act of opening the seal, which points to the New Testament or later church history, usually to a persecution. Joachim refers to the period of each persecution or war as a *tempus*, Latin for "time."

Somewhat eccentrically, even by Joachim's standards, the fifth *tempus* in each age is longer than all of the others—sixteen generations as opposed to six. Joachim explained the anomaly by appealing once more to the story of Hezekiah and the sundial. When God moved the sundial's shadow back ten degrees, he was indicating that Hezekiah's *tempus*, the fifth *tempus*, would last ten generations longer than all the ones that had preceded it. As a result, the times of the sixth and seventh persecutions would be much shorter, almost simultaneous with one another, occupying together the space of two generations (see table 7). There would then follow a time of peace; for when the angel opened the seventh seal, in Revelation 8:1, there was a silence in heaven for half an hour.[40]

Joachim sets out the basics of this reading of history in his two earliest surviving works, one titled the *Genealogy*, written in 1176, and the other called *On an Unknown Prophecy*, written in 1184 during Joachim's first visit to the papal court at Veroli.[41] The *Genealogy* represents his initial attempt to sort out the implications of his vision on Mount Tabor. *Unknown Prophecy* grew out of a particular circumstance at the papal court. An anonymous prophecy, thought to be associated with a Roman Sibyl, was found tucked away in the papers of a recently deceased cardinal. Lucius III asked Joachim, freshly arrived from his Easter and Pentecost visions at Casamari, to interpret its content.[42] Most of Joachim's analysis focused on the eventual conversion of the Jews at the end of time, but he does begin with an overview of Christian history and its parallels with the travails of the ancient Israelites, essentially recapitulating material from the *Genealogy*.[43]

The fourth *tempus* is the most crucial for understanding the crusade. The rise of the Assyrians occurred at the time when Israel divided into two kingdoms—Judah (including the tribes of Judah and Benjamin, as well as the priests of Levi) and Israel (the other ten tribes). Elsewhere for Joachim the division of Israel into two parts would be a favored harbinger for the schism of the Latin and Greek churches. Here he focuses on Israel's war against Chaldea, which led

Table 7: Joachim's First Presentation of the Seven *tempores*

Enemies of the Israelites	Persecutors of the Church
1. Egyptians	1. Jews
2. Medians	2. Romans/Pagans
3. "Other Nations"	3. Goths, Vandals, Swabian Lombards
4. Assyrians	4. Saracens
5. Chaldeans	5. Contemporary Events
6. Medians and Persians	6. Unknown
7. Antiochus	7. Unknown

to the destruction of the ten tribes of Israel (not to be confused with Nebuchadnezzar's later destruction of Judah). The historical parallel with the threat of Chaldea was the rise of Islam, a connection Joachim made fairly consistently throughout his writing. Just as the Assyrians had devastated the ten tribes, so did the Saracens lay waste to countless Greek churches in the seventh century. For a time it seemed that Constantinople might not survive, but Charlemagne, revered King of the Franks, scored so many victories against Islam that all Christians could rejoice under his protection.[44]

So little had the crusades touched Joachim's consciousness—despite his own pilgrimage to the Holy Land—that the threat from Islam seemed to have ended there. The fifth persecution, in concord with the Babylonian Captivity, was ongoing. "A fifth persecution from a new and worse Babylon thus awaits us, in which Mother Sion will be led into Babylon."[45] What is this new Babylon, he asks. "Is it a Chaldean capital? Hardly!" But Joachim hesitates to elaborate—like an older Gerhoh of Reichersberg (whose books Joachim may have discovered at Veroli), he does not want to commit incendiary thoughts to parchment, but he adds, with a wink to his audience, "who this king of Babylon is—I reckon you understand me."[46] He would follow this formula, and fill in the gaps, in his *Book of Concords.* The ongoing fifth persecution of the church refers back to the Babylonian Captivity and forward to current events. The villain, the chief persecutor, is the Western Roman Emperor, since, "going back to the days of Henry I, Emperor of the Germans, certain intractable problems have troubled the church."[47]

How different that view is from the model Joachim developed in *The Exposition of the Apocalypse* (see table 8). He waffles a bit on some of the images. He also leaves gaps in some of his summaries of the seven *tempores.* But a fairly consistent model does emerge from his examinations and reexaminations of Revelation's sevenfold tribulations. The seven persecutors of the church are each led by a forerunner of Antichrist, or in the case of the seventh persecutor, by Antichrist himself.[48]

Most immediately striking, in connection to the crusades, is that the fourth and fifth persecutors of the church are now both Islamic—the Arab followers of Muhammad who devastated the churches of Greece, and the Moors who had expanded into Spain. The German emperor, the fifth persecutor from *The Book of Concord,* and the Investiture Controversy have disappeared. Joachim says that the fifth persecutor is a Moor, "commonly called Mesemutus, the heretical leader of another sect of men, followers of the first sect

Table 8: The Seven Seals, from the *Exposition of the Apocalypse*

Seven Seals	Enemies of Israel	Persecutors of the Church
1. Rider on a White Horse	1. Egypt	1. Herod and the Jews, persecuting the early church
2. Rider on a Red Horse	2. Canaanites	2. Nero and the Romans, persecuting martyrs
3. Rider on a Black Horse	3. Syrians, and the division of Israel	3. Constantius and the Heretics, opposed to church doctors
4. Rider on a Pale Horse	4. Assyrian destruction of the ten tribes	4. Muhammad and Saracens, persecuting hermits and virgins
5. Souls hidden under the altar in Heaven	5. Babylonian captivity of Judah	5. Mesemutus—Saracen expansion into Spain and North Africa
6. Earthquake, Blackened Sun, Bloodied Moon, etc.	6. Rebuilding the Temple, with twin persecutions described in the books of Judith and Esther	6. Twin persecutions: the eleventh king foretold in Daniel and Antichrist
7. Silence in Heaven	7. Period of peace after rebuilding Jerusalem	7. Beginning of Third Status

of Saracens; he rules mightily through his successors in parts of Africa and the Maghreb."[49] Joachim is a bit cagier about the identities of the last two persecutors, but he has no doubt that at least one of them will be connected to Islam. At the end of his summation of the sixth persecution, he says that Saracen leaders "will begin to interrogate and torture Christians, to lacerate them with whips, to compel them to accept their rites and deny the name of Christ, especially at the prompting of pseudo-prophets who have abandoned the Christian people. All of this we see happening in the world today."[50]

In 1184, Joachim's perspective had been similar to Gerhoh's. The prophetic future had drifted westward. The Last Days would chiefly concern questions of papacy and empire, a final resolution to the intractable problems of the Investiture Controversy. In the aftermath of Hattin, the future had changed—dominated now by bloodthirsty Saracens who tortured Christians and forced them into apostasy.

Only later in the *Exposition* does Joachim suggest with precision who one of the final two persecutors might be. He does so when commenting on the seven-headed beast ridden by the Whore of

Babylon and described in Revelation 17:10. Each of the heads symbolizes a king. The verse reads, "Five have fallen. There is another one. He has not yet come, and when he does come, it is good that that time will be brief." Joachim focuses specifically on the phrase, "There is another one." "On account of the convergence of the times, I think this one to be Saladin, that famed king of the Turks, who recently captured the city where Christ suffered."[51] Saladin was also the name of the sixth persecutor written on the sixth head of the red dragon and shown to Richard the Lionheart.

As preserved in *The Book of Figures*, the sixth head of the dragon stands out for two reasons. First, it is one of only two heads whose name is written in red—the other is Nero. Saladin was thus put on par with history's most infamous persecutor of Christians. Second, the sixth head is the only one to wear a golden crown, even though it does not represent the only king in the group. Under this new model, the fourth, fifth, and sixth persecutors were all Muslims. As the second *status* careened toward its catastrophic end, Islam, Saladin, and the Holy Land had assumed starring roles.

The various overlapping groups of seven all but demanded that Muhammad, as chief persecutor of the fourth *tempus*, directly align with the figure unleashed from behind the fourth seal in Revelation 6:8: "And behold, a pale horse, and his name that sat on him was 'Death,' and Hell followed with him." According to Joachim, the pale horse represents "that cruel people whose hateful progeny we grieve to say has occupied such a vast space of land. Whom could we more properly call 'death' than that damned Muhammad, who caused the deaths of so many thousands of men?"[52]

To provide more detail, Joachim turned to another of Revelation's lists of seven: the seven angels with seven trumpets. When the fourth angel sounded his horn, in Revelation 8:12, a third part of the sun, moon, and stars were darkened. This fourth *tempus*, in Joachim's exegetical system, pertained especially to hermits and virgins. The message of the fourth trumpet, then, is that one-third of the hermits and virgins, particularly in Egypt, abandoned their faith, tempted by Muhammad's "heresy." In place of lives of chastity and self-abnegation, Muhammad promised lives of extravagance and indulgence, in this world and in the next.[53] Despite Joachim's familiarity with Islam, greater than most of his predecessors who had engaged in similar prophetic speculations, he did not move beyond the scornful parodies of the earliest crusade chronicles. And perhaps no wonder. Muhammad, as a forerunner of Antichrist, was literally, and literarily, a parody of Christ.

The First Crusade does not appear directly in this model, but it is there by implication, lurking in the eschatological shadows. Specifically, in Revelation 13, John of Patmos saw a beast emerge from the sea. Like the dragon, it had seven heads and ten horns. One of the heads had suffered a grave wound, seemingly unto death, miraculously it had survived and filled the entire world with wonder. That head represented Islam, and the wound was the First Crusade.

> In the year of the Lord 1015 [*sic*] as they say, a wondrous sign appeared in sky. Countless stars fell here and there, wandering the heavenly roads like birds. In the wake of this sign, Christians everywhere were moved by the admonition of Pope Urban to go beyond the sea to liberate the Holy Sepulcher. Such boldness filled Christians that it seemed plausible pagans everywhere had been laid low and reduced to nothing, with Christ victorious.[54]

Victory was contagious. From what Joachim had heard, after the crusade Saracens in Egypt were paying tribute to Christians in Constantinople. The Norman king of Sicily was claiming cities in North Africa and setting up colonies there. Christian kings in Spain were scoring victories over the heirs of Mesemutus. "After so many triumphs over that once unbeatable people, who would not have thought the Christians had been raised in glory and who would not have believed the head of that beast utterly defeated?"[55]

Joachim originally developed this reading in a commentary on the life of St. Benedict, securely datable to 1187, likely in the immediate aftermath of Hattin. There he identifies the seventh head of the beast as "a new breed of Saracen, inhabiting the eastern lands." It had once appeared dead, but now, "because of our sins," it had revived ready to make war on the church.[56] Three years later, putting the final touches on the red dragon, Joachim corrected this point and associated the near fatal wound with the dragon's sixth head: "Then after a few years its wound will be healed, and the head, and the king who will be over it—it could be Saladin, if he still lives, or another one in his place—will put together a greater army than before and will raise general war against God's elect, and many martyrs will be crowned in those days."[57]

Against such an epic background, the Second Crusade fit uncomfortably. Joachim did, however, find a place for it in his *Book of Concord*, in a discussion of the Cistercian Order, and in particular of Bernard of Clairvaux. Bernard was a type of Moses. His friend and companion Eugenius was the high priest Aaron, Moses's brother. And just as Moses wrote the book of Leviticus for Aaron, so had Bernard written *On Consideration* for Eugenius, in which he explained the failure of the Second Crusade. The two men had raised great armies of pilgrims to fight against the enemies of the faith, but most of them had died, a catastrophe foretold in scripture. As the Israelites had rebelled and threatened to stone Moses and Aaron to death, so too had the new Chosen People raised voices against Bernard and Eugenius, complaining that they had been led out of the safety of their own secular Egypt for the dangers of travel to the Promised Land.[58] Not a crucial chapter in salvation history and ultimately not one worth working into the grander themes of the *Exposition of the Apocalypse*, the Second Crusade was at least a remarkable failure, prelude to a much greater one forty years later.

For with Saladin, the apocalyptic drama had resumed. The fourth head of the dragon, who was Muhammad, had returned through his new general. And that fourth head was also the fourth beast described in Daniel 7—a beast unlike any other, with iron teeth and claws, ready to maim and devour its enemies, and with ten horns, three of which were displaced by an eleventh horn with eyes and a mouth that spoke blasphemies. Given all of these convergences around the fourth *tempus,* Joachim was now able to identify this eleventh king from the book of Daniel (who was, once upon a time, Antiochus IV Epiphanes) as a ruler of the Saracens in the East. In dense, allegoric language, Joachim outlines how desperate this situation was growing:

> For wickedness is on the rise. New Babylon has been given into the hand of the beast in its kingdom, to be struck down. Gentile power will grow stronger because of our sins, so that in this time the eleventh and final king will rule in the kingdom of the Saracens. The false prophets, whom the devil has not ceased to draw together before him to augment our anguish, see the chance to work their deceits. The Gentiles will meet with them and make a pact of peace, and they will preach as if their power is from God and their kingdom is the kingdom of the faithful, and as if the religion of those who worship a crucified man is false.[59]

It was time to panic, but how to sort all of these crises out? To start with the first: New Babylon referred, as usual for Joachim, to the German Empire. The prophecy that Germany would fall before the beast was, at the time of the writing of the *Exposition*, ripped from the headlines, given that word Frederick's drowning had just reached Europe. It was also a fulfillment of Revelation 16:12, where an angel poured out the sixth bowl of God's wrath, and the Euphrates ran dry "to prepare the way for kings from the East." "This passage cannot be read without weeping," Joachim observes. "The terrible beginning of it has started. Recently it happened to the renowned army of that great and mighty Emperor Frederick and to the armies of other Christian people. They crossed the sea in a vast multitude, and hardly any of them returned home, having accomplished almost nothing."[60] Not a perfect fit, but the idea of a catastrophe at a river evoked Frederick's death. Joachim may also have had in mind the armies of Philip and Richard and the outcome of the rest of the crusade, but it seems unlikely. The description of so few returning home alive seems better to fit the story of Frederick's followers. New Babylon, the final incarnation of Rome, had fallen before the beast.

That still leaves unexplained the false prophets whom Joachim described as mesmerized by the devil and who had made peace with the Saracens. These prophets are, in Joachim's symbolic universe, Christian heretics. He calls them "Patarenes." A century earlier, "Patarene" had been the name given to Milanese church reformers who were important allies to Gregory VII in his struggles against the German emperor. By the time Joachim wrote, the label was associated with heretics often called "Cathars"—their shadowy origins often attributed to missionaries from a Bulgarian sect known as Bogomils.

The Patarenes had thus become a byword for another East-West conspiracy, a product of Christendom's encounter and subsequent contamination from unhealthy Eastern climes. As such, Joachim was able to imagine Patarenes taking the place of Moors as the fifth head of the dragon. With reference to Revelation 13, he writes, "And so in the fourth *tempus* there appeared a beast who rose from the Abyss, and in the fifth another beast arose from the earth. They are, respectively, the Saracen sect, which opposed the fourth angel sounding a trumpet, and the Patarene sect, which opposed the fifth."[61]

This alliance between the Patarenes and the Saracens grew not out of allegory but actual diplomacy, or so Joachim believed. While visiting Messina in 1195, he met a man who confirmed it. "Remarkably, last year, a man, who seemed trustworthy and God-fearing, arrived from somewhere near Alexandria, where he had been held in chains. He said that he had learned from an important Saracen that the Patarenes had sent legates to the Saracens, in search of fellowship and peace, which they obtained."[62]

Such were the enemies of the Last Days: Heretics allied with Saracens, Turks to the East, Ethiopians in the South, Moors in the West, and other barbarians (as German pilgrims had told Joachim) in the North.[63] Joachim had fully absorbed the vision of crusading once promoted by Bernard of Clairvaux (who also preached against

Cathars), when he had preached simultaneous crusades against Saracens and pagans everywhere.

Christendom in the Last Days had entered a time of total war. The second *status* would end with a two-front campaign against both these adversaries, Muslims and Patarenes. It would happen thus, because, as noted before, in Joachim's system, the final two enemies would follow closely upon one another in the sixth *tempus*, leading into the peaceful Sabbath of the third *status*. This dual procession of enemies had begun to assume ever greater importance in Joachim's thought—so much so that he read it back into his analysis of the Old Testament and changed those models accordingly. In his earliest writings, the *Genealogy* and the *Unknown Prophecy*, Israel's sixth war had been against the Chaldeans, set against the background of the rebuilding of Jerusalem and its Temple. The seventh war occurred over three centuries later, fought against Antiochus Epiphanes. In the remodeled history, Israel's sixth and seventh wars occur quickly, one after the other, fought first against Holofernes, as described in the book of Judith, and second against Haman, as described in the book of Esther. After successive victories, Israel entered into a long historical Sabbath, a time of relative peace before Antiochus's persecution, when the composition of authentic Old Testament histories ended.

A similar dual procession of enemies, Joachim believed, would occur for Christians, too. The first one had started. Writing around 1190, Joachim believed it would comprise two great battles. A prince fighting first against Babylon (which is to say, Germany) and another prince against Christ and his Church. "In the first, he [the prince in the East] will be allowed to conquer; in the other, he will be conquered."[64] This passage had begun to be fulfilled when Frederick Barbarossa (leader of New Babylon) drowned and his army dispersed. The second battle would occur when a new army representing the church—perhaps Richard the Lionheart's—took the fight back to Saladin.

Around the time of this second battle, the seventh persecutor, the last Antichrist, would appear. He would announce himself almost immediately, based on the theory of dual persecutions in the sixth *tempus*. Joachim announces their close connection in one of his more subtle visual flourishes: The sixth and seventh heads of the red dragon, Saladin and Antichrist, grow out of the same neck. "That king who is called Antichrist and a multitude of false prophets with him, will arise in the West, I think, and will come to the aid of that king who is head of the pagans. He will make great signs before him and his army, just as Simon Magus once made before Nero."[65]

Who would this heretical prince be—a heretical emperor or a priest? Joachim had different answers at different times. For much of the 1190s he seemed to anticipate that in the face of the seventh persecution, a reformed, spiritual papacy, would lead Jews and schismatic Christians back into the fold.[66] In his final years, he seems to have grown disillusioned with the papacy as an agent of apocalyptic change and to have looked to the German Empire instead.[67] In his commentary of the Apocalypse, he is evasive. The belief that the heretical Western Antichrist would be in league with his Islamic Eastern counterpart, working miracles before the Saracens, suggests that he was still trying to process the news of a Paterene-Muslim peace summit.

Whatever the case, Christian armies would prevail, eventually. After they had triumphed over the sixth head, which was the Saracen persecutor and probably Saladin, the devil "will again rouse the dead beast—that is, the pagans—and will bring to their aid false prophets; and again there will be a bitter fight, and Christ's army will conquer them more forcefully than before. And the beast and the false prophet will be handed over into a lake of burning fire. Whoever is left will be converted to the Lord."[68]

At that point, finally, the third *status*, a time of peace governed by Spiritual Men, would begin, but it would not bring an end to all conflict.[69] Rather, Antichrist would skulk off to the far corners of the earth, literally so, according to scripture and medieval maps. He would traverse the Caspian Gates, sealed by Alexander the Great and raise up the armies of Gog—for Joachim, a person and not a tribe. The place of Gog within salvation history is one of the great mysteries in his writing.[70] He associates him variously with Nimrod, the builder of the tower of Babel; Antiochus, the desecrator of the Temple; and Titus, who oversaw the destruction of Jerusalem in 70 CE—an impressive pedigree of concordances.[71]

Earlier, Joachim had associated Antiochus with the seventh enemy of Israel, but in his more developed thought he became the eighth persecutor of Jews, who rose to power after a long period of peace, just as Gog would arise at the end of the peaceful third *status*. Or else the key to understanding it all was to make Titus into the eighth persecutor of the Jews, appearing years after the end of the first *status*, just as Gog, the eighth persecutor of the Christians, would appear years after the second *status*. Joachim ever flexible, if not fickle, never settled on a single interpretation.[72]

Similarly, he never precisely defined the relationship between Gog and Antichrist. In *The Book of Figures* and in *The Introductory Book*, he identifies Gog as the last, greatest Antichrist. He is symbolized not by one of the dragon's heads but by his tail—the last persecutor of the Christians. Toward the end of the *Exposition*, however, Joachim disavows this reading. "Although I have already said it in the preface to this book, Gog does not in fact seem to be Antichrist, but he is rather a prince of Antichrist's army." Antichrist will be the "author of his seduction" and will cause Gog to lead armies into the West.[73] Whatever the case, Gog kept his own status as the creature's tail, ready to snap into action at the end of the third *status* and to bring the age of Spiritual Men to an end.

For all Joachim's originality, his historical model is in many ways traditional, not far removed from those of Adso, Pseudo-Methodius, and Lambert of Saint-Omer. Indeed, he is the culmination of the ideas that this book has been following: a great, anti-Christian enemy would be defeated in the East. A period of peace would follow—for Pseudo-Methodius, it would be brought about by a Last World Emperor; for Joachim, by the work of Spiritual Men. And then there would ensue, according to both systems, a war against Gog, who would lead northern barbaric tribes—Scythians whom Alexander the Great had long ago imprisoned behind the Caspian Gates—into war against Christendom, only for Christ to strike those tribes down.[74]

Joachim recounted some version of this story to King Richard during the latter's winter in Sicily. Roger of Hovedon, an English chronicler and pilgrim on the Third Crusade, was there to witness their meeting. "At that time," Roger writes, "there was an abbot in Calabria from the Cistercian order, called Abbot Joachim of Corazzo. He had the spirit of prophecy and was preaching to the people about things that were to come."[75] Richard gladly listened to Joachim's words, and he and his followers found them delightful.

According to Roger, Joachim spoke on Revelation 12:1–6, which describes a woman "clad in the sun" who cried and suffered and then gave birth to a male child, destined one day to govern the world with an iron rod. At the same time, a seven-headed dragon appeared in the skies and stood before the woman, ready to devour her offspring. The boy was taken up to heaven, and the woman fled. For God had prepared a hiding place for her where she was to be nourished for 1,260 days (both the sum of days in 42 months and the projected year of the end to the second *status*). The woman, Joachim explained, symbolized the church, wearing the sun of justice, that is, Christ. Her labor pains symbolized the difficulty with which the church redeemed souls. The seven-headed dragon was the devil, each head representing a persecutor of Christianity. It is a familiar list: Herod, Nero, Constantius, Muhammad, Mesemutus, Saladin, and Antichrist. Five of these kings, Joachim, notes, have already fallen. One is here, and one is not yet come—a reference to Revelation 17:10. The one "who is," as mentioned in Revelation, was Saladin.

> *One is*—that is Saladin, who right now oppresses God's church, and he has reduced it, along with the Lord's Sepulcher and the holy city of Jerusalem and the land where the Lord's feet stood, into slavery. But he will lose the kingdom of Jerusalem, and he will be killed. And the kites' ravenous hunger shall end, and there will be great slaughter such as never was from the world's beginning; and their homeland shall be made desert and their cities laid low and Christians will return to their lost pastures and nest in them.[76]

Roger has Joachim promise Richard that he will defeat Saladin and that the Franks will resettle in the Holy Land. He also told Richard that a passage from Revelation referred directly to current events, that John of Patmos had written these words as if he were alive in the year 1190: "Five have fallen, one is, and another has not yet come, and when he comes, it is good that that time will be brief." Also surprising, Roger has Joachim quote the British wizard Merlin, who had become a respected, albeit fictional, prophetic voice throughout Europe by the end of the twelfth century. "The kites' ravenous hunger shall end," is one of a sizable group of suitably obscure sayings, in circulation in the twelfth century, attributed to Merlin.[77]

If there was any doubt as to the meaning of this prediction, according to Roger, Joachim turned to face Richard directly and said, "All these things God has set aside and will allow to happen through you. He will give you victory over your enemies, and he will glorify your name for eternity, and you will glorify him, and in you he will be glorified, if you persevere in your work."[78] Yet at the time Roger wrote, he would have known that this prediction had not come to pass. Perhaps he was lampooning the prophet for the boldness of his words. More likely he intended to prod Richard with the phrase "if you persevere in your work." After negotiating a truce with Saladin that had left Jerusalem under Muslim lordship, Richard left the Holy Land in October 1192. Saladin died five months later. If only the king had persevered in his work, what might have happened?

More surprising was Joachim's next utterance, according to Roger. The final Antichrist is alive and fifteen years old, though he had not yet come to power. Ever in search of a glorious new war, Richard wants to know "Where was Antichrist born? And where will he reign?" Roger pauses before giving Joachim's answer and recites a short list of witnesses, apparently feeling the need to confirm what he is about to say, and then he again quotes Joachim: "it is believed that Antichrist has been born in Rome, and he will obtain the apostolic see, as the Apostle said, 'And he will be raised up and praised over all that is called God and worshipped, so that he might sit in the Temple of God, presenting himself as if he were God.'"[79] Antichrist would be the pope. Or Joachim felt so in 1190.

Nebuchadnezzar's Dream

It is impossible to know how seriously Richard took Joachim's predictions. Mainly, it provided for him an opportunity to insult the current pope. "If Antichrist is born in Rome and will possess the apostolic throne," the king said, according to Roger, "then I know that he is that Clement who is now pope." Roger adds by way of explanation, "He said these things because he really hated that pope."[80] Richard followed this comment, according to Roger, with his own brief disquisition about the Last Days—a retelling of the traditional life of Antichrist, who would be born in Babylon, enthroned in Jerusalem, and struck down by Christ after three and one-half years.[81] Apparently, Richard preferred established prophetic patterns over newfangled calculations.

Roger of Hovedon felt similarly, or at least his suspicions about Joachim grew with time. A few years later, he retold the story as part of a new and longer chronicle. The changes he made were minor but striking, particularly Richard's reaction at hearing that Saladin would lose control of Jerusalem. Roger has the king asking Joachim when this will happen. "After seven years have passed from the day of Jerusalem's capture." Then Richard wonders, "Then why did I bother coming here so quickly?" Joachim responds, "Your arrival is essential, since the Lord will grant you victory over his enemies and will exalt your name above all the other princes of the earth."[82]

The predicted course of events was nearly accurate. Richard did attain victories at Acre and Jaffa but failed to capture Jerusalem. Saladin also lost control of Jerusalem six years after its conquest (it is possible Roger miscounted when he wrote "seven," or else, like Joachim and John of Patmos, he simply liked the number seven). It happened because Saladin died, not because he was defeated. Prophecy is a tricky ally.

Did Joachim have a similar sense, that God had played a trick on him, or at least that his prophetic system had failed, despite his greater proximity to the end of history? Possibly. At some point

Table 9: Joachim's Later Reading of the Seven Seals

Seven Persecutors: The Red Dragon from the *Book of Figures*	Seven Persecutors: *Introductory Book* to the *Exposition of the Apocalypse*
1. Herod	1. Herod
2. Nero	2. Nero
3. Constantius	3. Constantius
4. Muhammad	4. Chosroes
5. Mesemutus	5. Unnamed German Emperor
6. Saladin	6. Saladin or a successor
7. Antichrist	7. Antichrist

during the construction of his commentary on Revelation, he developed yet another list of the church's seven persecutors, one that greatly reduces the importance of Islam (see table 9).[83]

Muhammad has been replaced with the Persian emperor Chosroes (defeated by Heraclius on the eve of the birth of Islam), and the Moors have been replaced by the Germans. Saladin remains significant, but now a Saracen outlier.

Around 1196, about the same time that Joachim was working on *The Introductory Book*, he composed one other short treatise of apocalyptic history, this one titled *On the Final Tribulations*.[84] Using a method more compatible with his overall view of history, he crafted a threefold vision of persecution and prophecy: there had been three great wars fought by the Jews, and three fought by the church. The first of the Jewish conflicts was for the Promised Land, which ran from Moses to David. Christians struggled in a similar way to found their church, beginning with Christ and continuing to Constantine. The second Jewish war comprised the years of the Babylonian Captivity and the rebuilding of Jerusalem. Its Christian counterpart ran from Constantine to Joachim's own day, comprising nine centuries of troubles during the second *status*. Finally, the third Jewish war was the Maccabean revolt, the worst of the three because in it Antiochus fought not just against Jews, but against God—just as Gog, the counterpart to Antiochus, would also make war on heaven.[85] With this model, Joachim had written Islam out of salvation history altogether.

In the same text, when Joachim treated the image of the dragon's wounded head, he again made no reference to Islam. Once upon a time, that seemingly fatal injury had referred to the First Crusaders' victory. Now, in the aftermath of the Third Crusade, which ended in 1192, Joachim believed that the wound referred either to the defeat of the king of the North, who is an unnamed eleventh king and seventh persecutor of the church, or else to the millennial imprisonment of Satan, described in Revelation 20.[86] Muslims are, again, nowhere to be found. Truer to his modern, post-humous reputation, Joachim had abandoned crusading and kept his gaze fixed within the bounds of Christendom. As he observes in the *Exposition*, "Perhaps it will happen that Christians will prevail against [Islam] by preaching more than fighting."[87]

But was that really his final word on the subject? (And even if it were, would it matter? The fact that Joachim might have subscribed to one view at his death in 1202 would have concerned his medieval readers less than it does modern historians, who have better tools to parse the chronology of his thought.) In that last passage, the most important word is "perhaps"—*forte* in Latin. In light of so many failures in the East, an embittered and disappointed Joachim found it just as likely that Christendom might defeat Islam through words rather than with weapons. It is a sigh of disgust rather than a missionary's call to lay down weapons for rhetorical arms.

From a broader perspective, Joachim did not have any final answers. He did not suddenly realize that the dragon's fourth head was a Persian monarch, not an Arab prophet. Rather, as noted, he had a collection of images and ideas to draw on according to historical circumstance, literary necessity, and personal inclination. And one of his most revolutionary historical ideas concerned exactly this question—the place of Islam in history. It was an idea so startling that it seemed to catch Joachim himself off guard. And, appropriately, it came to him as he meditated on Nebuchadnezzar's dream. In a flash of insight, he realized that a thousand years of interpretive tradition had been wrong.

Such an embrace of novelty could be dangerous. In his own defense, Joachim appealed again to his temporal perspective: "We who live near the end of time can assemble many details about the end of things, details which lay hidden from the ancients."[88] Effectively, Joachim understood Daniel's visions better than Daniel. An angel in Daniel 12 had sealed God's secrets, and they would remain locked until the end of time; but in the 1190s, the Last Days were at hand. Seals were being broken.[89]

This new reading of Nebuchadnezzar appears in the fifth and final part of the *Book on Concord* (see table 10). Joachim's decision to place it there by itself is revealing. The *Book on Concord* was the introduction to his entire system of thought, the key that unlocked all of his other writings. In this most fundamental work, the very last thing

Table 10: Joachim's Reading of Nebuchadnezzar's Dream

Parts of Statue: Traditional Reading	Parts of Statue: Joachim's Reading
1. Gold: Babylon	1. Gold: Assyria, Chaldea, Persia
2. Silver: Persia	2. Silver: Greece
3. Bronze: Greece	3. Bronze: Rome
4. Iron: Rome	4. Iron: Islam

he wanted his readers to know about were the prophecies of Daniel, beginning with Nebuchadnezzar's dream.

What Joachim had realized was that the accepted interpretations of the metals needed revision. His first move was to combine all the Eastern kingdoms—Assyria, the Chaldeans, the Persians—into one single metal, not two, as Jerome believed, or three, as Lambert had done. The statue's gold head represented all of them. For "even though kings changed in Babylon, the eastern kingdom remained intact under all of them."[90] The silver torso represented the Macedonian empire. It began with Alexander the Great and endured, in Joachim's system, until the Maccabeean Revolt, when the third, bronze kingdom absorbed it. According to Daniel 2:39, this bronze empire would dominate the entire world. Joachim writes, "I do not see how anything could apply more appropriately to this passage than does that decree of Caesar Augustus, that a census of the whole world be taken."[91]

Rome is thus the bronze midsection of the statue. It survived many struggles and usually proved victorious. Passing over its earliest victories, Joachim focuses instead on what he terms the "final" or "outermost" battles of the sixth century, when "Emperor Justinian fought against the Persians and conquered them, fought against the Vandals and Goths who had invaded Africa and Italy and wiped them out, and then closed out the rest of his life in a time of peace, the enemies of Rome effectively purged."[92]

Historically, Joachim's analysis leaves something to be desired. But it makes an important point in the context of salvation history. At the time of Justinian, Rome was as powerful as it ever had been. It dominated the world, completely oblivious to the threat of a new kingdom. Joachim phrased his argument so tentatively—in newspaper parlance, he buried the lede—that readers might miss what had happened. The Iron Kingdom, the last, enduring earthly empire, was no longer Rome.

That distinction went to Islam. Rome had once defeated all of her enemies, but starting with the emperor Heraclius, she could not conquer the Saracens, "who have spread across the earth like locusts." They violently stole lands from Rome, and more recently, Joachim adds, with a nod toward the First Crusade, "what Christians had once recovered overseas, they have lost again to the same triumphant enemy, with many Christian dead. They are truly," he concludes, "an unyielding people, like iron."[93]

It was the Saracens' most characteristic trait. Unlike all other persecutors of the church, Saracens endured. The Jews had attacked Christians until in 70 CE, Rome stormed Jerusalem and scattered their nation. The Romans themselves became the second persecutor, but under Constantine they converted to Christianity. All the heretical kings, the third great persecutor, were likewise defeated. But the fourth persecutor, Muhammad and his followers, survived. They returned in the sixth *tempus* and reversed what had seemed a steady advance of Christianity—and according to at least one of Joachim's models, they were the chief persecutors of the fifth *tempus* as well.[94]

Islam existed in concord with the Babylonians, also known as the Assyrians, who had been the fourth enemy of Israel. In concord with Islam, Babylon had also come back to life after seeming pacified, if not dead, for Babylon was also the sixth enemy of Israel. A resurgent Babylon, a resurgent Islam, the wounded sixth head of the dragon resurrected.

> What is there to be said about the fourth enemy? I have seen one of the heads appear as if killed, dead. And then its battle wound was healed, and now we see it raised up above the hills and exceeding the heights of mountains. In the same way, that fourth persecution against Israel occurred through the Assyrian Kingdom, and it likewise remained strong through to the time of the sixth seal.[95]

The structure here is dazzlingly original. But the core argument is familiar. Babylon and Islam are inextricably linked, existing in harmony, or in concord, with one another across millennia, and the wars of the Jews against Nebuchadnezzar prefigured the wars of the Christians against Antichrist, be it Saladin or else the shadowy heretical king who, even as Joachim wrote his increasingly nightmarish commentaries, was making overtures of alliance toward Christ's most fearsome enemy, Muhammad, "this fourth, unyielding beast."[96]

Make no mistake—the beast would be defeated, its destiny written in the statue's feet, iron mixed with clay. Joachim, who had had the opportunity, both in Sicily and the Holy Land, to witness Islam's ethnic diversity, could write, "Although that people takes its origin from iron, it will not be as sturdy as it once was, on account of the various mixed peoples who will comprise it. Part of the kingdom will be sturdy, and part will be vulnerable on account of the mixed human seeds it will contain."[97] The stone from the mountain, uncut by human hand, would find the statue's weak spot and eradicate all trace of its rule, as well as all trace of the previous kingdoms.

Despite this apparently utopian conclusion to the second *status*, it would not be the end of Antichrist, and perhaps not the end of Islam, either. On at least one occasion, when discussing the defeat of the Saracens at the end of the sixth *tempus*, Joachim indicated that—with possibly a few exceptions—they would not convert like the Jews or disappear from the earth; rather, they would withdraw from the field of battle. "The lamb will fight through his followers and will conquer those peoples and give this clear sign: That fierce storm will end in such a way that the remaining unbelieving peoples will scatter to the four corners of the earth, not daring to cross their borders to swallow up God's elect."[98] As Joachim knew from Revelation 20:7, Satan (or rather Antichrist, in whom the devil would live as if he were a house) would seduce the nations, notably Gog and Magog. Then would begin the final battle of the third *status*—a heretic king possessed by the devil, leading an army of barbarians, whose number presumably included the final dregs of the Saracens, Christendom's most constant foe.[99]

Joachim believed himself close enough to see the curtain wall of humanity's destination but not to know what lay beyond it. As he observed at one point, "Whether things will turn out like this or in some other way, I don't know. God knows."[100] At times he seems to have wanted to eliminate the crusade altogether from his prophetic model. But apart from a couple of minor departures, the Saracen threat runs throughout his many oracular pronouncements, a nightmare war between East and West that would endure, like iron, even to the Last Days.

Conclusion

The Ongoing Madness of Antichrist

THE SKEPTICAL RALPH the Black took note of Joachim of Fiore's writing. In a short section near the end of his world history completed around the year 1200, he describes Joachim as a Cistercian monk who "went from being almost illiterate to having sudden understanding and who wrote about the Apocalypse and the opening of the Seven Seals." Joachim compared persecutions in the Old and New Testaments, and warned that the reign of Antichrist and the Day of Judgment were at hand. Ralph does not offer a final verdict, but he does observe that "Geoffrey of Auxerre, formerly the abbot of Clairvaux, wrote a more prudent commentary on the Apocalypse."[1]

Geoffrey, Ralph's preferred exegete, was indeed a man capable of great prudence. He was secretary to Bernard of Clairvaux and the monk who raised questions about how (during the German miracle tour) people who had been deaf-mutes from birth could suddenly understand and speak languages they had never before heard. His commentary on the Apocalypse was as different as possible from Joachim's. Instead of a verse-by-verse analysis emphasizing how the Bible had foretold the future, he composed a series of sermons that dealt primarily with moral and spiritual questions, focusing on how the images of Revelation could be applied to a monk's daily life.[2]

Joachim, however, challenged Geoffrey's diplomatic mind-set. Joachim, Geoffrey wrote, was not just whispering blasphemies about the kingdom of heaven and the resurrection—he was publicizing them, too. Where did Joachim get his ideas? "He is a person born among the Jews, trained for many years in Judaism, and he has not yet vomited it all out." Crypto-Judaism explained his unusual name. "Joachim" was more Jewish than Christian, and as Geoffrey darkly observes, he had never heard of anyone once Jewish keeping his name after baptism.[3] Ralph may not have accepted, or known of, Geoffrey's charges against Joachim. But the character of his prophecies was enough to give pause to a cautious observer such as he.

A similarly dismissive attitude marks Ralph's final verdict on the crusade. One of the last entries in his universal history concerns the death of Saladin, "the lord of Damascus, prince of Syria, Sultan of Babylon, king of the lands of Egypt, who conquered Jerusalem and almost all of Palestine and many Saracen kingdoms, a man of indescribable glory, raised high by victories unheard of." Saladin had planned to return to Mecca, Ralph says, slightly inaccurately, since Saladin had never been, but he died on the way. It is an impressive enough mistake, though, since Saladin had in fact hoped to perform the hajj, the pilgrimage to Mecca expected of all Muslims, at the end of his life. Upon his death, Saladin's sons wrecked the peace that he had created. They fought against one another, just as Christian princes continued to engage in destructive civil wars. "This is the land of the Lord and the fullness thereof, and Saracens and Christians deservingly brought wickedness to their faith. And so let man's wickedness be punished on land and sea."[4]

Ralph's historical instinct would be a long-standing one: to see Saladin, against a backdrop of double-dealing, backstabbing, and slaughter by both Christians and Muslims, as the only honorable man in the whole drama of the Third Crusade. The overall conclusion Ralph draws is equally prescient—a desire for Westerners to wash their hands of the Holy Land once and for all.

One of Ralph's contemporaries, a monk of Winchester named Richard of Devizes, pronounced an even more stinging indictment against the crusade at the conclusion of a highly idiosyncratic narrative of the years from 1189 to 1192. Despite his status as a monk, Richard brought a formidable store of classical learning to his history, viewing contemporary events with a satiric, secular eye. His most perceptive reader, the historian Nancy Partner, has described his work as "a pastiche of classical allusion," almost unmarked by biblical citation and completely absent the kind of overarching interpretation of Christian history typical of early crusade literature. It is truly a wonder, Partner observes, "how a twelfth-century monk could conceive of a specifically holy war so completely dominated by ordinary earthly considerations. If God were present at all to the author's

210   *Conclusion*

imagination, He would seem to have been a sadly feckless partisan of His own cause."[5]

The character King Richard, as Richard of Devizes imagines him, felt similarly. After recovering from a long illness, the Lionheart was ready to lead a final attack on Jerusalem, but all of his key followers, due in large part to machinations by the French, had decided to abandon the campaign. The last scene in the chronicle is of King Richard refusing an invitation to visit Jerusalem, because "the appropriate contempt that he carried in his great heart could not accept as a favor from the gentiles what he could not possess as a gift from God."[6] Just a few lines earlier, when Richard realized that his crusade would not end in victory, he phrased his disappointment in starker terms, speaking directly to God: "Oh, how unwillingly would I desert you in such a time of need, if I were to you what you are to me, my Lord and advocate! Know that my banners henceforth shall lie low not because of me but because of you! Know that it is not because of the indolence of my army that you, my king and my God, and not your little king Richard, are defeated on this day."[7]

The scene is wholly fanciful. The historian Richard had no access to the emotional world of his namesake, and in any case it was Richard the Lionheart who took the lead in negotiating a truce with Saladin. Instead of a historically accurate reconstruction of events, what Richard of Devizes offers is a deliberately provocative reading aimed at an audience ready to consider his controversial ideas.[8] Richard the Lionheart's cry of rage would have resonated for anyone who had followed a movement born out of the euphoric belief that God was working salvation at the center of the earth only to abandon the soldiers who were his tools. It is a fitting epitaph for twelfth-century crusading as a whole. God had failed.

But that was not the final word in the Middle Ages. Just as Joachim of Fiore had a large stock of images and ideas to draw on as he constructed his prophetic models, so too did and do medieval and modern readers of crusade history. In this book my purpose has been to highlight one strand of thought, which is both prominent in the sources and underappreciated in modern historical writing—a belief that the First Crusade was an apocalyptic event in the usual sense of the word. The 1099 conquest of Jerusalem had been foretold in the books of the Bible, in the book of Daniel, and in the "Apocalypse" proper, the book of Revelation. The establishment of a Christian kingdom of Jerusalem brought the Last Days closer to hand, although just how close remained a point of debate.

This apocalyptic reading of the crusade is as old as the crusade itself, apparent in the earliest chronicles—the anonymous *Deeds of the Franks* and the *Book* of Raymond of Aguilers—and in most of the next generation of sources as well. The connection to Nebuchadnezzar's dream was initially pronounced by an actual crusader, Bohemond of Antioch. The crusade was the rock that had struck the statue's feet. In doing so it had brought to an end all Eastern empires and raised in their place the great mountain of the Latin church. The chroniclers whose books Bohemond most directly influenced (Baldric of Bourgueil, Guibert of Nogent, Robert the Monk, and Ralph of Caen) all embraced this message, but it was the encyclopedist Lambert of Saint-Omer who labored most to give it a precise shape, searching the Bible, Orosius, Augustine, Isidore of Seville, and elsewhere for the historical figures and resonances that foreshadowed and created the crusade.

This idealized reading of history was, from the start, difficult to maintain. The knights who had achieved victory were imagined as paragons of virtue, warriors who had purged themselves in the fires of penance and been honed into inexorable weapons of divine vengeance. The survivors who returned home could not possibly live up to the legends they had inspired, though a notable few seemed to have made claims to moral infallibility. Also eroding the triumphant legacy of the First Crusade was a steady stream of uncomfortable news from the East. Alongside grand failures, like the crusade of 1101 and the Field of Blood, there must have been hundreds of tales like that of Corba of Thoringé, painful memories or shattered lives created by the desire to capture and hold Jerusalem. Even the good news—Baldwin I's almost unbroken record of conquest and expansion—was problematic, coming wrapped in the uncomfortable truth that survival in the Holy Land meant accommodation with an East whose dress, manners, and piety seemed in every respect an attack on Western virtue, if not a concession to Antichrist. One did not need a Second Crusade to find reason for disillusionment with the First.

But the Second Crusade—that glorious, brutal fiasco—did happen. The myth of the apocalyptic crusade might have survived sociopathic veterans like Thomas of Marle. It could survive Christ's failure to return right away, since according to most accepted prophetic models, there would be a waiting period between victory in Jerusalem and the final showdown with Antichrist, Gog, and Magog. The apocalyptic crusade might have even survived the fall of Edessa, which, after all, had been a fairly peripheral element of the original crusade story. What it could not endure was the Second Crusade as preached by Bernard of Clairvaux, framed as a call to reenact the "efforts of your forebears" and endorsed by God through hundreds of miracles.

The wounds left by this expedition did at least lead to some marvelously creative thought. The historian Otto of Freising, himself a survivor (and possibly an early enthusiast for the Second Crusade), who had spent some time reading through Lambert of Saint-Omer's *Liber floridus*, perfected the idea of *translatio imperii*: the belief that the legitimate practice of empire had gradually migrated to the West. Less recognized, but equally profound, was his decision to write the Holy Land out of the future. For Otto managed to keep traditional prophetic models, just without reference to earthly Jerusalem. Gerhoh of Reichersberg, like Otto an early supporter of the Second Crusade, took this idea further, developing a set of rules that denied any need for Antichrist to be Jewish or for the wars against him to occur in the Middle East. By the time Ralph the Black made his contributions to history and theology, he could comfortably dismiss crusade and pilgrimage as dangerous distractions from the more important battles to be fought at home and in the soul.

The urge to crusade might have died altogether, as Ralph wanted it to, were it not for the spectacular fall of Jerusalem in 1187 (though of course Ralph himself was immune to the ensuing panic). Promoters of the new crusade, however, were chary of mentioning the First Crusade. It no longer made sense as a focal point in salvation history. Christian Jerusalem had ceased to be a quest fulfilled and had become instead a Holy Grail, a relic newly lost and for decades and centuries thereafter tantalizingly out of reach.

The exception to this tendency was Joachim of Fiore. Joachim did confine the First Crusade to the nooks and crannies of his prophetic system—literally, hidden beneath a dragon's scar—but it played a crucial role in his thought. More surprisingly (certainly I was surprised by it) was the fearful and spiteful tone he adopted toward Islam, revealed in part through his belief that Saracens and heretics were actively conspiring against Christians, and brought more fully to light in his wholly original interpretation of Nebuchadnezzar's dream. Islam was the iron empire, the enduring adversary that would stalk Christendom till the end of time.

With Joachim, moreover, the intellectual path traced in this book comes full circle, back to Bohemond. Both men, Bohemond and Joachim, saw the Latin West as the rock destined to bring down the statue of all earthly rule, whose metals (all four of them according to Bohemond or else just the iron according to Joachim) pointed to Islam. It is a historical vision shared by most of the prophets, theologians, preachers, and chroniclers examined in this book. It is a grim view as well, a world divided between East and West, with Greek, Syrian, and Armenian Christians serving as a sort of treacherous, effeminate buffer zone between the two.

This stark vision was not the only option, even if in the twelfth century it was the dominant one. Nor did it die away in the thirteenth century. Readers in medieval libraries were similar to a certain breed of Internet troll. They would, with far less effective search engines, scour available evidence, readily accept barely justifiable attributions (leading to prolific authorial voices like Pseudo-Augustine or Pseudo-Methodius), and presume that highly suspect or badly outdated materials spoke directly to their own situation. So even if Joachim of Fiore at the end of his life moved away from his vitriolic, anti-Islamic intellectual stance, as some of his modern apologists suggest, it would be of little matter to a reader confronted with book 5 of his *Book of Concord* or with the bulk of the material in his *Exposition of the Apocalypse.* Any reader who accepted the challenge of reading these books would walk away thinking that Joachim had foreseen this endless and endlessly destructive conflict with the Saracens.

In a similar fashion, despite Godfrey of Bouillon's failure to usher in a last-world empire at Jerusalem, any reader who came across one of the enormously impressive copies of the *Liber floridus* in circulation would still be confronted with a detailed exposition of why the sixth age had come to end in 1099. Such a reader might respond to this presentation in two ways. One would be to recognize the error in Lambert's reading of history. Crusader Jerusalem had collapsed, and apart from a brief and unsatisfying period of joint Christian-Muslim possession of the city in the early thirteenth century, the West had never reclaimed its prize. The other response would be to try to reconcile Turkish rule in Jerusalem with the possibility that a new age in salvation history had begun with King Godfrey. That was likely the path pursued by many readers, since scribes continued to copy the *Liber floridus* into the thirteenth century. It even enjoyed a resurgence in popularity in the fifteenth, its texts and images and interpretations of the crusade relevant enough to merit the investment of time, money, and artistry needed to make further copies.[9] How exactly a prophetic book rooted in so particular a moment spoke to readers three centuries later is unclear. Like iron, apocalyptic expectations endure.

And then as now, prophetically minded readers of current events found new texts, ideas, and images to mull over. The leaders of the Fifth Crusade (1217–21), in the course of their campaign, discovered two Arabic books, which they believed forecast imminent Christian victories in Egypt and which they consulted as they formulated actual battlefield strategies. As news of westward Mongol expansion reached Europe, prophets in the Latin homeland believed Genghis Kahn to be the long-awaited Prester John or else the long-dreaded Gog of Magog, once imprisoned by Alexander the Great, now turned loose on the world.[10] In the face of continual failure, prophetic hope springs eternal.

By and large I have focused less on events and more on ideas, many of them rather bookish, rooted in scripture, history, myth, geography, and prophecy. It might be fair to ask if such a conceptual vocabulary, on the face of it born of a rare combination of erudition and naïveté, could have had any effect on the actual conduct of war. Put more simply, did the crusaders actually believe this nonsense?

Apart from a small circle of modern scholars, most of them French, the idea of an apocalyptic crusade has not found a receptive audience among specialists.[11] The eminent historian Jonathan Riley-Smith pronounced authoritatively about apocalyptic beliefs during the First Crusade, "It is difficult to believe, however, that hysteria affected more than a minority of crusaders."[12] The word choice is revealing, since it points to a basic misunderstanding of what the Apocalypse actually is—not a set of fringe beliefs but rather the last book of the Christian Bible, crucial to the practice of faith and no more a product of hysteria or superstition than the (utterly irrational, if we can set aside our own spiritual and cultural baggage) compulsion to perform penance, which Riley-Smith thought a much more credible explanation for going to war.[13]

As should be apparent from the preceding pages, an embrace of the apocalyptic, by crusaders or historians, does not necessarily lead to hysteria or fear or despair. In the twelfth century, it indicated a wish to understand history and a belief that humanity still had an important role to play in God's plan for salvation. It was a call to arms, allegorically and literally. And presumably, as calls to arms go, it was an effective one, especially compared to a penitential model. "Confess your sins and enter battle with serene intention and a pure mind, ever mindful of the dangers of greed, glory, and hatred," does not compare favorably, from a warrior's perspective, to "Your enemies are polluted and demonic slaves of Antichrist who deserve pitiless slaughter and in whose bloodshed you may revel. Consign them to hell, and even as you do, you shall see the gates of heaven open before you."

A dedicated apocalypticist need not stop there. New levels of meaning, interpretation, and storytelling could be layered on top of this message. And they could be communicated simply to most any audience. The idea that Jerusalem was the center of the earth and a microcosm of it, for example, might be demonstrated either through a carefully drawn world map or else by an informed preacher with a stick, able to scratch an "O" and a "T" into the dirt. Local pilgrims had learned to see caskets stuffed with bones of questionable authenticity as sources of miraculous power and portals to heaven. How much more thunderously might these emotions have resounded in the hearts of soldiers primed to paint the streets of Jerusalem in the blood and entrails of their enemies?

From a different perspective, warriors have been ubiquitous in this story. One of them, Bohemond of Antioch, was the source of the book's eponymous concept—the crusade as fulfillment of Nebuchadnezzar's dream—though he likely had help from Bruno of Segni and other representatives of the papal court in honing his message. Bernard of Clairvaux successfully recruited vast armies for the Second Crusade, relying on a language colored by popular prophecies about the Last Emperor. The bishop and historian Otto of Freising advised two kings, led German foot soldiers through Anatolia, meditated on prophecies about a conquering king from the West with the initial "C," and then tried to make sense of it all through a theory about the western movement of government. And Richard the Lionheart sought out Joachim of Fiore, listened to a sermon about how a seven-headed dragon revealed the outcome of his own crusade, and then responded with a defense of the traditional prophetic school of Pseudo-Methodius and Adso of Montier-en-Der.

A fascination with the Last Days and an excitement at the thought that they might actually be at hand were places where clerical learning and knightly valor met. The First Crusade had represented a moment of joyous apocalyptic celebration, out of which a great dream or revelatory illusion had been born. The remainder of the twelfth century was spent trying to reconcile this vision of imminent peace with the relentless and dreary slog of history.

A more pressing question to readers not confined to the contentious realm of academic politics is whether these thought-worlds from the

216   *Conclusion*

twelfth century offer any lessons for the twenty-first. To draw one-to-one parallels across nine centuries of history is a fraught business.[14] But at the same time, it would seem obtuse not to recognize what a powerful motivation apocalyptic thought remains in modern belief systems.

The most obvious recent historical analog is the conflict of the West (a deeply felt sense of identity shared across the centuries with crusaders) with the Islamic State (or ISIS or ISIL). William McCants, in his book *The ISIS Apocalypse*, has argued that much of the Islamic State's tactics and outlook is comprehensible only when viewed through the lens of Muslim apocalyptic tradition. The group's decision in 2015 to attack the Syrian village of Dabiq, held by Syrian rebels and described in a contemporary news report as "an unimpressive cluster of clay-brick farmsteads and houses," was born out of a prophecy attributed to Muhammad: "The Hours will not come until the Romans land at al-A'maq or in Dabiq. An army of the best people on earth at that time will come from Medina against them." In harmony with ideas presented here, the Romans have transformed into a symbol for the West more generally. Western (and particularly American) incursions into the region are part of a crusade. The road to the End Times would run through the Dabiq, preparing the way for the appearance of the Mahdi, the redeemer of Islam. And soon after will arrive the Day of Judgment (according to some Muslim traditions to be carried out in Jerusalem by Jesus, just as twelfth-century Christian prophets would have expected.)[15]

A focus on the Islamic State or other comparable terrorist organizations, however, ignores the ways in which any number of popular Western writers, preachers, pundits, and proselytizers adopt the same vocabulary. To take only one representative title: *Countdown to the Apocalypse: Why ISIS and Ebola Are Only the Beginning*.[16] Evangelical Protestants ally with Orthodox Jewish groups in hopes of seeing the Temple rebuilt (and consequently, the Dome of the Rock and al-Aqsa Mosque leveled), each side with its own apocalyptic scenario in play—a phenomenon detailed in Gershom Gorenberg's *The End of Days*. Because of a verse from Numbers 19:2, Christian and Jewish groups alike anxiously await the birth of a perfect red heifer in Israel, which might serve as a purifying agent to enable the construction of this Third Temple in Jerusalem. In 1969, an Australian Christian named Dennis Michael Rohan set fire to the minbar (or pulpit) in al-Aqsa Mosque originally installed by Saladin, in hopes of enabling the rebuilding of the Temple. A similar ideology is suspected of motivating Baruch Goldstein to open fire on worshippers at the mosque of Abraham in the Cave the Patriarchs in Hebron, killing 29 people and wounding 125.[17] The suicide bombings, shootings, assassinations, and everyday madness inspired by the Temple Mount (or Haram al-Sharif) in Jerusalem demonstrates just how closely allied twelfth- and twenty-first-century passions are. As in 1099, the heart of Jerusalem remains the most contested real estate on earth.

It is possible to dismiss Western apocalypticists like the ones mentioned earlier as isolated eccentrics, lunatics, lone gunmen, or fringe elements. But that is too easy an out. Philippe Buc has argued powerfully in his book *Holy War, Martyrdom, and Terror* for the continuities in Western tradition (over two millennia) that bring together ideas of crusade and terror, martyrdom, purge, and purity. It is not a purely Christian worldview that Buc analyzes (it encompasses in his work not just the crusades and the sixteenth-century Wars of Religion but also the Terror of the French Revolution and Stalinist trials, among other phenomena, and probably set the stage for how social and political scientists ought to be interpreting the digital tempest of the alt-right), but it does draw heavily on the fundamental "grammar" of Christian exegesis.[18]

Buc offers a specific salutary reminder of how alive the language of crusading can be with Lieutenant General William G. Boykin, who served as the U.S. Undersecretary of Defense for Intelligence from 2002 to 2007, the foundational years of the War on Terror. While in office, he maintained an active sideline as an itinerant preacher, helping to set American foreign policy in scriptural context. To account for why his men had prevailed in a 1993 firefight in Somalia against the Muslim leader Osman Ali Atto, for example, the general explained, "I knew that my God was bigger than his. I knew that my God was a real God and his was an idol." In another of his sermons, he stressed, "I want to impress upon you that the battle that we're in is a spiritual battle...Satan wants to destroy this nation, he wants to destroy us as a nation, and he wants to destroy us as a Christian army."[19] The sentiment (though not the words, which lack the requisite sophistication) could have been drawn from Baldric, Guibert, or Robert, rather than a twenty-first-century policy maker at the highest levels of the US government, expected to help to set the tone of Western-Islamic engagement. More recently, (as of this writing) the decision by the Trump administration to recognize Jerusalem as the capital of Israel and to move the embassy there would seem only the latest prophetic gambit in an ongoing struggle to control apocalyptic history, an act to inspire hope among radical Christians, Jews, and Muslims alike.

To ask the obvious question: Is there any lesson to be drawn between the overlaps between medieval and modern approaches (fringe and mainstream) to religious violence? Might policy makers have avoided the grisly missteps of the Iraq War if they had taken religious ideologies more seriously, as opposed to (from all appearances) seeing them only as poses of fanaticism easily dispensed with once the material advantages of democratic capitalism were made plain? Might the rise of the Islamic State have been foreseen or the humanitarian catastrophes along the Turkish-Syrian-Iraqi borders been avoided or ameliorated? Could the chimeric Israeli-Palestinian peace process be ushered toward a satisfying conclusion with a more frank and sensitive recognition of the dark apocalyptic energy radiating from the Temple Mount? Perhaps. As this book will have made clear, however, prophecies are easier to interpret after the fact. Put another way, historians ought not to be in the business of predicting the future.

On the other hand, historians should be in the business of telling cautionary tales. If a reader leaves this book with a deeper respect for the sophistication, the attractiveness, and the sheer staying power of apocalyptic ideas, some useful purpose will have been served.

To turn the previous line of argument on its head, the survival and influence of apocalyptic thought in the twenty-first century world reaffirms the case for its reality and importance in the Middle Ages. If a largely literate and educated population whose faith has been tempered by Reformation and Enlightenment still looks with hope (and probably some greater fear than did medieval Christians) toward the Last Days, there is no reason to think that Christian audiences who regularly passed through church doors topped by graphic images of Christ sitting in judgment over newly resurrected bodies would have dismissed apocalyptic ideas as mere hysteria. Entering into the age of crusades, the Apocalypse was simply one aspect of the experiences and perceptions of medieval Christian's life, a significant one, and an everyday one as well, part of the imaginative floor plan around which belief and practice would necessarily arrange themselves.[20]

This argument need not stand in opposition to other motives advanced to explain the crusades. To suggest that crusaders (and the contemporary historians who wrote about them) viewed their campaign as intimately connected to the Apocalypses of Daniel, John of Patmos, and Pseudo-Methodius does not preclude the likelihood that a desire for penance motivated crusaders and historians alike. The whole point of the Last Judgment is to weigh sins outstanding—not purged by penance—and to impose punishment or reward as appropriate. Motivations, as we have known since Freud (or Shakespeare, or Homer) are overdetermined. Guibert of Nogent certainly knew it. In the introduction to his crusade chronicle, he admits that he will get some details wrong. "Is it any wonder if we make mistakes in reporting the deeds of others when we are hardly able—I do not say 'to express in words' but—to order our own thoughts and deeds silently in our minds? How can I speak about Intentions, which are so impenetrable that the very acumen of the inner man can barely discern them?"[21] There is room for apocalyptic enthusiasm, a fear of sin, hatred, love, greed, and vainglory in one army and in a single mind. Historians who wish to find a simple answer to complex psychological phenomena would do well to learn from Guibert.

Penance, the pilgrimage of life, the apocalyptic destination of a Jerusalem, which might be geographical or allegorical—it is all part of a single story of salvation. In 1106 a warrior born in southern Italy declared Christian victory over Antichrist in a war fought in the shadows of a gold, silver, bronze, iron, and clay statue. History itself may have ended. Nearly a century later a prophet born in the same lands realized that that war had not ended and wrote that its fires would burn through to the final military engagements at the end of time. Not only was history ongoing, but it seemed to extend beyond what had once looked like Armageddon into a new age of peace, with yet another fiery battle to be fought against armies called from all the earth's corners, a statue looming above it all on unsteady feet, ready to fall, but its ultimate meaning still sealed.

ACKNOWLEDGMENTS

This book is the culmination of about fifteen years of reading, research, writing, fellowship support, conference presentations, talks with colleagues, and conversations with friends. It wouldn't exist without all of the above, and at the end of this long road, I have forgotten more of these acts of kindness and generosity than I should have done. In terms of research support, I was fortunate enough to receive a MacArthur Fellowship (2008–12) which made all aspects of my professional life easier. It came on the heels of an NEH Fellowship (2007–8), which allowed me to live in Paris for a year, and an ACLS Burkhardt Fellowship (2006–7), which allowed me to spend a year in the American Academy in Rome. The friendships I formed there (and the good grace with which the Fellows bore with my endless discussions of crusader cannibalism) have grown ever more important with the passage of time. And as an added bonus, I became a character in Tom Bissell's book *The Apostle*, in the chapter describing our trip to Jerusalem. Corpus Christi College in Oxford allowed me to spend a term in 2014 as a visiting scholar and also made it possible for me to pass a few hours in the library's vault with the manuscript of Joachim of Fiore's *Book of Figures*. Chapter 12 of this book could not have happened without that time in England. Through it all, my department at the University of Tennessee has been supportive with leave time, allowing me to keep returning to this work—most recently a year spent at the Tennessee Humanities Center, where most of this book was actually written. Writing is a solitary process best undertaken in communities, I have learned. The communities mentioned above, as well as my colleagues in medieval and Renaissance studies in Knoxville (at the Marco Institute) and the many graduate students with whom I have closely worked have won my endless gratitude. I have to mention in particular Tom Burman, Bob Bast, Matthew Gillis, Anne-Hélène Miller, Mary Dzon, Katie Hodges-Kluck, Thomas Lecaque, Brad Phillis, and Lydia Walker.

I have too many colleagues to thank. I have tried to make acknowledgments as appropriate throughout the book. A few need special mention. Peggy Brown has been a true friend and a valued academic consigliere throughout. Damien Kempf generously shared his knowledge of Robert the Monk manuscripts whenever I had a particular question (which was often). Ed Peters has given sage advice when I needed it (which, again, was often). Bill North, who has a keener insight into the workings of the Reform Papacy than anyone in the world, I think, helped me get a handle on what Bruno and Paschal might have been up to. Luigi Russo has similarly helped me understand Bohemond. Cecilia Gaposchkin has kept me up to date on liturgy about the crusades and has reassured me that, from that side of the story, my ideas are not as wildly off-base as I sometimes fear. Philippe Buc has always been willing to Skype in from Vienna at a moment's notice to discuss holy war. John Nielsen helped straighten me out about the real Nebuchadnezzar. Brett Whalen and Matt Gabriele have read chunks of the manuscript in advance and offered their thoughts. Jonathan Phillips, William Purkis, Bernard Hamilton, Susan Edgington, Steve Biddlecombe, and Carol Sweetenham made me feel very welcome in London. Christopher Tyerman, Peter Frankopan, and Mark Whittow (who passed away during the final stages of editing this manuscript) did the same in Oxford. Cheers and thanks to my research assistant, Katie Kleinkopf, who helped get this book across the finish line. Much gratitude to Will Fontanez as well, who put together the book's maps. The editorial support at

Oxford University Press came to me highly recommended and has exceeded all expectations—gratitude to Tim Bent, Joellyn Ausanka, and Mary Sutherland.

There are lots of other people to thank, but I will close by thanking my wife, Meredith McGroarty, for living with this book (and living with me living with this book) for so long. And thanks to my son, Edward, who turned up for the final four years of its writing and who has taught me to draw all sorts of new connections between past, present, and future, how we choose to remember, live, and dream it respectively.

NOTES

PREFACE

1. I have discussed the specifics of this shift in Jay Rubenstein, *Guibert of Nogent: Portrait of a Medieval Mind* (New York: Routledge, 2002), 95–101 and 108–9.
2. Norman Cohn, *The Pursuit of the Millennium: Revolutionary Millenarians and Mystical Anarchists of the Middle Ages* (London: Secker and Warberg, 1957).

CHAPTER 1

1. Daniel 2:10.
2. Following the description of Paul-Alain Beaulieu, "Nebuchadnezzar's Babylon as World Capital," *Journal of the Canadian Society of Mesopotamian Studies* 3 (2008): 5–12.
3. 2 Kings 24:4.
4. 2 Kings 24:14.
5. Daniel 2: 28.
6. Daniel 2:45–46.
7. These two visions are in Daniel 7 and 8.
8. Daniel 12:9.
9. On this theme, Anathea E. Portier-Young, *Apocalypse against Empire: Theologies of Resistance in Early Judaism* (Grand Rapids, MI: Eerdmans, 2011); on the process of its compilation, Carol A. Newsom with Brennan W. Breed, *Daniel: A Commentary* (Louisville: Westminster John Knox Press, 2014), 8–14.
10. Jerome, *Commentariorum in Danielem libri III <IV>*, ed. F. Glorie, CCSL 75A (Turnhout: Brepols, 1964), 1.2.31/35, 794–95.

CHAPTER 2

1. Orderic Vitalis, *Ecclesiastic History*, ed. Marjorie Chibnall, 6 vols. (Oxford: Oxford University Press, 1969–1980), 6.11, 70–71.
2. Anna Komnene, *The Alexiad*, trans. E. R. A. Sewter and Peter Frankopan (London: Penguin Classics, 2009), 13.10, 383–84.
3. I have written about Bohemond's preaching tour and its role in inspiring these three writers in Jay Rubenstein, "The Deeds of Bohemond: Reform, Propaganda, and the History of the First Crusade," *Viator* 47 (2016): 113–35. The definitive work on Bohemond's preaching itinerary is Luigi Russo, "Il viaggio di Boemondo d'Altavilla in Francia (1106): un riesame," *Archivo Storico Italiano* 163 (2005): 3–42.
4. *Hystoria de via et recuperatione Antiochiae atque Ierusolymarum*, ed. Edoardo D'Angelo (Florence: Edizioni del Galluzzo, 2009), 140, 135.
5. Orderic Vitalis, *Ecclesiastical History* 6.11, 70–71. Bohemond would have passed close to Orderic's monastery of Saint-Evroult in May, when he journeyed from Chartres to Rouen; Russo, "Il viaggio," 40.
6. In addition to Russo, "Il viaggio," see R. B. Yewdale, *Bohemond I, Prince of Antioch* (Princeton, NJ: Princeton University Press, 1924), 108–12; Réginald Grégoire, *Bruno de Segni, exégète médiéval et théologien monastique* (Spoleto: Centro Italiano di Studi sull'Alto Medioevo,

1965), 46–47, and more recently, Jean Flori, *Bohémond d'Antioche, Chevalier d'Aventure* (Paris: Payot, 2007), 253–73.

7. On Bruno, William Linden North, "In the Shadows of Reform: Exegesis and the Formation of a Clerical Elite in the Works of Bruno, Bishop of Seigni (1078/9–1123)," (PhD diss., University of California-Berkeley, 1998), 402. On the role of the Gregorian papacy unleashing crusade violence, see Gerd Althoff, *"Selig sind, die Verfolgung ausüben": Päpste und Gewalt im Hochmittelalter* (Darmstadt: Wissenschaftlich Buchgesellschaft, 2013).

8. The hagiographic material about Léonard appears as *Vita et miracula S. Leonardi*, in *AASS*, *Nov.* 3 (Brussels: Socii Bollandiani, 1910), 149–82. Unless otherwise noted, the miracles cited come from a second book of miracles, titled simply *Liber alter miraculorum*, henceforth *Liber alter S. Leonardi*. The hagiographers frequently comment on the great size of the chains with which local lords used to enforce harsh justice on their subjects. The vicomte of Limoges, for example, had one massive chain specially forged to bind individual prisoners to the top of a column outside his castle. He called it "the Moor's chain," *catena maura*; 156B.

9. *Vita et miracula S. Leonardi*, from the first book of miracles, prologue, 150.

10. William of Malmesbury, *Gesta Regum Anglorum*, ed. R. A. B. Mynors, R. M. Thomson, and M. Winterbottom (Oxford: Clarendon Press, 1998), 4.387, 692–93. William writes that the chains Bohemond took back from Antioch were made of silver. Orderic Vitalis, *Ecclesiastical History*, 5.10, 376, says that Richard brought them to Noblat instead of Bohemond.

11. Galeran's text is preserved as the second chapter of *Liber alter S. Leonardi*, 161–69; with a revised version on 178–82. See also Russo, *Boemondo*, 159.

12. *Liber alter S. Leonardi* 2.2.1, 161C.

13. Paul M. Cobb, *The Race for Paradise: An Islamic History of the Crusades* (Oxford: Oxford University Press, 2014), 72. On the Danishmendid Sultanate, Claude Cahen, *The Formation of Turkey: The Seljukid Sultanate of Rum: Eleventh to Fourteenth Century*, trans. and ed. P. M. Holt (New York: Pearson, 2001), 11–14.

14. "Persarum doli"; *Liber alter S. Leonardi* 2.2.2, 161D.

15. Two good recent accounts are: Luigi Russo, *Boemondo. Figlio del Guiscardo e principe di Antiochia* (Avellino: Elio Sellino, 2009), 139–41; and Flori, *Bohémond*, 219–20.

16. Christopher MacEvitt, *The Crusades and the Christian World of the East: Rough Tolerance* (Philadelphia: University of Pennsylvania Press, 2008), 58–63.

17. MacEvitt, *Rough Tolerance*, 76–77. See also Thomas S. Asbridge, *The Creation of the Principality of Antioch, 1098–1130* (Woodbridge: Boydell Press, 2000), 51.

18. "quasi fauces quaedam angustissimus introitus"; *Liber alter S. Leonardi* 2.2.2, 161D.

19. *Liber alter S. Leonardi* 2.2.2, 161E. The description of the style of warfare characteristic of the crusades finds its reflection in modern scholarship: Carole Hillenbrand, *The Crusades: Islamic Perspectives* (Edinburgh: Edinburgh University Press, 1999), 511–16; and R. C. Smail, *Crusading Warfare, 1097–1193*, 2nd ed. (Cambridge: Cambridge University Press, 1995), 75–83.

20. *Liber alter S. Leonardi* 2.2.3, 162A–C.

21. Revelation 12:7–9. On Michael and the Normans, see Elizabeth Lapina, *Warfare and the Miraculous in the Chronicles of the First Crusade* (University Park: Penn State University Press, 2015), 81–83; on saintly intervention during the crusade, Lapina, *Warfare and the Miraculous*, 37–53.

22. *Liber alter S. Leonardi* 2.2.4, 162D.

23. On Bohemond and Alexius's relationship, J. Shepard, "When Greek meets Greek: Alexius Comnenus and Bohemond in 1097–8," *Byzantine and Modern Greek Studies* 12 (1988): 185–277. Also, Peter Frankopan, *The First Crusade: The Call from the East* (Cambridge, MA: Harvard University Press, 2012), esp. 133–35 and 160–62.

24. *Liber alter S. Leonardi* 2.2.5, 162E.

25. Galeran mentions Tancred's prayers, along with those of his *clientes ac familiares*, in his later, revised version of the *Miracula S. Leonardi* 3, 180C. On Tancred's disinterest in

freeing Bohemond, Ralph of Caen. *Gesta Tancredi, RHC Oc.* 3 147, 709, and the analysis of Flori, *Bohémond*, 221–23.

26. *Liber alter S. Leonardi* 2.2.5, 163B.

27. *Liber alter S. Leonardi* 2.2.9, 165D. See also Galeran's revised version of the story, where Léonard tells Bohemond in a vision, "You are confined and bound by the chains of your oath": *Compede artaris, ligatus es sacramenti vinculis; Miracula S. Leonardi* 3, 181A.

28. *Liber alter S. Leonardi* 2.2.6, 163–64.

29. *Liber alter S. Leonardi* 2.2.7, 164B,C. The story of Richard's capture and eventual freedom appears in the chapter of the miracle collection just before Galeran's account of Bohemond's adventures: *Liber alter S. Leonardi* 1, 159–60. Galeran wrote his own version of Richard's story as a chapter in his *Miracula S. Leonardi* 2, 177–79.

30. *Liber alter S. Leonardi* 2.2.7, 164C,D.

31. The chosen heroes are described as "reclining around his bed": "discumbunt in circuitu thori electi heroes"; *Liber alter S. Leonardi* 2.2.8, 164E.

32. *Liber alter S. Leonardi* 2.2.8, 164E.

33. *Liber alter S. Leonardi* 2.2.8, 164E,F.

34. *Liber alter S. Leonardi* 2.2.8, 164–65.

35. *Liber alter S. Leonardi* 2.2.9, 165B, with reference to Hebrews 12:6.

36. Galeran, *Miracula S. Leonardi* 3, 181A. Compare to *Liber alter S. Leonardi* 2.2.10, 165E; Richard's visions appear at 2.2.6, 164A.

37. "Per eundem Danismannum, qui nos captivavit, sanctus Leonardus nos liberabit"; *Liber alter S. Leonardi* 2.2.10, 165F.

38. *Liber alter S. Leonardi* 2.2.11, 166B.

39. Cobb, *Race for Paradise*, 71–77 and 105–7.

40. *Liber alter S. Leonardi* 2.2.11, 166D.

41. See Flori, *Bohémond*, 227–31. Bezants were gold coins minted at Byzantium.

42. *Liber alter S. Leonardi* 2.2.16–17, 168D,E.

43. *Liber alter S. Leonardi* 2.2.14, 167C,D.

44. *Miracula S. Leonardi* 3, 182F.

45. *Liber alter S. Leonardi* 2.2.18, 168E. Galeran reduced these figures slightly, to three weeks of fighting and a territorial expansion of around three days, in his revised version of the story: *Vita et miracula S. Leonardi* 3, 182F.

46. Flori, *Bohémond*, 242–43; Russo, *Boemondo*, 142–45; Asbridge, *Principality of Antioch*, 55–56.

47. Emily Albu discusses this legend of Bohemond in the broader context of Norman culture: "Bohemond and the Rooster: Byzantines, Normans, and the Artful Ruse," in *Anna Komnene and Her Times*, ed. Thalia Gouma-Peterson (New York: Garland, 2000), 157–68. Her essay never directly questions the veracity of the rooster story, though she does observe of another Norman ruse described by Anna alone that "the story is not precisely true," 164.

48. Anna Komnene, *Alexiad*, 11.12, 331.

49. On the links forged between crusaders and the Capetians, James Naus, *Constructing Kingship: The Capetian Monarchs of France and the Early Crusades* (Manchester, UK: Manchester University Press, 2016); on Bohemond and Philip I, Nicholas Paul, "A Warlord's Wisdom: Literacy and Propaganda at the Time of the First Crusade," *Speculum* 85 (2010): 534–66. Paul offers a different evaluation of Bohemond's character from the one presented here, points addressed in Rubenstein, "Deeds of Bohemond."

50. Guibert of Nogent, *Dei gesta per Francos*, ed. R. B. C. Huygens, CCCM 127 (Turnhout: Brepols, 1996), 1.5, 105–6.

51. Guibert establishes his expectation of war against Antichrist, centered around Jerusalem, in his version of Urban II's sermon at Clermont: *Dei gesta* 2.4, 113–14.

52. "Syria servit ei, mittunt nova dona Sabaei/Parthus, Arabs, Medus cupiunt sibi jungere foedus./Mulcet eum donis rex magnificus Babylonis/Soldanus, Persas pavet, et fugit illius enses,/Africa formidat, devotaque munus ei dat"; Marbod of Rennes, "Commendatio Jerosolymitanae expeditionis," in PL 171, col. 1672B,C.

53. "In toto mundo non est homo par Boemundo...Per Totum Mundum fert fama boans Boemundum / Et reboet mundus quia tanta facit Boemundus"; Marbod, "Commendatio," col 1672A and 1672C.
54. On the siege of Dyrrachium, Russo, *Boemondo*, 179–86, and Flori, *Bohémond*, 275–84.
55. Flori, *Bohémond*, 282–84 and 291–92; Frankopan, *Call from the East*, 190–92.
56. *Narratio Floriacensis de captis Antiochia et Hierosolyma et obsesso Dyrrachio*, RHC *Oc.* 5, 14, 362. Paul, "Warlord's Wisdom," 562–66, sees this text as part of Capetian propaganda, intended to conceal how ill-conceived the marriage between Constance and Bohemond had proven.
57. We learn these points in the form of a deathbed confession from Guy in *Narratio Floriacensis*, 15, 362.
58. "O Danai fortes, decet en meminisse priorum: Esto memor, miles, quae sit origo tua... Troia Miceneis ignibus usta perit"; Rodulfus Tortarius, *Carmina*, ed. Marbury B. Ogle and Dorothy M. Schullian (Rome: American Academy in Rome, 1933), Ep. 7, 305, lines 205–6, 210.
59. "Quaeso recorderis, habuit quas Gallia vires:/Orbem quae Romam straverat haec domuit;" Rodulfus Tortarius, *Carmina*, 304, lines 166–67.
60. Orderic Vitalis, *Ecclesiastical History* 6.11, 102–3. Anna Comnena claims that Alexius deliberately implicated Guy and others in treachery through forged letters, but she says that Bohemond ultimately was not deceived. Perhaps Orderic's informants were? Anna Komnene, *Alexiad* 13.4, 366–69; also, Chibnall's note, in the *Ecclesiastical History*, 6, 102, n.1. See also the comments in Robert Bartlett, *The Making of Europe: Conquest, Colonization, and Culture Change, 950–1350* (Princeton, NJ: Princeton University Press, 1993), 88, where he argues that acquisitiveness for its own sake is a peculiarly Norman trait.
61. "Cui cum succumberet orbis, non hominem possum dicere, nolo deum"; Flori, *Bohémond*, 296.
62. It was in fact a revision of the *Vita et miraculi S. Leonardi*, that survives only in an incomplete copy. The pagination in the AASS is 173–82.
63. Galeran, *Miracula S. Leonardi* 3, 180D.
64. The "little apocalypse" appears in all three of the synoptic gospels: Matthew 24, Mark 13, and Luke 21. The war for heaven is described in Revelation 12.
65. *Miracula S. Leonardi* 3, 180E.

CHAPTER 3
1. On the many events of March 25, as well as Bohemond's visit: Lambert of Saint-Omer. *Liber Floridus: Codex Autographus Bibliotheca Universitatis Gandavensis*, ed. A. Derolez and I. Strubbe (Ghent: E. Story-Scientia, 1968), fol. 27v. Lambert noted the concurrence of events on March 25 also on fol. 2r.
2. Lambert, *Liber floridus*, fol. 3v.
3. For the liturgical calendar references, Lambert, *Liber floridus*, fol. 31v; fol. 28r; fol. 29r; and fol. 29v; the version of Fulcher's *Historia* in the autograph copy, which is missing a quire, begins on fol. 110v; the annals are on fol. 43v.
4. Lambert, *Liber floridus*, fol. 1v.
5. Mark 13:32. Also, Matthew 24:36, which does not specify that the Son does not know. Luke 21, another version of the "Little Apocalypse," does not include this verse. Lambert refers to these verses on *Liber floridus*, fol. 23r, where he adds that Christ does in fact know when the day will be.
6. See, for example, Paula Fredriksen, "Tyconius and Augustine on the Apocalypse," in *The Apocalypse in the Middle Ages*, ed. Richard K. Emmerson and Bernard McGinn (Ithaca, NY: Cornell University Press, 1992), 20–37.
7. Matthew 24:32–34.
8. Richard Landes, "The Fear of an Apocalyptic Year 1000: Augustinian Historiography, Medieval and Modern," *Speculum* 75 (2000): 97–145 (111 and n.53); Jerome, *Commentariorum in Danielem* 1.2, 794–95.

9. Augustine, *De civitate Dei*, ed. B. Dombart and A. Kalb, 2 vols., CCSL 47–48 (Turnhout: Brepols, 1955), 2: 15.2, 454.

10. "Babylonia, quasi prima Roma, cum peregrina in hoc mundo Dei ciuitate procurrate"; Augustine, *De civitate Dei* 18.2, 594. Augustine explains here why he must list the "kings of Assyria."

11. R. A. Markus, *Saeculum: History and Society and the Theology of St. Augustine* (Cambridge: Cambridge University Press, 1970), 46–47.

12. James T. Palmer, *The Apocalypse in the Early Middle Ages* (Cambridge: Cambridge University Press, 2014), 31–32; Markus, *Saeculum*, 51–53.

13. I am basing this summary on what appears to be Augustine's earliest rendering of this model, as presented in Auguste Luneau, *L'histoire du salut chez les Pères de l'Eglise. La doctrine des ages du monde* (Paris: Beauchesne, 1964), 286–88.

14. Based on citations indexed in Albert Derolez, *The Autograph Manuscript of the Liber Floridus: A Key to the Encyclopedia of Lambert of Saint-Omer* (Turnhout: Brepols, 1998), (with additional reference on fol. 100r). The passages on the resurrection are cited at *Liber floridus* fols. 92v–93r, 220r (Derolez cannot identify the source of this quotation; *Autograph Manuscript*, 155), and 228v. The Sibylline prophecies are quoted on fol. 56r. The faulty reference on Paradise on fol. 100r, and on Christ in Hell on fol. 97v. Lambert also cites a passage from *On the City of God* on the possible humanity of monstrous creatures on fol. 53r and a passage on numerology from Augustine's *De Musica* on fol. 85v. I am not including a summation of the Ten Commandments on fol. 98r, which Derolez suggests was based on an Augustinian text (*Autograph Manuscript*, 95).

15. Palmer, *Apocalypse*, 87–95 discusses the implicit apocalyptic message of Isidore's presentation.

16. Bilbiothèque municipale Saint-Omer, MS 717, fols. 1v–63v. See entry 9, appendix II, in Derolez, *Autograph Manuscript*, 193, for a brief description of this manuscript.

17. The long excerpt covers fols. 190v–202r and is titled in the table of contents, on fol. 4v, *Gesta Romanorum imperatorum*. On fol. 202r, Lambert announces that he is changing sources and will now use Marcellinus instead of Orosius to complete the history, starting at the year 446. On fols. 19r and 52r, he uses Orosius for geographic information. On fol. 142v he quotes Orosius's judgment on Moses. On fols. 153r–153v, he draws on Orosius for information on Alexander. And fols. 166v–167v contain a highly abridged version of Orosius's *Historia*.

18. Markus, *Saeculum*, 161. Following Marcus, James J. O'Donnell, *Augustine: A New Biography* (New York: Harper, 2006), 250, characterizes Orosius's work as a misreading of Augustine's ideas in *City of God*.

19. See the commentary in Peter Van Nuffelen, *Orosius and the Rhetoric of History* (Oxford: Oxford University Press, 2012), 3–9 and 196–99. The edition of Orosius used here is: Orose, *Histoire (contre les Païens)*, ed. and trans. Marie-Pierre Arnaud-Lindet, 3 vols. (Paris: Belle Lettres, 1990–1991), cited as by volume, book, chapter, and page number. Orosius refers to Augustine's *City of God* in vol. 1, prologue, 8.

20. Peter Brown, *Augustine of Hippo: A Biography* (London: Faber and Faber, 1967), discusses these two sections on, respectively, 299–312 and 313–29.

21. Orosius, *Histories* 1, 2.19, 126–27. These points are echoed in Augustine, *De civitate Dei* 3.29, 95.

22. Orosius, *Histories* 3, 7.28, 74–75.

23. Orosius, *Histories* 3, 7.20, 55.

24. I have discussed these points in Jay Rubenstein, "Lambert of Saint-Omer and the Apocalyptic First Crusade," in *Remembering the Crusades: Myth, Image, and Identity*, ed. Nicholas Paul and Suzanne Yeager (Baltimore: Johns Hopkins University Press, 2012), 69–95.

25. Orosius, *Histories* 3, 7.2, 20.

26. See the comments in Nuffelen, *Orosius and the Rhetoric of History*, 153–56.

27. Orosius, *Histories* 1, prologue, 9, provides a brief discussion of the Last Days.

28. During the early years of Babylon and the later years of Rome, Macedon and Carthage are variously prominent on the historical stage. The habit of seeing the geographic

empires as chronologically divided is, however, an engrained, if faulty, historical habit—for example, Nuffelen, *Orosius and the Rhetoric of History*, 47, and Suzanne Conklin Akbari, *Idols in the East: European Representations of Islam and the Orient, 1100–1450* (Ithaca, NY: Cornell University Press, 2009), 35.

29. Orosius, *Histories* 1, 2.1, 187.

30. See Nuffelen, *Orosius and the Rhetoric History*, 153, who states strongly that Orosius did not hold to this calculation.

31. "Ordo regnorum principaliter regnantium"; Lambert, *Liber floridus*, fol. 19v.

32. As Nuffelen, *Orosius and the Rhetoric of History*, 48, notes, Orosius's list is related to that of the *Historiarum Philippicarum libri XLIV* by the (probably) third-century historian Justin, a list which is also similar to Lambert's: Assyria, Medes, Persia, and Macedon.

33. Orosius, *Histories* 1, 2.9–10, 87–88.

34. On Orosius's significance in the development of *translatio imperii*, Werner Goez, *Translatio Imperii: Ein Beitrag zur Geschichte des Geschichtsdenkens und der politischen Theorien im Mittelalter und in der frühen Neuzeit* (Tübingen: J. C. B. Mohr, 1958), 46–49, and Akbari, *Idols in the East*, 35–37. An east to west trajectory for history was also crucial to Hugh of Saint-Victor's diagram of the mystic ark: Conrad Rudolph, *The Mystic Ark: Hugh of Saint Victor, Art, and Thought in the Twelfth Century* (Cambridge: Cambridge University Press, 2014), 200–203.

35. Wolfenbüttel, Herzog August Bibliothek, MS Guelf. 1 Gud. lat., fol. 69v.

36. This passage is not preserved in the autograph manuscript but appears in Wolfenbüttel, Herzog August Bibliothek, MS Guelf. 1 Gud. lat., fol. 32v.

37. Augustine, *De civitate Dei* 18.2, 593; also, 18.22, 612; and 18.27, 618. Nuffelen's argument in *Orosius and the Rhetoric of History*, 198, n.64, that Augustine based these passages on Orosius is more convincing than that of Conrad Trieber, "Die Idee der Vier Weltreiche," *Hermes* 27 (1892): 321–44, who suggests (322, n.2) that Orosius depends on Augustine. Both Nuffelen and Trieber note that Augustine/Orosius are building on older, indeed pre-Christian, historiographic traditions.

38. "Babylonia, quasi prima Roma...Roma quasi secunda Babylonia"; Augustine, *De civitate Dei* 18.2, 594.

39. Augustine, *De civitate Dei* 18.22, 612 and 18.46, 643–44.

40. Lambert, *Liber floridus*, fol. 232v. The passage appears in the upper right-hand corner of his diagram of Nebuchadnezzar's dream, and the image to which I will return in the next chapter.

41. On this model, see Luneau, *L'histoire du salut*, 45–46.

42. Orosius, *Histories* 1, 1.1, 5 specifies the conjunction between Ninus and Abraham. He identifies Ninus explicitly as the founder of Assyria at *Histories* 1, 1.4, 43. Orosius says that the era between Creation and Abraham lasted for 3,184 years. On why Lambert used a different calculation, see Rubenstein, "Lambert of Saint-Omer," 83.

43. "Mundi Aetates usque ad Godefridum Regem"; Lambert, *Liber floridus*, fol. 20v.

44. "Octavianus, Christus, apostoli, evangeliste, martyres, confessores, virgines. In hoc anno Domini MXCIX Godefridus dux cepit Hierusalem indictione VII" and "VI etas usque ad captam Hierusalem annos MXCIX"; Lambert, *Liber floridus*, fol. 20v.

45. I am generally in sympathy with the eschatological reading of this diagram presented by Suzanne Lewis, "Encounters with Monsters at the End of Time: Some Early Medieval Visualizations of Apocalyptic Eschatology," *Different Visions: A Journal of New Perspectives on Medieval Art* 2 (2010): 76 [http://differentvisions.org/Issue2PDFs/Lewis.pdf], but am obviously reluctant to say that Lambert believed that the Sixth Age had in fact ended in 1099, as she argues on 62–65, although it is a possibility.

46. Daniel 2:21.

47. Guibert, *Dei gesta* 7.14, 289–90. I have written on the context of this poem in more detail in "Miracles and the Crusading Mind: Monastic Meditations on Jerusalem's Conquest," in *Prayer and Thought in Monastic Tradition: Essays in Honour of Benedicta Ward SLG*, ed. Santha Bhattacharji, Dominic Mattos, and Rowan Williams (London: Bloomsbury, 2014), 197–210 (esp. 209). The sentiment can be found in Psalm 101:2123 (NRSV 102:2022).

48. Peter the Venerable, "Sermo de laude dominici sepulchri," in Giles Constable, ed., "Petri
    Venerabilis sermones, tres," *Revue bénédictine* 64 (1954): 224–72 (232–54, cited here at 247).
49. Guibert, *Dei gesta* 2.4, 113.

CHAPTER 4

1. Kevin L. Hughes, *Constructing Antichrist: Paul, Biblical Commentary, and the Development of
   the Doctrine in the Early Middle Ages* (Washington, DC: Catholic University of America Press,
   2005), 1–27, gives a fine introduction to the biblical foundation of Antichrist theory.
2. One could add to this list the prophecy of the Tiburtine Sibyl, which tells essentially the
   same story. Here are examples of these prophecies circulating alongside crusade
   narratives: The Sibylline prophecy appears in: Paris, MS BnF *lat.* 6041A, fols. 124v–127r
   (which contains Raymond of Aguilers's Chronicle); and Rome, MS Vat. Lat. 1795, fols.
   85v–88v (which contains Robert the Monks's *Historia*). Versions of Adso's *Life of Antichrist*
   appear in Rome, MS Vat. Reg. Lat. 631, fols. 77r–76v (which contains Baldric's *Historia*
   and Fulcher abbreviated); Vienna, Österr. Nationalbibl., MS 480, fols. 185v–186v (which
   contains Robert's *Historia* and an excerpt from Fulcher); and St. Petersburg, National
   Library of Russia, MS Lat. Q.v.IV.n.3, cited in Derolez, "Abbey of Saint Bertin," 5 and n.7
   (which also contains Fulcher Abbreviated). The *Liber floridus* manuscripts, of course,
   contain Fulcher Abbreviated, Pseudo-Methodius, and Adso, although only three include
   all three texts now. The text of Adso is published in its many medieval versions as Adso
   Dervensis, *De ortu et tempore Antichristi*, ed. D. Verhelst, CCCM 45 (Turnhout: Brepols,
   1976); Methodius as Pseudo-Methodius, *Apocalypse*, ed. and trans. Benjamin Garstad
   (Cambridge, MA: Harvard University Press, 2012); the Tiburtine Sibyl in *Sibyllinische Texte
   und Forschungen*, ed. Ernst Sackur (Halle: Max Niermeyer, 1898), 117–87.
3. Lambert, *Liber floridus*, fol. 110; noted by Penelope C. Mayo, "The Crusaders under the
   Palm: Allegorical Plants and Cosmic Kingship in the *Liber Floridus*." *Dumbarton Oaks Papers*
   27 (1973): 29–67 (45, n.52).
4. Lambert, *Liber floridus*, fols. 217r–220r.
5. "Nascetur Antichristus perditionis filius de tribu Dan. quia Dan fuit filius Iacob genitus de
   Bala ancille Rachelis; Nascetur Antichristus in Corozaim. nutrietur in Bethsaida. regnabit
   in Capharnaum. Ingreditur in Iherusalem et sedebit in templo Dei quasi sit Deus; post
   hec modicum temporis interficiet eum Dominus spiritu oris sui. Tunc Iudei convertentur
   ad Dominum ex omni tribu filiorum Israhel: c.xl.iiii": Lambert, *Liber floridus*, fol. 62v, and
   figure 4. In the full text of Pseudo-Methodius in the *Liber floridus*, Lambert gives the usual
   figure that there will be 144,000 redeemed from the Jews; fol. 219v.
6. "Quod infortunium cernentes que in Iudea erant mulieres Wandalos et Hunos, qui tunc
   forte Orientis regna inuaserant, maritos acceperunt. Quapropter tempore ab illo non de
   Abraham, sed de Wandalorum semine descendisse creduntur"; Lambert, *Liber floridus*,
   fol. 81r.
7. "Antichristus sedens super Leviathan serpentem diabolum signantem bestiam crudelem
   in fine"; Lambert, *Liber floridus*, fol. 62v.
8. Lewis, "Encounters with Monsters," 58–60, and Mayo, "Crusaders under the Palm," 64.
9. Orderic Vitalis, *Ecclesiastical History* 4.8, 186–89. Chibnall keeps the Latin "Cornardus,"
   but in context, the translation to "Horny" seems justified.
10. William of Malmesbury, *Gesta regum* 1, 4.314, 558–61, following the translation of Mynors,
    Thomson, and Winterbottom.
11. Using the translation from Guibert of Nogent, *Monodies and On the Relics of Saints: The
    Autobiography and a Manifesto of a French Monk from the Time of the Crusades*, trans. Joseph
    McAlhany and Jay Rubenstein (London: Penguin Classics, 2011), 32.
12. Jeffrey Bowman, "Beauty and Passion in Tenth-Century Córdoba," in *The Boswell Thesis:
    Essays on John Boswell's Christianity, Social Tolerance, and Homosexuality*, ed. Mathew Kuefler
    (Chicago: University of Chicago Press, 2006), 236–53; John Boswell, *Christianity, Social
    Tolerance, and Homosexuality: People in Western Europe from the Beginning of the Christian Era to
    the Fourteenth Century* (Chicago: University of Chicago Press, 1981), 198–200.

13. Guibert, *Dei gesta* 1.5, 103. Akbari, *Idols in the East*, 283, suggests that an association between Islam and sodomy was more typical of the colonial era. Guibert was, perhaps, sadly ahead of his time.
14. Adso, *De Antichristo*, 27.
15. Adso, *De Antichristo*, 28.
16. "Epistola Methodii," published in Adso, *De Antichristo*, 151.
17. "Epistola Methodii," published in Adso, *De Antichristo*, 152, citing Romans 9.27.
18. Peter the Venerable, "Sermo de laude," 252, with reference to Genesis 4 and 1 Kings 18.
19. *Chanson d'Antioche*, ed. Suzanne Duparcq-Quioc (Paris: Paul Geuthner, 1978), 11, 26, lines 171–78. On both the Chanson in crusade history and on the conflation of Jews and Muslims in the Latin Christian imagination, see Philippe Buc, *Holy War, Martyrdom, and Terror: Christian Violence in the West, ca. 70 C.E. to the Iraq War* (Philadelphia: University of Pennsylvania Press, 2015), 280–82.
20. On this theme, Susanna A. Throop, *Crusading as an Act of Vengeance, 1095–1216* (Aldershot: Ashgate, 2011), though Throop emphasizes vengeance as a judicial idea.
21. It was such an unlikely mixture that it forced Lambert to tamper with the content of scripture. Mayo, "Crusaders under the Palm," 60, argues that Lambert did not intend the axe man to represent the statue, but clearly he did. He tells us as much on the left-hand side of the page: "The dream of Nebuchadnezzar, King of the Chaldeans, about the statue and the tree at the end of the fourth age of the world, which the prophet Daniel interpreted during the Babylonian captivity"; Lambert, *Liber floridus*, fol. 232v.
22. Though this association seems to have been lost on the copyist of the Wolfenbüttel manuscript, who depicted the Antichrist with a beard seated atop the dragon on fol. 72r.
23. "Somnium Nabugodonosor regis Chaldeorum. quod interpretavit Daniel propheta dum esset in transmigratione Babylonis. de statua et arbore in fine quarte etatis mundi"; Lambert, *Liber floridus*, fol. 232v.
24. "Mundus in prima etate habens caput aureum. et in secunda pectus argenteum. et in tertia ventrem aeneum. et in quarta femur ferreum. et in quinta tibias plumbeas. et in sexta pedea luti"; Lambert, *Liber floridus*, fol. 232v.
25. Rudolph, *Mystic Ark*, 12 and 127; see also 75.
26. Philip of Harveng. *De somnio regis Nabuchodonosor*, in PL 203, cols. 585–592 (cols. 585D–586D).
27. "Cecidit Babilon illa magna cum qua fornicati sunt reges terre"; Lambert, *Liber floridus*, fol. 232v. The verses are Revelation 18:2–3; also 14:8.
28. No historical record survives of any event of this sort from the reign of Nebuchadnezzar, though the story may grow out of events that happened during the reign of Nabonidus, one of Nebuchadnezzar's successors; see Newsom, *Daniel: A Commentary*, 127–30.
29. Mayo, "Crusaders under the Palm," 65–66, notes that the ends of the fourth and sixth ages are also linked by conquests of Jerusalem.
30. Lambert, *Liber floridus*, fol. 232v, and see table 2, chap. 3.
31. Pseudo-Methodius, *Apocalypse* 13, 128; Psalm 78:65 in non-Vulgate numbering.
32. Pseudo-Methodius, *Apocalypse* 13–14, 130–33.
33. "nisi venerit discessio primum et revelatus fuerit homo peccati filius perditionis"; 2 Thessalonians 2:3.
34. Palmer, *Apocalypse in the Early Middle Ages*, 118–19; Hughes, *Constructing Antichrist*, 29–37.
35. The belief that Godfrey styled himself "advocate of the Holy Sepulcher" is a myth. See my arguments in Rubenstein, *Armies of Heaven*, 101–3.
36. Adso, *De Antichristo*, 26.
37. "Epistola Methodii," published in Adso, *De Antichristo*, 149.
38. Paris, BnF Arsenal, MS 1102, fol. 102r (which contains Fulcher and Raymond of Aguilers). The verse is Revelation 19:11, which begins, "And I saw heaven opened, and behold a white horse." Raymond d'Aguilers, *Liber*, ed. John Hugh Hill and Laurita Littleton Hill, trans. Philippe Wolff (Paris: P. Geuthner, 1969), 150, and Revelation 14:20; discussed with great subtlety in Buc, *Holy War, Martyrdom*, 269–72.

39. The first manuscript is London, BL MS Add. lat. 8927 (which contains Fulcher's *Historia* and Raymond's *Liber*), quoted at fol. 134v; on this text, see Amnon Linder, "The Liturgy of the Liberation of Jerusalem," *Mediaeval Studies* 52 (1990): 110–31. The other is Paris, BnF, MS *lat.* 5132 (which contains a problematic version of the chronicle of Raymond of Aguilers) published as John France, "The Text of the Account of the Capture of Jerusalem in the Ripoll Manuscript, Bibliothèque nationale (latin) 5132," *English Historical Review* 103 (1988): 640–57, quoted here at 657. Cecilia Gaposchkin, *Invisible Weapons: Liturgy and the Making of Crusade Ideology* (Ithaca, NY: Cornell University Press, 2017), 141–56 and 179–91, sets this material in a broader liturgical context; my thanks to the author for sharing a copy of the manuscript in advance of publication.

40. France, "Unknown Account," 642.

41. France, "Unknown account," 652–53. The prophecy is Isaiah 11:10, "And his sepulcher will be made glorious." The passage also references the parable of the vineyard workers, Luke 20:9–18.

42. France, "Unknown Account," 652. The blood imagery perhaps comes from Leviticus 1:5.

43. On Godfrey's propaganda program, Rubenstein, *Armies of Heaven*, 136–37 and 298–301; also Jean Flori, *L'Islam et la Fin des Temps: L'interprétation prophétique des invasions musulmanes dans la chrétienté médiévale (VIIe–XIIIe siècle)* (Paris: Éditions du Seuil, 2005), 264–65.

44. Guibert, *Dei gesta* 2.4, 113–14.

45. Baldric, *Historia*, 107–9; Rubenstein, *Armies of Heaven*, 284–86; and Buc, *Holy War and Martyrdom*, 102–5.

46. Robert, *Historia*, 5–6. Discussed cautiously in Anne Latowsky, *Emperor of the World: Charlemagne and the Construction of Imperial Authority* (Ithaca, NY: Cornell University Press, 2013), 217–18. Robert perhaps intended these passages at least in part to promote Capetian interests, a program discussed by James Naus, "The *Historia Iherosolimitana* of Robert the Monk and the Coronation of Louis VI," in *Writing the Early Crusades: Text, Transmission, and Memory*, ed. Marcus Bull and Damien Kempf (Woodbridge: Boydell & Brewer, 2014), 105–15.

47. Ekkehard, in *Frutolfs und Ekkehards Chroniken und die anonyme Kaiserchronik*, ed. and trans. F.-J. Schmale and I. Schmale-Ott, Ausgewählte Quellen zur deutschen Geschichte des Mittelalters XV (Darmstadt: Wissenschaftliche Buchgesellschaft, 1972), 144. Matthew Gabriele, *Empire of Memory: The Legend of Charlemagne, the Franks, and Jerusalem before the First Crusade*, 139–41; Buc, *Holy War and Martyrdom*, 284–85; Latowsky, *Emperor of the World*, 219–20.

48. Discussed in Rubenstein, *Armies of Heaven*, 63–65, and by Matthew Gabriele, "Against the Enemies of Christ: The Role of Count Emicho in the Anti-Jewish Violence of the First Crusade," in *Christian Attitudes towards Jews in the Middle Ages: A Casebook*, ed. M. Frassetto (New York: Routledge, 2005), 84–111.

CHAPTER 5

1. Historians have usually attributed this version of the text to an otherwise unknown writer named Bartolph de Nangis. But there is no real evidence that any writer named Bartolph actually existed. The book instead seems to be a lightly revised and abridged version of the earliest copy of Fulcher's history.

2. My account of the creative process behind this text grows directly out of Albert Derolez, "The Abbey of Saint-Bertin, the Liber Floridus, and the Origin of the Gesta Francorum Hierusalem expugnantium," *Manuscripta* 57 (2013): 1–28. I am not, however, confident that Bohemond or a member of his entourage delivered the copy of Fulcher to Saint-Omer as Derolez suggests (28). Bohemond began his tour at Saint-Léonard de Noblat in February 1106, which is when (apparently) this copy of Fulcher's text ended.

3. The title of the text is *Gesta Francorum Iherusalem expugnantium*. To avoid confusion with the *Gesta Francorum*, and to dispense with the name Bartolph de Nangis, I will simply refer to it as "Fulcher Abbreviated": Fulcher Abbreviated in RHC *Oc.* 3, 2, 492.

4. I make this argument based on Derolez's reconstruction of the text's composition in "Abbey of Saint-Bertin." The copy of Fulcher's chronicle made at Saint-Bertin falls into two parts,

     separated roughly by this description and the map of Jerusalem. Derolez labels them "EA" and "EB." In composing the first half, EA, the scribes at Saint-Bertin appear to have been working on their own initiative. In transcribing the second half, EB, they appear to have been copying the version of Fulcher used in the *Liber floridus*. The break between EA and EB corresponds closely to the travel guide/map section of the text, meaning that the codicological project became a collaborative one between Saint-Bertin and Saint-Omer just as it became a cartographic project as well; see Derolez, "Abbey of Saint-Bertin," 8–11.

5. Later recensions of Fulcher's history also include a different and much shorter travel guide, although it is located in the same place in the text. Either the monks of Saint-Bertin found Fulcher's guide unsatisfying and replaced it, or else Fulcher himself decided to condense his original description when he revised his book. Compare the versions in Fulcher Abbreviated 31–33, 509–12, and Fulcher, *Historia* 1.26, 281–92.

6. Fulcher notes that the Temple was in a state of disrepair in the third draft of his chronicle; in the second, he mentions that Baldwin's role in damaging the roof. Fulcher, *Historia* 1.26.9, 291.

7. Fulcher Abbreviated 35, 515.

8. Fulcher Abbreviated 31, 510. When Lambert made his copy of the map, based on copies that appear in Leiden, Universiteitsbibliotheek, MS lat. Vossianus 31, fol. 85r, and in Paris, BnF lat. 8865, fol. 133r, he shifted the Latin Church of St. Mary to the northern side of the main road in Jerusalem, which is where it is properly located. His motives are obviously not transparent, but it does raise the possibility that there was some real interest in making the map as accurate as possible.

9. I have made a case for why the map in the *Liber floridus* was based on the one in the Saint-Bertin manuscript in Jay Rubenstein, "Heavenly and Earthly Jerusalem: The View from Twelfth-Century Flanders," in *Visual Constructs of Jerusalem*, ed. Bianca Kühnel, Galit Noga-Banai, and Hanna Vorholt (Turnhout: Brepols, 2014), 265–76. Without Derolez's article, however, I was unable to see just how close the working relationship between Lambert and Saint-Bertin was.

10. See, for example, Robert Ousterhout, "Flexible Geography and Transportable Topography," *Jewish Art* 24 (1997/98): 393–404; Milka Levy-Rubin, "From Eusebius to the Crusader Maps: The Origin of the Holy Land Maps," in *Visual Constructs of Jerusalem*, 253–63; Hanna Vorholt, "Studying with Maps: Jerusalem and the Holy Land in Two Thirteenth-Century Maps," in *Imagining Jerusalem in the Medieval West*, ed. Lucy Donkin and Hanna Vorholt (Oxford: Oxford University Press, 2012), 163–99 (esp. 163–70); and Albert Derolez, "*Codex Aldenburgensis*, Cotton Fragments Vol. 1, and the Origins of the *Liber Foridus*," *Manuscripta* 49 (2005): 139–63. Unfortunately, I was unable to consult the recently published Hanna Vorholt, *Shaping Knowledge: the Transmission of the* Liber floridus (London: Warburg Institute, 2017).

11. On the development of this tradition in the thirteenth century, Robert Konrad, "Das himmlische und das irdische Jerusalem im mittelalterlichen Denken. Mystische Vorstellung und geistliche Wirkung," in *Speculum historiale. Festschrift Johannes Spörl*, ed. C. Bauer (Freiburg: Alber, 1965), 523–40. The lone twelfth-century attempt to locate Jerusalem here is in Oxford, St. John's College, MS 17, fol. 6r, though the name "Jerusalem" may have been a later addition to the map. Anna-Dorothee von den Brincken, "Jerusalem on Medieval Mappae Mundi: A Site Both Historical and Eschatological," in *The Hereford World Map: Medieval World Maps and Their Context*, ed. P. D. A. Harvey (London: British Library, 2006), 355–79, describes the Oxford map as "a most striking example of shoddy workmanship." (362). Among other oddities, it locates Carthage in Europe. Sylvia Schein, *Gateway to the Heavenly City: Crusader Jerusalem and the Catholic West (1099–1187)* (Aldershot: Ashgate, 2005), 141–57, discusses the tradition of Jerusalem as the center of the earth and its eschatological significance. Hugh of Saint-Victor placed Jerusalem at the center of his own eccentric exercise in historical and moral geography: Rudolph, *Mystic Ark*, 166–67.

12. Peter the Venerable, "Sermo de laude," 238–39.

13. *Gesta Francorum*, 98. Samu Niskanen, "The Origins of the *Gesta Francorum* and Two Related Texts: Their Textual and Literary Character." *Sacris Erudiri* 51 (2012): 287–316, argues for the centrality of the travel guide to the historical vision of the *Gesta*.

14. The guide in the *Gesta Francorum*, in addition to the *Gesta* manuscripts, appears in: London, BL MS Harley 3904, fols. 63v–65r (Tudebode); Paris, BnF, MS *lat.* 5135A, fols. 37v–39r (Tudebode); and Paris, BnF *lat.* 15074, fols. 68v–69v (Robert the Monk).

15. Three examples of travel guides appended to different crusade chronicles: Tudebode manuscript, Paris, BnF, MS *lat.* 4892, follows the crusade chronicle with the "First Guide" from the *Gesta Francorum*, but then offers a much more elaborate geographic overview of the world—fols. 236r–243r; Paris, BnF, MS *lat* 5129, inserts a travel narrative between Robert the Monk's *Historia* and the metrical history by Gilo of Paris; Rome, Vat. Ottob. lat. 1089, fols. 54r–54v, follows Baldric's chronicle with the travel guide that Wilkinson, *Jerusalem Pilgrimage, 199–1185*, names "Qualiter."

16. Fulcher, *Historia* 2.5.2–3, 377–78; 2.57.1, 596–97; and 2.60.2, 602–3. Verena Epp, *Fulcher von Chartres: Studien zur Geschichtsscreibung des ersten Kreuzzuges* (Düsseldorf: Droste, 1990), 104–27, sees Fulcher's increasing interest in nature as evidence of a growing sense of self and possibly a breaking away from training he would have received at Chartres.

17. Especially, Akbari, *Idols in the East*, 66–111.

18. Lambert, *Liber floridus*, fol. 61v. Lambert bases his description on Isidore of Seville, but as Derolez, *Autograph Manuscript*, 82, observes, he adds the detail about the human face.

19. "serpentes horribiles…Corcodrillus pre cunctis animantibus hominem odit"; Brussels, BR, MS 9823–9834, fol. 137r. Fulcher of Chartres, *Historia* 3.49.3–4, 778–79, refers to the same legend.

20. Vatican, MS Reg. lat. 572, fol. 67r. Described and transcribed in *Gesta Francorum*, 103.

21. Newsom, *Daniel*, 262; Jerome, *In Daniel*, 1.2.31–35, 794.

22. The maps are discussed above, in chap. 2. On the legend of Gog, Magog, and Alexander, Andrew Runni Anderson, *Alexander's Gate, Gog and Magog, and the Inclosed Nations* (Cambridge, MA: Medieval Academy of America, 1932).

23. Alexander imprisons Gog and Magog at Pseudo-Methodius, *Revelations* 8.10, 100. Lambert passes over these details on *Liber floridus*, fol. 218r.

24. Stated with awareness of the difficulty of defining the genre of romance; see, for example, Sarah Kay, *The* Chanson de geste *in the Age of Romance: Political Fictions* (Oxford: Oxford University Press, 1995), 7–12 and 48–52. Lambert's Alexander material does at least largely conform to the characteristics of Romance described in that latter passage—an emphasis on the journey, self-discovery, and the "modification of the self" apparent in the hero.

25. Drawn mainly from the Latin life by Julius Valerius, discussed in George Cary, *The Medieval Alexander*, ed. D. J. A. Ross (Cambridge: Cambridge University Press, 1956), 24–26.

26. Lloyd L. Gunderson, *Alexander's Letter to Aristotle about India* (Meisenheim am Glan: Verlag Anton Hain, 1980), esp. 92–122.

27. Cary, *Medieval Alexander*, 91–95.

28. Lambert, *Liber floridus*, fols. 152v–162r. Discussed in Derolez, *Autograph Manuscript*, 129–34. This section of the manuscript is especially complicated, since a bifolio has been relocated to the end of the codex and since Lambert attached a folding leaf to fol. 153r.

29. Later copyists of the *Liber floridus* shared this opinion, since at least two of them portrayed Alexander as clad in chain mail armor: Leiden University, MS Voss. lat. fol. 31, fol. 211r, and Paris, BnF MS *lat.* 8865, fol. 71v.

30. Akbari, *Idols in the East*, 81–82 notes this comparison and suggests that Lambert may have deliberately juxtaposed the Alexander material with Anselm of Bec's treatise on the Incarnation, *Cur Deus homo*; Derolez, *Autograph Manuscript*, 129–30, sees the placement of *Cur Deus homo* as more a scribal accident.

31. Lambert, *Liber floridus*, fols. 152v–153r. The easiest access to a fuller version of this story, complete with delightful detail about spells, costumes, and fraud, is in *The Greek Alexander Romance*, trans. Richard Stoneman (London: Penguin Classics, 1991), 35–43. Also,

Richard Stoneman, *Alexander the Great: A Life in Legend* (New Haven, CT: Yale University Press, 2008), 6–26.

32. Adso, *De Antichristo*, 146.

33. Akbari, *Idols in the East*, 89.

34. Lambert, *Liber floridus*, fols. 153r´–153v´. The manuscript is badly damaged here. I have filled in the gaps by referring to the Wolfenbüttel codex, fols. 87r–87v.

35. Josephus, *Jewish Antiquities*, Loeb Classical Library, vol. 7 of 8, trans. Ralph Marcus (London: William Heinemann, 1937), 11.8, 477.

36. Paraphrasing slightly Bohemond's self-description in Orderic Vitalis, *Ecclesiastical History*, 5.10, 378.

37. "orbem terrarum circumnavigare oceanumque"; Lambert, *Liber floridus*, fol. 158v.

38. Lambert, *Liber floridus*, fols. 156r and 3v.

39. Lambert, *Liber floridus*, fol. 64v. I have discussed the connections between Arthur's palace and the heavenly Jerusalem in my article, "Heavenly and Earthly Jerusalem," 274–76.

40. See the comments in Derolez, *Autograph Manuscript*, 84. Amy G. Remensnyder, *La Conquistadora: The Virgin Mary at War and Peace in the Old and New Worlds* (Oxford: Oxford University Press, 2014), 31–38, and elsewhere, discusses the early historical traditions of using the virgin as a symbol of holy war (though much later than Lambert; she begins her narrative with Las Navas de Tolosa in 1212).

41. Lambert, *Liber floridus*, fols. 271v–278r, and the commentary in Derolez, *Autograph Manuscript*, 175.

42. "Valentiniano regnante, anno domini ccclxvi fuerunt Troiani in finibus Germanie. de quibus orti sunt reges Galliorum"; Lambert, *Liber floridus*, fol. 263r; see commentary in Derolez, *Autograph Manuscript*, 171.

43. "Faramundus nepos Priami ducis Troiani Francorum regum omnium. primus rex fuit"; Lambert, *Liber floridus*, fol. 1v.

44. I am working from Lambert's own chronologies here. Troy was destroyed near the beginning of the fourth millennium of the world; Valentinian would have been reigning near the beginning of the sixth; Lambert, *Liber floridus*, fol. 32v.

45. "Toianischen Vranken," taken from the anonymous vernacular poem *Das Anno-Lied*, ed. Walther Bulst (Heidelberg: Carl Winter, 1946), §6, 10.

46. Lambert, *Liber floridus*, fol. 277v.

47. Colette Beaune, *The Birth of an Ideology: Myths and Symbols of Nation in Late Medieval France*, trans. Susan Ross Huston, ed. Frederic L. Cheyette (Berkeley: University of California Press, 1991), 233–40, makes note of the imaginative connections of Troy to crusading in twelfth-century historical writing and as such part of the creation of the ideology of nationhood, which she traces in her book. I would suggest only that this element of the story of the birth of France might have been still more significant than Beaune indicates.

48. Based on comparing Lambert's established chronologies with Troy-centered ones on fols. 99r and 257v.

49. Gubiert, *Dei Gesta* 2.17, 133, and 4.24, 226–27.

50. Baldric, *Historia*, 25.

51. Ralph of Caen, *Gesta Tancredi*, RHC *Oc.* 3, 98, 675.

52. The pilgrim Saewulf mentions that he learned from Greek guides about the possibility of visiting the ruins of Troy; see Wilkinson, *Jerusalem Pilgrimage 1099–1185*, 113.

53. *Chronicarum quae dicuntur Fredegarii Scholatici* 2.6, in MGH Scriptores rerum Germanicarum 2, 46.

54. *Gesta Francorum*, 21. Guibert of Nogent makes the same statement, that the Turks thought themselves *contribules*, of the same tribe as the Franks: *Dei gesta* 3.11, 159.

55. William of Tyre, *Chronicon*, ed. R. B. C. Huygens, 2 vols., CCCM 63, 63a (Turnhout: Brepols, 1986), 1.7, 114–15.

56. Guibert, *Dei gesta* 1.2, 89.

57. On the Charlemagne legend and the connection to Jerusalem, see Matthew Gabriele, *Empire of Memory*, 79–93.

58. To provide a representative, if incomplete list (arranged roughly according to subject matter) of how manuscript survivals combine crusade chronicles with the materials of mythic history, here are ten examples: (1) London, BL MS Add. 30898 contains the chronicle of Baldric of Bourgueil (merged with the Fulcher Abbreviated) with Solinus, *De mirabilibus mundi*, which is the first text in the codex; (2) Paris, BnF MS *lat.* 18417 combines Guibert of Nogent's chronicle with Valerius's abbreviated *Life of Alexander* and the letter to Aristotle; (3) Paris, BnF *n.a.l.* 310 contains Robert the Monk's chronicle and a variety of historical texts, including a *Life of Alexander* and two *Lives* of Charlemagne (Einhard and Notker Balbulus of musical sequences fame); (4) Rome, Vat. MS lat. 1795 contains Robert's chronicle, preceded by Dares Phrygius's history of Troy, Paul the Deacon's History, the Life of Alexander and letters to Aristotle and Dindymus, as well as the Tiburtine Sibyl; (5) London, BL MS Stowe 56 begins with Baldric's chronicle and follows it with Dares Phrygius's history of Troy, the story of Apollonius of Tyre (also included in the *Liber floridus*), Valerius's *Life of Alexander* followed by the letters, and Geoffrey of Monmouth's *History of the Kings of Britain*; (6) Paris, BnF *n.a.l.* 692 has Fulcher's chronicle preceded by Dares Phrygius's history of Troy (and the history of Symeon of Durham, as well); (7) Montpellier, Faculté de Médicine MS 142 follows Peter Tudebode's chronicle immediately with Geoffrey of Monmouth's prophecies of Merlin and, a few folios later, Pseudo-Turpin's *Life* of Charlemagne; (8) Montpellier, Faculté de Médicine MS 235 combines Robert's Chronicle with the Pseudo-Turpin material; (9) Paris, BnF MS *lat.* 6041A combines a highly irregular copy of Raymond of Aguiler's chronicle with Pseudo-Turpin and Geoffrey of Monmouth (and other historical and hagiographic material, the Sibylline prophecy among them); (10) Rome, Vat. MS Reg. lat. 658 contains Robert the Monk's chronicle and a list of the ten conquests of Jerusalem, including Charlemagne's on fol. 92r.

59. The manuscripts are: Brussels, BR MS 9823–34; Paris, BnF MS *lat.* 5129; and Rome, Vat. Reg. lat. 712.

60. One might add to this list (though it is not as highly developed a manuscript) Cambrai, MS BM 802, a twelfth-century manuscript that contains Robert the Monk, a travel guide to Jerusalem, a biography of Muhammad, a fragmentary description of the Lateran, and the story of Apollonius (included also in the *Liber floridus*). My thanks to Damien Kempf for sharing with me his notes on this manuscript.

61. Eivor Andersen Oftestad, "The House of God: The Translation of the Temple and the Interpretation of the Lateran Cathedral in the Twelfth Century," PhD diss., University of Oslo, 2010, 298. A longer version of the description has been published as *Descriptio Lateranensis Ecclesiae*, in *Codice topogografico della città di Roma* 3, ed. Roberto Valentini and Giuseppe Zucchetti (Rome: Tipografia del Senato, 1946), 319–73. I will be citing from BnF MS *lat.* 5129.

62. Lambert, *Liber floridus*, fol. 168r.

63. *Descriptio Lateranensis*, fols. 90r–90v, including the conversion of Constantine and Helena's journey to Jerusalem, as well as a fragment of the True Cross brought back by Heraclius after his defeat of Chosroes.

64. "In ecclesia lateranensi. que est caput mundi. que patriachalis et imperialis est: sedis est apostolice cathedra pontificalis. et eiusdem ecclesie ara principalis est. archa federis domini"; *Descriptio Lateranensis*, fol. 91r.

65. *Descriptio Lateranensis*, fol. 92r.

66. "donec deus congreget congregationem populi et propitius fiat. et tunc dominus ostendet hec. et apparebit maiestas domini et cetera"; *Descriptio Lateranensis*, fol. 93r.

67. *Descriptio Lateranensis*, fol. 93r. The Arch of Titus, of course, contains an image of a candelabrum and other plunder brought back from Jerusalem but not the Ark.

68. Charlemagne had famously made this a key element of his cultural program: Mary Garrison, "The Franks as the New Israel? Education for an Identity from Pippin to Charlemagne," in *The Uses of the Past in the Early Middle Ages*, ed. Yitzhak Hen and Matthew Innes (Cambridge: Cambridge University Press, 2000), 114–61.

CHAPTER 6

1. William of Malmesbury, *Gesta Regum Anglorum*, ed. R. A. B. Mynors, R. M. Thomson, M. Winterbottom, vol. 1 (Oxford: Oxford University Press, 1998), 3.344, 592–95.
2. More literally, holy battles: "prelia sancta"; Guibert, *Dei gesta* 1.1, 87.
3. Ralph of Caen imagines Tancred meditating on this conundrum: *Gesta Tancredi* 1, 605–6.
4. Augustine, Ep. 138 to Marcellinus, in PL 33, 12, col. 530; see also Frederick Russell, *The Just War in the Middle Ages* (Cambridge: Cambridge University Press, 1975), 16–26. The passages are Matthew 5:39–40 and Luke 6:29. Only Matthew specifies "the right cheek."
5. Ralph, *Gesta Tancredi* 1, 606.
6. For example, Jonathan Riley-Smith, *The First Crusaders (1095–1131)* (Cambridge: Cambridge University Press, 1997), 71: "the crusaders openly craved forgiveness." Riley-Smith builds his argument chiefly around charters, a literary genre based on a centuries-old habit of imagining every interaction of lay folk with the church as growing out of a desperate need (as imagined by monks) for forgiveness.
7. Robert, *Historia*, 6.
8. Fulcher, *Historia* 1.3.7, 136.
9. Baldric, *Historia*, 9.
10. Robert, *Historia*, 6. The surviving indulgence reads: "Whoever sets off for Jerusalem to liberate the church of God, for devotion alone and not to win prestige or money, can substitute that journey for all penance"; "Quicumque pro sola devotione, non pro honoris vel pecunie adeptione, ad liberandam ecclesiam Dei Hierusalem profectus fuerit, iter illud pro omni penitentia ei reputetur"; Robert Somerville, *The Councils of Urban II*, 1. *Decreta Claromontensia* (Amsterdam: Adolf M Hakkert, 1972), 74.
11. Orderic, *Ecclesiastical History* 2.3, 50–51.
12. "peregrini milites Sancti Sepulcri"; Robert, *Historia*, 18.
13. Baldric, *Historia*, 19.
14. Robert, *Historia*, 47. Discussed in Colin Morris, *The Sepulchre of Christ and the Medieval West: From the Beginning to 1600* (Oxford: Oxford University Press, 2005), 187.
15. Somerville, *Councils of Urban II*, 74.
16. Henrich Hagenmeyer, ed., *Epistulae et chartae ad primi belli sacri spectantes: Die Kreuzzugsbriefe aus den Jahren 1088–1100* (Hildesheim: Georg Olms, 1901, repr. 1973), 3, 137.
17. Ralph, *Gesta Tancredi*, 1, 606.
18. Dominique Barthélemy makes a similar suggestion about knights who experienced the power of St. Foy: "elle libère des chevaliers qui pourront piller les pauvres avec d'autant plus d'ardeur qu'ils se croiront bénis de Dieu"; *Chevaliers et miracles: La violence et le sacré dans la société fédodale* (Paris: Armand Colin, 2004), 101.
19. Burchard of Worms, *Libri decretorum*, PL 140, 20. 51, col. 995B; and Ivo of Chartres, *Decreti*, PL 161, 15.65, col. 877B. See also James A. Brundage, *Medieval Canon Law and the Crusader* (Madison: University of Wisconsin Press, 1969), 9 and n29.
20. Burchard, *Libri decretorum*, 20.51, col. 995C and Ivo, *Decreti*, 15.65, col. 877C; citing Jerome, Ep. 58. Discussed in Morris *Sepulchre of Christ*, 48–49.
21. Guibert, *Dei gesta* 5.25, 228–29.
22. Guibert of Nogent, *Monodies*, published as *Autobiographie*, ed. and trans. Edmond-René Labande (Paris: Belles Lettres, 1981); 3, 7, 328. Abbot Suger of Saint-Denis, a writer with a far broader experience of the world offers a similar judgment: Suger, *Vita Ludovici Grossi*, ed. H. Waquet (Paris: Belles Lettres, 1964), 7, 30–35, and 24, 172–79.
23. Guibert, *Monodies* 3.1, 143.
24. Guibert, *Monodies* 3.14, 158–59.
25. First mentioned at Albert of Aachen, *Historia Ierosolimitana, History of the Journey to Jerusalem*, ed. and trans. Susan B. Edgington (Oxford: Clarendon Press, 2007), 1.28, 52–53, as a part of Emicho's army. See also Edgington's comment in her edition of Albert, *Historia* n72, 52–53. Thomas resurfaces periodically, including at the siege of Jerusalem: Albert, *Historia* 5.46, 404–5. Jacques Chaurand, *Thomas de Marle, sire de Coucy* (Marle: Syndicat d'initiative de Marle, 1963), 31–50, calls attention to this crusading activity.

26. Albert, *Historia* 2.42, 134–35; 6.2, 406–7; and 6.45, 462–63; and Rubenstein, *Guibert of Nogent*, 104–7.

27. Orderic, *Ecclesiastical History*, 6.13, 396–97; Riley-Smith, *First Crusaders*, 136 and 144–45.

28. On his departure, Orderic Vitalis, *Ecclesiastical History* 5.9, 30; Also mentioned by Albert, *Historia* 4.48, 322–23. On the conflict with the king, Suger, *Vita Ludovici* 2, 16–19.

29. Suger, *Vita Ludovici*, 8, 34–43 (Guy of Rochefort); 11, 68–77 (Guy again); 19, 128–31 (Evrard, and Hugh of Le Puiset) and 27, 146–49 (Ralph of Beaugency).

30. Guibert, *Dei gesta*, 5.24, 227. On this theme generally, Naus, *Constructing Kingship*.

31. Ivo of Chartres, *Epistolae*, in PL 162, cols. 144D–145A. A specific date is not given, although Ivo implies the incident occurred shortly after Raimbold returned.

32. Jeremy Adams, "Returning Crusaders: Living Saints or Psychopaths?" in *From Knowledge to Beatitude: St. Victor, Twelfth-Century Scholars, and Beyond, Essays in Honor of Grover A. Zinn, Jr.*, ed. E. Ann Matter and Lesley Smith (Notre Dame: University of Notre Dame Press, 2013), 328–41, explores these tensions.

33. The list can be reconstructed from the introduction to the Primitive Rule of the Templars: Henri de Curzon, *Le règle du Temple* (Paris: Librairie Renouard, 1886), 6–7, 16–20. Also, Malcolm Barber, *The New Knighthood: A History of the Order of the Temple* (Cambridge: Cambridge University Press, 1994), 6–19; Barber, "The Origins of the Order of the Temple," *Studia Monastica* 12 (1970): 219–40; and Anthony Luttrell, "The Earliest Templars," in *Autour de la Première Croisade: Actes du Colloque de la Society for the Study of the Crusades and the Latin East (Clermont-Ferrand, 22–25 juin 1995)*, ed. M. Balard (Paris: Publications de la Sorbonne, 1996), 193–202.

34. The rule describes them as "manifestum est gentili," "famously for heathen"; *La règle du Temple*, ed. Henri de Curzon (Paris: Librairie Renouard, 1886), 22, 32–33.

35. A frequently translated and readily available work; for example, Bernard of Clairvaux, *Liber ad milites templi de laude Novae militiae*, in *S. Bernardi Opera*, ed. J. Leclercq, C. H. Talbor, H. M. Rochais, and G. Hendrix, 9 vols. (Rome: Editiones Cistercienses and Turnhout: Brepols, 1957–98), vol. 3, 213–39 [in English as *In Praise of the New Knighthood: A Treatise on the Knights Templar and the Holy Places of Jerusalem*, trans. M. Conrad Greenia (Kalamazoo, MI: Cistercian Publications, 2000), whose translation I have largely followed here]. The introduction to the translation, 10–13, notes the difficulty in dating the treatise. Paul Rousset, *Les origins et les caractères de la Première Croisade* (Neuchatel: à la Baconnerie, 1945), 162–68, draws a comparison between the First Crusaders and the Templars, as does Purkis, *Crusading Spirituality*, esp. 100–102, though Purkis emphasizes the originality of Bernard's rhetoric. Barber, "Origins," 237–38, places the foundation of the Templars into the context of eleventh-century violence and justification of the crusade in a way similar to what is suggested here.

36. Bernard uses the pun in *De laude* 2, 216. Greenia offers the not entirely satisfactory translation of "not knighthood but—knavery"; Greenia, *In Praise of the New Knighthood*, 37.

37. Bernard describes the psychology and the accoutrement of the worldly *militia* in *De laude* 1–2, 214–16. Jean Leclercq, *Monks and Love in Twelfth-Century France: Psycho-historical Essays* (Oxford: Oxford University Press, 1979), presents an extended argument on behalf of Bernard's familiarity with the knightly psychology.

38. Bernard, *De laude* 3, 217 and 1, 214–15.

39. Bernard, *De laude* 4, 220–21.

40. Bernard, *De laude* 4, 221. Caroline Walker Bynum, "Monsters, Medians, and Marvelous Mixtures: Hybrids in the Spirituality of Bernard of Clairvaux," in *Metamorphosis and Identity* (New York: Zone Books, 2005), 113–62, discusses the centrality of this sort of imagery in Bernard's thought (Templars at 124–25).

41. Bernard, *De laude* 5, 222.

42. Bernard, *De laude* 5, 223.

43. "nova militia Dei"; Guibert, *Dei gesta* 7.21, 303, and 1.1, 87, where he speaks of the new path to salvation. Alan Forey, *The Military Orders: From the Twelfth to the Early Fourteenth Century* (Toronto: University of Toronto Press, 1992), 11–12, recognizes the connection

between this passage and the Templar ethos but emphasizes that the Templars were a religious order, unlike the Franks on crusade, who were merely like one.

44. Guibert expresses his distaste for the commoners' greed at Guibert, *Dei gesta* 6.22, 262 but praises their rough equality at 5.25, 226–27. See also Baldric, *Historia*, 26. and Albert of Aachen, *Historia*, 2.43, 136–37.

45. Baldric, *Historia*, 101.

46. Baldric, *Historia*, 25.

47. Guibert, *Dei gesta* 6.7, 238.

48. Guibert, *Dei gesta* 1.1, 85–86.

49. Baldric, *Historia*, 8.

50. Robert, *Historia*, 71.

51. Guibert, *Dei gesta* 6, prologue, 233.

52. Anselm of Havelberg, *Dialogi*, ed. Migne, PL 188, col. 1156B.

53. Suger, *Vita Ludovici* 31, 250–57.

CHAPTER 7

1. Elizabeth Sibbery, *Criticism of Crusading, 1095–1274* (Oxford: Clarendon Press, 1985) argues that the crusade enterprise remained generally popular throughout the Middle Ages, except for a period of intense criticism after the failures of the Second Crusade. Martin Aurell, *Des chrétiens contre les croisades, xiiᵉ–xiiiᵉ siècle* (Paris: Fayard, 2013) finds more evidence for criticism, though little before the Second Crusade.

2. Orderic Vitalis, *Ecclesiastical History* 5.10, 322–23.

3. Orderic Vitalis, *Ecclesiastical History* 5.10, 324–25.

4. Guibert, *Die gesta* 7.24, 314.

5. William J. Purkis, *Crusading Spirituality in the Holy Land and Iberia, c.1095–c.1187* (Woodbridge: Boydell Press, 2008), 114–19.

6. In general, the chroniclers who discuss the crusade of 1101 write as if there were only one army. Albert of Aachen is the exception, and because of his positive reputation as a historian, I have given his testimony primacy. The best modern description of the crusade of 1101 remains that of James Lea Cate, in *A History of the Crusades*, ed. Kenneth M. Setton et al., 6 vols. (Madison: University of Wisconsin Press, 1969–89), 1:343–67.

7. Albert, *Historia* 8.3, 588.

8. Albert, *Historia* 8.4, 590.

9. Orderic, *Ecclesiastical History* 5.10, 330, 334. I say that he had access to Albert's sources because Orderic imagines Alexius unleashing lions and leopards on the crusaders, which seems a garbled version of the crusaders killing the tamed lion.

10. Albert exonerates Alexius of any wrongdoing, though he does find fault with Raymond: *Historia* 8.8–9, 596–99, and 8.46, 634–37. Orderic, as noted, suspects Alexius, as does, unsurprisingly, Guibert, *Dei gesta* 7.24, 313. William of Malmesbury, *Gesta regum* 4.383, 682–83, indicates his agreement with Guibert and Orderic.

11. Based mainly on the descriptions of Albert, *Historia* 8.11–17, 600–611.

12. Orderic, *Ecclesiastical History* 5.10, 338–39.

13. Albert, *Historia* 8.19, 610–13. Susan Edgington translates *raptas* as "seized," which is certainly possible, though "raped" seems equally justified by the context. In *Historia* 8.20, 612–13, Albert describes briefly the more general massacre by the Turks of all the Christians who could not escape on horseback.

14. Albert, *Historia* 8.25–31, 618–23.

15. Albert, *Historia* 8.32, 624–25.

16. Orderic, *Ecclesiastical History* 5.10, 324.

17. Guibert, *Dei gesta* 7.23, 313.

18. Orderic Vitalis, *Ecclesiastical History* 5.10, 324–27; on Odo Arpin in particular, Riley-Smith, *First Crusaders*, 154.

19. Ekkehard, *Hierosolymita*, 24–25, 30–31.

20. Orderic Vitalis, *Ecclesiastical History* 5.10, 338–41; Albert, *Historia* 8.37–39, 628–31; Guibert, *Dei gesta* 7.24, 314–15 and 7.23, 313, where Guibert reports Hugh's death.

21. Corba's story is partly retold in Georges Duby, *The Knight, the Lady, and the Priest: The Making of Modern Marriage in Medieval France*, trans. Barbara Bray (New York: Pantheon, 1983), 245–47; the source material is *Chroniques des comtes d'Anjou et des seigneurs d'Amboise*, ed. Louis Halphen and René Poupardin (Paris: Auguste Picard, 1913), 101. According to the chronicle, news of Aimery's death came from Stephen of Blois, after he returned from Antioch.
22. *Chroniques des comtes d'Anjou*, 102–3.
23. Urban II directed as much in a letter to followers in Bologna: Hagenmeyer, *Epistulae* 3, 137–38.
24. On these details, Guibert, *Dei gesta* 7.24, 316; Albert, *Historia* 9.6, 644–45 and 10.39, 754–55; Orderic, *Ecclesiastical History* 5.10, 346–47 and 350–51; and Fulcher of Chartres, *Historia* 2.17–20, 436–46.
25. Albert, *Historia* 10.39, 754–55.
26. Orderic, *Ecclesiastical History* 5.10, 352–53.
27. Albert, *Historia* 8.21, 615–16.
28. Guibert, *Dei gesta* 7.24, 315.
29. Duby, *The Knight, the Lady*, 247; Riley-Smith, *First Crusade and the Idea of Crusading*, 129. Cate, in "The Crusade of 1101," in Setton, *History of the Crusades* (see n. 6), describes William IX as a "light-hearted young man."
30. Fulcher, *Historia* 2.16, 433.
31. Guibert, *Dei gesta* 7.24, 315.
32. William, *Historia regum* 4.383, 682. The vocabulary is highly classicizing: *manubiis* for "spoils" and *inferias* for "sacrifices made for the fallen war dead."
33. On the role of Genoa in the establishment of the crusader states, Martin Hall and Jonathan Phillips, eds., *Caffaro, Genoa and the Twelfth-Century Crusades* (Farnham: Ashgate, 2013). On the Norwegian Crusade, Fulcher, *Historia* 2.44, 543–48.
34. Albert, *Historia* 7.67, 578–79.
35. Guibert, *Dei gesta*, 7.39, 338–39.
36. "Un Épisode de la Lutte entre Baudouin Ier et les Habitants d'Ascalon," printed as Appendix I in Huygens's edition of GN, 355–60. It survives in four manuscripts; see Huygens's introductory comments, 68–69.
37. "Un Épisode," 360.
38. Fulcher Abbreviated, 42, 520.
39. Fulcher, *Historia* 2.1, 352–54. As Hagenmeyer observes in his notes to Fulcher's chronicle, 353, n.5, the later, highly revised text of Fulcher's *History* contained in Cambridge University Library MS 2079, known as the L manuscript, also does not contain this barbed observation.
40. Albert, *Historia* 9.48, 706–7.
41. William, *Chronicon* 11.14, 517–19. The Muhammad character from Albert has been identified as Bektash ibn Tutush, who died in 1104 (see Edgington's comment in her edition of Albert, 707, n.89). The battle for Sidon occurred in 1110, which would suggest they were two different characters. The converted-Muslim-Baldwin character's historicity is so lightly attested, however, that any conclusion is tentative.
42. William of Tyre, *Chronicon* 11.14, 518.
43. "Ibn Rust on the Rūs," in *Ibn Fadlān and the Land of Darkness: Arab Travellers and the Far North*, trans. Paul Lunde and Caroline Stone (London: Penguin Classics, 2012), 127. Thanks to Peter Frankopan for this reference.
44. On these points, see S. G. Bruce, "'Lurking with Spiritual Intent': A Note on the Origin and Functions of the Monastic Roundsman (*circator*)," *Revue Bénédictine* 109 (1999): 75–89 (esp. 87).
45. Christopher Tyerman, *God's War: A New History of the Crusades* (Cambridge, MA: Harvard University Press, 2006), 202; Hans Eberhard Mayer, *Mélanges sur l'histoire du royaume latin de Jérusalem*, Mémoires de l'Academie Inscription et Belles-Lettres 5 (Paris: Imprimerie Nationale, 1984), 69–72, makes a case for Baldwin's homosexuality without reference to the convert Baldwin.

46. The phenomenon of Frankish settlers going native in the twelfth century was an enduring, if not a common one. Famously, Usama Ibn Muqidh, *The Book of Contemplation: Islam and the Crusades* (London: Penguin Classics, 2008), 153–54.
47. Galterius Cancellarius, *Bella Antiochena*, ed. Heinrich Hagenmeyer (Innsbruck: Wanger'schen Universitäts Buchhandlung, 1896), *Bella Antiochena* 1.prologue, 61. The word for metaphor is in fact *metaphora*.
48. Galterius, *Bella Antiochena* 1.prologue, 62.
49. Galterius, *Bella Antiochena* 1.prologue, 1.1, 62–63.
50. Galterius, *Bella Antiochena* 1.1, 63–65. "Sackcloth and ashes" is taken from Matthew 11:21, which mentions Corozain and Bethsaida, both cities associated in later tradition with Antichrist. The root verse is Jonah 3:6–8, in reference to Nineveh. Thomas S. Asbridge and Susan B. Edgington identify Cereb as al-Athrib in their translation: *Walter the Chancellor's Antiochene Wars: A Translation and Commentary* (Burlington, VT: Ashgate, 1999), 83, n.38.
51. "simulata pace"; Galterius, *Bella Antiochena* 1.2, 66–67.
52. Galterius, *Bella Antiochena* 1.4, 69–70. On the association of "Belial" with Islam, Scott G. Bruce, *Cluny and the Muslims of La Garde-Freinet: Hagiography and the Problem of Islam in Medieval Europe* (Ithaca, NY: Cornell University Press, 2015), 30–39.
53. Galterius, *Bella Antiochena* 1.4, 71.
54. Galterius, *Bella Antiochena* 1.6, 73–74.
55. Lapina, *Warfare and the Miraculous*, 37–40.
56. Galterius, *Bella Antiochena* 1.7, 77.
57. Galterius, *Bella Antiochena* 2.3, 83, and more generally 2.2–2.3, 80–83. The madwoman is described as *lunatica mulier*.
58. Galterius, *Bella Antiochena* 2.3, 84 and 2.4, 86; Fulcher, *Historia* 3.3.4, 622–24.
59. Galterius, *Bella Antiochena* 2.4, 87.
60. Galterius, *Bella Antiochena* 2.5, 88, where Walter describes the apparent cowardice of the Turcopoles.
61. On pornography and martyrdom stories, Thomas Sizgorich, *Violence and Belief in Late Antiquity: Militant Devotion in Christianity and Islam* (Philadelphia: University of Pennsylvania Press, 2009), 124–26.
62. Galterius, *Bella Antiochena* 2.7, 91–93.
63. Galterius, *Bella Antiochena* 2.7, 93 and 2.15, 112.
64. Galterius, *Bella Antiochena* 2.15, 110–11.
65. Galterius, *Bella Antiochena* 2.14, 109.
66. Galterius, *Bella Antiochena* 2.14, 107–8 and 2.16, 114–15.
67. Jonathan Riley-Smith, "The Venetian Crusade of 1122–1124," in *I Comuni Italiani nel Regno Crociato di Gerusalemme*, ed. Gabriella Airaldi and Benjamin Z. Kedar (Genoa: Università di Genova, Istituto di Medievistica, 1986), 339–50.
68. What follows is a narrative summary of material presented in detail in Jay Rubenstein, "Putting History to Use: Three Crusade Chronicles in Context," *Viator: Medieval and Renaissance Studies* 35 (2004): 131–68.
69. Copied (with slight stylistic revision) from Rubenstein, "Putting History to Use," 134.

CHAPTER 8
1. Hugh's legation is mentioned in Otto of Freising, *Chronica sive historia de duabus civitatibus*, ed. Walther Lammers (Berlin: Rütten & Loening, 1960), 7.33, 566.
2. Otto of Freising, *Gesta Frederici seu rectius cronica*, ed. Franz-Josef Schmale (Berlin: Deutscher Verlag der Wissenschaften, 1965), 1.36, 200.
3. Odo of Deuil, *De profectione Ludovici VII in orientem*, ed. Virginia Gingerick Berry (New York: Columbia University Press, 1948), 6–7. See also John G. Rowe, "The Origins of the Second Crusade: Pope Eugenius III, Bernard of Clairvaux, and Louis VII of France," in *The Second Crusade and the Cistercians*, ed. Michael Gervers (New York: St. Martin's Press, 1992), 79–89; Theodore Evergates, "Louis VII and the Counts of Champagne," in

Gervers, *Second Crusade and the Cistercians*, 109–17; Jonathan Phillips, *The Second Crusade: Extending the Frontiers of Christendom* (New Haven, CT: Yale University Press, 2007), 61–66; Penny J. Cole, *The Preaching of the Crusades to the Holy Land, 1095–1270* (Cambridge, MA: Medieval Academy of America, 1991), 37–41.

4. Otto, *Gesta Frederici*, prologue, 114–17; and see Schmale's nn.14 and 15 on 117 for the discussion that follows.
5. Otto discusses the two Babylons at length in *Chronica* 7.3, 502–5.
6. Discussed in the Bible in Ezra 1. Cyrus, according to Herodotus, conquered Babylon by first diverting the Euphrates and lowering its water level so that his armies could pass, a story repeated in Otto, *Chronica* 2.11, 124, though the river is named as the Ganges.
7. Gabriele, *Empire of Memory*, 123–28.
8. A historical overview of Bernard's role in the crusade is offered by Marco Meschini, *San Bernardo e la seconda crociata* (Milan: Ugo Mursia, 1998).
9. Otto, *Gesta Frederici* 1.36, 200.
10. The Latin text of *Quantum praedecessores* is printed in Rolf Große, "Überlegungen zum Kreuzzugsaufruf Eugens III. von 1145/46. Mit einer Neuedition von JL 8876," *Francia* 18 (1991): 85–92 (90–92). Quoted here at 90.
11. *Quantum praedecessores*, 91.
12. Odo, *De profectione*, 8–9.
13. Bernard, *Ep.* 247.2, in *S. Bernardi Opera*, ed. J. Leclercq, C. H. Talbot, H. M. Rochais, and G. Hendrix, 9 vols. (Rome: Editiones Cistercienses and Turnhout: Brepols, 1957–1998), vol. 8, 141, with reference to Psalm 39:6 and Isaiah 4:1.
14. From Book VI of the *Vita prima* (though, in the manuscript tradition, it almost never circulates bound together with the *Vita prima*), in Migne, Patrologia Latina 185, col. 381B,C.
15. On the difficulties facing Conrad, Phillips, *Second Crusade: Extending the Frontiers*, 88–95; Otto, *Gesta Frederici* 1.31, 188–90, saw the sudden spread of peace throughout Germany in 1146, enabling the crusade, as miraculous.
16. Ephraim of Bonn, *Sefer Zekhirah*, in *The Jews and the Crusaders: The Hebrew Chronicles of the First and Second Crusades*, trans. Shlomo Eidelberg (Hoboken, NJ: KTAV Publishing, 1996), 122. Also described by Otto, *Gesta Frederici* 1.39, 206–9. See also Phillips, *Second Crusade*, 84–86, and Cole, *Preaching of the Crusades*, 43–45; Meschini, *San Bernardo*, 102–5.
17. Isaiah 63:3 speaks of the Lord crushing Gentiles in a winepress.
18. Ephraim, *Sefer Zekirah*, 123 and 127.
19. Ephraim, *Sefer Zekirah*, 127–28.
20. Bernard, *Ep.* 363, 317.
21. Bernard, *Ep.* 365, 321. On Guibert's attitude toward Peter the Hermit, Jay Rubenstein, "How, or How Much, to Reevaluate Peter the Hermit," in *The Medieval Crusade*, ed. Susan J. Ridyard (Woodbridge: Boydell, 2004), 22–41. It is possible that Bernard had read Guibert's history, since a twelfth-century copy of it was included among the holdings of the library at Clairvaux. It is today MS Florence, Bibl. Laurentianae, Ashb. 1054.
22. Bernard, *Ep.* 365, 321. The reference is to 2 Maccabees 12:44.
23. Bernard, *Ep.* 363, 316–17.
24. Bernard, *Ep.* 363, 316, drawing on Psalm 58:15 (Ps 59:15, NRSV) and Wisdom 3:6.
25. Bernard, *Ep.* 365, 321, and *Ep.* 363, 316. The passage is Romans 11:25–26.
26. Bernard McGinn, "Saint Bernard and Eschatology," in *Bernard of Clairvaux: Studies presented to Dom Jean Leclercq* (Spencer, MA: Cistercian Publications, 1973), 161–85.
27. Bernard, *Ep.* 56, in *Sancti Bernardi opera* 7, 148. Discussed in McGinn, "Bernard and Eschatology," 169–70.
28. Following the Vulgate numbering of the Bible Song 1:6 (Song 1:7, NRSV). *Sermo* 33 appears in *Sancti Bernardi opera* 1, 233–45. McGinn, "Bernard and Eschatology," 173, dates the sermon to "just before 1139." Leclercq, in his introduction to the sermons, xv–xvi, notes that it is difficult to date particular sermons after the first twenty-four, but says that Bernard continued working on the sermons beginning in 1138.

29. Bernard, *Sermo* 33, 3.4, 236.
30. The passage about the kisses is in *Sermo* 3, 14–17.
31. Bernard, *Sermo* 33, 3.5, 236 and 6.11, 241; Psalm 90:5 (Ps. 91:5 NRSV). Discussed in McGinn, "Bernard and Eschatology," 173–74.
32. Bernard, *Sermo* 33, 7.14, 243.
33. Bernard, *Sermo* 33, 3.6, 237, and 7.14, 243; Psalm 90:6 (Ps. 91:6 NRSV).
34. Bernard, *Sermo* 33, 7.16, 243–44; Psalm 90:6 (Ps. 91:6 NRSV).
35. Bernard, *Sermo* 33, 7.15–16, 244.
36. Bernard, *Sermo* 33, 7.16, 245, with reference to 2 Thessalonians 2:4, a key biblical source for Antichrist, referred to by Bernard also at *Sermo* 33, 5.9, 240; Psalm 90:6 (Ps. 91:6 NRSV).
37. Bernard, *Sermo* 33, 4.7, 238.
38. Bernard, *Sermo* 33, 6.13, 243. McGinn, "Bernard and Eschatology," 175, mistakenly observes that Bernard did not use the image of the fourth hour of the watch here but did so only in a later sermon on Psalm 90.
39. Bernard, *Sermo* 33, 7.16, 245.
40. Bernard, "*Sermo in psalmum* Qui habitat," *Opera Sancti Bernardi* 4, 404–11; and Jean Leclercq, "Une parabole restituée à Saint Bernard," in *Études sur Saint Bernard et le texte de ses écrits, Analecta Sacri Ordinis Cisterciensis* 9 (1953): 133–36 (quoted here at 133). See also McGinn, "St. Bernard and Eschatology," 177.
41. The student was Geoffrey of Auxerre; McGinn, "Bernard and Eschatology," 180, quoted in Leclercq, "Une parabole," 133. Fritz Radcke, *Die eschatologischen Anschauugen Bernhards von Clairvaux: Ein Beitrag zur historischen Interpretation aus den Zeitanschaungen* (Langensalza: Wendt & Klauwell, 1915), argues that Bernard's sense of history was built on the belief that he was living in the *ferreum regnum*, the iron kingdom, which would imply a connection to Nebuchadnezzar's dream; however, Radcke draws the language of the iron kingdom from the Tiburtine Sibyl rather than from Bernard's actual words. Bernard combines the imagery with the four horsemen in the introduction to *Parobola* 6, in *Sancti Bernardi Opera* 6.2, 287–88.
42. Bernard, *Ep.* 363, 312.
43. Adriaan H. Bredero, *Bernard of Clairvaux: Between Cult and History* (Grand Rapids, MI: Wm. B. Eerdmans, 1996), 267–75.
44. Bernard, *Ep.* 363, 312.
45. Bernard, *Ep.* 363, 315, and more generally 3–5, 313–15.
46. Bernard, *Ep.* 458, 435.
47. Bernard, *Ep.* 457, 432. On the Second Crusade as a general campaign against unbelief, Giles Constable, "The Second Crusade as Seen by Contemporaries," *Traditio* 9 (1953): 213–79, and more generally, Jonathan Phillips, *Second Crusade: Extending the Frontiers*.
48. Bernard, *Ep.* 457, 433.
49. Bernard, *Ep.* 457, 432, with reference to Romans 11:25–26.
50. Hans-Dietrich Kahl, "Die Kreuzzugseschatologie Bernhards von Clairvaux und ihre missionsgeschichtliche Auswirkung," in *Bernard von Clairvaux und der Beginn der Moderne*, ed. Dieter R. Bauer (Innsbruck: Tyrolia-Verlag, 1996), 262–315 (294–97).
51. Odo, *De profectione*, 70–71.
52. Arnold is one of three authors of the *Vita prima Sancti Bernardi Claraevallis abbatis*, ed. Paul Verdeyen, CCCM 89B (Turnhout: Brepols, 2011), in particular comments at 2.24, 106. The others are Geoffrey of Auxerre and William of Saint-Thierry.
53. Geoffrey of Auxerre, *Vita prima S. Bernardi* 3.17–19, 145–47, esp. 3.19, 146.
54. Odo, *De profectione*, 8–11.
55. Benedicta Ward, *Miracles and the Medieval Mind: Theory, Record and Event, 1000–1215*, rev. ed. (Aldershot, Scolar Press, 1987), 182–83, where she specifies 235 paralytics cured and 172 blind, a total of 407, which does not include the deaf and dumb cured, the demon-possessed exorcised, and the one dead person raised to life; see also Meschini, *San Bernardo*, 64, observing that the number of miracles cannot be counted; "siamo tuttavia nell'ordine delle centinaia."

56. *Liber sextus vitae S. Bernardi*, in Migne, ed., PL 185, col. 377B,C. Using one's own saliva to heal the sick has gospel precedent—see for example Mark 8:23.

57. *Liber sextus*, col. 378C,D (on the dangerous crowds) and col. 387C,D, on there being too many miracles to remember.

58. Ward, *Miracles and the Medieval Mind*, 110–31; Henry Mayr-Harting, "Functions of a Twelfth-Century Shrine: The Miracles of St. Frideswide," in *Studies in Medieval History Presented to R. H. C. Davis*, ed. Henry Mary-Harting and R. I. Moore (London: Hambledon, 1985), 193–206; and more recently, Rachel Koopmans, *Wonderful to Relate: Miracle Stories and Miracle Collecting in High Medieval England* (Philadelphia: University of Pennsylvania Press, 2011).

59. *Liber sextus*, col. 376B.

60. *Liber sextus*, col. 377A. I am presuming that "dux Conradus" in this passage should be "rex Conradus."

61. *Liber sextus*, col. 382B.

62. *Liber sextus*, col. 383B.

63. Using the translation in Guibert, *Monodies and on the Relics of Saints*, 206.

64. *Liber sextus*, col. 375C, with reference to Wisdom 10:21.

65. *Liber sextus*, col. 399B.

66. *Liber sextus*, cols. 402B,C and 408C,D.

67. *Liber sextus*, cols. 384D–385A. The story grew in the retelling: Conrad of Eberbach, *Exordium magnum Cisterciense, sive narratio de initio Cisterciensis ordinis*, ed. Bruno Griesser, CCCM 138 (Turnhout: Brepols, 1994), 2.19, 93–96, has the man fall and break his neck. Bernard heals him by rubbing his own saliva along the facture.

68. Odo, *De profectione* 1, 10. The section title here is stolen from Christopher Hill, *The Experience of Defeat: Milton and Some Contemporaries* (London: Faber and Faber, 1984).

69. Odo, *De profectione* 7, 130.

70. Odo, *De profectione* 7, 132.

71. Suger, *Ep.* 6, in *Oeuvres* 2, ed. Françoise Gasparri (Paris: Belles Lettres, 2001), 39; on Louis's time in Antioch, see Phillips, *Second Crusade: Extending the Frontiers*, 207–12.

72. Martin Hoch, "The choice of Damascus as the Objective of the Second Crusade: A Re-evaluation," in *Autour de la Première Croisade*, 359–69.

73. Phillips, *Second Crusade: Extending the Frontiers*, 216–27 provides an excellent summary and analysis of the evidence for the events of the siege.

74. Phillips, *Second Crusade: Extending the Frontiers*, 222–24; Rubenstein, "Putting History to Use," 154–57; Alan J. Forey, "The Failure of the Siege of Damascus in 1148," *Journal of Medieval History* 10 (1984): 13–25.

75. Bernard, *De consideratione* in *Sancti Bernardi opera* 3, 2.1, 410.

76. Bernard, *De consideratione* 2.1, 411, referencing Psalm 113B:2 (Ps 115:2, NRSV). The word for "nations" is *gentes*.

77. Bernard, *De consideratione* 2.1, 411. Kahl, "Die Kreuzzugseschatologie," 272 reads Bernard as admitting to being a false prophet here.

78. Bernard, *De consideratione* 2.2, 412.

79. Bernard, *De consideratione* 2.3, 412, and Judges 19:30.

80. Bernard, *Ep.* 521, 483.

81. Bernard, *De consideratione* 2.3, 412, and Judges 20.

82. Phillips, *Second Crusade: Extending the Frontiers*, 270–72, and Timothy Reuter, "The 'Non-crusade' of 1149–50," in *The Second Crusade: Scope and Consequences*, 150–63; Giles Constable, "The Crusading Project of 1150," in *Montjoie: Studies in Crusade History in Honour of Hans Eberhard Mayer* (Aldershot: Variorum, 1997), 67–75.

83. Bernard, *Ep.* 256.4, 164–65.

84. Bredero, *Bernard of Clairvaux*, 36 and 86–87 (on Godfrey) and 81–85 (on Bernard's ill health); and Phillips, *Second Crusade*, 190–94.

85. The Würzburg annalist describes the gradual return of maimed prisoners from the East: *Annales Herbipolenses*, MGH SS 16, 5.

86. Bredero, *Bernard of Clairvaux*, 86, observes that Bernard's critics sometimes accused him "of refusing to take full responsibility for matters in which he involved himself," which would certainly apply in this case.
87. Bernard, *De consideratione* 2.4, 413.
88. Bernard, *Ep.* 386, printed in PL 182, ed. Migne, col. 590B.
89. Bernard, *Ep.* 386, col. 590C,D.
90. Bernard, *Ep.* 386, cols. 590D–591A.
91. *Vita prima* 3.10, 140. Bernard himself wrote on the doctrine of mankind replacing fallen angels; see Peter Raedts, "St. Bernard of Clairvaux and Jerusalem," in *Prophecy and Eschatology*, ed. Michael Wilks (Woodbridge: Boydell & Brewer, 1997), 69–82, 172.
92. Bernard, *Ep.* 386.3, col. 591A.
93. *Vita prima* 3.9, 139.
94. *Vita prima* 3.10, 140–41.
95. *Annales Herbipolenses*, 3.
96. Walter Map, *De Nugis Curialium, Courtiers' Trifles*, ed. and trans. M. R. James, rev. C. N. L. Brooke and R. A. B. Mynors (Oxford: Clarendon Press, 1983), 1.24, 80–81. On the 1163 push for canonization, Bredero, *Bernard of Clairvaux*, 43–46. The choreography of the scene is inspired by 1 Kings 17:17–24, when Elijah raised a boy from the dead.
97. *Vita prima* 4.30–34, 179–83; compare to *Liber sextus*, cols. 376B,C; 377C; 381A–C; 388B,C; 390D; 397A,B; and 399A.
98. Kahl, "Die Kreuzzugseschatologie," 289–91.
99. Bernard, *Vita S. Malachiae episcopi*, in *Sancti Bernardi opera* 3, preface, 307. Both McGinn, "Bernard and Eschatology," 184, and Kahl, "Die Kreuzzugseschatologie," 267–68 and 271, see Bernard becoming increasingly apocalyptic in outlook toward the end of his life, with Kahl accenting the calling of the crusade as the chief impetus and McGinn stressing disappointment with the failure of the crusade.

CHAPTER 9

1. Otto, *Gesta Frederici* 1.36, 200.
2. Otto, *Gesta Frederici* 1.50, 224. I am translating *credulus* as naïve.
3. Hans-Werner Goetz, *Das Geschichtsbild Ottos von Freising: Ein Beitrag zur historischen Vorstellungwelt und zur Geschichte des 12. Jahrhunderts* (Cologne: Böhlau, 1984), 22–49. The details of Otto's life are also given in broad strokes by Charles Christopher Mierow in his translation *The Two Cities: A Chronicle of Universal History to the Year 1146 A.D., by Otto, Bishop of Freising* (New York: Columbia University Press, 1928), 3–18; and in more detail, P. Leopold Josef Grill, "Das Itinerar Ottos von Freising," in *Festschrift Friedrich Hausmann*, ed. Herwig Ebner (Graz: Akadem. Druck- u. Verlagsanst., 1977), 153–77. Elisabeth Mégier, "Tamquam lux post tenebras, oder: Ottos von Freising Weg von der Chronik zu den Gesta Frederici," *Mediaevistik* 3 (1990): 131–267, offers a useful study of Otto's life in connection with his writing.
4. Otto, *Gesta Frederici* 1.43, 210.
5. Otto, *Gesta Frederici* 1.45, 216; on the processes of creating this peace, Knut Görich, "Fürstenstreit und Friedensstiftung vor dem Aufbruch Konrads III. zum Kreuzzug," *Zeitschrift für die Geschichte des Oberrheins* 158 (2010): 117–36; Mégier, "Tamquam lux," 217.
6. Otto, *Gesta Frederici* 1.47, 218.
7. Otto, *Gesta Frederici* 1.48, 220–22.
8. Otto, *Gesta Frederici* 1.48, 222; Mégier, "Tamquam lux," 221.
9. Otto, *Gesta Frederici* 1.49–62, 222–62; on the issues and Otto's connections, Constant J. Mews, "Accusations of Heresy and Error in the Twelfth-Century Schools: The Witness of Gerhoh of Reichersberg and Otto of Freising," in *Heresy in Transition: Transforming Ideas of Heresy in Medieval and Early Modern Europe*, ed. John Christian Laursen, Cary J. Nederman, and Ian Hunter (Aldershot: Ashgate, 2005), 43–57, esp. 51–54; also Karen Bollermann and Cary J. Nederman, "Standing in Abelard's Shadow: Gilbert of Poitiers, the 1148 Council of Rheims, and the Politics of Ideas," in *Religion, Power, and Resistance*

from the Eleventh to the Sixteenth Centuries: Playing the Heresy Card, ed. Karen Bollermann, Tomas M. Izbicki, and Cary J. Nederman (New York: Palgrave Macmillan, 2014), 13–36, esp. 19–20.

10. *Annales Herbipolenses,* 5; also, Phillips, *Second Crusade: Extending the Frontiers,* 169 and 184, and Grill, "Das Itinerar," 160–61.

11. As reported in *Annales Reicherbergenes,* MGH SS 17, 462.

12. On the literary background to Otto's self-referential observation, Tuomas M. S. Lehtonen, "History, Tragedy and Fortune in Twelfth-Century Historiography, with Special Reference to Otto of Freising's *Chronica,*" in *Historia: The Concept and Genres in the Middle Ages,* ed. Tuomas M. S. Lehtonen and Päivi Mehtonen (Helsinki: Societas Scientiarum Fennica, 2000), 31–49.

13. Otto, *Gesta Frederici* 1.64, 264.

14. From an exegesis of 1 Kings 22, in Lincoln Cathedral MS 26, fol. 113r, with the relevant excerpt printed in Radulfus Niger, *De re militari et triplici via peregrinationis Ierosolimitane,* ed. Ludwig Schmugge (Berlin: Walter de Gruyter, 1977), 70, n.319; mentioned in Aurell, *Chrétiens contre les croisades,* 147. See also Schmugge's biographical introduction to Ralph in *De re militari,* 4, on Ralph's teacher Gerard Pucelle, who served briefly at Barbarossa's court.

15. Otto's vocabulary: "pro dilatione terminorum vel commoditate corporum"; *Gesta Frederici* 1.66, 270.

16. Goez, *Das Geschichtsbild,* 280–81, discusses Otto's final assessment of the crusade's benefits, without sufficiently taking into account, I think, Otto's own experience of its failures.

17. Otto, *Gesta Frederici* 1.66, 270. The last line is an oblique reference to 1 Corinthians 14:32, where Paul warns the church about the potential difficulties created by having too many prophets.

18. Otto, *Gesta Frederici,* prologue, 114 and 118; Mégier, "Tamquam lux," 215.

19. The idea dissected at length by Werner Goez, *Translatio Imperii,* esp. on Otto, 113–20. Goez demonstrates that Otto drew on a variety of sources for his historical model, but argues that he was the first to put them together in an overarching, systematic fashion. He does not include the *Liber floridus* among those possible sources. More succinctly summed up in eschatological perspective by Hubert Glaser, "De monte abscisus est lapis sine manibus (Daniel 2: 45): Die geschichtliche Rolle des Reformpapsttums im Spiegel der Weltchronik Ottos von Freising," in *Papsttum und Kirchenreform, historische Beiträge. Festschrift Georg Schwaiger,* ed. Georg Schwaiger, Manfred Weitlauff, and Karl Hausberger (St. Ottillien: EOS Verlag, 1990), 151–91, on 188.

20. Joseph Staber, "Eschatologie und Geschichte bei Otto von Freising," in *Otto von Freising: Gedenkgabe zu seinem 800. Todesjahr,* ed. Joseph A. Fischer (Freising: Verlag des Historischen Vereins Freising, 1958), 106–26, esp. 121–23.

21. Otto, *Chronica,* prologue, 10.

22. Codex Jenensis Bose q. 6. Schmidt's edition of Otto includes reproductions of all of the illustrations, following *lxx* of the introduction.

23. Otto, *Chronica* 5.31, 420.

24. See the commentary in Goetz, *Geschichtsschreibung und Geschichtsbewußtsein* 211–13.

25. Otto, *Chronica* 1.2, 60 (the discussion of the shape of the world is in 1.1).

26. As discussed in chapter 5. This cartographic sensibility is never straightforward and rarer than assumed, but Otto is one of its clearest practitioners; see Stephen McKenzie, "The Westward Progression of History on Medieval Mappaemundi: An Investigation of the Evidence," in Harvey, *Hereford World Map,* 335–44.

27. Otto, *Chronica* 1.2, 60, with reference to Psalm 84:7.

28. Otto, *Chronica* 2.13, 128.

29. Otto, *Chronica,* prologue, 14.

30. Conrad had not been crowned emperor by the pope, but he did use an imperial title, particularly when he corresponded with the Byzantine emperor—e.g., Otto, *Gesta Frederici*

1.26, 170, addressing Emperor John II Comnenos: "Conradus Dei gratia Romanorum imperator augustus"; in the same chapter, 176, to Manuel Comnenos: "Conradus Dei gratia Romanorum imperator augustus."

31. Kahl, "Die Kreuzzugseschatologie," 300–302 suggests that Bernard held this belief about Conrad, though Kahl acknowledges that it is impossible to prove the point conclusively. The "C" prophecy appears in one of the revisions of Adso's *Life of Antichrist*, usually called "Pseudo-Alcuin," published by Verhelst in *De Antichristo*, 117–28, with the key passage on 125. See also Gabriele, *Empire of Memory*, 123–25.

32. Otto, *Chronica* 2.13, 128.

33. Otto, *Chronica* 6.36, 492. He repeats the "mountain" imagery in the introduction to Book 7, 496. Also, Goez, *Das Geschichtsbild*, 264–66; Glaser, "De monte abscisus," 170–71; Staber, "Eschatologie und Geschichte," 125.

34. Otto, *Chronica* 6.36, 492.

35. Otto, *Chronica* 7.10, 516. I translate *perfidissimus* as "utterly treacherous."

36. Otto, *Chronica* 7.9, 514, with reference to 2 Timothy 3:1; Goez, *Das Geschichtsbild*, 269–71.

37. Otto, *Chronica* 7.9, 514.

38. On the links between history and morality (in the exegetical sense), Xavier Biron Ouellet, "Affectivité et sense chrétien de l'histoire dans la *Chronica sive Historia duabus civitatibus* d'Otton de Freising," *Memini* 16 (2015): 45–62.

39. Otto, *Chronica* 5.9, 396.

40. Otto, *Chronica* 7.7, 510.

41. Otto, *Chronica* 7.7, 508.

42. Otto, *Chronica* 7.2, 502.

43. Otto, *Chronica* 7.3–4, 502–6.

44. All in Otto, *Chronica* 4, 506. On the different levels of blood, Thomas Madden, "Rivers of Blood: An Analysis of One Aspect of the Crusader Conquest of Jerusalem," *Revista Chilena de Estudios Medievales* 1 (2012): 25–37, an oddly entertaining mathematical analysis of the evidence, in which I make a narrative cameo.

45. Otto, *Chronica* 7.5–6, 506–8; Otto's original monastery at Morimond occupied a similar geographic frontier: Grill, "Das Itinerar," 155.

46. The one exception is a bit of whimsy that the Turks surrendered Jerusalem to the Egyptians in 1098 because the former feared the presence of Frankish ambassadors in the latter's army: Otto, *Chronica* 7.4, 504–6.

47. Otto, *Chronica* 7.4, 504; an echo of a passage from the *Gesta Francorum*, 55–56, where the Turkish general Kerbogha asks his mother if the Franks' leaders are in fact gods.

48. Grill, "Das Itinerar," 159–60.

49. Otto, *Chronica* 7.33, 556.

50. Otto, *Chronica* 7.34, 556–58. On this encounter, and the possible basis of the battle in history, Martin Gosman, "Otto de Freising et le Prêtre Jean," *Revue belge de philologie et d'histoire* 61 (1983): 270–85; Akbari, *Idols in the East*, 86–88. On the connection of Prester John with the Magi and their wealth, Richard C. Trexler, *Journey of the Magi: Meanings in History of a Christian Story* (Princeton, NJ: Princeton University Press, 1997), 72–75 and 125–30.

51. The relevant material has been collected in Keagan Brewer, ed. and trans., *Prester John: The Legend and Its Sources* (Farnham: Ashgate, 2015), 30–42.

52. Otto, *Chronica*, Letter to Frederick, 4. Seven symbolizes God's rest after creation and eight the eternal age that will succeed history: Peter Darby, *Bede and the End of Time* (Farnham: Ashgate, 2012), 65–92; Mégier, "Tamquam lux," 205.

53. Otto, *Chronica* 7.34, 560. Mégier, "Tamquam lux," 215–16, offers a similar reading: In the *Gesta Frederici*, Frederick provides the peace/restraining force on Antichrist which, at the end of the *Two Cities*, only the monks had seemed capable of offering.

54. Brett Edward Whalen, *Dominion of God: Christendom and Apocalypse in the Middle Ages* (Cambridge, MA: Harvard University Press, 2009), 91. The most detailed examination of Book 8 remains (though obviously dated) Max Büdiger, "Die Entstehung des achten

Buches Otto's von Freising: ein universalhistorische Studie," *Sitzungsberichte. Akademie der Wissenschaften in Wien, Philosophish-Historische Klasse* 98 (1881): 325–65.

55. Otto, *Chronica*, Letter to Rainald of Dassel, 8.
56. Otto, *Chronica* 8, prologue, 584.
57. Otto, *Chronica* 8.1, 568.
58. Otto, *Chronica* 8.4, 594, and more generally 592–94. The reference to Job appears to be Habakkuk 1:16. See also Bollermann and Nederman, "Standing in Abelard's Shadow," 27.
59. Otto, *Chronica* 8.3, 592.
60. Otto, *Chronica* 8.1, 588. Compare to Adso, *De Antichristo*, 23. His Jewish descent was incorporated, for example, into the *Glossa ordinaria*; see Hughes, *Constructing Antichrist*, 217–18.
61. Otto, *Chronica* 8.5–7, 594–96.
62. Pseudo-Methodius, *Apocalypse* 14, 136–39 and Adso, *De Antichristo*, 27–28.
63. *Epistola Methodii*, in Adso, *De Antichristo*, 151. Robert E. Lerner, "Refreshment of the Saints: The Time after Antichrist as a Station for Earthly Progress in Medieval Thought," *Traditio* 32 (1976): 97–144 (112) (written at a time when the various versions of Adso has not been thoroughly delineated) describes Otto's structure of the conversion of the Jews as a "clear divergence" from his sources.
64. Though as Mégier, "Tamquam lux," 217, points out, there was an irony that must have been intentional on Otto's part in his description of how Bernard told Ralph that a monk could not leave his monastery to preach.
65. Otto, *Chronica* 8.2, 590.
66. Otto, *Chronica* 8.3, 593.
67. For comparison, even Augustine, who heavily allegorized all of these prophetic images, did not dismiss the possibility that Antichrist would sit in the ruins of the Temple in Jerusalem; he did not embrace the idea, but he did accept it as a possibly valid reading: *De civitate Dei* 20.19, 731.
68. Otto, *Chronica* 8.2, 588–90.
69. Otto, *Chronica* 8.7, 596.
70. The Latin text with commentary is in Karl Young, *The Drama of the Medieval Church* (Oxford: Clarendon Press, 1933), 369–96; translated as *The Play of Antichrist*, trans. John Wright (Toronto: Pontifical Institute, 1967). Conventional wisdom dates the play to 1160, though with no real certainty.
71. Helmut Plechl, ed., *Die Tegernseer Briefsammlung des 12. Jahrunderts*, MGH Die Briefe der deutschen Kaiserzeit 8 (Hannover: Hahnsche, 2002), 93, 123–24.
72. Paris, MS BnF *nouv. acq. lat.* 310. The Josephus version is attributed to Rufinus. Thanks to Brad Phillis for the reference.
73. *Ludus Antichristi*, 373, lines 49–54.
74. Anne Latowsky, *Emperor of the World*, 149–60, focuses on these elements of the play to discuss its place in a tradition of imperial panegyric, downplaying its prophetic implications in a world very much at war over Jerusalem.
75. *Ludus Antichristi*, 377, lines 146–50.
76. Björn Weiler, "Suitability and right: Imperial succession and the norms of politics in early Staufen Germany," in *Making and Breaking the Rules: Succession in Medieval Europe, c. 1000–1600*, ed. Frédérique Lachaud and Michael Penman (Turnhout: Brepols), 71–86, esp. 76–77.
77. *Ludus Antichristi*, 379, lines 193–94.
78. *Ludus Antichristi*, 381, lines 263–66.
79. Based on a reference to an expedition against Milan that appears in a dedicatory letter. Frederick did not announce his designs on Milan until March 1157; Otto, *Chronica*, 5, n.12. Grill, "Das Itinerar," 164, notes two instances in Book 4 where Otto seems to have made revisions based after returning from Crusade.
80. Staber, "Eschatologie und Geschichte," 118–19.

CHAPTER 10

1. On Gerhoh's life and thought, see Damien Van den Eynde, *L'œuvre littéraire de Géroch de Reichersberg* (Rome: Pontificum Athenaeum Antonianum, 1957); Peter Classen, *Gerhoch von Reichersberg: eine Biographie mit einem Anhang über die Quellen, ihre handschrifliche Überlieferung und ihre Chronologie* (Mainz: Wiesbaden, 1960); Erich Meuthen, *Kirche und Heilsgeschichte bei Gerhoh von Reichersberg* (Leiden: Brill, 1959); Anna M. Lazzarino del Gross, *Società e potere nella Germania del XII secolo: Gerhoch di Reichersberg* (Florence: Casa Editrice Leo S. Olschki, 1974); Alois Weissthanner, "Regesten des Freisinger Bischofs Otto I. (1138–58)," *Analecta Cisterciensia* 14 (1958): 151–222, esp. §1, 153; §142, 200–201; and §159, 207. Goetz, *Das Geschichtsbild*, 80–81, draws a distinction between the *Symbolismus* of this historical thought of Gerhoh (and Rupert of Deutz and Hildegard of Bingen), as opposed to the *Figuralismus* of Otto, though he notes points of similarity and engagement between the two writers throughout his text.
2. The details of the Alexander-Barbarossa wars are most easily accessible in Marshall W. Baldwin, *Alexander III and the Twelfth Century* (New York: Newman Press, 1968), 43–83 and 135–53.
3. Gerhoh of Reichersberg, *Libri iii de investigatione Antichristi*, ed. Friederich Scheibelberger (Linz: M. Quirein, 1875), 1.57, 112.
4. Gerhoh of Reichersberg, *De quarta vigilia noctis*, in MGH *Libelli de lite* 3 (Hannover: Hahn, 1897), 1, 503
5. MS Österreischische Nationalbibliothek 427; see Kempf and Bull's introduction to Robert, *Historia*, xlii.
6. Gerhoh of Reichersberg, *Libellus de ordine donorum*, in *Opera Inedita*, ed. D. Van den Eynde, O. Van den Eynde, A. Rijmersnaei, and P. Classen, 2 vols. (Rome: Speicilegium Pontificii Antoniani, 1955), 1, 84–85.
7. Gerhoh, *Epositio Psalmorum*, in *Opera Inedita* 1, 257. The verse is Song of Songs 6:3 (6:4, NRSV).
8. Gerhoh's use of crusade histories noted by Buc, *Holy War, Martyrdom*, 281.
9. Gerhoh, *Expositio Psalmorum*, in *Opera Inedita* 1, 260.
10. Gerhoh could be careless with history. He elsewhere writes that Robert Guiscard (d. 1085) rescued Urban II (r. 1088–99) from a siege of Rome; *De investigatione* 1.23, 56–57.
11. Gerhoh, *Expositio Psalmorum*, in *Opera Inedita* 1, 262; Gerhoh quotes the liturgy for the second Sunday of Advent here as prophecy.
12. Gerhoh, *Expositio Psalmorum*, in *Opera Inedita* 1, 437.
13. Wolf Zöller, "The Regular Canons and the Liturgy of the Latin East," *Journal of Medieval History* 43 (2017): 367–83. On the apostolic ideal within the broader rhetoric of twelfth-century reform, Giles Constable, *The Reformation of the Twelfth Century* (Cambridge: Cambridge University Press, 1996), 125–67; on Gerhoh's place within this tradition in Germany, Peter Classen, "Gerhoch von Reichersberg und die Regularkanoniker in Bayern und Österreich," in *La vita comune del clero nei secoli XI e XII* (Milano: Vita e Pensiero, 1962), 304–40.
14. Gerhoh, *Expositio Psalmorum*, in *Opera Inedita* 1, 263. The four churches Gerhoh had in mind were the Holy Sepulcher, the Temple of the Lord/al-Aqsa, St. Mary on Mount Zion, and the Church of the Ascension on the Mount of Olives.
15. Gerhoh, *Expositio Psalmorum*, in *Opera Inedita* 1, 263. Reference is to Psalm 33:8 (34:7, NRSV)
16. Gerhoh, *Expositio Psalmorum*, in *Opera Inedita* 1, 262, refers to the king of Babylon blaspheming his god Muhammad after the defeat at Ascalon.
17. Gerhoh, *Expositio Psalmorum*, in *Opera Inedita* 1, 263.
18. Eynde, *L'œuvre littéraire*, 292–324, divides Gerhoh's expositions of the Psalms into ten groups, written at different points. Group 3, into which Psalm 33 falls, was written sometime between late 1146 and summer 1147; group 4, into which Psalm 39 (Ps 40, NRSV) falls, was written in 1148.
19. Gerhoh, *Expositio Psalmorum*, in *Libelli de lite* 3, 437, mentions Edessa as the triggering event for the new crusade.

20. Gerhoh of Reichersberg, *Expositio Psalmorum*, in MGH *Libelli de lite* 3, 434.
21. Gerhoh, *Expositio Psalmorum*, in *Libelli de lite* 3, 436, with reference to Numbers 10:2.
22. Gerhoh, *Expositio Psalmorum*, in *Libelli de lite* 3, 436, with reference to Philippians 1:21.
23. Gerhoh, *Expositio Psalmorum*, in *Libelli de lite* 3, 434. The Latin for the final passages reads: "Inde mihi cuilibet fideli et catholico iucunda est in hoc psalmo preteritorum temporum commemoratio et cum presentibus eorum collatio."
24. Gerhoh, *Expositio Psalmorum*, in *Libelli de lite* 3, 437.
25. Gerhoh, *De investigatione* 1.67, 139–40.
26. Gerhoh, *De investigatione* 1.69, 140–43.
27. Gerhoh, *De investigatione* 1.70, 143–44.
28. Gerhoh, *De investigatione* 1.70, 144; he says he had learned the story from *rex Romanorum*, which could refer to Frederick Barbarossa, but in context seems to indicate Conrad.
29. Gerhoh, *De investigatione* 1.71, 144–45.
30. "Ecce quis finis!"; Gerhoh, *De investigatione* 1.71, 145.
31. Gerhoh, *De investigatione* 1.72, 145–46; commented on in Schein, *Gateway*, 138.
32. Gerhoh brings up Simony's connection to Jerusalem in *De investigatione* 1.73, 147, in connection with financial disputes between the Patriarch and the Hospital, whose amicable relations he believed stretched back to apostolic times.
33. Gerhoh, *De investigatione* 1.79, 155–56.
34. Gerhoh, *De investigatione* 1.80, 157, with reference to Luke 21:11.
35. Gerhoh, *De investigatione* 1.80, 157–58. The "Little Apocalypse": Matthew 24, Mark 13, and Luke 21.
36. Gerhoh, *De investigatione* 1.4, 23; Jerome, *Epistulae*, CSEL 54, ed. Isidore Hilberg (Venice: Österreichische Akadamie der Wissenschaft, 1910), 53.9, 463.
37. Gerhoh uses the language of tropes and types at *De investigatione* 1.2, 15 and 1.33, 74. In the latter case, he speaks of how current events are congruent to a type from the ancient world, *typo antiquitatis*.
38. Gerhoh, *De investigatione* 1.2, 14–15, all with reference to Adso, *De antichristo*, 23; Meuthen, *Kirche und Heilsgeschichte*, 144–45. Gerhoh's argument would seem to have escaped the lynx-eye of Robert Lerner, who observes in *The Feast of Saint Abraham: Medieval Millenarians and the Jews* (Philadelphia: University of Pennsylvania Press, 2001), 136, n.45, that the argument that Antichrist would be from the tribe of Dan was not contradicted until Joachim of Fiore. Corrected by Gian Luca Potestà, *Il tempo dell'Apocalisse: Vita di Gioacchino da Fiore* (Rome: Laterza, 2004), 243–44.
39. Gerhoh, *De investigatione* 1.3, 16–20. He refers several times in *De investigatione* to his indecision about the schism, e.g., preface, 11–12 and 1.63, 128. More generally on the rich semiotic tradition of Babylon: Andrew Scheil, *Babylon under Western Eyes: A Study of Allusion and Myth* (Toronto: University of Toronto Press, 2016).
40. Daniel 9:27 and Mark 13:14, cited in Gerhoh, *De investigatione* 1.4, 21.
41. Gerhoh, *De investigatione* 1.4, 21.
42. 1 Corinthians 3:16, cited in Gerhoh, *De investigatione* 1.4, 20.
43. Gerhoh, *De investigatione* 1.45, 92–93.
44. Gerhoh, *De investigatione* 1.4, 21–22 and 1.46, 93–94.
45. Gerhoh, *De investigatione* 1.4, 23–24.
46. Hildegard at least knew Gerhoh indirectly, in that she advised Bishop Eberhard of Bamberg on the latter's Christological disputes with Gerhoh; see the note and the translated letters in *The Letters of Hildegard of Bingen* 1, trans. Joseph L. Baird and Radd K. Ehrman (Oxford: Oxford University Press, 1994), esp. 31 and 31r, 94–99. Given Hildegard's fame, Gerhoh certainly knew of her and her work.
47. Hildegard, *Scivias*, ed. Adelgundis Führkötter and Angela Carlevaris, 2 vols., CCCM 43–43a (Turnhout: Brepols, 1978) vol. 2, 3.11, 576–77 and 3.11.14, 584.
48. Hildegard, *Scivias* 2, 3.11.37–39, 598–600.
49. Gerhoh, *De investigatione* 1.88, 173–74, with reference to Colossians 3:16.
50. See the introductory comments in Gerhoh of Reichersberg, *Letter to Pope Hadrian about the Novelties of the Day*, ed. Nikolaus M. Häring (Toronto: Pontifical Institute, 1974), 11–12.

As mentioned, Gerhoh makes extensive use of Bernard's *De consideratione*, a text discussed at length in chapter 8.

51. See, for example, Morrison, "Exercise of Thoughtful Minds," 361–62.
52. Gerhoh returns to this historical model periodically throughout *De investigatione*; the sections most closely pertaining to the "building phase" of the temple are 1.14, 37 and 1.31, 71.
53. Gerhoh, *De investigatione* 1.14, 36; 1.33, 72; and 1.90, 179.
54. Gerhoh, *De quarta* 12, 511–12. Gerhoh makes a similar argument in fact in *De investigatione* 1.32, 73, where he writes that the softening of Nebuchadnezzar's heart, apparent in the various stories of Daniel, points toward the eventual conversion of Rome to Christianity.
55. Gerhoh, *De investigatione* 1.14, 37–38; 1.34, 75–76; and 1.90, 178.
56. Gerhoh, *De investigatione* 1.90, 179; also 1.15, 38.
57. Matthew 14:22–33. The version of the story in Mark 6:47 does not include the details about Peter.
58. Gerhoh, *De quarta* 12, 512. Whalen, *Dominion of God*, 97–98, discusses this passage and reads it as an early expression of the "Angelic Pope" legend.
59. Gerhoh, *De quarta* 11, 508–9; Gerhoh's appreciation of Gregory increased later in his life, as noted by Meuthen, *Kirche und Heilsgeschichte*, 138.
60. Gerhoh, *De quarta* 1, 508.
61. Gerhoh, *De quarta* 11, 510.
62. Gerhoh, *De investigatione* 1.50, 101.
63. Gerhoh, *De quarta* 14, 514, following 1 John 4:3, "Every spirit that does not acknowledge Jesus is not from God and is Antichrist."
64. Gerhoh, *De quarta* 10, 508.
65. Gerhoh, *De investigatione* 1.20, 52.
66. Hildegard does not name Henry but makes his identity clear. The passages quoted here are from *Liber divinorum operum*, ed. A. Derolez and P. Dronke, CCCM 92 (Turnhout: Brepols, 1996) 3.5.7, 416–17 and 3.5.15, 432.
67. Gerhoh, *De quarta*, 18, 521.
68. Gerhoh, *De investigatione* 1.90, 180.
69. Gerhoh, *De quarta* 21, 525.
70. On Ralph's life, George B. Flahiff, "Ralph Niger: An Introduction to His Life and Works," *Mediaeval Studies* 2 (1940): 104–26, and Schmugge's introduction to *De re militari*, 3–10. On Ralph's attitude toward crusading, George B. Flahiff, "*Deus Non Vult*: A Critic of the Third Crusade," *Mediaeval Studies* 9 (1947): 162–88, and Aurell, *Chrétiens contre les croisades*, 139–60. Schmugge was able to reconstruct Niger's life impressively through his exegetical works: *De re militari*, 6–7. On the political character of Ralph's thought, Philippe Buc, "Exégèse et pensée politique: Radulphus Niger (vers 1190) et Nicolas de Lyre (vers 1330)," in *Représentations, pouvoir et royauté à la fin du Moyen Age*, ed. Joël Blanchard (Paris: Picard, 1995), 145–64.
71. Radulfus, *Chronica: Eine englische Weltchronik des 12. Jahrhunderts*, ed. Hanna Krause (Frankfurt am Main: Peter Lang, 1985), 51–53 (the theoretical overview of world historical models); 15 (the fourth age beginning at David); 33 (beginning of the fifth age); 34 (Babylon and Rome).
72. Radulfus, *Chronica*, 29.
73. Radulfus, *De re militari*, 2.74, 160, and see also n.2, and Matthew 24:12.
74. Ulf Büngten and Willy Tegel, "European Tree-ring Data and the Medieval Climate Anomaly," *Pages* 19:1 (2011): 14–15. Thanks to James Palmer for this reference.
75. Radulfus, *Chronica*, 250–51 and 260–61.
76. Radulfus, *Chronica*, 269–70. The language Ralph uses here is similar to that in his exegesis of 1 Kings, discussed in chap. 7, though he does not single out Otto of Freising here for blame, as he did in his commentaries.
77. Radulfus, *De re militari* 4.54, 224.
78. Radulfus, *Chronica*, 93–94.

79. Radulfus, *De re militari*, prologue, 92, and 3.86, 194.
80. Radulfus, *De re militari*, prologue, 94.
81. A point emphasized by Radulfus, *De re militari* 2.21, 141.
82. Radulfus, *De re militari* 3, prologue, 162, with reference to James 3:2.
83. Radulfus, *De re militari* 2.74, 159.
84. Radulfus, *De re militari* 3.66, 187–88.
85. Radulfus, *De re militari* 3.82, 193. Aurell, *Chrétiens contre les croisades*, 150 goes as far as to compare Ralph to Candide, "avant les Lumières," urging that one tend to one's own garden.
86. Radulfus, *Chronica*, 9 and 210–11 (he writes that "the holy places of Jerusalem were profaned").
87. "tam vitium quam Sarracenum"; Radulfus, *De re militari*, 2.73, 159. Ralph suggests here that pure-hearted crusaders who had conquered vice could conquer Jerusalem (though the process of attaining such purity was daunting).
88. Radulfus, *De re militari* 3.91, 197.
89. Radulfus, *De re militari* 3.90, 196; discussed in Kedar, *Crusade and Mission*, 109–12. In his chronicle, Radulfus, *Chronica*, 289, would criticize Frederick Barbarossa for not trying to convert Muslims during his march through Anatolia on the Third Crusade.
90. "Homines sunt eiusdem conditionis nature cuius et nos sumus"; Radulfus, *De re militari* 3.90, 196; Aurell, *Chrétiens contre les croisades*, 156.
91. Radulfus, *De re militari* 3.65, 186.
92. Radulfus, *De re militari* 3.84, 194.
93. Radulfus, *De re militari* 3.83, 193–94.
94. See also the commentary in Aurell, *Chrétiens contre les croisades*, 145.

CHAPTER 11

1. The best modern account of the Third Crusade and its background, as well as the most readable, is to be found in the relevant chapters of Thomas Asbridge, *The Crusades: The Authoritative History of the Holy Land* (New York: Ecco, 2010), culminating with his description of Hattin and the capture of Jerusalem, 343–64; also, Anne-Marie Eddé, *Saladin*, trans. Jane Marie Todd (Cambridge, MA: Belknap-Harvard, 2011), 203–37.
2. *Audita tremendi* as printed in PL 202, cols 1539C–1542D. I am following Psalm 78:1–3 (Ps 79:1–3, NRSV) as used by Gregory at cols. 1539D–1540C; Baldric, *Historia*, 8.
3. *Audita tremendi*, col. 1541A,B.
4. *Audita tremendi*, col. 1540D, with reference to Psalm 73:12 (Ps 74:12, NRSV)
5. Vatican MS Reg. lat. 658.
6. "Postea anno dominice incarnationis m. c. lxxxvii. iiii. nonas iulii capta est terra Iherosolimitana a Salahadino rege Damasci et Babilonis…undecima vice"; Vat. Reg. lat. 658, fol. 92v. The scribe notes as well that Acre had been recaptured, meaning that the manuscript was written after 1191.
7. Augustine, *De civitate Dei* 15.20, 485.
8. *Audita tremendi*, col. 1541B.
9. W. L. Warren, *Henry II* (Berkeley: University of California Press, 1973), 538, n1; Frank Barlow, *Thomas Becket* (London: Guild Publishing, 1986), 272.
10. John D. Cotts, *The Clerical Dilemma: Peter of Blois and Literate Culture in the Twelfth Century* (Washington, DC: Catholic University of America Press, 2009), presents a remarkably nuanced, sympathetic, clear-eyed analysis of Peter's career: esp. 179–88 on the Becket conflict; On the intellectual connections between Peter and Ralph, John D. Cotts, "The Exegesis of Violence in the Crusade Writings of Ralph Niger and Peter of Blois," in *The Use of the Bible in Crusader Sources*, ed. Elizabeth Lapina and Nicholas Morton (Leiden: Brill, 2017), 273–95.
11. Michael Markowski, "Peter of Blois and the Conception of the Third Crusade," in *The Horns of Hattin*, ed. Benjamin Z. Kedar (Jerusalem: Yed Izhak Ben-Zvi, 1992), 261–69.
12. The best introduction to this text is Alexander Marx, *Die Passio Raginaldi von Petrus von Blois: Märtyertum, Emotionalität, und Eschatologie* (master's thesis, University of Vienna,

2014); the best overview of Reynald's career, Bernard Hamilton, "The Elephant of Christ, Reynald of Châtillon," in *Religious Motivation: Biographical and Sociological Problems for the Church Historian*, ed. Derek Baker (Oxford: Blackwell, 1978), 97–108.

13. Peter of Blois, *Passio Raginaldi principis Antiochie*, in *Tractatus duo*, ed. R. B. C. Huygens, CCCM 194 (Turnhout: Brepols, 2002), 42, with reference to Hebrews 11:24–26.

14. William of Tyre, *Chronicon* 18.1, 809. William's account does not justify the more glamorous descriptions of Reynald's violence. On Reynald's early career, Asbridge, *Crusades*, 252–57 and 304–5.

15. Peter, *Passio*, 44–45, with reference to Job 28:15 and Proverbs 17:3; Carole Hillenbrand, "The Imprisonment of Reynald of Châtillon," in *Texts, Documents and Artefacts: Islamic Studies in Honour of D. S. Richards*, ed. C. F. Robinson (Leiden: Brill, 2003), 79–102.

16. Hillenbrand, "Imprisonment," 99.

17. Hamilton, "Elephant of Christ," 106–7, argues for the latter interpretation.

18. Asbridge, *Crusades*, 324–25 and 343; Eddé, *Saladin*, 193–95.

19. Peter, *Passio*, 51 and 54.

20. Peter, *Passio*, 51–52.

21. Peter, *Passio*, 53.

22. Peter, *Passio*, 59.

23. Radulfus, *Chronicle*, 278.

24. On these points, Eddé, *Saladin*, 210–11.

25. Bahā' al-Dīn Ibn Shaddād, *The Rare and Excellent History of Saladin*, trans. D. S. Richards (Aldershot: Ashgate, 2002), 75.

26. Peter, *Passio*, 45 and 43.

27. Peter, *Passio*, 67.

28. Peter, *Passio*, 33–38 and 73.

29. Peter, *Passio*, 70.

30. Aurell, *Des Chrétiens contre les croisades*, 158–59, assumes that it is a knight.

31. Peter, *Passio*, 70, and Leviticus 24:16.

32. Peter, *Passio*, 70 and 63.

33. Peter, *Passio*, 40 and 46.

34. Peter, *Passio*, 54–55.

35. Peter, *Passio*, 40.

36. Peter, *Passio*, 57.

37. Marx, *Die Passio*, 165–82, esp. 177–79.

38. Peter, *Passio*, 34; noted in Schein, *Gateway*, 181.

39. Peter, *Conquestio*, 78. The Latin is closer to: "He badly avenges an insult who cuts off his own nose."

40. Noted in Schein, *Gateway*, 162.

41. Reported in Jaroslav Folda, *Crusader Art in the Holy Land: From the Third Crusade to the Fall of Acre* (Cambridge: Cambridge University Press, 2005), 50–51.

42. Asbridge, *Crusades*, 378–81; John Gillingham, *Richard I* (New Haven, CT: Yale University Press, 1999), 87–89.

43. Henry of Albano, *Tractatus de perigrinante civitate Dei*, PL 204, cols. 251–400, at cols. 357D-358A.

44. Henry, *Tractatus*, col. 353D.

45. Henry, *Tractatus*, cols. 352B,C and 357C.

46. Henry, *Tractatus*, col. 360A, with reference to Proverbs 26:11.

47. Henry, *Tractatus*, col. 355B.

48. Henry, *Tractatus*, col. 358D.

49. Henry, *Tractatus*, col. 359C,D.

50. Henry, *Tractatus*, col. 359B,C.

51. Cole, *Preaching of the Crusades*, 65–71; Asbridge, *Crusades*, 371–72; Schein, *Gateway*, 176–78; Henry, *Tractatus*, col. 357A,B.

52. As discussed in Damien Kempf, "Towards a Textual Archaeology of the First Crusade," in *Writing the Early Crusades*, 116–26 (esp. 123–26).

53. "non ut decuit decoratus/Aule regali. nichilominus imperiali"; Vat. MS lat. 2001, fol. 92v.
54. "Pollens intrepidi ducis exemplo Gotefridi/Nusquam deficiat. sibi pax et gloria fiat"; Vat. MS lat. 2001, fol. 92v.
55. "Nulli. Pacificum. Sarraceno. Fredericum. Dirigat. Iste. Liber Ubi. Sit. Locus. A Nece Liber"; Vat. MS lat. 2001, fol. 1r.
56. Asbridge, *Crusades*, 382 and 420–22. The precise circumstances and the ultimate explanation for why Frederick drowned are unclear. Asbridge's reading that he suffered a heart attack seems plausible.

CHAPTER 12
1. See Gillingham, *Richard I*, 130–39 more generally.
2. The best introduction to Joachim's life is Potestà, *Il tempo dell'Apocalisse*. In English, Bernard McGinn, *The Calabrian Abbot: Joachim of Fiore in the History of Western Thought* (New York: MacMillan, 1985), and more briefly and with important updates Robert Lerner, *Feast of Saint Abraham*, 5–22. Two incomplete medieval biographies survive, printed in Herbert Grundmann, "Zur Biographie Joachim von Fiore und Rainers von Ponza," *Deutsches Archiv für Erforschung des Mittelalters* 16 (1960): 437–546 (528–44).
3. The best introduction to this dense system is a set of diagrams collected by Joachim's students shortly after his death: Joachim, *Book of Figures*, published as Gioacchino da Fiore, *Il Libro delle Figure*, ed. Leone Tondelli, Marjorie Reeves, and Beatrice Hirsch-Reich, 2 vols., 2nd ed. (Turin: Società Editrice Internazionale, 1953). See also Alexander Patschovsky, ed., *Die Bildwelt der Diagramme Jochims von Fiore* (Ostfildern: Jan Thorbecke Verlag, 2003), and Bernard McGinn, "Image as Insight in Joachim of Fiore's *Figurae*," in *Envisioning Experience in Late Antiquity and the Middle Ages: Dynamic Patterns in Texts and Images*, ed. Giselle de Nie and Thomas F. X. Noble (Burlington, VT: Ashgate, 2012), 93–118.
4. Joachim, *Book of Figures*, *tavola* 14.
5. R. W. Southern, "Presidential Address: Aspects of the European Tradition of Historical Writing: 3. History as Prophecy," *Transactions of the Royal Historical Society*, 5th Series, 22 (1972): 159–80 (174).
6. See, for example, Joachim, *Liber de Concordia noui ac veteris testamenti*, ed. E. Randolph Daniel (Philadelphia: American Philosophical Society, 1983), 3.1.1, 208.
7. Lerner, *Feast of Saint Abraham*, 33; Lerner uses the expression "paths not taken" on 1. He frames his argument against R. I. Moore's famous thesis about medieval persecution presented in *The Formation of a Persecuting Society: Authority and Deviance in Western Europe, 950–1250* (Oxford: Blackwell, 1987). Brett Edward Whalen, "Joachim of Fiore and the Division of Christendom," *Viator* 34 (2003): 89–108, takes a similar approach in reference to Moore in connection with Joachim's view of the historical role of the Greeks.
8. "While most of his comments about Islam are negative and look forward to the coming destruction of Christianity's nemesis, a passage in a treatise written sometime in the 1180s...expresses a more positive view: 'In the future, the same Saracen people, who are now given to the Christian people as a scourge, may be converted to God at the same time as the Jewish people, just as the Roman people, once given to the children of Israel as a scourge, were converted'"; Bernard McGinn, "Joachim of Fiore," in *Christian-Muslim Relations: A Bibliographic History*, David Thomas and Alexander Mallett, 4th ed. (Leiden: Brill, 2012), 83–85 (85). A more developed presentation of the case appears in Alexander Patschovsky, "Semantics of Mohammed and Islam in Joachim of Fiore," in *Conflict and Religious Conversation in Latin Christendom: Studies in Honour of Ora Limor*, ed. Israel Yuval and Ram Ben-Shalom (Turnhout: Brepols, 2014), 115–31. More generally, E. R. Daniel, "Apocalyptic Conversion: The Joachite Alternative to the Crusades," *Traditio* 25 (1969): 127–54.
9. "The Christians will triumph, when the time comes, not by battle but by preaching"; Daniel, "Apocalyptic Conversion," 136. Daniel argues that Joachim was ambivalent about the crusade, not necessarily opposed to it at the time of the Third Crusade, but that he had rejected it at the end of his life.
10. Potestà, *Il tempo dell'Apocalisse*, 4.

11. Grundmann, "Zur Biographie," 529 and n. *a*; McGinn, *Calabrian Abbot*, 19.
12. "aritmeticae spiritualis"; Joachim of Fiore, *Enchiridion super Apocalypsim*, ed. Edward K. Burger (Toronto: Pontifical Institute, 1986), 82.
13. Grundmann, "Zur biographie," 541.
14. Grundmann, "Zur biographie," 529.
15. Joachim, *Liber de Concordia*, 2.1.16, 92, places Bernard and the Cistercians as the moment of flowering of monastic orders; 4.2.2, 417, he labels Bernard as another Moses; Potestà, *Il tempo dell'Apocalisse*, 39–43.
16. Federico Farina Benedetto Fornari, *L'architettura cistercense e l'abbazi di Casamari* (Casamari: Edizioni Casamari, 1981), 51–66.
17. Antonio Maria Adorisio, *Dinamiche librarie cistercensi: da Casamari alla Calbria. Origine e dispersione della biblioteca manoscritta dell'abbazia di Casamari* (Casamari: Edizioni Casamari, 1996); 28–32 on Joachim's experiences there. Also, Potestà, *Il tempo dell'Apocalisse*, 9.
18. Potestà, *Il tempo dell'Apocalisse*, 342–44, suggests that we ought to read these visions more symbolically than literally.
19. McGinn, *Calabrian Abbot*, 21–22; Lerner, *Feast of Saint Abraham*, 8–9; Potestà, *Il tempo dell'Apocalisse*, 36–38.
20. Luke of Cosenza notes that Joachim began working on all three books during his stay at Casamari: Grundmann, "Zur biographie," 539–40.
21. Further complicating any reading of them is, until recently, the lack of any usable critical editions. Of the three major works, the only one available in a fully realized edition is *Psalterium decem cordarum*, MGH Quellen zur Geistgeschichte des Mittelalters 20, ed. Kurt-Victor Selge (Hannover: Hahnsche, 2009). The edition of the *Liber de concordia*, cited in n.6, is in need of revision and contains only the first four books. Book 5 of the *Liber de concordia* and the entire *Expositio in Apocalypsim* are available in early modern Venetian editions published in 1519 and 1527 respectively. Critical editions are in preparation.
22. In addition to the materials already cited, the most concise and still authoritative presentation of Joachim's thought is Marjorie Reeves, *The Influence of Prophecy in the Later Middle Ages: A Study in Joachimism* (Oxford: Oxford University Press, 1969), 16–27; also, Whalen, *Dominion of God*, 103–8.
23. On the coincidence of Hezekiah (or Ozias) and Rome, see Marjorie Reeves and Beatrice Hirsch-Reich, *The Figurae of Joachim of Fiore* (Oxford: Clarendon Press, 1972), 126.
24. For example, Joachim, *Liber de concordia*, 2.1.21, 101–102 and 3.1.1, 209; in Book 5, fols. 134rb–134va. The scriptural importance of the number 42 for Joachim lay first of all in Daniel 12:7, which refers to "time, times, and half a time," which could be read as reference to 3.5 years (1 + 2 + .5), or 42 months. See *Liber de concordia*, preface, 15. Revelation 11:2 and 13:5 both refer to a period of 42 months; Revelation 11:3 and 12:6 refer to 1,260 days, which breaks down into 42 months of 30 days each; Potestà, *Il tempo dell'Apocalisse*, 29–32.
25. These diagrams are laid out most clearly in Joachim, *Liber de concordia*, 88–92, and in Joachim, *Book of Figures, tavole* 9 and 10.
26. See Daniel's introductory comments to *Liber de concordia*, xxxvii–xl. Thanks also to Brett Whalen, for sharing with me a draft of an article-in-progress, "Rewinding History: Joachim of Fiore and the Sundial of Hezekiah."
27. Joachim, *Liber de concordia* 5.117, fol. 132va. Whalen, *Dominion of God*, 178–80 and 215–16, notes the connection between Joachim's positive assessment of the papacy and later apocalyptic predictions of a heroic, angelic pope.
28. Many of Joachim's modern admirers have described his system as emerging all at once, Athena-like from his head, during his visions at Mount Tabor and Casamari. That view has become difficult to maintain, especially in light of recent work by Gian Luca Potestà, who has placed Joachim's ideas more carefully into the context of twelfth-century thought. Potestà, *Il tempo dell'Apocalisse*, 168–69, suggests that Joachim may have had access to the early lost draft of *De investigatione Antichristi*, which Gerhoh had submitted for papal approval, during his visits to the curia. See also Potestà's comments on

resonances between Gerhoh and Joachim at 5–10, 39–44, 108–10, 168–69, 173–74, 200–201, and 243. Whalen, *Dominion of God*, 100–124 superbly situates Joachim's in the broader world of "reformist apocalyptic thought."

29. Joachim, *Liber de concordia* 3.1.6, 267: "It nevertheless may happen that the Saracen people, who today have been given as a scourge to the Christian people, will convert to God at the same time as the Jewish people, just as the Roman people, who had once been given as a scourge to sons of Israel, also converted."

30. Joachim of Fiore, *Dialogi de prescientia dei et predestinatione electorum*, ed. G. L. Potestà (Rome: Istituto Storico Italiano per il Medio Evo, 1995), 95–96.

31. On the dating of this treatise, Potestà, *Il tempo dell'Apocalisse*, 46.

32. Grundmann, "Zur biographie," 532–33.

33. As suggested by McGinn, *Calabrian Abbot*, 20 22 and 24.

34. Joachim of Fiore, *De vita Sancti Benedicti et de officio Divino secundum eius doctrinam*, ed. Cipriano Baraut, in "Un trato inédito de Joaquin de Fiore: De vita Sancti Benedicti et de officio Divino secundum eius doctrinam," *Analecta Sacra Tarracoensia* 24 (1951): 31–122; here at 28, 93.

35. Joachim, *Expositio*, fol. 175rb.

36. Reeves, *Influence of Prophecy*, 12–13.

37. Discussed at length by Julia Eva Wannenmacher, *Hermeneutik der Heilsgeschichte: De Septem Sigillis und die sieben Siegel im Werk Joachims von Fiore* (Leiden: Brill, 2005). Wannenmacher includes an edition of a short work called *De septem sigillis*, 336–55, which she reads as Joachim's final word on the subject.

38. Potestà, *Il tempo dell'Apocalisse*, 299–301.

39. The *Liber introductorius* is published at the beginning of the *Expositio in Apocalypsim*; the *Enchiridion* is published in the edition by Burger, as cited in n12; Potestà, *Il tempo dell'Apocalisse*, 327–31, argues that the *Enchiridion* was an earlier draft that left Joachim dissatisfied, mainly because of its failure to treat the Investiture Controversy adequately.

40. Revelation 8:1. Discussed in Joachim, *Book of Figures*, tavola 9; Joachim, *Liber de Concordia* 3.1.1, 211–12, among other places. Joachim further explained the dual wars/persecutions of the sixth tempus by an appeal to the imagery of manna in the Old Testament: the Israelites were told to gather twice the needed amount of manna on the sixth day so that on the seventh, the Sabbath, they might rest; Joachim, *Enchiridion*, 15–16, and elsewhere.

41. Joachim, *Genealogia*, published as: Gian Luca Potestà, "Die Genealogia. Ein frühes Werk Joachims von Fiore und die Anfänge seines Geschichtsbildes," *Deutsches Archiv für Erforschung des Mittelalters* 56 (2000): 55–101 (91–96); and Joachim, *De prophetia ignota*, published as: Matthias Kaup, *De prophetia ignota: Eine frühe Schrift Joachims von Fiore* (Hannover: Hahnsche, 1998). See also Whalen, *Dominion of God*, 103–6; Potestà, *Il tempo dell'Apocalisse*, 57–60; and McGinn, *Calabrian Abbot*, 22–24.

42. Joachim provides a date for the text at 1.2, 180–82 and 1.4, 184.

43. The diagram is a summary of Joachim, *De prophetia ignota* 1.4, 184–90. Kaup discusses the connection of this passage to later discussion of the seven seals on 30–42. The list in *Genealogia* 3, 95–96, is nearly identical. The chief differences are that the earlier text explicitly draws a connection to the seven seals and that the earlier list includes the Persians (but not the Swabians) among the third persecutors of the church.

44. Joachim, *De prophetia ignota* 1.4, 186.

45. Joachim, *De prophetia ignota* 1.4, 192.

46. Joachim, *De prophetia ignota* 2.2, 194.

47. Joachim, *Liber de concordia* 3.2.5, 301.

48. Following Joachim, *Expositio*, fols. 114ra–120rb.

49. Joachim, *Expositio*, fol. 116rb.

50. The Latin reads: "incipient Christianos interrogare suppliciis: laniare tormentis: compellentes eos transire ad ritum suum negato nomine Christiano; suggerentibus id: maxime pseudoprophetis: qui de populo Christiano egressuri sunt: sicut et presens seculi probat dies"; Joachim, *Expositio*, fol. 120rb.

51. Joachim, *Expositio*, fol. 197ra.
52. Joachim, *Expositio*, fol. 116ra/b.
53. Joachim, *Expositio*, fol. 130ra.
54. Joachim, *Expositio*, fols. 164vb–165ra.
55. Joachim, *Expositio*, fol. 165ra.
56. Joachim, *De vita Sancti Benedicti* 24, 53. Described as a "jumble of half-finished works" by Potestà, *Il tempo dell'Apocalisse*, 68–69, Joachim nonetheless provides a date of 1187 in the text at *De vita* 35, 65.
57. Joachim, *Book of Figures*, tavola 9.
58. Joachim, *Liber de concordia* 4.2.2, 416–19; and Numbers 14.
59. Joachim, *Expositio*, fol. 167vb.
60. Joachim, *Expositio*, fol. 134vb.
61. Joachim, *Expositio*, fol. 134rb. Heinrich Fichtenau, *Heretics and Scholars in the High Middle Ages: 1000–1200*, trans. Denise A. Kaiser (University Park, PA: Penn State University Press, 1998), 52–104, provides a traditional overview of the spread of Catharism, including the connection to the Patarene movement. Mark Gregory Pegg, *A Most Holy War: The Albigensian Crusade and the Battle for Christendom* (Oxford: Oxford University Press, 2009), and R. I. Moore, *The War on Heresy* (Cambridge, MA: Belknap Press, 2012), in different ways, have undermined conventional readings of the Cathars and seen them more as products of a persecuting mentality rather than as an outgrowth of the Bogomil heresy—a reading which dovetails nicely with Joachim's belief in an international Saracen-Patarene conspiracy, as described here.
62. Joachim, *Expositio*, fol 134rb.
63. Joachim, *Expositio*, fol. 134va.
64. Joachim, *De vita Sancti Benedicti* 24, 53.
65. Joachim, *Book of Figures*, tavola 9.
66. Whalen, *Dominion of God*, 118–22.
67. Potestà, *Il tempo dell'Apocalisse*, 360–66.
68. Joachim, *Expositio*, fol. 210vb.
69. Joachim literally asks, "Who knows how brief this Sabbath might be?"; Joachim, *Expositio*, fol. 210va.
70. Discussed at length in Robert E. Lerner, "Antichrists and Antichrist in Joachim of Fiore," *Speculum* 60 (1985): 553–70. The literal "four corners" reference appears in Revelation 20:8, "he shall go out to deceive the nations which are in the four corners of the earth, Gog and Magog."
71. On Nimrod: Joachim, *De Vita Sancti Benedicti* 35, 72; on Antiochus: Joachim, *Liber de concordia* 4.1.46, 404 and *Liber introductorius*, fol. 9r; on Titus: Joachim, *Enchiridion*, 25–26 and 62.
72. Noted in Lerner, "Antichrists," 562.
73. Joachim, *Expositio*, fols. 10vb–11ra and 213ra/b. At *Expositio*, fol 168rb, Joachim in fact identifies Gog as Antichrist. Lerner, "Antichrists," 564–66, evaluates this evidence and concludes that Gog was the last Antichrist, though his reading may presume too much consistency in Joachim's own thought.
74. On their origins behind the Scythian gates, Joachim, *Expositio*, fols. 211vb and 210ra/b.
75. Roger of Hovedon (published as Benedict of Peterborough), *Gesta regis Henrici Secundi et gesta regis Ricardi*, ed. William Stubbs, Rolls Series, 2 vols (London: Longmans, 1867), 2:151.
76. Roger of Hovedon, *Gesta regis* 2:151–52.
77. The prophecy as attributed to Merlin appears in Geoffrey of Monmouth's *Historia regum Britanniae*. "Peribit milvorum rapacitas et luporum dentes hebetabuntur," 7.3; see Gottfried von Monmouth, *Historia Regum Britannia*, ed. Albert Schulz (Magdeburg: E. Anton, 1854), 94. Joachim also cites Merlin in *Vita Benedicti* 29, 63.
78. Roger of Hovedon, *Gesta regis*, 2:153.
79. Roger of Hovedon, *Gesta regis*, 2:153–54, with reference 2 Thessalonians 2:4.

80. Roger of Hovedon, *Gesta regis*, 2:154.
81. Roger of Hovedon, *Gesta regis*, 2:154.
82. Roger of Hovedon, *Chronica*, ed. William Stubbs, Rolls Series, 4 vols. (London: Longmans, 1868–1871), vol. 3, 77–78.
83. Joachim, *Liber introductorius*, fols. 10ra–10va.
84. On the dating, I am following Potestà, *Il tempo dell'Apocalisse*, 327–39.
85. Joachim, *De ultimis tribulationibus*, published as Kurt-Victor Selge, "Ein Traktak Joachims von Fiore über die Drangsale der Endzeit: 'De ultimis tribulationibus,'" *Florensia* 7 (1993): 7–35; 21–22 for the three Jewish wars, and 23–26 for the Christian wars.
86. Joachim, *De ultimis tribulationibus*, 28–29.
87. Joachim, *Expositio*, fol. 164vb.
88. Joachim, *Liber de concordia* 5.111, fol. 127rb.
89. Joachim, *Liber de concordia* 5.118, fol. 133vb, and Daniel 12:9.
90. Joachim, *Liber de concordia* 5.110, fol. 127rb.
91. Joachim, *Liber de concordia* 5.110, fol. 127rb, with reference to Luke 2:2.
92. Joachim, *Liber de concordia* 5.110, fol. 127va. A rare discussion of this passage appears in Whalen, *Dominion of God*, 116–17; Whalen places it in the context of Joachim's ambivalent attitude toward crusading. Another in Potestà, *Il tempo dell'Apocalisse*, 277; also Patschovsky, "Semantics of Mohammad," 118–19.
93. Joachim, *Liber de concordia* 5, 110, fol. 127va.
94. Joachim lays out this bleak assessment of Christian-Muslim relations in *Expositio*, fol. 163va/b.
95. Joachim, *Expositio*, fol. 116va.
96. Joachim, *Expositio*, fol. 163va. In the *Liber de concordia* 5.115, fol. 13vb, Joachim describes these shadowy enemies as "Patarenes, evil doers, false Christians, and many others."
97. Joachim, *Liber de concordia* 5, 110, fol. 127va.
98. Joachim, *Expositio*, fol. 120rb. Patschovsky, "Semantics of Mohammad," 126-28 and n. 40, sees Joachim's reference to a remnant of the unbelieving peoples, *de reliquiis gentium*, as referring to a general conversion of Muslims (as opposed to a conversion of the remaining heretics, pagans, and Muslims who are not scattered to the four corners of the earth by a military defeat).
99. Joachim, *Liber introductorius*, fol. 11ra; and, for the image of Antichrist as Satan's home, Joachim, *Liber de concordia* 5.116, fol. 132rb.
100. Joachim, *Expositio*, fol. 147vb.

CONCLUSION

1. Ralph, *Chronicon*, 286–87. A similar description of Joachim appears in Ralph of Coggeshall, *Cronicon Anglicanum*, ed. Joseph Stevenson, Rolls Series (London: Longman, 1875), 67–68. Since Ralph of Coggeshall wrote later than Ralph the Black, they would appear to have drawn on a common source. Curiously, Ralph of Coggeshall makes Saladin the fifth persecutor, which does not fit any of Joachim's own writings.
2. Published as Goffredo di Auxerre, *Super Apocalypsim*, ed. Ferruccio Gastaldelli (Rome: Edizioni di storia e letteratura, 1970); in English as *Geoffrey of Auxerre: On the Apocalypse*, trans. Joseph Gibbons (Kalamazoo, MI: Cistercian Publications, 2000).
3. A fragmentary text printed in Grundmann, "Joachim von Fiore und Rainer von Ponza," 546. Lerner, *Feast of Saint Abraham*, 24–29, is inclined to accept Joachim's Jewish origins. On the wider context of the dispute between Joachim and Geoffrey, Potestà, *Il tempo dell'Apocalisse*, 204–7.
4. Opening reference to the Vulgate Psalm 23:1 (Ps 24:1, NRSV): "Domini est terra et plenitudo eius, et Sarazeni et Christiani pariter fidei in iniquitatem pro merito contulerunt, et mari et terra iniquitas hominum puniatur"; Ralph, *Chronicon*, 306–7.
5. Nancy F. Partner, *Serious Entertainments: The Writing of History in Twelfth-Century England* (Chicago: University of Chicago Press, 1977), 151 and 174–75.

6. Richard of Devizes, *The Chronicle of Richard of Devizes*, ed. John T. Appleby (London: Thomas Nelson, 1963), 84.

7. Richard of Devizes, *Chronicle*, 82.

8. Partner, *Serious Entertainments*, 145.

9. The later codices of the text that survive: Leiden, Universiteitsbibliotheek MS Lat. Vossianus 31 (thirteenth century); Paris BnF MS *lat.* 8865 (thirteenth century); Genoa, Biblioteca Durazzo-Giustiniani MS A IX 9 (fifteenth century); Chantilly, Musée Condé MS 724 (fifteenth century); Douai, Bibliothèque municipale MS 796 (fifteenth century); Paris, BnF MS lat. 9675 (fifteenth century); and The Hague, Royal Library MS 27 A 23 (sixteenth century).

10. Oliver of Paderborn describes the use of prophecy during the Fifth Crusade in *The Capture of Damietta*, translation published in Jessalynn Bird, Edward Peters, and James M. Powell, *Crusade and Christendom: Annotated Documents in Translation from Innocent III to the Fall of Acre, 1187–1291* (Philadelphia: University of Pennsylvania Press, 2013), esp. 108–9 and 224–25. On the ambiguous role of the Mongols in prophetic thought, Felicitas Schmieder, "*Nota sectam maometicam atterendam a tartaris et christianis*: The Mongols as Non-believing Apocalyptic Friends Around the Year 1260," *Journal of Millennial Studies* 1 (1998): 1–11; more generally, Robert E. Lerner, *The Powers of Prophecy: The Cedar of Lebanon Vision from the Mongol Onslaught to the Dawn of the Enlightenment* (Ithaca, NY: Cornell University Press, 2008).

11. The most important French exceptions are Paul Alphandéry, *La Chrétienté et l'idée de croisade*, ed. Alphonse Dupront, 2 vols. (Paris: Albin Michel, 1954), and Jean Flori, *Pierre l'Ermite et la première croisade* (Paris: Fayard, 1999).

12. Riley-Smith, *First Crusade and the Idea of Crusading*, 35. "Hysteria" earns a place in Riley-Smith's index. Given Riley-Smith's skepticism of apocalyptic associations with the crusade, it is ironic that the cover of the 2003 Continuum reprint of the volume is illustrated with a fourteenth-century picture of crusaders as knights following Christ into the Last Battle, as foretold in Revelation 19:11–16.

13. The core of Riley-Smith's book *The First Crusaders*; see also Marcus Bull, *Knightly Piety and the Lay Response to the First Crusade: The Limousin and Gascony, c. 970–c. 1130* (Oxford: Clarendon Press, 1993).

14. Rubenstein, *Armies of Heaven*, 324–25.

15. William McCants, *The ISIS Apocalypse: The History, Strategy, and Doomsday Vision of the Islamic State* (New York: St. Martin's Press, 2015), quoted at 102; 99–119 more generally. The news report mentioned is Jamie Seidel, "The apocalyptic prophecy behind Islamic State's death cult," December 9, 2015, http://www.news.com.au/world/the-apocalyptic-prophecy-behind-islamic-states-death-cult/news-story/e28d3e633341c2db7f7c1e8d3f957f2b, accessed September 8, 2016. On Jesus as judge in Islamic traditions, Tarif Khalidi, ed. and trans., *The Muslim Jesus: Sayings and Stories in Islamic Literature* (Cambridge, MA: Harvard University Press, 2001), 32–34.

16. By the Southern Baptist preacher and TV/radio personality Robert Jeffress (New York: FaithWorks, 2015).

17. Gershom Gorenberg, *The End of Days: Fundamentalism and the Struggle for the Temple Mount* (Oxford: Oxford University Press, 2000), esp. 7–29, 203–8, and 107–10.

18. See also Philippe Buc, "Evangelical Fundamentalist Fiction and Medieval Crusade Epics," *Cahiers de Recherches Médiévales et Humanistes*, forthcoming.

19. William Arkin, "The Pentagon Unleashes a Holy War," October 16, 2003, http://articles.latimes.com/2003/oct/16/opinion/oe-arkin16 (accessed on September 8, 2016).

20. James T. Palmer, *The Apocalypse in the Early Middle Ages* (Cambridge: Cambridge University Press, 201), esp. 18–22.

21. Guibert, *Dei gesta*, preface, 82 (quoted in Rubenstein, *Guibert of Nogent*, 94).

SELECT BIBLIOGRAPHY

ABBREVIATIONS

AASS:	Acta Sanctorum
BL:	British Library
BM:	Bibliothèque municipale
BR:	Bibliothèque royale
BnF:	Bibliothèque nationale de France
CCCM:	Corpus Christianorum Continuatio Mediaevalis
CCSL:	Corpus Christianorum Series Latina
CSEL:	Corpus Scriptorum Ecclesiasticorum Latinorum
GN:	Guibert of Nogent (ed. Huygen)
MGH SRM:	Monumenta Germaniae Historica, Scriptores rerum Merovingiarum
MGH SS:	Monumenta Germaniae Historica, Scriptores
PL:	Patrologia Latina
RHC Oc.:	Recueil des Historiens des Croisades, Historiens Occidentaux. Paris: Imprimerie Royale, 1844–1895, 5 vols.

PRIMARY SOURCES

Adso Dervensis. *De ortu et tempore Antichristi*. Edited by D. Verhelst. CCCM 45. Turnhout: Brepols, 1976.

Andrew of Saint-Victor. *Expositionem super Danielem*. Edited by Marcus Zier. CCCM 53F. Turnhout: Brepols, 1990.

Anna Komnene. *The Alexiad*. Translated by E. R. A. Sewter and Peter Frankopan. London: Penguin, 2009.

Annolied. Edited by Walther Bulst. Heidelberg: Carl Winter, 1946.

Anselm of Havelberg. *Dialogi*. In PL 188, cols. 1139A–1248B.

Arnold of Bonneval, William of Saint-Thierry, and Geoffrey of Auxerre. *Vita prima Sancti Bernardi Claraevallis abbatis*. Edited by Paul Verdeyen. CCCM 89B. Turnhout: Brepols, 2011.

Augustine. *De civitate Dei*. Edited by B. Dombart and A. Kalb. 2 vols. CCSL 47–48. Turnhout: Brepols, 1955.

Bahā' al-Dīn Ibn Shaddād. *The Rare and Excellent History of Saladin*. Translated by D. S. Richards. Aldershot: Ashgate, 2002.

Baldric of Bourgueil. *The* Historia Ierosolimitana *of Baldric of Bourgueil*. Edited by Steven Biddlecombe. Woodbridge: Boydell, 2014.

Bernard of Clairvaux. *Sancti Bernardi Opera*. Edited by J. Leclercq, C. H. Talbor, H. M. Rochais, and G. Hendrix. 9 vols. Rome: Editiones Cistercienses; Turnhout: Brepols, 1957–98.

Chanson d'Antioche. Edited by Suzanne Duparcq-Quioc. Paris: Paul Geuthner, 1978.

Chroniques des comtes d'Anjou et des seigneurs d'Amboise. Edited by Louis Halphen and René Poupardin. Paris: Auguste Picard, 1913.

Conrad of Eberbach. *Exordium magnum Cisterciense, sive narratio de initio Cisterciensis ordinis*. Edited by Bruno Griesser. CCCM 138. Turnhout: Brepols, 1994.

Ekkehardi chronica. In *Frutolfs und Ekkehards Chroniken und die anonyme Kaiserchronik*, edited and translated by F.-J. Schmale and I. Schmale-Ott. Ausgewählte Quellen zur deutschen Geschichte des Mittelalters XV. Darmstadt: Wissenschaftliche Buchgesellschaft, 1972.

Ephraim of Bonn. *Sefer Zekhirah.* In *The Jews and the Crusaders: The Hebrew Chronicles of the First and Second Crusades*, translated by Shlomo Eidelberg, 117–36. Hoboken, NJ: KTAV Publishing, 1996.

Eugenius III. *Quantum praedecessores.* Printed in Große, Rolf. "Überlegungen zum Kreuzzugsaufruf Eugens III. von 1145/46. Mit einer Neuedition von JL 8876." *Francia* 18 (1991): 85–92.

"Fulcher Abbreviated" (or Bartolph of Nangis). *Gesta Francorum.* In RHC *Oc.* 3, 2, 491–543.

Fulcher of Chartres. *Historia Hierosolymitana.* Edited by Heinrich Hagenmeyer (Heidelberg: Carl Winter's Universitätsbuchhandlung, 1913). Translated by Frances Rita Ryan as *A History of the Expedition to Jerusalem, 1095–1127.* Knoxville: University of Tennessee Press, 1969.

Galterius Cancellarius. *Bella Antiochena.* Edited by Heinrich Hagenmeyer. Innsbruck: Wanger'schen Universitäts Buchhandlung, 1896.

Gerhoh of Reichersberg. *De quarta vigilia noctis.* In MGH *Libelli de lite* 3. Hannover: Hahn, 1897.

———. *Letter to Pope Hadrian about the Novelties of the Day.* Edited by Nikolaus M. Häring. Toronto: Pontifical Institute, 1974.

———. *Libellus de ordine donorum.* In *Opera Inedita*, edited by D. Van den Eynde, O. Van den Eynde, A. Rijmersnaei, and P. Classen. 2 vols. Rome: Spicilegium Pontificii Athenaei Antoniani, 1955.

———. *Libri iii de investigatione Antichristi.* Edited by Friederich Scheibelberger. Linz: M. Quirein, 1875).

Gesta Francorum et aliorum Hierosolimitanorum. Edited by Rosalind Hill. London: Nelson, 1962.

The Greek Alexander Romance. Translated by Richard Stoneman. London: Penguin Classics, 1991.

Gregory VIII. *Audita tremendi.* In PL 202, cols. 1539C–1542D.

Guibert of Nogent. *Dei gesta per Francos.* Edited by R. B. C. Huygens, CCCM 127A. Turnhout: Brepols, 1996. Translated by Robert Levine as *The Deeds of God through the Franks.* Woodbridge, Boydell, 1997.

———. *Monodies.* Published as *Autobiographie*, edited and translated by Edmond René Labande. Paris: Belles Lettres, 1981. Translated by Joseph McAlhany and Jay Rubenstein as *Monodies and On the Relics of Saints: The Autobiography and a Manifesto of a French Monk from the Time of the Crusades.* London: Penguin Classics, 2011.

Hagenmeyer, Heinrich, ed. *Epistulae et chartae ad primi belli sacri spectantes: Die Kreuzzugsbriefe aus den Jahren 1088–1100.* Hildesheim: Georg Olms, 1901. Repr., 1973.

Henri de Curzon. *Le règle du Temple.* Paris: Librairie Renouard, 1886.

Henry of Albano. *Tractatus de perigrinante civitate Dei.* In PL 204, cols. 251–400.

Hildegard of Bingen. *The Letters of Hildegard of Bingen* 1, translated by Joseph L. Baird and Radd K. Ehrman. Oxford: Oxford University Press, 1994.

———. *Liber divinorum operum.* Edited by A. Derolez and P. Dronke. CCCM 92. Turnhout: Brepols, 1996.

———. *Scivias.* Edited by Adelgundis Führkötter and Angela Carlevaris. 2 vols. CCCM 43 and 43a. Turnhout: Brepols, 1978.

Hystoria de via et recuperatione Antiochiae atque Ierusolymarum. Edited by Edoardo D'Angelo. Florence: Edizioni del Galluzzo, 2009.

Ibn Fadlān and the Land of Darkness: Arab Travellers and the Far North. Translated by Paul Lunde and Caroline Stone. London: Penguin Classics, 2012.

Jerome. *Commentariorum in Danielem libri III <IV>.* Edited by F. Glorie. CCSL 75A. Turnhout: Brepols, 1964.

Joachim of Fiore. *Book of Figures.* Published as Gioacchino da Fiore, *Il Libro delle Figure.* Edited by Leone Tondelli, Marjorie Reeves, and Beatrice Hirsch-Reich. 2 vols. 2nd ed. Turin: Società Editrice Internazionale, 1953.

———. *De prophetia ignota.* Published as Matthias Kaup, *De prophetia ignota: Eine frühe Schrift Joachims von Fiore.* Hannover: Hahnsche, 1998.

———. *De ultimis tribulationibus.* Published as Kurt-Victor Selge, "Ein Traktak Joachims von Fiore über die Drangsale der Endzeit: 'De ultimis tribulationibus.'" *Florensia* 7 (1993): 7–35.

———. *De vita Sancti Benedicti et de officio Divino secundum eius doctrinam.* Edited by Cipriano Baraut. In "Un trato inédito de Joaquin de Fiore: De vita Sancti Benedicti et de officio divino secundum eius doctrinam." *Analecta Sacra Tarracoensia* 24 (1951): 31–122.

———. *Dialogi de prescientia dei et predestinatione electorum.* Edited by G. L. Potestà. Rome: Istituto Storico Italiano per il Medio Evo, 1995.

———. *Enchiridion super Apocalypsim.* Edited by Edward K. Burger. Toronto: Pontifical Institute, 1986.

———. *Expositio magni Prophete Abbatis Joachim in Apocalypsim.* Venice, 1527.

———. *Genealogia.* Published as: Gian Luca Potestà. "Die Genealogia. Ein frühes Werk Joachims von Fiore und die Anfänge seines Geschichtsbildes." *Deutsches Archiv für Erforschung des Mittelalters* 56 (2000): 55–101.

———. *Liber de Concordia noui ac veteris testament.* Venice, 1519. Also, edited by F. Randolph Daniel. Philadelphia: American Philosophical Society, 1983.

———. *Psalterium decem cordarum.* MGH Quellen Zur Geistgeschichte des Mittelalters 20. Edited by Kurt-Victor Selge. Hannover: Hahnsche, 2009.

Lambert of Saint-Omer. *Liber Floridus: Codex Autographus Bibliotheca Universitatis Gandavensis.* Edited by A. Derolez and I. Strubbe. Ghent: E. Story-Scientia, 1968.

Ludus Antichristi. In *The Drama of the Medieval Church,* edited by Karl Young, 369–96. Oxford: Clarendon Press, 1933.

Map, Walter. *De Nugis Curialium, Courtiers' Trifles.* Edited and translated by M. R. James, rev. ed., C. N. L. Brooke and R. A. B. Mynors. Oxford: Clarendon Press, 1983.

Marbod of Rennes. "Commendatio Jerosolymitanae expeditionis." In PL 171, col. 1672.

Narratio Floriacensis de captis Antiochia et Hierosolyma et obsesso Dyrrachio, RHC *Oc.* 5, 356–62.

Odo of Deuil. *De profectione Ludovici VII in orientem.* Edited and translated by Virginia Gingerick Berry. New York: Columbia University Press, 1948.

Orderic Vitalis. *Ecclesiastical History.* Edited and translated by Marjorie Chibnall. 6 vols. Oxford: Oxford University Press, 1969–1980.

Orosius. *Histoire (contre le Païens).* Edited and translated by Marie-Pierre Arnaud-Lindet. 3 vols. Paris: Belle Lettres, 1990–1991.

Otto of Freising. *Chronica sive historia de duabus civitatibus.* Edited by Walther Lammers. Berlin: Rütten & Loening, 1960. Translated as *The Two Cities: A Chronicle of Universal History to the Year 1146 by Otto, Bishop of Freising.* Translated by Charles Mierow. New York: Columbia University Press, 1956.

———. *Gesta Frederici seu rectius cronica.* Edited by Franz-Josef Schmale. Berlin: Deutscher Verlag der Wissenschaften, 1965. Translated as *The Deeds of Frederick Barbarossa.* New York: Columbia University Press, 1953.

Peter of Blois. *Tractatus duo.* Edited by R. B. C. Huygens, CCCM 194. Turnhout: Brepols, 2002.

Peter Tudebode. *Historia de Hierosolymitano itinere.* Edited by John Hugh Hill and Laurita Young Littleton Hill. Notes translated by Philippe Wolff. Paris: Paul Geuthner, 1977.

Peter the Venerable. "Sermo de laude demonici sepulchri." In "Petri Venerabilis sermones, tres," edited by Giles Constable. *Revue bénédictine* 64 (1954): 224–72.

Philip of Harveng. *De somnio regis Nabuchodonosor.* In PL 203, cols. 585–92.

Pseudo-Methodius. *Apocalypse.* Edited and translated by Benjamin Garstad. Cambridge, MA: Harvard University Press, 2012.

Radulfus Niger. *Chronica: Eine englishce Weltchronik des 12. Jahrhunderts.* Edited by Hanna Krause. Frankfurt am Main: Peter Lang, 1985.

———. *De re militari et triplici via peregrinationis Ierosolimitane.* Edited by Ludwig Schmugge. Berlin: Walter de Gruyter, 1977.

Ralph of Caen, *Gesta Tancredi,* RHC *Oc.* 3, 587–710.

Raymond of Aguilers, *Liber.* Edited by John Hugh Hill and Laurita Littleton Hill, notes translated by Philippe Wolff. Paris: P. Geuthner, 1969. Translated as *Historia Francorum qui ceperunt Iherusalem.* Translated by John Hugh Hill and Laurita Lyttleton Hill. Philadelphia: American Philosophical Society, 1968.

Richard of Devizes, *The Chronicle of Richard of Devizes*. Edited by John T. Appleby. London: Thomas Nelson, 1963.

Robert the Monk. *The Historia Iherosolimitana of Robert the Monk*. Edited by D. Kempf and M. G. Bull. Woodbridge: Boydell, 2013. Translated as *Robert the Monk's History of the First Crusade: Historia Iherosolimitana*. Translated by Carol Sweetenham. Aldershot: Ashgate, 2005.

Roger of Hovedon. *Chronica*. Edited by William Stubbs. Rolls Series. 4 vols. London: Longmans, 1868–1871.

———. Published as Benedict of Peterborough. *Gesta regis Henrici Secundi et gesta regis Ricardi*. Edited by William Stubbs. Rolls Series. 2 vols. London: Longmans, 1867.

Suger. *Oeuvres*. Edited by Françoise Gasparri. 2 vols. Paris: Belles Lettres, 1996–2001.

———. *Vita Ludovici Grossi*. Edited by H. Waquet. Paris: Belles Lettres, 1964. Translated as *The Deeds of Louis the Fat*. Translated by Richard C. Cusimano. Washington, DC: Catholic University of America Press, 1992.

Tiburtine Sibyl. In *Sibyllinische Texte und Forschungen*, edited by Ernst Sackur, 117–87. Halle: Max Niermeyer, 1898.

Vita et miracula S. Leonardi. In AASS, *Nov*. 3. Brussels: Socii Bollandiani, 1910.

Wilkinson, John. With Joyce Hill and W. F. Ryan. *Jerusalem Pilgrimage, 1099–1185*. Cambridge: Hakluyt Society, 1988.

William of Malmesbury. *Gesta Regum Anglorum*. Edited by R. A. B. Mynors, R. M. Thomson, and M. Winterbottom. 2 vols. Oxford: Oxford University Press, 1998–1999.

William of Tyre. *Chronicon*. Edited by R. B. C. Huygens. 2 vols. CCCM 63, 63a. Turnhout: Brepols, 1986. Translated as *History of the Deeds Done Beyond the Sea*. Translated by August C. Krey. 2 vols. New York: Columbia University Press, 1943.

SECONDARY SOURCES

Adams, Jeremy. "Returning Crusaders: Living Saints of Psychopaths?" In *From Knowledge to Beatitude: St. Victor, Twelfth-Century Scholars, and Beyond, Essays in Honor of Grover A. Zinn, Jr.*, edited by E. Ann Matter and Lesley Smith, 328–41. Notre Dame: University of Notre Dame Press, 2013.

Akbari, Suzanne Conklin. *Idols in the East: European Representations of Islam and the Orient, 1100–1450*. Ithaca, NY: Cornell University Press, 2009.

Albu, Emily. "Bohemond and the Rooster: Byzantines, Normans, and the Artful Ruse." In *Anna Komnene and Her Times*, edited by Thalia Gouma-Peterson. New York: Garland, 2000.

Alphandéry, Paul. *La Chrétienté et l'idée de croisade*. Edited by Alphonse Dupront. 2 vols. Paris: Albin Michel, 1954.

Althoff, Gerd. *"Selig sind, die Verfolgung ausüben": Päpste und Gewalt im Hochmittelalter*. Darmstadt: Wissenschaftlich Buchgesellschaft, 2013.

Anderson, Andrew Runni. *Alexander's Gate, Gog and Magog, and the Inclosed Nations*. Cambridge, MA: Medieval Academy of America, 1932.

Asbridge, Thomas S. *The Creation of the Principality of Antioch, 1098–1130*. Woodbridge, UK: Boydell Press, 2000.

———. *The Crusades: The Authoritative History of the Holy Land*. New York: Ecco, 2010.

Aurell, Martin. *Des chrétiens contre les croisades, xiie–xiiie siècle*. Paris: Fayard, 2013.

Autour de la Première Croisade: Actes du Colloque de la Society for the Study of the Crusades and the Latin East (Clermont-Ferrand, 22–25 juin 1995). Edited by M. Balard. Paris: Publications de la Sorbonne, 1996.

Barber, Malcolm. *The New Knighthood: A History of the Order of the Temple*. Cambridge: Cambridge University Press, 1994.

Barthélemy, Dominique. *Chevaliers et miracles: La violence et le sacré dans la société féodale*. Paris: Armand Colin, 2004.

Beaulieu, Paul-Alain. "Nebuchadnezzar's Babylon as World Capital." *Journal of the Canadian Society of Mesopotamian Studies* 3 (2008): 5–12.

Beaune, Colette. *The Birth of an Ideology: Myths and Symbols of Nation in Late Medieval France*. Translated by Susan Ross Huston. Edited by Frederic L. Cheyette. Berkeley: University of California Press, 1991.

Bredero, Adriaan H. *Bernard of Clairvaux: Between Cult and History*. Grand Rapids, MI: Wm. B. Eerdmans, 1996.

Bruce, Scott G. *Cluny and the Muslims of La Garde-Freinet: Hagiography and the Problem of Islam in Medieval Europe*. Ithaca, NY: Cornell University Press, 2015.

Brundage, James A. *Medieval Canon Law and the Crusader*. Madison: University of Wisconsin Press, 1969.

Buc, Philippe. "Exégèse et pensée politique: Radulphus Niger (vers 1190) et Nicolas de Lyre (vers 1330)." In *Représentations, pouvoir et royauté à la fin du Moyen Age*, edited by Joël Blanchard, 145–64. Paris: Picard, 1995.

———. *Holy War, Martyrdom, and Terror: Christian Violence in the West*, ca. 70 C.E. to the Iraq War. Philadelphia: University of Pennsylvania Press, 2015.

Budiger, Max. "Die Entstehung des achten Buches Otto's von Freising: ein universalhistorische Studie." *Sitzungsberichte. Akademie der Wissenschaften in Wien, Philosophish-Historische Klasse* 98 (1881): 325–65.

Bull, Marcus. *Knightly Piety and the Lay Response to the First Crusade: The Limousin and Gascony, c. 970–c. 1130*. Oxford: Clarendon Press, 1993.

Bull, Marcus, and Damien Kempf. *Writing the Early Crusades: Text, Transmission, and Memory*. Woodbridge, UK: Boydell, 2014.

Bynum, Caroline Walker. *Metamorphosis and Identity*. New York: Zone Books, 2005.

Cary, George. *The Medieval Alexander*. Edited by D. J. A. Ross. Cambridge: Cambridge University Press, 1956.

Cate, James Lea. "The Crusade of 1101." In *A History of the Crusades*, edited by Kenneth M. Setton et al., 1:343–676. Madison: University of Wisconsin Press, 1969–89.

Classen, Peter. *Gerhoch von Reichersberg: eine Biographie mit einem Anhang über die Quellen, ihre handschrifliche Überlieferung und ihre Chronologie*. Mainz: Wiesbaden, 1960.

———. "Gerhoch von Reichersberg und die Regularkanoniker in Bayern und Österreich." In *La vita comune del clero nei secoli XI e XII*. Milano: Vita e Pensiero, 1962, 304–40.

Cobb, Paul M. *The Race for Paradise: An Islamic History of the Crusades*. Oxford: Oxford University Press, 2014.

Cole, Penny J. *The Preaching of the Crusades to the Holy Land, 1095–1270*. Cambridge, MA: Medieval Academy of America, 1991.

Constable, Giles. "The Second Crusade as Seen by Contemporaries." *Traditio* 9 (1953): 213–79.

Cotts, John D. *The Clerical Dilemma: Peter of Blois and Literate Culture in the Twelfth-Century*. Washington, DC: Catholic University of America Press, 2009.

———. "The Exegesis of Violence in the Crusade Writings of Ralph Niger and Peter of Blois." In *The Uses of the Bible in Crusader Sources*, edited by Elizabeth Lapina and Nicholas Morton. Leiden: Brill, 2017, 273–95.

Cowdrey, H. E. J. "Cluny and the First Crusade." *Revue Bénédictine* 83 (1973): 285–311.

Daniel, E. R. "Apocalyptic Conversion: The Joachite Alternative to the Crusades." *Traditio* 25 (1969): 127–54.

Derolez, Albert. "The Abbey of Saint-Bertin, the *Liber Floridus*, and the Origin of the *Gesta Francorum Hierusalem expugnantium*." *Manuscripta* 57 (2013): 1–28.

———. *The Autograph Manuscript of the* Liber Floridus*: A Key to the Encyclopedia of Lambert of Saint-Omer*. Turnhout: Brepols, 1998.

———. "*Codex Aldenburgensis*, Cotton Fragments Vol. 1, and the Origins of the *Liber Floridus*." *Manuscripta* 49 (2005): 139–63.

Eddé, Anne-Marie. *Saladin*. Translated by Jane Marie Todd. Cambridge, MA: Belknap-Harvard University Press, 2011.

Emmerson, Richard K., and Bernard McGinn, eds. *The Apocalypse in the Middle Ages*. Ithaca, NY: Cornell University Press, 1992.

Epp, Verena. *Fulcher von Chartres: Studien zur Geschichtsscreibung des ersten Kreuzzuges*. Düsseldorf: Droste, 1990.

Flahiff, George B. *Deus Non Vult:* A Critic of the Third Crusade." *Mediaeval Studies* 9 (1947): 162–88.

———. "Ralph Niger: An Introduction to His Life and Works." *Mediaeval Studies* 2 (1940): 104–26.

Flori, Jean. *Bohémond d'Antioche, Chevalier d'Aventure.* Paris: Payot, 2007.

———. *L'Islam et la Fin des Temps: L'interpretation prophétique des invasions musulmanes dans la chrétienté médiévale (VIIe–XIIIe siècle).* Paris: Éditions du Seuil, 2005.

———. *Pierre l'Ermite et la première croisade.* Paris: Fayard, 1999.

Folda, Jaroslav. *Crusader Art in the Holy Land: From the Third Crusade to the Fall of Acre.* Cambridge: Cambridge University Press, 2005.

Forey, Alan. "The Failure of the Siege of Damascus in 1148." *Journal of Medieval History* 10 (1984): 13–25.

———. *The Military Orders: From the Twelfth to the Early Fourteenth Century.* Toronto: University of Toronto Press, 1992.

Frankopan, Peter. *The First Crusade: The Call from the East.* Cambridge, MA: Harvard University Press, 2012.

Gabriele, Matthew. *Empire of Memory: The Legend of Charlemagne, the Franks, and Jerusalem before the First Crusade.* Oxford: Oxford University Press, 2011.

Gaposchkin, Cecilia. *Clamouring to God: Crusade, Ideology, Liturgy, and Devotion, 1095–1500.* Ithaca, NY: Cornell University Press, forthcoming.

Gervers, Michael, ed. *The Second Crusade and the Cistercians.* New York: St. Martin's Press, 1992.

Glaser, Hubert. "De monte abscisus est lapis sine manibus (Dan 2, 45): Die geschichtliche Rolle des Reformpapsttums im Spiegel der Weltchronik Ottos von Freising." In *Papsttum und Kirchenreform, historische Beiträge. Festschrift Georg Schwaiger,* edited by Georg Schwaiger, Manfred Weitlauff, and Karl Hausberger, 151–91. St. Ottillien: EOS Verlag, 1990.

Goetz, Hans-Werner. *Das Geschichtsbild Ottos von Freising: Ein Beitrag zur historischen Vorstellungwelt und zur Geschichte des 12. Jahrhunderts.* Cologne: Böhlau, 1984.

———. *Geschichtsschreibung und Geschichtsbewußtsein im hohen Mittelalter.* Berlin: Akademie Verlag, 1999.

Goez, Werner. *Translatio Imperii, Ein Beitrag zur Geschichte des Geschichtsdenkens und der politischen Theorien im Mittelalter in der frühen Neuzeit.* Tübingen: J. C. B. Mohr, 1958.

Görich, Knut. "Fürstenstreit und Friedensstiftung vor dem Aufbruch Konrads III. zum Kreuzzug." *Zeitschrift für die Geschichte des Oberrheins* 158 (2010): 117–36.

Gosman, Martin. "Otto de Freising et le Prêtre Jean." *Revue belge de philologie et d'histoire* 61 (1983): 270–85.

Grégoire, Réginald. *Bruno de Segni, exégète médieval et théologien monastique.* Spoleto: Centro Italiano di Studi sull'Alto Medioevo, 1965.

Grill, P. Leopold Josef. "Das Itinerar Ottos von Freising." In *Festschrift Friedrich Hausmann,* edited by Herwig Ebner, 153–77. Graz: Akadem. Druck- u. Verlagsanst, 1977.

Grundmann, Herbert. "Zur Biographie Joachim von Fiore und Rainers von Ponza." *Deutsches Archiv für Erforschung des Mittelalters* 16 (1960): 437–546.

Hall, Martin, and Jonathan Phillips, eds. *Caffaro, Genoa and the Twelfth-Century Crusades.* Farnham: Ashgate, 2013.

Hamilton, Bernard. "The Elephant of Christ, Reynald of Châtillon." In *Religious Motivation: Biographical and Sociological Problems for the Church Historian,* edited by Derek Baker, 97–108. Oxford: Blackwell, 1978.

Harvey, P. D. A., ed. *The Hereford World Map: Medieval World Maps and Their Context* London: British Library, 2006.

Hillenbrand, Carole. *The Crusades: Islamic Perspectives.* Edinburgh: Edinburgh University Press, 1999.

———. "The Imprisonment of Reynald of Châtillon." In *Texts, Documents and Artefacts: Islamic Studies in Honour of D. S. Richards,* edited by C. F. Robinson, 79–102. Leiden: Brill, 2003.

Hoch, Martin. "The Choice of Damascus as the Objective of the Second Crusade: A Re-evaluation." In *Autour de la Première Croisade,* 359–69.

Housley, Norman. *Contesting the Crusades*. Oxford: Blackwell, 2006.

Hughes, Kevin L. *Constructing Antichrist: Paul, Biblical Commentary, and the Development of the Doctrine in the Early Middle Ages*. Washington, DC: Catholic University of America Press, 2005.

Kahl, Hans-Dietrich. "Die Kreuzzugseschatologie Bernhards von Clairvaux und ihre missionsgeschichtliche Auswirkung." In *Bernard von Clairvaux und der Beginn der Moderne*, edited by Dieter R. Bauer, 262–315. Innsbruck: Tyrolia-Verlag, 1996.

Kay, Sarah. *The Chanson de geste in the Age of Romance: Political Fictions*. Oxford: Oxford University Press, 1995.

Kedar, Benjamin Z. *Crusade and Mission: European Approaches toward the Muslims*. Princeton, NJ: Princeton University Press, 1984.

Konrad, Robert. "Das himmlische und das irdische Jerusalem im mittelalterlichen Denken. Mystische Vorstellung und geistliche Wirkung." In *Speculum historiale. Festschrift Johannes Spörl*, edited by C. Bauer, 523–40. Freiburg: Alber., 1965.

Koopmans, Rachel. *Wonderful to Relate: Miracle Stories and Miracle Collecting in High Medieval England*. Philadelphia: University of Pennsylvania Press, 2011.

Kühnel, Bianca, Galit Noga-Banai, and Hanna Vorholt, eds. *Visual Constructs of Jerusalem*. Turnhout: Brepols, 2014.

Landes, Richard. "The Fear of an Apocalyptic Year 1000: Augustinian Historiography, Medieval and Modern." *Speculum* 75 (2000): 97–145.

Lapina, Elizabeth. *Warfare and the Miraculous in the Chronicles of the First Crusade*. University Park, PA: Penn State Press, 2015.

Latowsky, Anne. *Emperor of the World: Charlemagne and the Construction of Imperial Authority*. Ithaca, NY: Cornell University Press, 2013.

Lazzarino del Gross, Anna M. *Società e potere nella Germania del XII secolo: Gerhoch di Reicersberg*. Florence: Casa Editrice Leo S. Olschki, 1974.

Leclercq, Jean. *Monks and Love in Twelfth-Century France: Psycho-historical Essays*. Oxford: Oxford University Press, 1979.

Lehtonen, Tuomas M. S. "History, Tragedy and Fortune in Twelfth-Century Historiography, with Special Reference to Otto of Freising's *Chronica*." In *Historia: The Concept and Genres in the Middle Ages*, edited by Tuomas M. S. Lehtonen and Päivi Mehtonen, 31–49. Helsinki: Societas Scientiarum Fennica, 2000.

Lerner, Robert E. "Antichrists and Antichrist in Joachim of Fiore." *Speculum* 60 (1985): 553–70.

———. *The Feast of Saint Abraham: Medieval Millenarians and the Jews*. Philadelphia: University of Pennsylvania Press, 2001.

———. *The Powers of Prophecy: The Cedar of Lebanon Vision from the Mongol Onslaught to the Dawn of the Enlightenment*. Ithaca, NY: Cornell University Press, 2008.

———. "Refreshment of the Saints: The Time after Antichrist as a Station for Earthly Progress in Medieval Thought." *Traditio* 32 (1976): 97–144.

Levy-Rubin, Milka. "From Eusebius to the Crusader Maps: The Origin of the Holy Land Maps." In Kühnel, Noga-Banai, and Vorholt, *Visual Constructs of Jerusalem*. Turnhout: Brepols, 2014, 253–63.

Lewis, Suzanne. "Encounters with Monsters at the End of Time: Some Early Medieval Visualizations of Apocalyptic Eschatology." *Different Visions: A Journal of New Perspectives on Medieval Art* 2 (2010) [http://differentvisions.org/Issue2PDFs/Lewis.pdf].

Linder, Amnon. "The Liturgy of the Liberation of Jerusalem." *Mediaeval Studies* 52 (1990): 110–31.

Luneau, Auguste. *L'histoire du salut chez les Pères de l'Eglise. La doctrine des ages du monde*. Paris: Beauchesne, 1964.

MacEvitt, Christopher. *The Crusades and the Christian World of the East: Rough Tolerance*. Philadelphia: University of Pennsylvania Press, 2008.

Madden, Thomas. "Rivers of Blood: An Analysis of One Aspect of the Crusader Conquest of Jerusalem." *Revista Chilena de Estudios Medievales* 1 (2012): 25–37.

Markowski, Michael. "Peter of Blois and the Conception of the Third Crusade." In *The Horns of Hattin,* edited by Benjamin Z. Kedar, 261–69. Jerusalem: Yed Izhak Ben-Zvi, 1992.

Markus, R. A. *Saeculum: History and Society and the Theology of St. Augustine.* Cambridge: Cambridge University Press, 1970.

Marx, Alexander. *Die Passio Raginaldi von Petrus von Blois: Märtyertum, Emotionalität, und Eschatologie.* Master's thesis, University of Vienna, 2014.

Mayer, Hans Eberhard. *Mélanges sur l'histoire du royaume latin de Jérusalem.* Mémoires de l'Academie Inscription et Belles-Lettres 5. Paris: Imprimerie Nationale, 1984.

Mayo, Penelope C. "The Crusaders under the Palm: Allegorical Plants and Cosmic Kingship in the *Liber Floridus.*" *Dumbarton Oaks Papers* 27 (1973): 29–67.

McGinn, Bernard. *Anti-Christ: Two Thousand Years of the Human Fascination with Evil.* New York: Columbia University Press, 1999.

———. *The Calabrian Abbot: Joachim of Fiore in the History of Western Thought.* New York: Macmillan, 1985.

———. "Image as Insight in Joachim of Fiore's *Figurae.*" In *Envisioning Experience in Late Antiquity and the Middle Ages: Dynamic Patterns in Texts and Images,* edited by Giselle de Nie and Thomas F. X. Noble, 93–118. Burlington, VT: Ashgate, 2012.

———. "Saint Bernard and Eschatology." In *Bernard of Clairvaux: Studies Presented to Dom Jean Leclercq,* edited by M. Basil Pennington. Spencer, MA: Cistercian Publications, 1973, 161–85.

Mégier, Elisabeth. "Tamquam lux post tenebras, oder: Ottos von Freising Weg von der Chronik zu den Gesta Frederici." *Mediaevistik* 3 (1990): 131–267.

Meschini, Marco. *San Bernardo e la seconda crociata.* Milan: Ugo Mursia, 1998.

Meuthen, Erich. *Kirche und Heilsgeschichte bei Gerhoh von Reichersberg.* Leiden: Brill, 1959.

Mews, Constant J. "Accusations of Heresy and Error in the Twelfth-Century Schools: The Witness of Gerhoh of Reichersberg and Otto of Freising." In *Heresy in Transition: Transforming Ideas of Heresy in Medieval and Early Modern Europe,* edited by John Christian Laursen, Cary J. Nederman, and Ian Hunter, 43–57. Aldershot: Ashgate, 2005

Moore, R. I. *The War on Heresy.* Cambridge, MA: Belknap Press, 2012.

Morris, Colin. *The Sepulchre of Christ and the Medieval West: From the Beginning to 1600.* Oxford: Oxford University Press, 2005.

Naus, James. *Constructing Kingship: The Capetian Monarchs of France and the Early Crusades.* Manchester: Manchester University Press, 2016.

———. "The *Historia Iherosolimitana* of Robert the Monk and the Coronation of Louis VI." In *Writing the Early Crusades: Text, Transmission, and Memory,* edited by Marcus Bull and Damien Kempf, 105–15. Woodbridge, UK: Boydell & Brewer, 2014

Niskanen, Samu. "The Origins of the *Gesta Francorum* and Two Related Texts: Their Textual and Literary Character." *Sacris Erudiri* 51 (2012): 287–316.

North, William Linden. "In the Shadows of Reform: Exegesis and the Formation of a Clerical Elite in the Works of Bruno, Bishop of Seigni (1078/9–1123)." PhD diss., Berkeley, CA, 1998.

Nuffelen, Peter Van. *Orosius and the Rhetoric of History.* Oxford: Oxford University Press, 2012.

Oftestad, Eivor Andersen. "The House of God: The Translation of the Temple and the Interpretation of the Lateran Cathedral in the Twelfth Century," PhD diss., University of Oslo, 2010.

Ousterhout, Robert. "Flexible Geography and Transportable Topography." *Jewish Art* 24 (1997/98): 393–404.

Palmer, James T. *The Apocalypse in the Early Middle Ages.* Cambridge: Cambridge University Press, 2014.

Partner, Nancy F. *Serious Entertainments: The Writing of History in Twelfth-Century England.* Chicago: University of Chicago Press, 1977.

Patschovsky, Alexander, ed. *Die Bildwelt der Diagramme Jochims von Fiore.* Ostfildern: Jan Thorbecke Verlag, 2003.

———. "Semantics of Mohammed and Islam in Joachim of Fiore." In *Conflict and Religious Conversation in Latin Christendom: Studies in Honour of Ora Limor,* edited by Israel Yuval and Ram Ben-Shalom, 115–31. Turnhout: Brepols, 2014.

Paul, Nicholas. *To Follow in Their Footsteps: The Crusades and Family Memory in the High Middle Ages.* Ithaca, NY: Cornell University Press, 2012.

———. "A Warlord's Wisdom: Literacy and Propaganda at the Time of the First Crusade." *Speculum* 85 (2010): 534–66.

Pegg, Mark Gregory. *A Most Holy War: The Albigensian Crusade and the Battle for Christendom.* Oxford: Oxford University Press, 2009.

Phillips, Jonathan. *Holy Warriors: A Modern History of the Crusades.* New York: Random House, 2010.

———. *The Second Crusade: Extending the Frontiers of Christendom.* New Haven, CT: Yale University Press, 2007.

Phillips, Jonathan, and Martin Hoch, eds. *The Second Crusade: Scope and Consequences.* Manchester: Manchester University Press, 2001.

Portier-Young, Anathea E. *Apocalypse against Empire: Theologies of Resistance in Early Judaism.* Grand Rapids, MI: Eerdmans, 2011.

Potestà, Gian Luca. *Il tempo dell'Apocalisse: Vita di Gioacchino da Fiore.* Rome: Laterza, 2004.

Purkis, William J. *Crusading Spirituality in the Holy Land and Iberia, c. 1095–c.1187.* Woodbridge: Boydell Press, 2008.

Radcke, Fritz. *Die eschatologischen Anschauungen Bernhards von Clairvaux: Ein Beitrag zur historischen Interpretation aus den Zeitanschauungen.* Langensalza: Wendt & Klauwell, 1915.

Raedts, Peter. "St. Bernard of Clairvaux and Jerusalem." In *Prophecy and Eschatology,* edited by Michael Wilks, 169–82. Woodbridge: Boydell & Brewer, 1997.

Reeves, Marjorie. *The Influence of Prophecy in the Later Middle Ages: A Study in Joachimism.* Oxford: Oxford University Press, 1969.

Reeves, Marjorie, and Beatrice Hirsch-Reich. *The Figurae of Joachim of Fiore.* Oxford: Clarendon Press, 1972.

Riley-Smith, Jonathan. "Crusades as an Act of Love." *History* 65 (1980): 177–92.

———. *The First Crusade and the Idea of Crusading.* London: Athlone, 1986.

———. *The First Crusaders (1095–1131).* Cambridge: Cambridge University Press, 1997.

Rousset, Paul. *Les origines et les caractères de la Première Croisade.* Neuchatel: à la Baconnerie, 1945.

Rubenstein, Jay. *Armies of Heaven: The First Crusade and the Quest for Apocalypse.* New York: Basic Books, 2011.

———. "The Deeds of Bohemond: Reform, Propaganda, and the History of the First Crusade." *Viator* 47:2 (2016): 113–35.

———. *Guibert of Nogent: Portrait of a Medieval Mind.* New York: Routledge, 2002.

———. "Lambert of Saint-Omer and the Apocalyptic First Crusade." In *Remembering the Crusades: Myth, Image and Identity,* edited by Nicholas Paul and Suzanne Yeager, 69–95. Baltimore: Johns Hopkins University Press, 2012.

———. "Putting History to Use: Three Crusade Chronicles in Context." *Viator: Medieval and Renaissance Studies* 35 (2004): 131–68.

Rudolph, Conrad. *The Mystic Ark: Hugh of Saint Victor, Art, and Thought in the Twelfth Century.* Cambridge: Cambridge University Press, 2014.

Russell, Frederick. *The Just War in the Middle Ages.* Cambridge: Cambridge University Press, 1975.

Russo, Luigi. *Boemondo. Figlio del Guiscardo e principe di Antiochia.* Avellino: Elio Sellino, 2009.

———. "Il viaggio di Boemondo d'Altavilla in Francia (1106): un riesame." *Archivo Storico Italiano* 163 (2005): 3–42.

Scheil, Andrew. *Babylon under Western Eyes: A Study of Allusion and Myth.* Toronto: University of Toronto Press, 2016.

Schein, Sylvia. *Gateway to the Heavenly City: Crusader Jerusalem and the Catholic West (1099–1187).* Aldershot: Ashgate, 2005.

Shepard, J. "When Greek Meets Greek: Alexius Comnenus and Bohemond in 1097–8." *Byzantine and Modern Greek Studies* 12 (1988): 185–277.

Sibbery, Elizabeth. *Criticism of Crusading, 1095–1274.* Oxford: Clarendon Press, 1985.

Sizgorich, Thomas. *Violence and Belief in Late Antiquity: Militant Devotion in Christianity and Islam.* Philadelphia: University of Pennsylvania Press, 2009.

Southern, R. W. "Presidential Address: Aspects of the European Tradition of Historical Writing: 3. History as Prophecy." *Transactions of the Royal Historical Society*, 5th Series, no. 22 (1972): 159–80.

Staber, Joseph. "Eschatologie und Geschichte bei Otto von Freising." In *Otto von Freising: Gedenkgabe zu seinem 800. Todesjahr*, edited by Joseph A. Fischer, 106–26. Freising: Verlag des Historischen Vereins Freising, 1958.

Stoneman, Richard. *Alexander the Great: A Life in Legend*. New Haven, CT: Yale University Press, 2008.

Throop, Susanna A. *Crusading as an Act of Vengeance, 1095–1216*. Aldershot: Ashgate, 2011.

Trexler, Richard C. *Journey of the Magi: Meanings in History of a Christian Story*. Princeton, NJ: Princeton University Press, 1997.

Trieber, Conrad. "Die Idee der Vier Weltreiche." *Hermes* 27 (1892): 321–44.

Tyerman, Christopher. "Were There Any Crusades in the Twelfth Century?" *English Historical Review* 110 (1995): 553–77.

Van den Eynde, Damien. *L'œuvre littéraire de Géroch de Reichersberg*. Rome: Pontificum Athenaeum Antonianum, 1957.

Vorholt, Hanna. "Studying with Maps: Jerusalem and the Holy Land in Two Thirteenth-Century Maps." In *Imagining Jerusalem in the Medieval West*, edited by Lucy Donkin and Hanna Vorholt, 163–99. Oxford: Oxford University Press, 2012.

Wannenmacher, Julia Eva. *Hermeneutik der Heilsgeschichte: De Septem Sigillis und die sieben Siegel im Werk Joachims von Fiore*. Leiden: Brill, 2005.

Ward, Benedicta. *Miracles and the Medieval Mind: Theory, Record and Event, 1000–1215*. Rev. ed. Aldershot: Scolar Press, 1987.

Weissthanner, Alois. "Regesten des Freisinger Bischofs Otto I (1138–1158)." *Analecta Cisterciensia* 14 (1958): 151–222.

Whalen, Brett Edward. *Dominion of God: Christendom and Apocalypse in the Middle Ages*. Cambridge, MA: Harvard University Press, 2009.

———. "Joachim of Fiore and the Division of Christendom." *Viator* 34 (2003): 89–108.

INDEX